WRIGHT AND NEW YORK

WRIGHT
AND NEW YORK

The Making of America's Architect

Anthony Alofsin

Yale University Press   New Haven and London

yalebooks.com/art

Designed and set in type by Lindsey Voskowsky
Printed in the United States of America by Sheridan Books

Library of Congress Control Number: 2018960100
ISBN 978-0-300-23885-3

A catalogue record for this book is available from the British Library.

This paper meets the requirements of ANSI/NISO Z 39.48–1992 (Permanence of Paper).

10 9 8 7 6 5 4 3 2 1

Frontispiece: Frank Lloyd Wright, c. 1926.

In memory of Bruce Brooks Pfeiffer (1930–2017)
Who opened the vaults of Taliesin

You can see for yourself how malignant circumstances have buffeted this man. This giant. This ingenious giant.
The New Yorker, 1930

CONTENTS

INTRODUCTION

When you think about Frank Lloyd Wright, you think of him as the architect of the prairies and Chicago, but there's another story—Wright and New York—that reveals a person and a life we've never known. Between 1925 and 1932 the city turned him around, moving him from personal and professional crisis to set the stage for his final decades as the American champion of modern architecture. Fifty-eight years old, broke, harassed, and seeking refuge, he found shelter and commissions for two buildings in the city—a vast modern cathedral and a new prototype for the skyscraper. They provided the context for this turnaround, freed him creatively, gave him a platform for his ideas, and, crucially, drew the attention of architects, critics, and writers.

That New York did this is ironic, as Wright loved to demonize urban life. Already in the mid-1920s he bemoaned the city as an unlivable urban nightmare run on greed. "The city is a prison," he told his son Lloyd. It grated on his sensibilities and affronted him with its clamor and speed. Its fleshy excesses appalled him. He ranted against New York, a place "fit for banking and not much else . . . a crime of crimes . . . humanity preying upon humanity . . . carcass . . . parasite . . . fibrous tumor . . . pig pile . . . incongruous mantrap of monstrous dimensions." As we might suspect from the intensity of his protest, Wright knew New York well.

He wandered its streets and chatted with passersby. He strolled the cobblestones of Greenwich Village, dined with pleasure in its restaurants, reeled in its movie palaces. He met artists and writers and fed off their energy and ambition. Yes, there were traffic, subways, noise, and stifling crowds. But Manhattan also challenged and changed him, becoming a force by which he defined himself. In this sense the architect was responding as many artists and writers had for generations: with repulsion and irresistible attraction. Although Wright always wanted to present himself as alone, self-made, and unique, he participated in a long tradition that continues today as new generations recoil at the terrors of the city while seeking to know it, celebrate it, and to find out who they are from within it. The New York Wright confronted resembled the Gotham defined cogently by cultural historian William R. Taylor as a village of ideas embedded in a larger, elusive sphere. In Taylor's terms, Gotham is the "cultural marketplace" where the commercial life of the city and the media it creates jostle with each other in a quest for self-expression. That description fits the world uncovered by Wright in the 1920s, a world defined not by a whole picture, but by partial yet potent views.[1]

Wright was, after all, a Midwesterner born in 1867. He came from a maternal lineage of self-righteous firebrand preachers. His immediate family was fractured, as his father divorced his mother when Wright was a boy and never saw his son again. He attended a progressive rural secondary school run by his aunts, but he became a college dropout. He benefited from neither rigorous academic training nor a luxurious Grand Tour. His formation as an architect came largely through apprenticeship under his mentor, the Chicago architect Louis Sullivan. But he had innate gifts: a powerful ability to visualize in three dimensions, skill in drawing, and a critical and curious mind. He also had endless ambition and indefatigable drive. New York is where both were tested and proved.

The period from 1925 to 1932 was also crucial for modern architecture in New York, and by extension for the entire United States. New York in the 1920s not only feted the Jazz Age with its excesses and saw the emergence of fecund literature, theater, and music, but it produced marvels of Art Deco architecture. Although the style is often dismissed as superficial, in part because of its dazzling glitz, it shook off its French influences to become the first widespread synthesis of a distinctive American architectural style. Art Deco's aesthetics extended from toasters to tall buildings and could be found from New York to El Paso to Portland. It was the idiom of the skyscrapers built for New Yorkers' homes and offices. Its buildings stepped back as its citizens stepped out. And its icons, such as the Chrysler Building, Rockefeller Center, and the Empire State Building, we still love today. As the authors of the monumental survey *New York 1930* observed about this period, "New York produced some of the tallest, zaniest, most inspired, entertaining, important— and, indeed, original—buildings of the twentieth century." This is the world of architecture that Wright confronted in the late 1920s. Not only did he understand it as a representation of money and power, but he saw it as antagonistic to his own evolving vision for the organic architecture of democracy.[2]

In this same period, the vibrant strands of American Art Deco collided with European Functionalism, which emphasized economy, rationality, and mechanization. The saga of the New World contesting the legacy of the Old World was playing out again, specifically in a struggle to define modern architecture. Much was at stake, not only how buildings and cities would look, but American identity itself. Could the country produce an autonomous modern architecture through Art Deco, its best design expression to date? Or would it defer to the powerful seduction of Functionalism, the forerunner of the International Style? As this book shows, Wright followed the contending camps and positioned his organic architecture—and his vision of America—as the only alternative to both. The fate of this third way was up for grabs. New York is both the crucible in which the drama takes place and a player itself.

The relationship between Wright and New York is convoluted, with ups and downs, twists and turns. The story here has a few twists of its own. Writing in the 1940s, Henry-Russell Hitchcock, the leading American architectural historian and Wright's friend, promulgated a narrative about the architect's influence abroad. "But," he noted, "it is a matter which ought to be pursued further." My first book on the architect, *Frank Lloyd Wright: The Lost Years, 1910–1922,* pursued that matter. I documented Wright's flight to Europe in 1909 with his lover, Mamah Borthwick Cheney; their embrace of the ideas of Ellen Key, a leading feminist of the day; Wright's work on the famous Wasmuth publications of his designs; and Europe's impact on Wright's aesthetics. I defined these years as Wright's primitivist phase, when his major innovation was exploring ornament, which Wright believed was loaded with the symbolic meanings of ancient and archetypal forms.[3]

Historians had neglected the years after the golden age of Wright's Prairie period. In 1969, a decade after the architect's death, theBritish architectural critic Reyner Banham observed Wright's achievement. "But," Banham noted, "there was an awkward passage in the chronological middle of his career that we know very little about." Banham identified Wright's Wilderness Years as the early 1910s to the early 1930s. "I believe," Banham declared, "that somewhere in those years he passed through some crucial experience, if not an actual crisis, that effectively separates his early career from his later work." Banham characterized the period with nuance as three wildernesses rolled into one: the professional, the spiritual, and the experience of the southwestern desert. They combined to fundamentally alter Wright's being and his career. But, as no critical history yet existed, Banham could not grasp the catalytic role New York played in Wright's transformation. Not yet clear was the interaction between city and desert that proved critical for the evolution of Wright's vision. This book makes the connection visible.[4]

As I pursued Wright in the 1920s, I encountered some fascinating figures. The Reverend William Norman Guthrie played the role of private guide to Wright's inner world and became the client who commissioned the visionary projects for New York: the Modern Cathedral and the apartment tower for the grounds of his church, St. Mark's Church in-the-Bowery. Everything about him was eccentric and idiosyncratic. Born in Scotland in 1868, Guthrie was raised on the Continent. His grandmother, the abolitionist Frances "Fanny" Wright, had started a utopian venture to help freed slaves in Tennessee, and the connection prompted Guthrie to study literature and theology at the University of the South in Sewanee, where he was ordained as an Episcopal minister in the late 1880s and became a lecturer and itinerant preacher. In 1911 he was appointed the rector of St. Mark's and quickly set out to overhaul church liturgy. Located on East 10th Street at Second Avenue, St. Mark's was one of the oldest churches in New York City, but Guthrie abandoned all of its traditions. He matched Wright in his zeal for the exotic, his devotion to primary spiritual sources, and his fierce efforts to reform not only his church but society at large. Guthrie prefigured New Age consciousness and created the milieu of what became the counterculture of the East Village. He saw in Native Americans the original spirit of America and even brought chiefs to his pulpit. He found in the Ancients, from Egypt to Greece, pure ideas and practices relevant for modern life. He sought the company of Hindu mystics and incorporated their chants into his services. And he instituted music, dramatic lighting, and rhythmic dancing by scantily clad young women as a means of spiritual elevation. Guthrie was a visionary who studied architecture, a radical who wanted to reform not just the Episcopal church but all religious practice, and a man of character who valued and nourished friendship. Wright found in him an ideal confidante, friend, and client. Their relationship is one of the great unsung connections between artist and patron in the history of modern art.

As I looked at the period as a whole, with Wright's turbulent life and Guthrie as motifs, an unexpected development occurred: New York itself began to emerge as Wright's savior from debt, professional insecurity, and tarnished reputation. A circle of figures appeared, ranging from the great practitioners of Art Deco architecture to young upstarts on the forefront of modernism. Beyond the realm of architects and designers, New York's literary world opened up to Wright. Its critics and editors engaged him as a professional writer, commissioning essays that provided income Wright desperately needed. Collectively they lifted Wright from the deepest doldrums to propel his life and work to new heights.

Wright's blooming as a writer and the extent of his writings are surprising. He emerged by the late 1920s as the most prolific American architect of the day, targeting the various camps of modern architecture and refining his reactions to the city. Though produced under duress, his literary output was so prodigious that it was, in the words of theorist

Kenneth Frampton, "something of a mystery." New York's critics, publishers, and architects gave him their imprimatur, establishing him not only as an architectural presence but as a professional writer and public lecturer.[5]

Seen through the kaleidoscope of New York, Wright's life appears as a complex story in American history. He is a figure wrapped in paradox and contradiction. Rather than a caricature or an impressionistic portrait, the Wright we encounter is vulnerable and relentless, selfish and tender, humiliated and haughty, by turns cold and warm, and often in possession of a sense of humor. He emerges more human than he has ever been portrayed, and in his humanity, his story is touching and uplifting. New York is the lens of this new perception: Wright arrived as one person and left as another. This transformation represents the turning point of his career and establishes the persona that the world would come to know. His zigzagging around the country and abroad prefigured the jet-setting celebrity. This is unsurprising, as Wright was the first star architect, the model for future generations of ambitious designers.

This picture suggests that over time there are many Wrights and many New Yorks, and our understanding comes from the moments we choose to view and the perspectives we take. While this book concentrates on 1925 to 1932, the narrative moves back and forth in time to encompass the arc of Wright's life. Wright traveled and moved a great deal during this period—sometimes even his lawyers couldn't find him. At some moments so much was happening simultaneously that we must return to the same time frame and look at it from a different perspective or with a different subject in mind. Like many complex and creative figures, Wright operated on several creative trajectories at once. His love life ricocheted from serenity to chaos. His architecture zoomed forward, slowed briefly, then resumed. His writing accelerated. The only constant Wright clung to was an inchoate sense of self, determined in his mind by destiny, in the service of an unyielding creative urge.

A variety of sources contribute to this narrative. Many come not only from Wright's letters but also from the family members, friends, clients, critics, and publishers with whom he corresponded. Written in candor and often with emotion, these letters not only speak about events but provide mood and psychological inclination—all dimensions of a human being that challenge a biographer.

In addition to parsing his letters and studying his designs, I turned to an obvious place for insight and accounts of this period, Wright's *Autobiography*. The first edition appeared in 1932 and is particularly important as the architect began writing it in 1926 and concluded in 1931, precisely during the pivotal years examined in this book. It is as close to a chronicle as we could ever hope for of the period, as he was passing through many events just before writing about them. The *Autobiography* provides the freshest insight into how Wright saw his own history, his turmoil, and his aspirations in the late 1920s before he retrospectively revised his text. Into his narrative he folded a few tantalizing fragments of his experience in New York.[6]

Wright's *Autobiography* was a critical and commercial success, but it was more impressionistic than coherent or complete. He acknowledged the challenges and limitations of writing autobiography: "As I have been writing away, myself autobiographical, I see why all autobiography is written between the lines. It must be so. No matter how skilled the writer or how spontaneous he may be, the implication outdoes his ability or undoes his intention." With the writer's own perceptions constantly changing, he went on to say, it is up to the reader to complete the text as "he who reads writes truth in between the lines for himself."[7]

This book intends to fill in those spaces "between the lines" to reveal a story richer than the one we have known about this American genius and the world he inhabited and attempted to transform. By concentrating on detail during a phase of Wright's life and by tying it into a broader narrative, it explores not a singular truth but a collage of truths and facts as well as misstatements and misunderstandings. Throughout this account, New York unfolds as the city transforms itself through architecture.

To grasp Wright's experience of New York in the mid-1920s, we need to ask what he knew of the city before then, how it affected him, and how his life slid to its low point. We begin, therefore, by returning to Wright and his plight in 1909, when he first visits Gotham.

1

POINTS OF DEPARTURE

By his forty-second birthday, June 8, 1909, Frank Lloyd Wright could see his stunning professional accomplishments and a life in disarray. In sixteen years of independent practice, he had defined a new idiom of architecture that was at once modern and, from his perspective, uniquely American. For Wright this had taken the form of "organic architecture," which bound together the transcendental philosophy, the design methods, and the symbolic language of his mentor Louis Sullivan and the reigning ethos of the Arts and Crafts movement. Interwoven in these ideas was the conviction that nature provided laws that could be abstracted for contemporary design. Wright's organic architecture respected its physical site, championed the idea of individualism, and used materials "honestly"—that is, for themselves. He had experimented with all the major styles of the late nineteenth century from Shingle style to the neocolonial, absorbing and transforming anything of value to him in an innate drive to abstract everything he saw. With the Ward Willits house, designed in 1901, he had crystallized the look and feel of his Prairie period style. Wright had dissolved the rooms of traditional houses into spaces that flowed continuously, linking the interior to the exterior. From then on, his art was a concert of theme and variation: with his aesthetic clearly defined, he explored different roof configurations (gabled or flat), changing palettes of materials, and color schemes meant to harmonize interiors, exteriors, and sites.

Wright's organic architecture spoke about the terrain and topography; in the Midwest, its low-pitched roofs hovered over the ground and ran parallel to the flattish land of the former prairies. For Wright, organic architecture was the material and spiritual manifestation of a democratic American identity, freed from the burdens of imitation and precedent. His houses had the elements that made houses recognizable as homes— roofs, doors, walls, and windows—but with their low-slung profiles and spare surfaces, they looked nothing like the late Victorian architecture and eclectic styles that had dominated American architecture.

Wright's houses also had ornament. Ornament was integral—built in, not added on—to the building whether it took the shape of a rug pattern, window glazing, masonry, or even a floor plan itself. Sullivan had revealed to Wright its role in architecture, and Wright had perfected his technique. Ornament was essential to the spirit of the design and inseparable from it. Of all the factors that made Wright different from the European modernists of the early twentieth century, his lifelong commitment to ornament placed him apart. Ornament was "a crime," in the words of Viennese architect and theorist Adolf Loos, the ultimate symbol of decadence and corrupt historicism. Its only rival was the dreaded use of the pitched roof.

Wright had dozens of successful applications of his organic ideas, mostly in residences in the Midwest. A few commissions moved further east, as seen in the home and estate of Darwin D. and Isabelle Martin in Buffalo in 1904. Darwin resembled many of Wright's other clients: a self-made, financially successful businessman rather than a member of high society, the usual patrons of famous architects. The Martins were devout and humble Christian Scientists, and Darwin became not only a major client but a friend and devoted supporter of Wright.[1]

Wright also designed major public buildings, demonstrating his facility in exploring the relationship of form and function and the expressive power of construction materials. At Unity Temple, the church in Oak Park, Illinois, rebuilt after a fire, Wright used amorphous concrete to make the somber masses appropriate to Unitarian practice while cradling a space within that was transcendent with light. At the Larkin Company Administration Building in Buffalo, where Martin was an executive, Wright identified the functions of the building with specific volumes so the building's purpose could be "read." Corner stairs had one tall mass assigned to them, the central core of the building to another. The working interior figured around a soaring atrium. Both buildings were as modern as any buildings anywhere.

Wright had made the case for his views on architecture in essays and local speeches, but in 1908 he reached a broader national audience when the *Architectural Record* published his article "In the Cause of Architecture." In the full-spread feature, the essay included a detailed explanation of his theories of organic design. His principles covered everything from building with the site, eliminating the inessential, to dissolving walls into screens of windows and creating color palettes. His platform included a call for individuality: because each client was unique, each client should have a distinctive design. The article included fifty-six pages of illustrations.[2]

Despite these successes, in 1909 Frank Lloyd Wright was still a regional architect. Though ascending in recognition, he was not a major player on the national scene, nor did he have a large-scale operation to compete with big firms in Chicago or New York. The *Architectural Record* had provided Wright a great service by publishing his work so comprehensively, but Wright disliked the grainy quality of the images on its pages. And some reviews of his work had been negative too. A couple of months before Wright's big splash, Russell Sturgis, architect, editor, and the leading American architectural critic, published a devastating critique of the Larkin Building in that same journal. "Few persons," Sturgis pronounced, "who have seen the great monuments of the past will fail to pronounce

Fig. 1 Mamah Borthwick Cheney, c. 1909.

this monument an extremely ugly building." In the very first paragraph, Sturgis described the Larkin Building as "a monster of awkwardness."[3]

Wright's awareness of his accomplishments, even criticism of them, and ambition to move forward collided with his feeling that he was creatively burned out. He had systematically perfected the style of his Prairie period, a phase later called his "First Golden Age," but he knew he was repeating himself instead of innovating. Professional fatigue coincided with a telling symptom of midlife crisis: a deep, passionate love affair that compromised him, his family, his lover, and her family. Wright had married his wife, Catherine Tobin, in 1889, when she was eighteen and he was twenty-two. Nicknamed Kitty, she had six children with him. Around 1904 he fell in love with Mamah Borthwick Cheney, a client in Oak Park (fig. 1). She was married to Eduard Cheney—they had two children—and for a time the couples had socialized together in Oak Park until the illicit love affair took hold.[4]

By late spring of 1909, Wright had found a way to address his domestic dilemma and creative malaise: a year-long stay in Europe. Announcing that he was taking leave from his practice to prepare a synoptic publication of his work for a great art publisher in Berlin, Wasmuth Verlag, he turned to a few clients, including Darwin D. Martin, to back him financially for this purpose. In private, he and Mamah informed their spouses that they were leaving their families to pursue a life together.

During the summer, the couple made plans for their European escape. They chose the Plaza Hotel in New York as their place of secret rendezvous and the first stop on their travels to Europe. For Wright, visiting New York was also his first chance to see Chicago's great rival for preeminence in American architecture. Three powerful forces coincided with his visiting Gotham: the pursuit of what he called a "spiritual hegira," the need for a new life with the woman he loved, and the revival of his creativity as an artist.

After signing a contract on September 22, 1909, to transfer his work to a local architect, Wright left Oak Park to head to New York. Mamah had left Oak Park earlier, in late June, taking her two children to spend time with a friend in Boulder, Colorado. In September she met Wright in New York at the Plaza, where they planned to stay until early October and then go to Berlin.[5]

The Plaza Hotel had opened only two years earlier, on October 1, 1907, after twenty-seven months of construction at the unprecedented cost of $12.5 million (fig. 2). The building replaced an existing hotel with the same name at the same location, and advertisements described it as "the most luxurious hotel in the world," a beacon to the elegant, the fashionable, and the wealthy. Henry Janeway Hardenbergh, who had produced the Waldorf-Astoria, the Dakota Apartments in New York City, and sumptuous hotels in Washington, D.C., and Boston, was the chief designer of the nineteen-story building set in the style of an opulent French chateau.

The Plaza, at the southeast corner of Central Park, opened onto a large traffic circle at whose center was Augustus Saint-Gaudens's gilt statue of William Tecumseh Sherman on horseback. Occupying an entire city block, it contained 753 units, with suites consisting of as many as seventeen rooms, and the latest technology, encompassing push-button maid service, electric dumbwaiters, separate room thermostats, and built-in vacuums.[6]

Opulence was its theme. The hotel had been responsible for the largest single order of gold-encrusted china and featured 1,600 crystal chandeliers. The richest of the rich, like Mr. and Mrs. Alfred Gwynne Vanderbilt, lived in its apartments, but guests could have rooms for the

Fig. 2 Plaza Hotel, c. 1910.

bargain rate of $2.50 a night. Wright preferred a suite on the lower floors, which were rumored to be the best. Although fully operational, the hotel was busy refining its guest offerings. A summer garden, intended to operate as a seasonal restaurant, would open in 1910 and later be known as the Rose Room. An outdoor café, the Champagne Porch, was planned for the Fifth Avenue side of the hotel between the building façade and a row of columns. With only ten tables, it would become the most desirable venue in New York.

The building's elaborate French chateau style conflicted with Wright's organic principles, but he liked its interiors, and its very ornateness seemed to him the right place to launch the new phase of his relationship with Mamah. They had been intimate for years, but quietly. Now they could luxuriate as a couple, anonymously, in the lap of high society. The furtive visit lasted only a few days, but it marked the beginning of a series of visits over the next fifteen years as Wright dipped in and out of the city.[7]

Still, the first visit stuck with him. Ironically, the city was old and new, as it had a long history but had not consolidated itself into the metropolis of "Greater Gotham" until 1898. Wright saw New York in its full splendor and mayhem. Certainly Chicago, Wright's main urban reference, was a thriving metropolis, loaded with industry, commerce, culture, dynamic architecture, and a multiethnic population. But New York, with a population of 4.7 million, was second in size only to London. Foremost among its attributes was its physical location: a city centered on the island of Manhattan surrounded by water, making it a global port and a world player in ways Chicago could never be. It was considered, as one commentator wrote, "one of the most beautiful, largest, and best of the world's great ports." Its waterways provided access from the Hudson River and Erie Canal, coastal trade with New England, and, of particular importance for Wright, access to the great transatlantic steamship companies, the Cunard and White Star lines, the North German Lloyd and the Hamburg-American lines, as well as other lines with English, German, French, Dutch, West Indian, and Central and South American ports.[8]

The location also had flaws, including indirect linkage between the railways and the city's network of wharfs and piers. But these hardly stood in the way of trade. New York imported vast quantities of everything imaginable, from works of art to cheese, from diamonds to hemp. It was the New World's center for the export of wholesale groceries and dry goods. Benefiting from its immigrant population, New York had already secured its status as the country's foremost manufacturing city. By 1905 the production of clothing there led all other trades, and by itself exceeded the total value of all factory goods in any other U.S. city except Chicago and Philadelphia. Production in Manhattan and the Bronx was valued then at around $1 billion.

New York resonated with history, from its seventeenth-century founding by the Dutch through its role in the Revolutionary War, during most of which it had been occupied by the British and used as a prison. The rocky land, with its brooks and ponds, had gone through continuous transformation. Fire had aborted Chicago's growth, and though its rebuilding created work opportunities for a diversity of immigrant populations, New York's identity was defined to a greater degree by the city's global mix. Nearly all of its area had been annexed in recent decades, and in 1909—some ten years after consolidation—the ratio of native-born New Yorkers to immigrants was 1.76 to 1. Of the foreign-born population, one-fourth were German, over one-fifth were Irish, nearly one-eighth were Russians (mostly Jews), one-ninth were Italians, and the remainder came from other European countries, Scandinavia, and even Canada. Over two-thirds of the city's entire population had foreign-born parents. By 1909 New York had more Germans than any city other than Berlin, and more Irish than Dublin. It was a city of ethnic villages, with Little Italy centered on Mulberry Street, Chinatown on Mott, a Jewish quarter on the upper Bowery, a German colony east on Second Avenue below 14th Street, two French quarters south of Washington Square near Bleecker Street and on the West Side between 20th and 34th Streets, in addition to Greek, Russian, Armenian, Arab, and "Negro" quarters on Thompson Street and in the West 50s.

The Lower East Side presented a challenging social problem, with its substandard housing, crushing density, and the health-threatening consequences of inadequate air, light, and substandard (if not nonexistent) sanitation. This tenement district was one of the most crowded in the world. Despite the progress made by many social welfare associations, deplorable living conditions persisted.

When Wright arrived in 1909, the physical layout of the city was very much in flux. The downtown port of Manhattan featured a hodge-podge of waterfront streets, with their irregularity extending north into what was called Greenwich Village. The gridding of the rest of the streets had occurred in the early nineteenth century, with divisions between east and west. Broadway was the most important avenue, symbolic of the city's growth. A narrow passage in the busy downtown, it shot north from Bowling Green, above the Battery, to 10th Street. Above 14th Street it veered west, disrupting the regularity of the street grid. Fifth Avenue had few residences between 34th and 45th Streets, but many fine ones above 50th Street. The Upper West Side and Riverside Drive were the newest residential areas of the city in 1909. The city's park system, with Central Park as its crown, extended into the boroughs. Many of these spaces were still wooded, yet several provided places for public gathering. Union Square, between Broadway and Fourth Avenue, was a favorite spot for workers' mass meetings, while Battery Park at the southern tip of Manhattan contained the New York Aquarium and a children's playground. The city's park property was valued at over $500 million, or $7.2 billion today.

"New York is a city in which many things happen, unprecedented in the history of urban humanity," read an article in the *Architectural Record*. "No other city in the world has ever added 500,000 inhabitants to its population every three years. In no other city does such a high level of real estate values prevail over so long a strip of land as the level of prices which are being paid for lots on Fifth Avenue, from Thirtieth Street to Fiftieth Street. In no other city has anything like $200,000,000 been invested in new buildings in any one year."[9]

Tall office buildings, called "sky-scrapers," responded to the narrow conditions of the Downtown—particularly in or around Wall Street—where businesses increasingly wanted to locate. On a stroll Wright could see dozens of skyscrapers that dwarfed anything that he had yet designed. The Metropolitan Life Insurance Company Building, 693 feet high, had just been completed in 1909. The Singer Sewing Machine Company Building, at 612 feet, was finished in 1908, after three years of construction. Its steel columns rested on pneumatic caisson piers, extending ninety feet down into bedrock. More than just offices and corporate headquarters, these buildings combined wide-ranging uses. Along Church Street, the Hudson Terminal Building, also completed in 1909, was twenty-two stories high, with four stories below ground, and served as the terminal of the downtown Hudson tunnels; it had a tenant population of ten thousand persons. Grand Central Station, the multilayered marvel of mixed transport, commerce, and retail, was still under construction, and the main terminal would not open until February 1913. Yet Wright could still grasp the scale of its structure, its lattice of transport systems whose workings would mesmerize the Italian Futurists and other avant-garde architects in Europe.

Wright could see not only skyscrapers, but also stirring examples of civic architecture and civil engineering. These included New York's bridges, some of which were just completed when he arrived. Of the four bridges connecting Manhattan and Long Island, three had been built between 1900 and 1910. The Manhattan Bridge, finished in 1909, was a wire-cable structure, the largest of the city's suspension bridges in

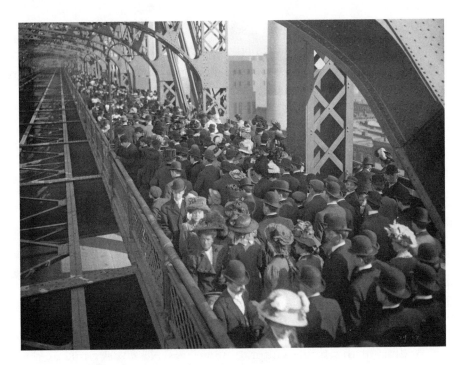

Fig. 3 Queensborough Bridge opening, c. 1909/10.

length and width. It had a double deck with a lower level for trolleys and wagons, and an upper level for foot traffic and elevated trains. The Queensborough Bridge, cantilevered from Second Avenue to Long Island City, was also completed in 1909 (fig. 3). It included sixteen-foot-wide sidewalks and tracks for electric carts. A dozen or so bridges crossed the Harlem River, and with the opening of the Pennsylvania–Long Island railway tube in 1910, the provision of these routes would continue to reduce the role of ferry boats.

The New York Wright saw was open for visitors. The Plaza, Wright and Mamah's refuge, was located at the northern edge of the hotel district, which ran between 23rd and 59th Streets, sandwiched between Fourth and Seventh Avenues. The city's early lodgings had been located in taverns near the tip of Manhattan, and few first-class hotels were to be found in the downtown business district except for the Astor House. Just as the increasing value of real estate caused buildings to soar upward, it also pushed them northward with the appearance of apartment-hotels, particularly on the Upper West Side.

There was a thriving cultural scene, one with deep roots (a London company gave its first dramatic performances at Pearl Street and Maiden Lane in 1732). Theater construction had boomed throughout the nineteenth century. The New Theatre had just been built in 1909 when Wright visited. Later known as the Century Theatre, it was located at 62nd Street and Central Park West, but with its poor acoustics and problematic location—the area around it was relatively undeveloped—it proved to be immediately unsuccessful. Musical societies, also with eighteenth-century roots, had flourished. In 1909, the principal concert venues were Carnegie Music Hall, as it was called then, and Mendelssohn Hall, originally a glee club, located on West 40th Street. The Metropolitan Opera, which gave its first season—German works exclusively—in 1884 and continued the tradition of Grand Opera, was supported by wealthy patrons. The city's oligarchy also funded art museums and cultural institutions. At the time of Wright's first visit, the Metropolitan Museum of Art was the largest public art gallery in the city.

Adding to this fertile cultural milieu was New York's role as the country's leading literary center, the home of major publishing houses and many authors. The "men of letters" lineage ran from Charles Brockden Brown—and his Gothic novels at the turn of the nineteenth century—to members of the Knickerbocker School, such as William Cullen Bryant and James Fenimore Cooper. The latter was a romantic corollary for Wright to add to his perpetual favorites: Emerson, Whitman, and Thoreau. An efflorescence of successful periodicals, particularly in the latter half of the nineteenth century, had emerged alongside magazines such as *Harper's* and *Scribner's*. The periodicals propelled the appearance of lower-priced monthlies and specialty publications, including religious weeklies. The city's ethnic mix offered a vast number of eager readers for these materials. While the American press was replete with numerous dailies, they did not dominate readership. By 1905, 127 of the city's 893 periodicals were printed in languages other than English, with twenty languages or dialects among them. The largest circulation of these foreign-language newspapers included German, Yiddish, and Italian publications, while others featured Bohemian, Greek, French, Croatian, Hungarian, and Slavonic dailies. New York was a frenetic collage of humanity and construction.[10]

The city was also an epicenter of architectural publishing, a critical component in the exchange of ideas, documentation, and criticism within the profession. Chicago had such exemplary journals as *Inland Architect and News Record,* Boston had *The Brick Builder* and the *Architectural Review,* while Philadelphia had the *Ladies' Home Journal,* where Wright's work had appeared. But New York was home of the *Architectural Record.* Launched in 1891, the *Record* became the leading national journal, for publishing work not only in the east but throughout the country. In its pages you could find drawings of the brick architecture of Dallas, when the city consisted of nothing more than a few buildings at a railroad crossing; hotels in Portland, Oregon; or civic buildings in Cleveland—all this alongside the latest works of major East Coast architects. It would play a major role in positioning Wright for posterity.

Wright and Mamah happened to arrive at a special moment of revelry for both the city and the region: the month-long celebration of the three hundredth anniversary of the discovery of the Hudson River and the one hundredth anniversary of Robert Fulton's first commercial use of the paddle steamer. The city was throwing itself a gigantic party, and Wright and Mamah were in attendance.

After four years of planning, the Hudson-Fulton Celebration feted the critical importance of the river to the city's development and its very status as a global center. The event drew international attention. German socialites and "European songbirds" sailed over for the festivities. On Thursday, September 30, 1909, a military parade took place in the afternoon, proceeding from 110th Street down Central Park West. The following day, twenty-five thousand people watched as a grand naval procession launched south from Newburg, midway between New York and Albany. A historical pageant was enacted in Brooklyn. On Saturday, there was a children's festival and parade as well as an evening carnival parade by German, Austrian, and Swiss societies. Electric illumination was a major theme, and Saturday evening culminated with the lighting of the warship fleet. As the *New York Times* reported: "New York burned the incandescent phantasmagoria of its week of celebration into the memory of its thousands of visitors last night in one last general illumination of fleet and river, city and highway of pageantry. After all, this is the electric

Fig. 4 Hudson-Fulton Celebration, 1909. Archway and reviewing stands on Fifth Avenue in front of the New York Public Library.

age." The entire city was lit up with a million incandescent bulbs and ten thousand arc lights (fig. 4). The parades and pageants spanned all phases of the city's history, from the Indian and Dutch to the English and Colonial periods. The Empire State was celebrated with replicas of a wigwam, skyscraper, and the Statue of Liberty. Several parades down Fifth Avenue went by the Plaza Hotel; it, too, was lit up, top to bottom. A drama of lights, fireworks, and celebrating throngs surrounded Wright and Mamah.[11]

Wright brought the perspective of a confirmed Midwesterner to this marvelous city, which was also a source of conflict for him. New York's architects were the followers of the École des Beaux-Arts, which Sullivan claimed had set American architecture back by fifty years. New York's architecture was the competition, the enemy. Instead of creating a new vocabulary, the style relied on classical precedents from Rome and Greece, filtered through the Renaissance, and used formulaic procedures to generate designs. It was, however, widely successful in creating iconic and functional civic buildings, not just in New York but in other major metropolitan centers. It was inconceivable to Wright that he would not one day build at the grand scale the city commanded, but up to that point he had contributed nothing. In 1909, he was conflicted, vulnerable, and unsure about his future. Yet that first trip to New York, short as it was, figured as part of a process of rupture from his Oak Park identity and the creation of a new life.

Wright embarked from New York with Mamah on October 5, 1909. Arriving in Berlin in mid-October, the couple made contact with Ernst Wasmuth, Wright's publisher, and settled into the Adlon Hotel, the Berlin equivalent of the Plaza in terms of luxury and celebrity. In Berlin they went to Darmstadt to see the Secessionist architect Joseph Maria Olbrich. Olbrich had also published his work with Wasmuth and had been recruited by the Grand Duke of Hesse to design an artists' colony. Wright saw him as his main competition in Europe, but upon arrival they discovered Olbrich had died. During their stay in Germany, Wright and Mamah bought art, mostly prints by Jugendstil and Secessionist artists, that fit with Wright's taste as a collector of Japanese woodblock prints, and were inexpensive and easy to transport.[12]

The couple's romantic idyll was brief. A Chicago newspaper reported that Mr. and "Mrs. Wright" were in Berlin, and once the papers discovered that the real Mrs. Wright was still in Oak Park, the lovers' cover was blown. In an article dated November 7, 1909, the *Chicago Tribune* described the architect's "affinity triangle," which was "unparalleled even in the checkered history of soul mating." The furor embroiled Wright in his first major public scandal, a harbinger of fiascos to come, an event exposing everyone—his family, Mamah, and her family—to public scrutiny and judgment. Splashed across the newspapers, the story established Wright as something of a madman—a caricature of infidelity and instability, which would plague him for decades. Afterwards, Wright kept a low profile, leaving Germany, visiting Paris, and eventually moving to Italy to prepare his publications while Mamah worked elsewhere as a translator.[13]

The Wasmuth venture resulted in two publications with confusingly similar names. *Ausgeführte Bauten und Entwürfe* (Built Work and Designs) was a double folio, featuring sumptuous lithographs of Wright's architectural designs. When eventually realized in 1910 and 1911, these images, often simply called the Wasmuth folios, became famous as introductions to Wright's work in Europe. *Frank Lloyd Wright: Ausgeführte Bauten,* the second publication, was a small picture book of photographic reproductions of built work and plan drawings. Wright intended it to be a supplement or "pendant" to the folios, and referred to it as his *Sonderheft,* or "special edition." Some commentators would later call it the "little Wasmuth" to distinguish it from the larger folios.

Producing these folios proved to be problematic, however, and their impact and Wright's intentions for them was long misunderstood. It turned out that Wright's excuse to go to Europe was only partly accurate; he had been invited to publish the picture book, not the folios, and instead of getting an advance, the entire project was a vanity project, paid for by Wright with funds from a couple of clients and friends. His true intention was to create a primer of his American "organic and democratic architecture." Wright would own, control, and distribute most of the publications. Two editions of the *Sonderheft* eventually came out, one for America and one for Europe, where the impact was coincidental to his plans. His intended market was the American home owner and entrepreneur, an audience he had only partly tapped yet ardently sought.[14]

Wright's letters to and from his few correspondents during his stay abroad give a sense of his inner conflicts. To Charles Robert Ashbee, the British Arts and Crafts architect whom he had met while Ashbee was touring the United States, Wright admitted he'd been in love with another woman "for some years" and that he was desperate to reconcile his situation. "I wanted to square my *life* with *myself,*" Wright explained to Ashbee. "I want to do this now more than anything else. I want to *live* true as I would *build* true, and in the light I have tried to do this thing."[15]

Wright opened himself up further in the spring of 1910 when he wrote the Reverend William Norman Guthrie, his confidant, for advice about his future with Mamah (fig. 5). Guthrie had been lecturing in Chicago, in the New Theater at Steinway Hall, where Wright had an office. He was also a colleague of Charles Robert Ashbee. With such proximity, Guthrie and Wright had fallen into the same circle, and by 1909 Wright had designed a house for Guthrie, intended as his

Fig. 5 Reverend William Norman Guthrie.

residence at Sewanee, University of the South, Guthrie's alma mater. Clearly, a relationship of mutual trust had developed between them.[16]

Guthrie answered the architect's letter by outlining all of Wright's problems: confounding the status quo, abandoning his family, seeking of individualistic liberties, and promoting feminism. He was writing as a friend who shared "something of the soul" with Wright, insisting that his judgment could be trusted even if Wright disagreed with it. Guthrie, who told Wright the truth as he saw it, felt the architect would not be able to vanquish the "established order." He could see how difficult it was for an individual like Wright to conform, but Guthrie claimed that if he didn't, Wright risked losing his ultimate goal: the full manifestation of his artistic powers. For the sake of "spiritual self-preservation," Wright had to stop rebelling, else the conflict would devour him and extinguish his creativity. "I claim a sacrifice you are capable of & sooner or later will make, even if your companion in revolt is not your companion in misery & refuses to see the truth," Guthrie added.

Guthrie's advice to his "dear brother" was to offer Wright a stark choice. Minimize the "friction" of moral and economic stress and return to his family, or risk losing his "raison d'être." If his architecture was sacred, then Wright had no time to lose. If he returned to his family, he would find that fulfilling his parental responsibilities, however inadequately, would nonetheless be a blessing. Finally, Guthrie reminded Wright that "to the highest the hardest standards are set," and assured him that his advice and criticism were given with deep love, empathy, and appreciation of their friendship. Wright took the advice seriously, but instead of changing his mind, it added to his guilt.

Despite the scandal, Wright's closest family members stayed in contact. Sisters Maginel and Jane, whom he nicknamed Jennie, and his mother, Anna Lloyd-Jones, all wrote to him. From Fiesole, where he was finishing his work on the Wasmuth folios, Wright sent his mother a long letter on July 4, 1910. In it he told her of his activities, including his publishing venture with Wasmuth and domestic matters in Oak Park. Wright might be able to dissemble and manipulate the details of his endeavors to his clients, but he could not lie to his mother.

"I have not replied to letters from Jennie and Maginel and am aware that I have written you no word for four months," he admitted. "I have had all your letters—I think—two from Maginel and three from Jennie. My neglect of them does not mean that I am insensible of what they contained or that it did not touch me and help me. I have been so troubled and perplexed that I have not known what to write."[17]

Wright then went into details about publishing, family, and money—always money. He told his mother that he had drawn twenty-five plates of the Wasmuth folios, but that six more plates and his introduction needed finishing. When completed, Wright imagined they would generate a considerable profit. He empathized with his brother-in-law Andrew Porter, Jane's husband, who was having problems getting his due salary, and he mentioned that he would like to farm a tract of land next to Andrew's when he returned. (That tract would later become Taliesin, the new home for himself and Mamah. He was already thinking about it in mid-summer, but he had no funds to buy the property.)

Wright's letter sidestepped his mother's censure at his failing to provide for his family. His younger children had complained that they couldn't take flute and piano lessons because "they had no money." Wright explained to his mother he had taught them that as their father he owed them everything and they owed him nothing. Nonetheless, he also commented on their self-centeredness: "In fact, they feel that but for their father's extravagance they would all have had much more. This doesn't look much like a farm to me." Even his children's needs could not keep him from "the struggle." He was willing to "die to them one and all" for the sake of his own fulfillment.

As an artist, Wright could not be held to the norms of society. "I dread the aspect my return must wear," he told his mother. "I am the prodigal—whose return is a triumph for THE INSTITUTIONS I have outraged." It would also rise up against Mamah, and he feared he would be forced to abandon her "to whatever fate may hold for her—probably a hard, lonely struggle in the face of a world that writes her down as an outcast to be shunned." They would be pushed into returning to their former lives, she forced to prostitute herself to her husband "for a roof and a bed and a chance to lose her life in her children," while he would return "to my dear wife and children who all along 'knew I would' and welcomed by my friends with open rejoicing and secret contempt."

Wright wanted unconditional approval for his behavior from his mother, but at that moment only Mamah provided the total confirmation he needed—and she had her own angst and doubts. Although he knew that his friends cared for him, Wright resented their efforts to dissuade him from making a life with her. While he expected that his affections would be "vulgarized, brutalized and spit upon," by the mob, he rankled at the thought of those closest to him forsaking him—"ticketed and labeled libertine and weakling"—in a frantic effort to save him. "Love is blind," Wright claimed, "but when love lies parallel to self-interest—of what is it capable?"

He was determined to show them all, telling his mother that the defamatory stories in the press about his character might have held some truth if he had eloped suddenly with the wife of his friend—but this was not the case. Both Wright and Mamah had fully informed their spouses of their plans before they left. "I may be the infatuated weakling," he declared to his mother, "she may be the child-woman inviting harm to herself and others—but nevertheless the basis of this whole struggle was the desire for a fuller measure of life and truth at any cost—and as such an act wholly sincere and respectable—within—whatever aspect it may have worn without."

Wright was anguished that his return would confirm him as the caricature portrayed by the press. He moaned the "bitter draught" was almost more than he could bear, particularly because he felt he'd been "clear and straightforward" with his family. Yet, in a letter to his mother he also described the shortcomings of both himself and Catherine: "the things the children have not had from me—nor from their mother—You know well enough what they are—I need not repeat them." "I have always as you know lived a divided life," he concluded, "but always with a HOPE—undefined—but a hope. Now it will be without the HOPE and so, perhaps more useful to others."[18]

Wright's "divided life" seems to have had several levels. He felt the tension between the life of an artist and that of a spouse with domestic obligations—a dilemma so common as to be banal. He was also torn between his belief that he and Mamah should set themselves up as a model of honest love and his fear of public condemnation of them as immoral. The conflict began fomenting a bitter resentment. No matter how prickly he had been previously, this feeling of resentful indignation would figure into the defensive and arrogant person into which Wright would grow.

A clue to his situation appears at the end of this letter to his mother, where in a postscript the ties of the women closest to him, his sisters and aunts, rendered him almost childlike, devoted, yearning both for their comfort and to comfort them. Aunt Nell's words on Christmas had made him feel again like her "favorite young nephew." "I would like to see," he concluded from Italy, "you and she and Aunt Jennie take a cottage for three months in this garden spot on earth—I would know how to tell you, how you could get most out of it—Love to Jennie and hers, Maginel and hers—I suppose I may look forward to seeing you all again before too long—As always, Frank." When Wright was the favorite among the women who adored him, he was perhaps as whole as he ever would be (fig. 6).

With drawings completed for the Wasmuth publications and Mamah having joined Wright in Fiesole, the couple traveled in the summer of 1910 from Italy through Bavaria and on to Vienna, where they saw the late phases of the artistic Secession movement. Wright was already aware of these efforts at artistic rebellions in Berlin, Darmstadt, and elsewhere

Fig. 6 From left, Jane, Nell, and Anna Lloyd-Jones.

against the status quo in Europe. It was in Vienna that Josef Hoffmann had co-founded the Wiener Werkstätte, where he and other designers and artists produced the artifacts and architecture of modern life. To Wright, the art and architecture of the Secession was modernism's cutting edge, though, in actuality, its creative apogee had peaked. Wright particularly admired the artist Gustav Klimt, which may seem quaint, but in 1910 the Cubist abstractions of Picasso and Braque were still fomenting, and the founding of the Bauhaus lay eight years in the future.[19]

Wright and Mamah considered going by train to Istanbul in mid-July, but they never got that far. According to his application for a visa to enter Turkey, Wright was forty-three years old, five feet eight inches tall, with brown eyes set in an oval face, sloping forehead, and slightly gray hair. The description of a middle-aged man said little about his inner world. At the risk of bigamy charges and falsifying a passport application, he identified Mamah as his wife. Instead of continuing further into exotic lands, the pressures Wright described to his mother—and had fully shared with Mamah—along with the practical reality of dwindling funds, drove Wright to face his dreaded return home. He would return through New York.[20]

2

FLEETING GLANCES

Wright returned to New York on October 6, 1910. He had traveled through Berlin and London and sailed from Southampton on the SS *Bluecher.* Mamah remained in Germany. Wright returned to a city at its densest population. Demographics divined the urbanity that was to follow: a metropolitanism that would incubate creativity, knowledge, news, and occasional disaster. Manhattan was at once a singular place and an analog to the nation. Through success and through failure, it became the mouthpiece for America itself. The grand arches of McKim, Mead & White's Pennsylvania Station, opened in 1910, expressed this in steel and marble. Covering eight acres of the city's downtown, the Beaux-Arts train station filtered visitors into and out of the city. From the suburbs to St. Louis, Penn Station was, as architect Charles McKim declared, "the entrance to one of the great metropolitan cities of the world."[1]

It was a fitting pronouncement for a city that was swiftly becoming *the* commercial and cultural mecca of the United States. In 1910 Gimbels opened its first major branch store in New York City, built with twelve thousand tons of Bethlehem Steel and comprising twenty-six acres of floor space. On the Thursday Wright returned, the city was witnessing fall rituals and the miscellany of urban life. The *New York Times* reported that Mr. and Mrs. John D. Rockefeller left their estate in Cleveland by private rail car attached to the Lake Shore Limited to spend the fall at their Pocantico Hills estate. Advertisers shifted into fall fashion with woolen apparel. A large throng had gathered around St. Patrick's Cathedral the day before, when it was consecrated by Archbishop Farley with three cardinals and hundreds of clergy in attendance—the pope sent a blessing. The New York Yankees had just beaten Philadelphia, seven to four. The city anticipated the arrival of five pilots who were set to compete that Saturday for a $25,000 prize for the fastest flight from Chicago to New York.[2]

But Wright's respite in New York was brief. He headed back to Oak Park, arriving on October 8 to face his unpleasant fate. He told Catherine he would never return to her and began figuring out how to support her and his children. Major tasks lay ahead. He faced professional challenges, legal hassles of his own making, and ensuring progress on the Wasmuth venture. Wright began setting up an office and searching for commissions, yet the restart was challenging. The Robie house in Chicago proved immediately problematic. Although the building was eventually referred to as his masterwork, Wright had done but a few sketches for it before leaving for Europe. With only the building's foundations in place, he handed its development and completion over to Hermann von Holst, a little known local architect. Marion Mahony, who had worked in Wright's office and had made the brilliant Japanesque perspectives of many designs, moved to von Holst's office and was largely responsible for developing the Robie house designs and overseeing its construction. George Mann Niedecken, who had built much of Wright's Prairie period furniture, assisted in fitting out the house. Wright had no hand in the project during most of the construction (he was in Europe the whole time), but he took legal action against von Holst for his fees. After seven months of hassle, Wright netted $108.29 from von Holst in a bitter moment. Wright also had to produce the long-postponed drawings for Francis Little's house outside of Minneapolis. The delay particularly galled Little as he, along with Darwin Martin, had backed Wright's Wasmuth venture, for which the architect still owed him $9,000.[3]

Because of his domestic scandal, many clients had abandoned Wright, but not all: Martin was still there, as were Queene and Avery Coonley, for whom he'd designed an estate in Riverside, Illinois. For Queene he designed a charming "playhouse" that served as a small coeducational school for children. Its tryptic of windows (now in the Metropolitan Museum of Art in New York) had simple, floating circles of reds and yellows, hinting at Wright's turn toward circular motifs and asymmetrical compositions.[4]

Wright went back to New York in mid-November to make an indulgent visit to Tiffany's and to work on an exhibition pavilion for the Universal Portland Cement Company. Rushed in design and construction for a mid-December opening, the pavilion used concrete articulated with surface ornament resonant of the late Secession motifs that had intrigued Wright.[5] He also visited his sister Maginel, who had just moved to Manhattan to pursue her career as an illustrator. Always affectionate toward her brother, she would later play a major role in sheltering him from an onslaught of vicissitudes.

Within three months of Wright's return to America, problems with Wasmuth in Germany increased. The disputes were about money— Wright's overdue payment for publication. In early January 1911, he decided a face-to-face confrontation with Ernst Wasmuth was necessary. For the fourth time in sixteen months, Wright went to New York. In the city, the eleventh National Annual Automobile Exhibition, under way at Madison Square Garden, included a display of electric vehicles. The regular affairs of High Society continued, as the *New York Times* reported, with dances, cotillions, receptions at private residences, as well as the circulation of European princes and princesses who arrived on the *Kronprinz Wilhelm* or the *Potsdam*. But there was no notice of Frank Lloyd Wright, and he continued on to make his second trip to Germany, departing the city in style on January 16, 1911, on the RMS *Lusitania*.

The Cunard liner, briefly the world's largest passenger ship, was the most luxurious passenger ship afloat, and so fast it was called the "Greyhound of the Sea." Four years later, however, it was unable to outrun a German U-boat, and its sinking helped propel the United States into war.[6]

The trip to Germany took place with no fanfare, as Wright's full purpose was hidden. Though he could legitimately tell people he was going to work with his publisher, he was also eager to see Mamah, who'd stayed behind.[7] Wright's negotiations with Wasmuth in Berlin succeeded, and by February 13, 1911, he had revised his publishing contract. No details of the brief reunion with Mamah surfaced, but they must have discussed their plans for a future together. Wright passed through New York yet again, arriving on March 30, 1911, on the SS *Mauretania,* which had surpassed the *Lusitania* as the largest ocean liner. By April 3, Wright was back in Oak Park.[8]

Wright had reasons for optimism that spring. The forces that had bored down when he'd first passed through New York appeared to resolve. He began planning the domestic sale of his Wasmuth publications—both the folios and the picture book—through mail-order sales, supported by an advertising campaign, and through bookstores. The task would preoccupy him for the next three years. Using his mother as signatory for a purchase agreement, Wright also bought a thirty-one-and-a-half-acre site surrounded by the farms of his uncles near Spring Green in Wisconsin. In this ancestral valley of the Lloyd-Jones clan, Wright began designing and building a refuge for himself and Mamah. He called it Taliesin, or "Shining Brow," after the shape-shifting Welsh bard whose forehead glowed. It lay near Tan-y-deri, the home he'd designed for his sister Jane and her husband Andrew Porter, and not far from the Hillside Home School operated by his aunts. The design of Taliesin drew on the familiar Prairie period vocabulary with overhanging pitched roofs, but the siting and use of rough masonry and huge base moldings created a mythic resonance, as if the abode were ancient and weathered. Jettisoning her married surname, Mamah returned from Europe in June 1911 after visiting Ellen Key, the Swedish feminist whose tracts she was translating. She stopped in New York to discuss the publication of her translation of Key's *Woman Movement* with G. P. Putnam and Sons. The book put forward

Key's idea that "Love is moral even without legal marriage, but marriage is immoral without love."[9]

Wright felt that despite his personal struggle and guilt, his spiritual hegira propelled him forward. He and Mamah were creating the life they had envisioned, fortified by a new home. And Wright's creativity experienced a rebirth as the golden age of the Prairie period gave way to a new phase of experimental primitivism.

This turn is so unique in American architecture that Wright's move to primitivism requires some explanation. His experience in Europe had spurred the change. In the work of the Secessionists, Wright saw in simple geometry a form language that resonated with symbolic meaning. The essence of primitivism lay in the belief that use of these timeless motifs returned art to the origins of creativity when culture was untainted. That purity would now provide the raw material for a new vocabulary to express modern life, one that was at once universal, ancient, modern, and abstract.

A universe of ancient forms found particularly in non-Western cultures was a source of inspiration. These forms retained a purity and spoke to the origins of human creativity and spiritual practices. Wright's primitivist architecture paralleled the interests of not only the Secessionists but also an emerging avant-garde including Picasso and Braque, who emulated African, Oceanic, and other non-Western sources. Wright's interest, however, arose independently of early modern art.

Wright described his perception of these developments as manifested by Secession artists, from Joseph Olbrich to Gustav Klimt, as a "splendid confirmation" of his own latent interests. It explained the appeal of other non-Western cultures for him, from Asia to Mesoamerica to Native North America. He developed his theory in a short book, *The Japanese Print.* Form could express "human ideas, moods and sentiments," and their meanings were specific: the circle represented infinity; the triangle, structural unity; the spire, aspiration and the spiral, organic process; and the square, integrity. For Wright, these geometric shapes contained "Spell Power." Whether in two or three dimensions, these shapes are so fundamental that we can call them "primary forms." Everything is built from them.[10]

The prevalence of these forms over time, across cultures, suggesting "pure" origins, was a romantic idea but an inspiration to artists from painters to composers. Primitivism perpetuated the fantasy of a golden age when art, spirit, and matter melded in a cultural harmony. But the fantasy in no way impeded the conviction. Wright's interest in primitivism continued for the next ten years, long before the exoticism of Egyptomania, Aztec revival, and even Babylonian revival animated American architecture in the 1920s. Primitivism also bonded Wright with the Reverend Guthrie, who believed in calling on universal sources for spiritual rebirth and the vitality of non-Western cultures, which he studied in detail.[11]

Two major projects became testing grounds for Wright's interest in primitivism. The first was Midway Gardens in Chicago, a commission from Ed Waller, an old friend and former client. This imaginative version of a beer garden would feature indoor and outdoor dining areas and a band shell for performances. Its decorative sculpture, murals, and patterned surfaces, cast on site, allowed Wright to develop a new approach to ornament, the first major development in his architecture since the innovations of his Prairie period.[12]

The second opportunity to experiment came with prospects for designing a new Imperial Hotel in Tokyo that would replace the existing outmoded building. In 1912, Wright learned that he was under consideration for a commission to design the hotel. Wright and Mamah left Taliesin in late December 1912, but they missed their boat to Japan and had to spend two weeks in California. While there, Wright was contacted about advertising in a special issue of *Arts and Decoration,* planned to be distributed at the New York Armory Show. Wright passed on the opportunity to promote his architecture at the epochal event that announced the presence of modern art in America.[13]

Finally, on January 11, 1913, Wright and Mamah departed for a five-month visit to Japan. The Imperial Hotel project started nearly simultaneously with Midway Gardens, but it would take almost a decade to complete. Wright assumed the project would proceed, but he had no contract. He produced a preliminary scheme that melded Japanese motifs with his Western sensibility, but the project hit a wall because the Meiji emperor had died six months earlier. A declaration of official mourning delayed discussion of the project and left it in limbo. Wright and Mamah left Japan and returned to the United States in late May 1913. En route they stopped in San Francisco, where, while staying at the elegant St. Francis Hotel, Wright supplied the *San Francisco Call* with a highly exaggerated account of his activities. The newspaper, for which Wright would later design his first skyscraper, reported on June 8 that Wright "has just returned from Japan, where he is superintending the construction of a new hotel in Tokyo. . . . Mr. Frank Lloyd Wright has built hunting lodges and summer homes of the royal family of Germany, as well as for many of our most wealthy Americans . . . [and] is also superintending the construction of several buildings for the emperor." It was a wonderful public relations ploy, but none of it was accurate.[14]

The designs for both Midway Gardens and the early phase of the Imperial Hotel came from Wright's studio at Taliesin. With Mamah settled and projects trickling in, Wright felt hopeful. He even had the good fortune of having his work promoted in Europe by Hendrik Petrus Berlage, considered the father of Dutch modern architecture. He had seen Wright's architecture in Chicago (but missed meeting the architect) and discussed it in March 1912 in a lecture on "New American Architecture" at the Swiss Society of Engineers and Architects in Zurich. The lecture and its subsequent publications in German and Dutch introduced Wright to Holland, Germany, and Switzerland and proved to be far more influential in spreading his name than the Wasmuth publications with their limited distribution.[15]

In the midst of Wright's professional revival, he and Mamah began to publicly present themselves as models for others. Mamah was the translator of the writings of Swedish feminist Ellen Key, and both she and Wright propagated Key's theory of love marriage, in which love, not social convention, bonded two people. A corollary notion promoted the liberating of children from rigid constraints of upbringing; they were the hope of the future and deserved their freedom. Wright made statements in the local press promoting their views—a noble gesture, but utterly naïve. As Guthrie had predicted, society rose up in opposition; the neighbors were appalled, and Wright and Mamah's children in no way benefited.

The movement toward serving as role models and creating a shared life in harmony did not last. While supervising construction at Midway Gardens with his son John, Wright received word of a fire at Taliesin on August 15, 1914. He rushed to Wisconsin to find a scene of horror. Julian Carlton, a servant from Barbados, had murdered Mamah, her two children, and four others working at the time. Deranged and psychotic, Carlton attacked his victims with a hatchet and intended to burn down Taliesin. Still recovering from the scandal of adultery, the Taliesin tragedy marked the start of a series of calamities for Wright that would take place over the next fifteen years.[16]

The horrific events were front-page news in the *Chicago Sunday Tribune*. "The Terrible Fate of Mamah Borthwick in her Bungalow of love," reported the newspaper as it recounted the details of not only the brutal murders but the debacle that involved Wright, Mamah, and their respective families (fig. 7). It was easy for the press, and later critics, to cast the tragedy as divine retribution against a couple that lived in sin and flaunted social convention. However, Herbert Fritz, a teenaged draftsman who survived the attack, provided an account that indicated Carlton's motive involved a grudge against a draftsman who'd harassed him and called him "a black son of a bitch" and was not a vendetta against Mamah or Wright.[17]

Wright's dream world was shattered. His younger sisters tried to comfort him in the aftermath. Jane was living at Tan-y-deri, and she did all she could while Wright hid out in a small bedroom at the back of his workshop. Maginel rushed from New York to Spring Green. "I went to the Valley to be with him," she recalled. "He wanted to ride, and so we rode by the hour, farther than we would have ridden in a happier time, as far as we could: over Pleasant Ridge, to Blue Mound, and on and on. He would stop the horses on a hill and stare down at the Valley, with its cloud shadows."[18]

Slowly, painfully, Wright moved from paralysis to rebuilding. The house had burned, but his studio had survived. "I went to the Valley again in May when the building was under way," Maginel recalled when she returned in spring 1915. "Jane, staunch as always in a crisis, had been working like a stevedore, and now I came to help her; she and I, with a

Fig. 7 Report on the Taliesin tragedy in the *Chicago Daily Tribune*, August 17, 1914.

neighbor or two, daily fed the twenty-five men at work on the building, as well as ourselves and our families. I was reminded of the threshing-time feasts of my childhood." Taliesin II, as it was later known, was rebuilt with shards of the burned Taliesin I cemented into the piers of the new construction. "Perhaps," Wright speculated, "new consciousness had to grow as a green shoot will grow from a charred and blackened stump."[19]

Wright mourned, feeling the deep grief that steals hopes of the future and deadens connections to the living. With his practice halted by the

Fig. 8 Miriam Noel at Taliesin.

fire, the Imperial Hotel in limbo, new prospects few, the love of his life murdered, New York was out of focus. Wright was alone except for mother and sisters.

But not for long. Shortly after Mamah's death, Wright met the woman who would eventually become his second wife, Miriam Maude Noel (fig. 8). She sent him a condolence note in December, and he invited her to meet at his office in Chicago. In her mid-forties, divorced with grown children, Miriam had worked in Paris as a sculptor and returned to the United States at the threat of war in Europe. At the time of their meeting, she claimed that as a fellow artist she could commiserate with Wright's suffering.[20]

"Rejoice . . . that you are worthy to bear so great affliction," she wrote the architect. As their correspondence progressed, Wright wrote her before Christmas 1914: "I hunger for the living touch of someone— something, immediately peculiar to myself—invariably 'mine.' Yes—at time almost *anyone* or *anything*." Miriam in turn likened him to a Greek warrior: "Let me crown your head with a wreath of violets and bind your hair with filets of gold, like Alcibiades at the Feast of Agathon." So began their life together, both figures burning with self-importance and passion, both grandiose, needy, and vulnerable.[21]

By various accounts, Miriam Noel was attractive and mysterious, spiritual and sensuous. Wright described her as "brilliant," but he also saw her as burdened with neuroses. Though Wright was still married to Catherine, who refused to grant him a divorce, he soon installed Miriam at Taliesin.

Wright and Miriam would spend much of the next ten years in flux and strife, bouncing between Taliesin, Los Angeles, Tokyo for long stretches, and New York. Wright's designs during the mid-1910s now moved on two tracks, one innovative, the other formulaic. He explored primitivist motifs as he began a long-term project, a whole complex for Aline Barnsdall, an oil fortune heiress, with her residence Hollyhock House as the initial focus on Olive Hill, a thirty-six-acre site in the Hollywood area of Los Angeles.[22]

Simplistically identified as Mayan revival, Hollyhock House was actually more complex. Ultimately constructed of stucco over structural clay tile block, Wright had intended it to be constructed of poured concrete—an update of his approach at Unity Temple. The mass with its inward sloping upper walls resembled the roofs of the Yamamura House in Japan he designed and built about the same time. Wright saw the structures as kindred spirits, an ode to universal motifs in the collective of archetypal forms.

For other commissions, Wright fell back on the Prairie period style, usually as an expedient. A commission for a home would come his way, but he was often distracted by personal issues or traveling. These homes were not without merit: a residence in Wichita, Kansas, for Henry J. Allen, newspaper editor and future governor of that state, was efficient, handsome, and appropriate for the client, but it was still a house Wright could have designed ten years earlier. Wright did somehow manage to work out a method for prefabricated, factory-built housing, the American System-Built Homes. A home buyer could order a kit of parts, Ready-Cut, to be shipped from the factory and built on the desired site. Despite advertising, strong designs, and some built models, the system did not catch on.[23]

Life at Taliesin, though bucolic, was not peaceful for Wright and Miriam. An aggrieved former housekeeper told the local newspaper that Miriam had accused Wright of cruelty, emotional torture, and flirting, alleging that he had violated the Mann Act. This recent law made it a crime to transport a woman across state lines for immoral purposes. An investigation followed and found no grounds for prosecution. Wright and Miriam survived that insulting intrusion into their life, and she accompanied him in late December 1916 on the first of their five visits to Tokyo as work resumed on the Imperial Hotel.[24]

Their quarrels and discord persisted. Wright drew up a contract with Miriam, signed by both and stamped with an ersatz seal like a real notarized document, that stipulated Wright would pay Miriam $60 a month for her services "to properly keep the house of Frank Lloyd Wright," and that this arrangement would continue as long as she remained with him. They were lovers, and the days of pretending she might be domestic help were long past. The instigator of the contract is unclear, but considering Miriam's fusty character, she may have demanded that Wright guarantee her an allowance, a reasonable demand since he'd used her money to rebuild Taliesin after the fire.[25]

Wright was always open with his mother Anna about his lovers, sharing his private fears and hopes first about Mamah and now his relationship with Miriam. Despite his adultery, which appalled her, his mother stuck close to her adored and only son, becoming quite involved in this newest relationship. "Had I the power to express myself clearly I know I could convince you of my loyalty to you and to Frank," Anna wrote to Miriam in July 1918. "Miriam," she continued, "you may go a long way before you find the sweet true spirit he manifests. There are few men as clean and pure in his conceptions of life, hence his artistic skill." For Anna, the solution to all their problems was marriage, and she pressed the issue for the next two years, ignoring the fact that Wright was still married to his first wife. Even more was at stake in resolving domestic conflict. Wright's aunts Nell and Jennie had died and left their Hillside Home School derelict. Wright told his mother he had plans for it, giving the first hint of the endeavor that would eventually become the Taliesin Fellowship. When Wright stated he wanted to use the campus to train young people, Anna asked how he could possibly propose such an undertaking with his own personal affairs so unsettled. Once again, she insisted that marriage was the answer.[26]

During these years of domestic struggles with Miriam, New York served as a marketplace for Wright's Japanese prints. He had long collected Japanese art and was a major dealer in woodblock prints. His frequent stays in Japan to work on the Imperial Hotel provided additional opportunities for increasing his vast holdings. A collector and a dealer, he targeted the Metropolitan Museum of Art for new sales (fig. 9). Wright would make at least three visits to New York over a five-year period for this purpose during the interludes when he returned to the United States.[27]

Wright's dealings with the Metropolitan Museum of Art began in the summer of 1917, when he started to negotiate print sales with Sigisbert Chrétien Bosch Reitz, the museum's curator of Far Eastern art. To spread the word of his holdings, Wright mounted an exhibition at the Arts Club of Chicago that lasted from November to early December and included a catalogue. He had assembled so many prints that, after receiving a copy of the exhibition catalogue, his friend Guthrie kidded him, "Are you alienating some more of these treasures? I hope not." Guthrie, who had gone to New York in 1911 when appointed rector of St. Mark's Church in-the-Bowery, had stayed in touch with Wright. Addressing Wright as "Dear Zealot," he also brought up their shared interest in primitivist sources, from Isis to "aboriginal Indians"; to them, Japanese woodblock prints were another aspect of "pure" design.[28]

In 1918, while Wright was residing at Taliesin between stays in Japan, he made two major sales to the Metropolitan Museum, one in July and the other in October, selling $20,000 worth of prints. Wright went to New York in October 1919 for further sales. He hosted a "print party" at the Hotel Astor, inviting experts and wealthy clients. Located in Times Square, the large and lavish hotel had long been a popular meeting place, with themed spaces, from a Flemish smoking room to an American Indian grill room, and ballrooms of various sizes. Wright needed only a relatively small venue for the prints, but the setting was festive and centrally situated, and resulted in several sales.[29]

Fig. 9 Metropolitan Museum of Art, New York, May 3, 1920.

Wright took advantage of this visit to New York to hire Antonin Raymond to assist him with the Imperial Hotel in Tokyo. Raymond, a thirty-year-old Bohemian-born architect who had come to New York in 1910 and worked for Cass Gilbert, the architect of the Woolworth Building, would become Wright's chief draftsman on the Imperial Hotel. Noémi Claude Raymond, his wife, worked with them as well.[30]

Hiring Raymond was a boon, but the print party was a bust. In July 1920, Frederick Gookin, Wright's close friend and noted expert on Japanese prints, broke the bad news that several of the sold prints had been retouched, or "revamped." The claim would have been disastrous for any dealer. Nevertheless, in the spring of 1921, Wright dropped back into New York while crisscrossing the United States to push print sales. Sometime between mid-April and late July, he spent two weeks in the city, probably still dealing with the print sales, before returning to Los Angeles and eventually heading to Japan.[31]

The challenges of building the Imperial Hotel and a dysfunctional relationship had dominated much of Wright's years in Japan. Progress had been slower on the hotel than he anticipated; a whole wing had yet to be constructed. An opening of the central section and the completed guest wing of the hotel had been planned for May 1922, but it was delayed because a severe earthquake hit Tokyo in April. When Wright left Japan, he had hoped that the whole building would be realized within six weeks; it took over a year. He had spent thirty-nine months in Japan during the previous six years. Arriving in Seattle on August 1, 1922, he and Miriam headed to Taliesin. Passing through Chicago en route, Wright indulged a tendency that worked both for and against him: trying to manipulate the press for his benefit, attacking whatever he objected to or defending his own ideas and actions. In this instance, he aimed for self-promotion. At his prompting, the *Chicago Daily Tribune* announced his return after spending several years working on the Imperial Hotel, built at a cost of $6 million, the equivalent of $83 million today.[32]

Arriving at Taliesin by August 20, Wright began to get Taliesin up and running in the fall of 1922. He also started to think about how and where to resurrect his practice in America and generate funds. He planned another visit to New York, as he told Bosch Reitz, explicitly to sell prints to meet operating expenses at Taliesin. Heading to the city in late October 1922, Wright passed through Buffalo, where he sold the Martins Japanese garments and objects.[33]

Wright's final sales to the Metropolitan Museum concluded by November 1922. He had sold the institution nearly four hundred Japanese prints, but, after the revamping debacle, his career as a major dealer was over. Although Wright made more money from the print sales than from his architectural commissions, he held on to none of it. The long-awaited divorce from his wife Catherine in November 1922 required settlement and alimony payments that absorbed much of this revenue. Living expenses consumed the rest. Wright's dealings with New York as the locus of his print market left a bittersweet taste. Two tense years would pass before Wright resumed contact with New York.[34]

Wright imagined that life on the west coast could solve at least his professional problems. In the fall of 1922 he informed his son Lloyd, who had already collaborated on several of Wright's projects, that he was considering moving to Los Angeles and would join him there. Wright and Miriam arrived in Los Angeles after the winter holidays, and by February 1923 they had rented 1284 Harper Avenue for a home and studio in what is now West Hollywood.[35]

Life in Los Angeles appeared promising but problematic. Work had gone badly at the Hollyhock House complex for Aline Barnsdall. During Wright's protracted absences he had turned the project over to Lloyd, and to Rudolf Schindler, Wright's former assistant at Taliesin. Problems mounted; fed up with Wright's absences, Barnsdall fired him, but their relationship somehow endured.

While in Los Angeles, Wright designed a series of houses that were just starting construction. Known as textile-block houses, their method of construction using patterned concrete blocks gave the appearance of a fabric pattern. Wright's assumption was that casting the blocks on site with the site's own material would save money, and this economical process would revolutionize construction methods. In doing so he was elevating the utilitarian concrete block into a wall material for exterior and interior use. But unlike other manufactured blocks, Wright's blocks were covered with the ornament patterns he had been developing over the past eight years, first at Midway Gardens and then extensively at the Imperial Hotel. Dynamic angular movements dominated their surface compositions, in contrast to the simpler geometry of his Prairie period. His insistent use of ornament, however, as described earlier, distanced him from modern architects who increasingly produced their abstract designs with flat, unadorned planes. For Wright, ornament as pattern remained central to his methods, and he used the textile block for almost all of his projects over the next ten years.[36]

Meanwhile, the Imperial Hotel still weighed on Wright. It finally opened on September 1, 1923—the very day the Great Kantō earthquake struck Japan, leveling much of Tokyo, devastating the port of Yokohama, and damaging the surrounding prefectures. Over one hundred thousand people died in what was the greatest natural disaster ever to hit the country. Wright read some accounts from newspapers in Los Angeles, but with ruptured communication and widespread destruction, he had no news about the fate of the Imperial until nearly two weeks after the earthquake had struck, when he received a telegram signed by his client and supporter Baron Okura: "Hotel stands undamaged as monument of your genius hundreds of homeless provided shelter by perfectly maintained service congratulations."[37]

The building's miraculous survival focused attention on Wright. The architect claimed that the secret of its survival was his designing two separate structural systems—one for the floors and one for the walls—that allowed the force of the tremors to be absorbed in two ways. Some critics disputed the claim, and in actuality the building survived due in part to luck and in part to its masonry mass. Nevertheless, newspapers circulated news of the feat widely and headlined Wright as the architect whose building defied disaster, a tag that became his first national public moniker, his first brand. It identified him more in the popular imagination than his Prairie period buildings ever had. Proud and pleased, Wright hoped that potential clients would take note.[38]

Although intent on establishing an architectural practice in Los Angeles, Wright bounced between the West Coast and the Midwest. Turning again to the press to promote his work, he updated his friend William T. Evjue, founder and editor of the *Madison Capitol Times,* with some exaggerated accounts of his practice. Claiming that he anticipated having offices in Chicago, Hollywood, and Tokyo, Wright explained he was laying out designs for a Hollywood Hills project and a summer resort in Tahoe, which would "cost millions." Both projects, the former on the site of the Doheny Ranch and the latter on Lake Tahoe, would fall through within two years. But for the time being, with wind in his sails and having finally received the divorce from Catherine, Wright married Miriam Maude Noel in Spring Green on November 19, 1923, fulfilling the wish of his mother, Anna. She never witnessed the event, though, having died eight months earlier. Wright hoped that the marriage would heal his fractured relationship with Miriam, as his mother suggested. Marriage, however, solved nothing, and by May 1924 Miriam had left Taliesin.[39]

On the professional front, Wright had limited visibility from the Taliesin tragedy to his return from Japan. His writing had been sporadic. He wrote a second paper that took up the banner "In the Cause of Architecture." Published by the *Architectural Record* in 1914, it mostly rehashed ideas covered in the Wasmuth introduction. Aside from a few short, scattered pieces, Wright published little in the 1910s while he was immersed in building the Imperial Hotel. But the survival of the hotel in a devasting earthquake generated sensational publicity, including Wright's own pamphlet, *Experimenting with Human Lives,* and a pair of articles that appeared in *Western Architect* in 1923.[40]

He pushed forward with his architectural practice in the late spring and summer of 1924. On the personal side, Wright considered himself liberated from Miriam, and by the fall he began to socialize. During a visit to Chicago on November 30, the artist Jerry Bloom invited him to a matinee at the Eighth Street Theatre featuring Tamara Karsavina, a renowned Russian ballerina. After the intermission, a beautiful woman entered the box where he sat. Olgivanna Hinzenberg was thirty years younger than the fifty-seven-year-old architect (fig. 10). They soon fell in love.[41]

If Miriam had been said to have a spiritual side, it paled compared with Olgivanna's otherworldly orientation. Olgivanna was born Olga Lazovich in 1897, and her maternal grandfather, Marko Miljanov, had been a Balkan general credited with preserving Montenegro's independence; her father had been chief justice of the country for almost thirty years. Later known as Olgivanna, in 1917, at age nineteen, she had married a Latvian architect named Valdemar Hinzenberg. She was pregnant within the year, giving birth to their daughter Svetlana. In 1919 she came under the influence of Georgi Ivanovich Gurdjieff, the charismatic Armenian-born mystic who taught dance techniques called Movements, which he claimed could transport his followers beyond the realm of ordinary senses. By the early 1920s, Olgivanna was one of his principal devotees. Gurdjieff helped her see her path as divinely charted, ordered by strict disciplinary routines, and devoted unquestionably to the service of an evolved master. She was not only one of the best dancers in Gurdjieff's institute, La Prieuré, located in Fontainebleau, just outside of Paris, but also a dance teacher.[42]

By the time Wright met Olgivanna, she was one of Gurdjieff's disciples charged with finding a center for the master in America—as well as the funds to support him and his enterprise. Without his knowing it, the circle identified Wright as either a potential funder—a gross error,

Fig. 10 Olgivanna Hinzenberg, c. 1924.

given his shaky finances—or a benefactor with an idyllic estate, Taliesin, for their activities. Also unknown to Wright, Bloom, who was on the Gurdjieffian fringe, may have orchestrated the meeting that fateful night in November for the purpose of introducing Wright to the beautiful and exotic Olgivanna.[43]

In any case, Wright was smitten and began courting Olgivanna in Chicago. A week-long trip to New York in December 1924 interrupted his pursuit of her, but the temporary separation gave Wright a chance to contemplate his new affection. He saw Olgivanna's Montenegrin roots as akin to his Welsh ancestry. The liberators and judges of her lineage were analogous to the outspoken preachers of his maternal family. He and Olgivanna saw themselves as free-spirited rebels, guided by principle, in the struggle for truth and justice.[44]

After his return from New York, Wright made plans to bring Olgivanna to Taliesin in January 1925 and pulled out all the stops to impress her. He had his Cadillac washed and recruited a new chauffer, who wore a special fur cap, to drive them from Madison to Taliesin, where he presented her to his draftsmen as "Mary," the new housekeeper.[45]

FLEETING GLANCES

Olgivanna not only filled the gap of the woman at his side, but would soon reveal dimensions of life—and New York—that Wright had never seen. She had her own recent experience of the city. She had arrived there from France on January 13, 1924, in the company of Gurdjieff on a three-month expedition to demonstrate his ideas and to survey the prospects for establishing a branch of the mystic's institute in the United States. His arrival marked a series of appearances that enthralled audiences, including many New York intellectuals and literati. One *New York Times* advertisement promoted in bold letters the Gurdjieff Institute's March 3 performance at Carnegie Hall: a "One Demonstration Only" event of "Ritual Dancing" and "Supernormal Phenomena."[46]

Olgivanna had stayed in New York after Gurdjieff's departure and returned to France in mid-June. Gurdjieff then capriciously ejected her from his institute in Versailles—implying that she had not met his lofty spiritual standards—and temporarily relegated her to working in Paris as "an attendant in a women's lavatory." He decided just as capriciously to rehabilitate her and sent her back to America in October with instructions to visit New York and Chicago and pursue her assignment of finding a new location for the institute. It was in pursuing her mission that she had first met Wright in Chicago.[47]

In February 1925, Olgivanna brought Wright back with her to New York. A new facet of the city opened. When he and Olgivanna arrived, they met with the leaders of Gurdjieff's institute, including the English writer and literary critic Alfred Orage, a proponent of radical politics and Eastern mysticism. Orage, an instrumental advocate for Gurdjieff's teachings in New York, actively organized groups to discuss his ideas as well as presentations of the dances in which Olgivanna had a lead role. On February 17, Olgivanna attended a meeting with Orage and Jean Toomer, a poet, novelist, and figure in the Harlem Renaissance. Also present was the author and playwright Zona Gale, a Wisconsinite whom Wright had briefly, yet unsuccessfully, pursued romantically.[48]

The meeting initially convened before Wright arrived, its purpose kept secret from other members of the institute, to discuss strategies for involving Olgivanna's new lover with their efforts. Wright arrived some time later. The details of the discussion remain undocumented, but if the group offered money for the use of Wright's Taliesin estate, he would have been thrilled, particularly since a major architectural project had just collapsed. Regardless of details, Wright was attracted to Gurdjieff's philosophy; it appealed to his metaphysical inclination. The mystic and the architect shared a mutual interest in "organic life"—the unity of existence, nature, and God with man's soul—and a belief that art was a means of revealing the cosmic order. Olgivanna's own mysticism, bolstered by Wright, would color their partnership. New York's role as a touchstone expanded. For Wright, it contained not only a mecca of skyscrapers but also an exotic coterie; for Olgivanna, her own esoteric circle. By March she was pregnant with their child. "It is now 1925," Wright noted. "Creative urge has gathered energy, once more. Objectives dimly felt, gropingly sought, are coming clearer now: confusion and disgraceful turmoil have ended. Sanity. The normal. Yes, it is the basis of all Freedom."[49]

3

NADIR

Returning from New York in midwinter 1925, Wright and Olgivanna settled into Taliesin, fashioning their life together, awaiting the birth of their child, and rebuilding—again—Wright's architectural practice. Progress came to a hard stop when a fire ravaged Taliesin on April 20. The conflagration destroyed the living room, bedrooms, kitchen, and dining room, but spared, as had the first fire in 1914, Wright's studio.

"The frustration of the life of the past seven years had ended in the destruction of everything the frustrated life had touched," Wright wrote as he tried to make sense of the event. "I sought comfort in that thought as one fine thing after another would rise out of its ashes and reproach me with a shameful sense of loss." To Wright, it was as if the gods had turned against him once again. He invoked the fate of the Old Testament prophet: "No doubt Isaiah still stood there in the storms that muttered, rolled and broke again over this low spreading shelter. . . . Had the angry prophet struck twice? He could strike again?" His mother was gone, his mentor Louis Sullivan had died in 1924, and Wright's three homes—Oak Park and Taliesin I and II—all slipped from him.[1]

Wright's family and friends rallied around the architect after the fire. His twenty-nine-year-old son David wrote his father with sympathy, and Guthrie and others sent word. Wright described his home as sensate to the struggles around him. "Taliesin's radiant brow though now marked by shame and sorrow should come forth and shine with serenity unknown before," he wrote. At least, in what he called his "third trial," he had "a little new soul long desired" who would help to replace what was lost. "I had," he added, "self-inflicted failure to bear. . . . But never have I been allowed to bear failure alone." The person who kept Wright from bearing failure alone was Olgivanna; the "little new soul" was the daughter they had conceived.[2]

Through spring and into the summer of 1925, the sense of shared struggle deepened the emotional bond between Wright and Olgivanna. He filed for divorce with Miriam and suggested a settlement in August. Miriam, who was in Los Angeles, had no idea that Olgivanna had replaced her at Taliesin, let alone that she was pregnant.[3]

The first phase of a protracted battle soon began. Both Miriam and Wright would fan the flames of the drama that followed, and both played the press for their own ends. He had still been basking in the fame of the Imperial Hotel's survival, but in the months ahead the press would turn on him, transforming him into a juicy subject of yellow journalism. Wire services, particularly the Associated Press and the Hearst papers, sent details of his escapades not only to papers in Chicago and New York but to small towns from Reading, Pennsylvania, to Manitowoc, Wisconsin.

The *Reading Times* reported in mid-November 1925 that both Wright and Miriam had withdrawn their divorce actions, and that Wright refused to admit that he was involved with another woman. Miriam, however, learned that Olgivanna had become "the newest affinity of her husband," according to one report. She therefore planned to file a new suit for separate maintenance. In an Associated Press wire story, Miriam claimed Wright had "bullied" her into agreeing to a divorce but that she opposed it upon discovering Olgivanna. "He'd fall in love," Miriam told the reporters, "with anyone who flattered him, told him he was the most wonderful man in the world. He proposes to discard me, toss me aside.

But I'll stop him if I have to raise a scandal." She already had raised a scandal, and it was generating the kind of publicity that would scare away new clients and frighten those few Wright still had.[4]

Miriam's campaign would hound Wright and Olgivanna for over three years. Tracking their movements, Miriam discovered that on December 2, 1925, Olgivanna had given birth to Iovanna Lazovich Lloyd Wright in Chicago. Miriam barged into the hospital and harassed Olgivanna in the room where she lay recovering. In the chaos Wright described as a "public charivari," he felt he had to rescue his family. Temporary shelter appeared in an offer from Olgivanna's brother Vladimir, whom they called Vlado, and his wife Sophie to have Olgivanna and her children stay with them in Hollis, a small residential neighborhood in Queens, New York. They insisted he go as well. "Of my brothers," Olgivanna recalled, "I was closest to Vlado who was sensitive, kind, and magnificently handsome."[5]

Wright's stay in Queens with his extended family gave him the opportunity to experience the city on his own from an enclave in the suburbs. Hollis was a small, middle-class residential neighborhood near what is now Jamaica, Queens. It had a few roots in Revolutionary battles but had remained largely rural until 1885, when developers transformed 126 acres of land into single-family houses. Hollis became part of New York City when it was amalgamated into Queens in 1898 (when Queens, in turn, was amalgamated into New York). In this modest community, Vlado and Sophie had found a rental house with enough room for his sister and her new family. The homes in Hollis were plain but sturdy row houses, two or three stories tall, prosaic American housing quite different from Wright's organic designs for middle-class Americans. When Wright arrived, Jamaica Avenue, a central thoroughfare, featured automobiles, trolleys, and even horse-drawn wagons for coal deliveries (fig. 11). For his solitary forays into Manhattan, he probably took the Hempstead branch of the Long Island Rail Road from Hollis Station, changing trains at Jamaica Station to a line that would deposit him at Pennsylvania Station in Manhattan. On exiting to the street, he could not avoid the Roman grandeur of McKim, Mead & White's masterpiece, with its thermal windows, great arches, and the light lattice structure of metal columns supporting the vast rail shed.[6]

Fig. 11 Jamaica Avenue, between Hollis Court Boulevard and 212th Street, October 26, 1928.

Wright and his family arrived in New York in the frenzy of the Christmas season. The *New York Times* informed the public of sales, parties, events, as well as the news. The paper included miscellany too: thirty-year-old Robert M. La Follette Jr., the brother of Philip, who would become one of Wright's lawyers in Wisconsin, was elected to the U.S. Senate to succeed their late father. The paper also ran a piece about a contingent of architects from the New York Chapter of the American Institute of Architects (AIA) who met with Senator James J. "Jimmy" Walker, city mayor-designate, to address the city's antiquated building code. The architects' goal was to improve relations between practitioners and the city and to reduce the byzantine permit requirements for small buildings.[7]

Wright accompanied his brother-in-law on his way to work. "I would go back to town with Vlado in the morning," he recollected, "to roam the streets of New York alone. I didn't care to see anyone for fear of revealing our whereabouts." Wright never mentioned visiting his sister Maginel, whose husband had died in 1925, or his friend Guthrie. He needed the solace, no doubt, and the rambling time in New York prompted his first attempts to come to terms with the city through his writing. As he put it, "I tried to write some impressions of the big city. 'In Bondage,' was one. 'The Usonian City' another."[8]

Wright originally called his first essay "Prelude to the City," only to later retitle the nine-page typescript "In Bondage." The text rang with a broad existential moan about modern life. In the "big machine New York," Wright expressed a pervasive sense of waiting—from crossing the street to getting stuck in an elevator. He felt inundated by "printed matter stacked in every hotel lobby, waiting at the gates of every train, waiting on the floor outside the hotel bedroom door." He saw the populace as automatons: "The throng seems to see nothing—the blind hurrying by" in the overwhelming presence of media, from electric signs to the crush of cabs and crowds. The pace was so kinetic that it diluted to numbness.[9]

Wright scrutinized materialism. "Men?" he questioned. They were "a drab characterless collection of items with no style." Their objects of everyday life were equally empty. "I have seen an enormous glut of everything—and have seen nothing of any true significance where any real life worth living is concerned. In apparel, furnishings, luxuries, motor cars or buildings, in whatever is bought and sold or may be had for love or money, I have looked for significance of *form:* some integrity in the making to justify the making. I see the extravagant pictures we are so busy making by way of these things all as *untrue.*"[10]

The city reeked of moral decay. The theater was louche: "New and old playhouses,—same plays of sex appeal, sex intrigue, sex satisfaction. Plays of vicarious sex, sex inhibitions, sex perversion. Plays on sex triumphant, sex foiled or sex despoiled—until the one passionate interest evident as the living new in urban pictures and 'shows' is 'Sex.' The shapely sexual leg is the living nerve, the never-failing 'motif' in this civilization of ours."[11]

For Wright, the images of things competed with reality itself. "Vaunted 'modernity' itself is everywhere attempting by attitudinizing or by general 'pictorialization' to vicariously recreate—yes—make shift to live in the *imitation* now wholly pictorial." He even criticized the romantic image of the American melting pot: "Perhaps we are improving upon famous hypocrisies of the past in this heterogeneous mix of Goldsteins, O'Tooles, Smiths, Jones, Telemachers, Petroviskis, Petersons, Carambas, Ledoux and Teufelmackers, all boiling together on the big-city gridiron while groping for a common denominator."[12]

Life in New York was dystopic, or so Wright, the maven of nature, seemed to suggest. Wright was by no means the only figure to bemoan modernism's displacement of life. But beyond his lament, the essay reveals dimensions of the architect himself. On the one hand, the intensity of his attack masked his own sense of being an outsider, his rage at not having, like a hardened New Yorker, a thick skin. On the other hand, the essay provided a platform to sort through his own position as an urban critic. He became the protagonist of his account: "The Artist alone can help us by interpretation and experience to arrive at such an expression of ourselves." The artificial was inevitable, but making "great art" could "be to the human-spirit what clear springs of water, blue sky, green-grass and noble trees are to parched human-senses."[13]

In his other essay drafted in Hollis, "The Usonian City," Wright acknowledged that "civilization has seemed to need and feature the city," but paradoxically, "Did civilization die *of* it?" If the city of the future was to produce a "modern" civilization, then "I believe the city, as we know it today," he wrote, "is to die." "The city is man," he declared, "the machine . . . a baleful shadow of the sentient man that once needed the city and built it and maintained it because he needed it." This philosophy would guide Wright's view of urbanism for the next thirty years in the creation of what he would call "Usonia." Here Wright uses the word "Usonian" for the first time. The term had a complex history—Wright did not invent it—and it resonated vaguely with the United States of North America. For the architect, "Usonia" included the entire continent of North America from Mexico to Canada.[14]

"Usonia" was an evolving vision, not only an antidote to the depredations of contemporary urbanism, but a distinctly "American" solution, in contrast to the European conceptions of the modern city. Wright, by his own declaration, was beyond the avant-garde: "Even at this hour— via *cubisme* and *futurisme*—comes philosophic assertion that machinery, in itself, is prophetic of a more citified and fortified city." Wright feared this vision of "Man entombed, at the mercy of his own appliances," this "future city" where "utilitarian mechanics along the line march toward the ultimate triumph of machine over man." "To it is all dire prophecy," he intoned. "And it is all false." The Machine Age—and its art—was not for him.[15]

Wright then shifted to consider his central socioeconomic concern, decentralization. Current conditions demanded a new configuration for living that was not European-inspired *urbanisme,* which attempted to harness science, technology, and art to manage urban spaces. America would require fundamental changes to the landscape. New road systems of great concrete arteries would be needed, and with these a revision of all services, from gas stations to "chain merchandising and chain servic-ing," as well as the creation of small, self-sustaining sites in the country, surrounded by nature, linked by the new transport systems. "Cities are great mouths," Wright wrote, and "New York the greatest mouth in the world." In Wright's Usonian world, local products would find a short haul to market as opposed to the long haul of the extant city.[16]

Both essays played important roles in Wright formulating his posi-tions on urban versus rural life, and each was a springboard for further development. His physical contact with New York stimulated both posi-tion papers. "The Usonian City," conceived in December, would be slot-ted directly into his 1932 *Autobiography.* It would provide the grounding for *The Disappearing City* in 1932, which was in turn the ideological basis of Broadacre City, which we will see in chapter 9 as the synthesis of his design for rational living away from the congested city. In 1925, however, Wright did not know the form that Broadacre City would take; the con-cept would evolve over the next decade. He was only responding to his perception of the outmoded features of the American city and the threat of European models that put mechanization above all else.

The essay "In Bondage" had a different fate. Its focus was the alien-ation of the individual and culture, and it became the basis for a redrafted essay, "The Pictures We Make," which Wright would update from New York in late spring 1927.[17]

So here was Wright trying to make sense of the city, venturing out from his safe house in Queens to grapple with the behemoth on the other side of the East River. His writing may even have been a consolation, a centering device in the midst of personal flux. Both pieces present his expository method of working over his text and often incorporating the essays into longer publications. He would later compose his *Autobiography* largely through this same method of collaging several essays into "books" and in turn making them a single, expandable tome.

In Hollis, Olgivanna was still recovering from childbirth. The stress of public exposure and postpartum depression had taken a toll on her, and she was not improving. Wright came up with the idea that to help her recovery, they could go to Puerto Rico, which would be warm and, as a U.S. territory, not require passports (which would have been a challenge for Olgivanna, who was still an illegal alien). They traveled there incognito after the holidays to see "what remained of Atlantis." Wright found the island lovely but the poverty appalling. Using vernacular spelling, he reported, "Porto Rico is beautiful but Porto Ricans are pitiful. . . . Gentle, apathetic. Poor beyond belief." After two months they returned to the United States. Still showing symptoms of depression, Olgivanna ate little and remained but a "shadow" physically. Despite his lawyer's warning that they could expect legal trouble from Wright's creditors and from Miriam, they headed back to Taliesin in the spring of 1926.[18]

Lying low had hindered Wright's efforts to find new projects and constrained what little work he already had. The office he'd set up in Los Angeles had dissolved, but he did make drawings on his own for a scheme he called Skyscraper Regulation, an architectural solution for dealing with the dark, urban canyons that resulted from tall buildings being placed too close together. His idea was to lay out a checkerboard of skyscrapers, controlled in height, along an eight-block grid. Wide boulevards with trees, shrubs, fountains, and gardens would provide open space, with roads reserved for automobiles and small delivery vans. Large trucks would move underground or in alleys. Sidewalks at the second floor would allow pedestrian movement above ground level, and the roofs of the buildings would be flat—not pointy spires—with gardens. Insightful in concept, it was unbuildable at the time, a vehicle for ideas.[19]

He was not having much success building anything in the mid-1920s, though he certainly tried. His new designs took advantage of a development in the ornament of his block patterns in which he methodically rotated basic geometric shapes to produce dynamic, nonrectilinear compositions with marked angularity. Wright took this method, first used for ornament and surface patterns, and applied it to entire floor plans for buildings. Even the elevations and roofs showed this angularity, a continuity of idea that made every element cohere harmonically, an update of his organic vocabulary. He also applied dynamic diagonal planning to entire complexes, using pathways as axes, to span vast tracts of the landscape. Between 1922 and 1926—despite personal turmoil—Wright produced thirty designs, ranging from a concrete commercial building in Los Angeles to an abstracted figural sculpture of Native Americans for a country club; from a vast and sepulchral shrine and compound in Death Valley to a speculative summer resort on Lake Tahoe featuring floating barges as cabins. Exploring a new direction in a search for lightness and strength in tall buildings, he designed the office headquarters for the National Life Insurance Company in Chicago. Commissioned by Albert M. Johnson, it was Wright's first attempt to create a tall core with floors cantilevered from it, the approach he would develop further in New York. Unfortunately, Johnson would renege on the project by the end of 1925.[20]

Despite his efforts, all of Wright's projects collapsed, one by one. The fate of his "Automobile Objective" for client Gordon Strong exemplified the professional rollercoaster Wright was riding. A successful businessman, Strong had contacted Wright about designing a resort on Sugarloaf Mountain, Maryland, near Washington, D.C. A savvy businessman, Strong realized that ownership of automobiles would increase and people would be looking for someplace to drive to. Wright shared that view and began thinking about how the car would transform American life; he liked motoring himself, and he loved buying fancy cars, appreciating them like a smoker enjoying a fine cigar.[21]

Strong knew architecture: he had built the Republic Building in Chicago, one of the city's tallest buildings. And he knew real estate: he was also president of the National Association of Building Owners and Managers, a sprawling real estate management company, and his own projects were located not only in Chicago but throughout the Washington, D.C., area. The property in Maryland was a rural estate that Strong intended to develop as a potential tourist resort. It was for this resort that Wright designed his "Automobile Objective" to capture the growing number of automobile tourists. The name implied that going to it by car was the "objective" of your journey. Although Strong was conservative in taste, he saw Wright as "the architect best adapted to dream out something that ordinary citizens would never think of." Wright and Strong soon entered into a contract.[22]

Wright began the design with a spiraling sculptural form, in the center of which was a theater. It evolved into a great internal dome onto which an optical projector, the latest model from Germany, would project images of the planets. A ramp led up and around the building's exterior (fig. 12). From the top, visitors could take in the vast panorama of the surrounding landscape they had just traversed. A second ramp led down. People could also leave their cars, which an attendant would take and park below, and walk down a pedestrian ramp. The ramps were cantilevered, a technique that Wright viewed as quintessentially "modern." A series of lounges and restaurants opened onto the walkways. After taking in the overlooks, visitors could pass through various lobbies into a broad promenade around the base of the dome and look down into the planetarium floor. Inside would be the large planetarium, two restaurants, an aquarium, and natural history exhibits.[23]

The project was monumental. Wright saw it as the spawn of a new world, liberated and defined by technology, from the choreography of cars to the cutting-edge projectors blasting the solar system onto the inner dome of the planetarium. "The perspectives are very attractive bits of artistic work which it is a pleasure to look at," Strong wrote after receiving drawings from Wright. Wright sensed a subtle skepticism, however, and replied cautiously: "I hope you will not let the 'artistic' character of the sketches prejudice you against the scheme." To elicit a touch of sympathy, Wright added that he continued to rebuild Taliesin after the fire, was trying to get the house enclosed before the onset of winter, and still struggled professionally. "If ever a fellow needed a friend," he told Strong, "I need one now."[24]

Wright planned to travel from Taliesin to Chicago and to present Strong with his drawings for the project. Initially Strong considered having a little party to celebrate, but before Wright's visit, he had begun to realize that the concept he had in mind for the site in Maryland and

Fig. 12 Automobile Objective for Gordon Strong, perspective drawing, 1925.

Wright's plans were entirely different. "I came to the further conclusion that your work would not be of practical value in this case," he wrote Wright in mid-October 1925. Strong explained that he saw the design "as a structure of complete unity and independence without any relation to its surroundings. It looks to me as if it were designed to be used anywhere in the United States—on any sloping hill or mere rise of ground."[25]

Strong, as smart and perceptive a client as Wright ever had, also recognized another quality of the scheme: while its function was modern, its form was archaic. "I must admit that the exterior ramps are archaeologically right. They prove overwhelmingly your close adherence to tradition. In devising the latest type of structure, you have gone straight back to the earliest." According to Strong, Wright had presented him with a ziggurat, and to underscore his point, he sent Wright an illustration of the Tower of Babel. He went on to explain how the famous tower had produced only confusion. "Hereafter, if anyone ever dares to say, within my hearing, that you are not the world's greatest architect, I am going to jam down the speaker's throat the fact that you are anyhow the world's greatest archaeologist and philologist." "Organic integrity!" Strong added sneeringly. "A highly formalized and standardized automobile observatory on my mountain!" With a clever mix of chastising sarcasm and condescension, Strong elaborated on the Tower of Babel as if Wright were not familiar with the image: "You will note in the foreground a gentleman, who according to the Bible, lost his voice, and according to the picture also lost his shirt: in endeavoring to explain that the structure under way possessed one thing anyhow—organic integrity."[26]

Wright had been fired again, this time with stinging criticism. His proposal lacked "organic integrity"! Few comments could have been more damning for Wright. Realizing he would not change Strong's mind, he replied angrily a week later. "I have given you a noble 'archaic' sculptured summit for your mountain," Wright wrote. Snarky and irritated, he continued, now trying to insult Strong: "I should have diddled it away with platforms and seats and spittoons for introspective or expectorating business men and the flappers that beset them, and infest the whole with 'eye'-talian squirt-guns and elegant balustrades together with the feeble phallus worship of pergola posts ad libitum, ad nauseam."[27]

Wright claimed the spiral precedent was everywhere, and that if he looked at a snail he'd be accused of stealing the idea of a house from it. Nevertheless, he had thought a double spiral—his symbol of organic process—would work for Strong's project. Wright included in his letter to Strong pictures of a spiral spring, a snail shell, an eggbeater, and a screw.

The failures of Wright's architectural projects not only impeded Wright's professional progress, but also deprived him of money to pay off his debts. The lone exception occurred in 1926—after Wright had returned from Puerto Rico—when Darwin Martin came to Wright's rescue with the commission for a cottage for his wife, Isabelle, on the edge of Lake Erie near the town of Derby, New York, twenty-two miles from their home in Buffalo. In April 1926, Wright visited the Martins in Buffalo to see their lakeside site. By Wright's standards the project was unassuming, but at least it was a paying prospect.[28]

While Wright's architectural work faltered, Miriam escalated her harassment of Wright and Olgivanna. In early June 1926, the *New York Times* reported that she had tried to storm the locked front gates at Taliesin.

She then had a warrant issued, demanding that Wright give her access to the homestead. She was still his wife and apparently legally entitled to entry. The *Chicago Daily Tribune,* which followed Wright's marital problems with glee, reported at the end of August that Miriam sued the "dancer" Olgivanna for $100,000 for alienation of affection.[29]

To help settle Wright's financial problems, his current lawyer, Levi Bancroft, insisted that the architect vacate Taliesin for three months with his family. Wright's absence would prevent Miriam from swooping down on them as she had done previously and deprive the press of opportunities to exploit the situation. Although Miriam was persecuting him, Wright pitied what he saw as her self-destructive behavior, regarding her as a victim of manipulative lawyers and the press. And Wright stayed put.[30]

Wright's resources were depleted from rebuilding Taliesin, the fire had damaged his Chinese and Japanese artifacts, and his architectural practice was on hold. To pay his debts, Wright mortgaged Taliesin for $43,000. Wright's lawyer told him to sign away everything: "plans, collections, drawing instruments, your tools in the studio and on the farm." In return the bank gave Wright a check for $1,500. It was all the money he had in the world.[31]

After formalizing their deal, the Bank of Wisconsin foreclosed on Wright's mortgage of Taliesin on September 6, 1926, taking possession of the building and all of its contents. With no income, the bank's foreclosure, and Miriam's ongoing harassment campaign, Wright traveled to Minnesota, where he had friends, Henry Thayer and his wife Frances. They found Wright a cottage to rent near Lake Minnetonka where he and his family could hide until things blew over. Olgivanna recalled that Wright had his old Uncle Enos drive them to the train station "in his rickety Ford" so they could avoid being recognized as they boarded a train for Minneapolis. Wright knew the area since he had designed a house for Francis Little at the lake's edge in Deephaven, sixteen miles from the city.[32]

From the moment Wright fled Taliesin, he became the subject of a manhunt. The Associated Press circulated reports that Olgivanna's ex-husband had taken legal action, prompted by Miriam's lawyers, to get possession of his daughter Svetlana. In October, he sued Wright for $250,000 for alienating his work and his child. The wire services continued to spread the news throughout the country and into the heartland of rural America. In Montana, the *Helena Daily Independent* had already carried a full-page exposé of the whole mess on October 2—the debacle of Wright's private life and Miriam's assault on Taliesin (fig. 13). Although Wright and Olgivanna kept forgetting to use their aliases—the Richardsons—they lived undetected for six weeks in Minnesota. With Olgivanna's encouragement, Wright began working on his autobiography. Through the Thayers they met Owen and Maud Devine; Maud would soon assist Wright by typing his handwritten texts.[33]

The court issued warrants, and the press posted a reward for finding Wright. The son of Wright's landlord had suspicions about the identity of the couple in the cottage and after a surreptitious visit alerted the authorities to the architect's whereabouts. On the evening of October 20, 1926, Wright, Olgivanna, her nine-year-old daughter Svetlana, and their ten-month-old child Iovanna had finished dinner. The children were asleep. Maud Devine was typing the manuscript of his autobiography. A cozy fire burned in the hearth. Suddenly, someone pounded on the door. When Wright opened it, a hoard of strangers muscled their way into the small cottage: a heavy-handed sheriff named Brown, a lawyer named Harold Jackson, Svetlana's father, and members of the press. "You are all under arrest," the sheriff announced. "Well, here they are . . . at last." Asked the lawyer, "Now where's the kid?" He proceeded to the bedroom, yanked the covers off Svetlana, and laughed. "Yeah!—here it is."[34]

Wright was informed that he was charged with abducting a child. Two policemen forced him outside (fig. 14). The sheriff escorted Olgivanna and her two daughters away as well. At the Hennepin County jail, the authorities separated Wright from his family. His anxiety surged. He bribed a guard with fifty cents to let him send Olgivanna a note.

The ponderous door of the animal cage slammed shut and automatically shot its steel bolt, he somewhat melodramatically recalled when he entered his cell in the Hennepin County jail late that night. His first sensation was suffocation as he took in the cell's narrow dimensions. A dirty, blood-stained mattress and a filthy water closet filled the space. At least, he assured himself, he was housed among the jail's "better elements," swindlers and bootleggers, as opposed to the violent offenders.[35]

Fig. 13 The full-page article on Wright's domestic troubles in the *Helena Daily Independent*, October 2, 1926.

Fig. 14 Frank Lloyd Wright under arrest at his cottage near Minneapolis, October 21, 1926.

Hailed just three years earlier for his design of the Imperial Hotel in Tokyo, the "Most Talked about Hotel in the World," Wright was reduced to a blurry figure, the subject of tabloids and local newspapers. The *Wisconsin State Journal* immediately published on its front page: "Wright and Olga in Minneapolis Jail."[36]

On the first morning of his imprisonment, Wright saw, courtesy of a nearby jail mate, the newspaper with his picture from the arrest. When the cell doors opened for the morning inspection, Wright stepped into the gangway, wide enough only for a single person, and ran into another prisoner. "You look funny in here," the man said to him. "Yes, I feel funny," the architect answered. His fellow inmate recommended his own lawyer to help him: William M. Nash, a Minneapolis native who had been county attorney in the early 1920s until being removed from office for taking bribes from criminals. His legitimate skills were undiminished, however, and Nash agreed to take on Wright's case. He quickly determined that Miriam's lawyers had prevailed upon Svetlana's father, Valdemar Hinzenberg, to file charges of abduction in Baraboo County, Wisconsin, near Wright's home. Nash also discovered there were no grounds for holding Wright, as no warrant was produced. When Wright was led into court in the morning, the Baraboo authorities, lacking the document, could not proceed with prosecution. The case was dropped.[37]

Unfortunately, however, the bogus abduction charges tipped off the federal authorities, who alleged that Wright had violated the Mann Act. He had faced the accusation in 1915, but this situation was more serious. "I had successfully shielded my little family from both press and camera until this episode," Wright noted about his second court appearance. "For twelve months I had beaten the reporters at their own game. . . . Now it all ended in this 'triumph' for them, rag, tag and bobtail." Pursued by the press and photographers, the couple was led to a public hearing, where each was served on a separate count, with bail set at $15,000 for both of them.[38]

The charges of violating the Mann Act propelled Wright's sisters into action. Jane rushed from her home in Philadelphia. Maginel phoned Nash for details and reassurances. Meanwhile, a federal officer interviewed Olgivanna alone and discovered that the couple had traveled to Puerto Rico earlier in the year. Returning from a territory without a passport meant Olgivanna had violated immigration laws. On top of charges that she had allegedly colluded in the abduction of her own child, she was now targeted as an illegal alien who had entered the country for "immoral purposes."[39]

Wright spent a second night in jail. A sympathetic jailor replaced the filthy, blood-stained mattress with a clean one, and Wright passed the evening listening to other inmates—most under more serious threat than he was—singing. "It was tremendous," he wrote later of the baritones reverberating in the void. "They sang familiar song after song. Some popular, some religious," until curfew. The music produced "a splendid sense of unity in their misery" that made Wright ashamed of his self-pity.[40]

The following morning, Wright and Olgivanna were released on bail. A preliminary hearing was set for the following week. By some accounts, the stress so affected Olgivanna that she considered suicide and collapsed before the hearing. She was later briefly hospitalized at a local sanatorium.[41]

After the hearing, Wright still could still not leave Minnesota until the prosecuting federal attorney cleared up some legal details. The architect floated around, hung out with the Thayers' son, Cleaver, and had his mail sent to him care of the Athletic Club of Minneapolis. His problems compounded. The federal charges made the Bank of Wisconsin nervous at the prospect of Wright having no means to repay them. In early November, the bank demanded the sale of Wright's Japanese prints collection to cover his debt.[42]

By Thanksgiving, still in Minneapolis, Wright hatched a scheme he thought would allow him to pay off the mortgage. He would incorporate himself and get ten of his friends to buy into Frank Lloyd Wright, Incorporated, for a cash kitty. As compensation, they would own both his assets and his designs, while he would be free to work. Wright's new lawyer in Wisconsin, Philip La Follette, was instrumental in this venture. A friend and graduate of Wright's aunts' Hillside Home School, La Follette was the son of the former Wisconsin governor who had run for president on the Progressive ticket in 1924. Philip himself was destined to become governor. Darwin Martin and Ferdinand Schevill, a friend and distinguished professor of Western European history at the University of Chicago, led the effort to incorporate Wright. The architect would soon ask former clients, family members (including Jane and Andrew Porter), friends in New York, anybody who might have a few dollars, to buy shares in his corporation. La Follette would control Wright's bills and expenses, provide the architect with a monthly allowance, and oversee the financial dealings of the corporation. Like all financial and personal matters connected with Wright, the fate of Wright, Incorporated, would be complicated and problematic.[43]

The move temporarily kept the Bank of Wisconsin at bay. The effort was also the starting point for what became, at the expense of his first set of children, the corporate ownership of his assets. Ultimately, this arrangement led to the creation of the Frank Lloyd Wright Foundation—

which to this day remains the owner of Wright's assets, designs, intellectual property, and his legacy enterprises.[44]

Although Wright was in serious trouble, he did not, as he acknowledged, suffer crises alone. Family and friends expressed sympathy and support. His thirty-three-year-old son John Lloyd Wright, who had been to the cottage hideaway, worried about his father's legal problems. "I feel very much concerned," he wrote his father, "but know that I cannot do much to help." Pilloried in much of the press, Wright received a strong letter of support from William Hanson Jr., editor at the *Capitol Times,* in his efforts to divorce Miriam. "With Miriam this has been a war of headlines," Hanson wrote, "bitter, unrelenting." "I hope you will not lose your fighting heart," he concluded. "Courage is the escape from all things." Even Aline Barnsdall, who had fired Wright in Los Angeles, empathized with the architect's plight. Dione Neutra, who had lived at Taliesin in 1925 while her husband Richard Neutra worked as one of Wright's assistants, wrote Wright about his being persecuted. Ferdinand Schevill expressed his solidarity by denouncing Miriam as "Satan's very own."[45]

Jane wrote her brother at length about his dire circumstances. Her first concern focused on settling the divorce with Miriam. "I think to work on Miriam in some way to get the divorce is the thing to do now—not thru force but thru her own highest 'strain'—her interest in metaphysics—perhaps a medium—someone who can bring her to reason to see that it is impossible for you to help her when you are ruined financially." Jane worried about Olgivanna, who was under a doctor's care, and offered her home, Tan-y-deri. Sounding like their late mother, Jane concluded: "I feel for you dear but it must be part of the Divine Plan—don't struggle except to do your work—destroy the bitterness which is the greatest enemy you have."[46]

Despite these testaments of support, Wright's troubles were hardly over. He had once again lost his studio. He had only one building project with a secure future—the lakeside cottage for the Martins. Everything else was tentative; Olgivanna and her daughters still suffered from the ordeal of jail, publicity, and constant instability. He and his family needed physical and emotional security, and Wright had to find some means of generating work and an income. New York again reentered his life.

4

REFUGE

The New York City to which Wright returned in late 1926 was dramatically different from the metropolis he had encountered in 1909, but its evolution was not a mystery. The dramatic skyscrapers, the stock market, airplanes, jazz, the Harlem Renaissance, radio, and even organized crime, which gave the 1920s their fame, did not appear from nowhere. All had developed from the preceding decades. The risk was large, but for greater New York, still barely twenty years old, "the ties that bound—subways, bridges, schools, amusement parks, police, theaters, jobs, water, public health, Tammany, the excitement and pride of living in a great city— overmatched the innumerable antagonisms and kept them with bounds." Squinting at risk, its citizens might assume "so far so good."[1]

With the cultural flux, modern art had made inroads in not just New York but America with the epochal Armory Show of 1913. Marcel Duchamp's *Nude Descending a Staircase* was one of several works that introduced the European avant-garde to Americans. In contrast to the art scene, the city's architectural evolution in the 1910s had developed erratically. Although the *Architectural Record* ran a short piece, "The Wild Men of Paris," profiling French painters, throughout the 1910s the publication demonstrated a pervasive architectural conservativism. The editors extensively published the work of traditionalists like Carrère & Hastings and John Russell Pope. Standard fare included "Gothic" residences, "Modern" colonial doorways, neoclassical libraries, and Spanish revival villas.

Though architecture leaned toward traditionalism, advances in media and technology had become woven into modern life. Times Square evolved into a rollicking visual spectacle, the forebear of the place we know today. Flashy movie palaces, like those built by Thomas Lamb, proliferated. From the lush interiors of the Rivoli (1917) or the Capitol (1919) theaters, Manhattanites could see Hollywood's latest (fig. 15). The "palaces" intoxicated visitors with flashing signage and grand marquees, their seemingly endless upholstered chairs, and climate-controlled interiors, bedecked with opulent neoclassical flourishes. Electricity was only one manifestation of energy physics: Einstein had ushered in the relativity of space and time. The two phenomena collapsed even further when, in 1915, the first transcontinental call was placed between San Francisco and New York.[2]

World War I had ended isolationist tendencies and fundamentally disrupted the cultural flow between Europe and America. American perceptions of Germany and Germans, formerly positive, became irresolutely negative. After two years of war, 116,708 U.S. soldiers had died and 204,002 had been wounded. As a percentage of the entire force deployed, this number was miniscule compared with that of European nations, some of which had lost almost a third of their enlisted military. Yet the war produced Ernest Hemingway's Lost Generation of artists and writers: Gertrude Stein, F. Scott Fitzgerald, and James Joyce, among many others, reacted to the horror of the conflict and its lasting reverberations.

In the 1920s, New York was overrun by a novel sight: the automobile. Already by 1920, 57th Street, with its various car showrooms, was considered to be the "automobile district." In less than ten years the car would become ubiquitous, with one out of every six Americans owning one.

Fig. 15 Capitol Theater, New York, built in 1919.

The automobile drove some of the city's greatest feats in civil engineering, such as the Holland Tunnel, which would connect Manhattan to Jersey City beneath the Hudson River in 1927, when construction started on the George Washington Bridge.[3]

Production of domestic architecture expanded. The Upper East Side swelled with new townhouses, while Elsie de Wolfe, the doyenne of interior decoration, shook high society loose from its stuffy Victorian furniture. The postwar economy swung into popular consumer culture. Through innovations in workplace technology, the average citizen suddenly had leisure time. Radio was on the rise, and innovative models for marketing and advertising flourished. The new sounds of jazz—tinny trumpets, sizzling snares—spilled forth from the city's speakeasies. The Harlem Renaissance was in full bloom, and African American artists, such as Langston Hughes, Duke Ellington, and Zora Neale Hurston, came to the fore. Further north, from the Bronx, came the roar of the Yankees' multiple wins throughout the 1923 World Series at their new stadium, and George Gershwin's 1924 *Rhapsody in Blue* suffused New York's Aeolian Hall.[4]

The sound was modern America, but the hall where the *Rhapsody* unfurled, a neoclassical building with four-story frontal Corinthian columns, suggested the dilemma of architects: What was the role of the classical tradition, and what was the image of modern architecture to be? Cass Gilbert's Woolworth Building (1913), located at 233 Broadway, had earlier synopsized the debate that would obsess architects for decades. Technologically advanced, but clad in the vaulting pinnacles of the neo-Gothic, the Woolworth Building looked at once forward and backward.

The dilemma increasingly engaged architects as the modern city expanded. Although occasional works of Functionalist architecture had appeared—the Flatiron Building and the Equitable Building—alongside factories and bridges, the hopes for the future identity of American modern architecture lay in a single building type: the skyscraper, or what the journalist John Taylor Boyd Jr. called in 1922 "the one supreme feature of modern architecture."[5]

The future of New York itself would turn on the skyscraper and its development, providing both images of modernity and a flood of creativity. One major stimulus occurred when the city enacted its 1916 planning code for "stepped-back structures." Architect and illustrator Hugh Ferriss delineated "wedding cake" buildings—monumental, shadowed, stepping, and ziggurat-like—that embodied the visual aura of evolving 1920s Manhattan. Dramatic renderings, they remained on paper but inspired others.[6]

From regulation came revolution. The dramatic profile liberated architects, and alongside the freedom to explore form was a burgeoning interest in the ancient and primitive, totally independent of Wright's earlier interest. Exoticism permeated the air, feeding on the Egyptomania following the discovery of King Tut's tomb in 1922. Wright had drawn from primitivist sources in the early 1910s with serious intention, but with the results so scattered, the effort was little understood. Now interest became widespread. In the 1920s, American architects began to look to non-Western cultures for the kernel of something "close to nature," something, in the words of art historian Patricia Morton, "simpler and more profound." The Aztecs, the Maya, and the ancient Egyptians inspired the revivalism. Even Cass Gilbert, architect of the neo-Gothic Woolworth Building, later in the decade fell under the sway of the exotic: his mid-block loft building in the fur district on West 30th Street included terra-cotta reliefs derived from ancient Assyrian sources.[7]

This exotic outburst suggests an ideal moment to pause to see how modern architecture had been evolving, and in doing so we get a better sense of how Wright fit and did not fit into its evolution. In Europe, among the varieties of modern currents that had floated across the continent, two fundamental directions began to emerge, an expressionist wing represented by a cadre of Dutch and German architects—they most appreciated Wright's work—and a rationalist wing that was antihistory, anti-ornament, and skeptical of Wright. By the early 1920s the rationalist wing began to dominate. The rationalists opposed historical reference and, with socialist leanings, emphasized mass housing and prefabrication characterized by simple surfaces, flat planes, and flat roofs. Generally, these efforts fell under the rubric of "Functionalism." By the late 1920s and early 1930s, images of Functionalism would be imported to New York, and it was eventually referred to as the "International Style" for its global ambitions.

During the 1920s, Le Corbusier emerged as the leader of the pack—and for Wright, his major competition. Born in 1887 as Pierre Jeanneret, a whole generation younger than Wright, in his earliest years he had worked through historic styles and systematically studied the fundamentals of architecture in search of the essence of construction and art. The young Franco-Swiss architect was also aware of Wright—he'd bought Wright's Wasmuth picture book during the war—though he never acknowledged him directly. For Le Corbusier and his sphere, the machine, as metaphor for technology, expressed the spirit of the times, the Machine Age. The house was a machine to inhabit. His domain was the city onto which the architect imposed his principles of *urbanisme,* in which he took on the central role of rationalizing the city's activities, buildings, space, and circulation systems.[8]

The American situation had been quite different. Its architects had little anxiety about historical reference while they created the most technologically advanced and tallest buildings in the world. Constructed of steel, efficient with the most powerful elevators and mechanical systems, and serving expanding commerce, they could still have cornices and ornaments as evidence of historical continuity.

Wright followed all these developments carefully. In contrast to Le Corbusier, for Wright, the house was a refuge, built by machines but an escape from them. As he explored his own aesthetic, even if his projects were doomed, he increasingly insisted that his organic architecture was the only viable style for a proper modern architecture.

The situation in the mid-1920s was, however, still fluid, as architects and critics competed to find a dominant and winning idiom. A new generation of big buildings emerged, mixing motifs and elements, often with rich visual effect, but too varied to be identified by a single style. The vast Barclay-Vesey Building (1923) at 140 West Street was the largest telephone building in the world. It featured a broad base bifurcated into two towers that cradled another soaring block. These big volumes had edge details of intertwined vines, exotic animals and birds, and even aborigines above the entries. Lewis Mumford, the young critic who would soon become Wright's protégé, described the lobby "as gaily . . . decorated as a village in a strawberry festival." It also was an international marker: the frontispiece for the English-language edition of Le Corbusier's *Towards a New Architecture,* which Wright would review.[9]

In 1924, John Mead Howells and Raymond Hood designed another landmark, the American Radiator Building at 40 West 40th Street. Two years earlier they had won the competition for the Chicago Tribune Tower with a controversial neo-Gothic skyscraper. But in New York for American Radiator (also known as the American Standard Building), Hood further abstracted the neo-Gothic and clad the building in black brick. The results were, according to the standard reference on the period, "condemned, applauded, and discussed." The pyramidal structure, rising twenty-three stories, featured terra-cotta friezes and Gothic pinnacles, each of which was coated in gold. The bronze-and-black granite base fed into a black marble and mirrored entrance hall. To some, the building itself communicated "glorious radiator." Even the carved ornament, allegories on the conversion of energy into matter, spoke of the heater product. As a journalist from the *Villager* commented soon after the skyscraper's construction, "New York is no blank; New York has a meaning, and Radiator gathers it up and distills it." The city surged with the chatter of a million voices—so, too, its buildings were to speak.[10]

In the midst of this excitement, New York could not anticipate the explosive impact that the 1925 *Exposition internationale des Arts décoratifs et industriels modernes* in Paris would have on American design. The exposition, which the United States bowed out of (the federal government saying it had nothing "modern" to present), woke Americans up. The existing disconnect could be seen in the 1925 issues of the *Architectural Record:* period rooms of America's country houses looked bloodless next to Konstantin Melnikov's Soviet pavilion or Le Corbusier's geometric composition at the Pavillon de l'Esprit Nouveau. They were the lone exceptions to—and reactions against—the dominating aesthetic of sensuality. Avoiding the challenge of expressing technology for its own sake, the architecture of French designers, with its focus on symmetry, muted classicism, and material sensuality, provided inspirations that resolved—for the moment—the dilemma of traditional versus modern by being both.

Energized by France, American architects and designers proceeded to create their version of the idiom that has since become synonymous with the Roaring Twenties: Art Deco. It provided in America the first great exuberant burst and the first large-scale expression of its modern culture since the grand Beaux-Arts architecture of Progressivism at the turn of the century. Art Deco broadly represented the Machine Age, and in New York it represented the Jazz Age as well. The term "Art Deco" was actually in limited use at the time: Zigzag style, Jazz Modern, Skyscraper style, and Modernistic, among other terms, were more common. Later in the decade the style morphed into the *moderne* or "Streamline" style, in which curves in buildings recalled the curves of locomotives and, by association, speed, power, and the machine. For our purposes, the term "Art Deco" works well.[11]

The firm of Buchman & Kahn emerged as major purveyors of commercial Art Deco building by the time Wright returned to the city in

December 1926. Trained at the École des Beaux-Arts, the designing partner Ely Jacques Kahn was fully aware not just of French stylistic motifs, but also of the vocabulary of the late Vienna Secession movement, which merged abstract geometries and primary motifs. He had already produced real buildings equivalent to Ferriss's stepped profile drawings; Kahn's name became synonymous with this architectural form. The firm's Insurance Center Building just north of Wall Street gave prominence to a bold zigzag banding that became a stylistic cue. Kahn's masterpiece, the Park Avenue Building, on Park between 32nd and 33rd Streets, would be finished in 1927. It pulled together color, texture, vibrant patterns, and a rich interplay of terra-cotta to efficiently house a pulsating commercial enterprise. Mumford approved, though it "may well serve to crystallize all the fumbling and uncertain elements in present-day architecture." Kahn's Squibb Building on Fifth Avenue (1929/30) comprised a composition of stacked vertical masses that receded in size as the building rose thirty-four stories. Between 1925 and 1931, Buchman & Kahn would build over thirty such buildings, many situated in the Garment District immediately south of Times Square and as far downtown as Wall Street (fig. 16).[12]

Art Deco flourished in New York. Its impact was so powerful that it had overtures of a national style, with examples cropping up from Gotham to the oil boomtown of Big Spring, Texas. It ushered in what would be some of New York's greatest architectural contributions to modern culture: the Chrysler Building (1930) by William Van Alen, the Empire State Building (1931) by William F. Lamb, and Radio City Music Hall (1932) by Edward Durell Stone and Donald Deskey. Jazz Age New York swaying with Art Deco towers characterized the city into which Wright walked. His response was to criticize the buildings and search for his own version of the skyscraper.

Wright's return in December 1926 began his longest stay in the city. He and Olgivanna were not alone when they returned. They had Wright's sister Maginel Wright Barney, a new cohort of receptive and supportive friends, and the verve of New York itself. The architect was swiftly approaching his sixties, a time when many slow down, but Wright's energy remained youthful. His return to New York would mark the

Fig. 16 120 Wall Street, E. J. Kahn, architect (c. 1930).

Fig. 17 Maginel Wright Barney.

beginning of a personal and creative transformation: he soon became a stellar figure on the national and international scene.

There *was* more than enough room for two artists in the Wright family, but the sister, whom we have encountered in passing, remains hidden (fig. 17). Maginel—illustrator of children's books and ladies' magazines—provided her home in New York as Wright's refuge when he and his young family lost their home in December. And her work, whose simple color-blocked forms set the tenor for nightly dreaming, captivated thousands of children.[13]

Frank's loving and devoted sister was a gifted and successful artist who, like her brother, knew personal losses. The youngest of the Wright siblings, Maginel was born in 1877, her name a contraction of those of her aunts Margaret Jones and Nell. She studied illustration at the Art Institute of Chicago and made enough money working for an engraving firm to take herself and her mother, Anna, to Europe in 1903. She married Walter "Pat" Enright, who was a political cartoonist, illustrator, and teacher at the Armour Institute in Chicago. They had a daughter, Elizabeth, in 1907, moved to New York in 1910 to expand their careers, and bought a seven-room townhouse at 41 West 12th Street. Enright had a studio in the Flatiron Building, and Maginel set up her workplace at home. Their young daughter, whose image appeared in several of Maginel's illustrations, recalled watching her mother work: "I can see her now as I saw her then, her drawing board tilted against the worktable before her. In her dark curly hair two or three pencils were stabbed like geisha ornaments, and a watercolor brush was often gripped between."[14]

Maginel and Walter lived in the bohemian milieu of Greenwich Village. Their friends included the artist and critic Gelett Burgess, who wrote for *The Smart Set, Collier's,* and *Century;* the painter William Glackens; Maud Tousey Fangel, an illustrator; and Wallace Morgan, another prolific illustrator whose work appeared in several newspapers. In 1912 Maginel was elected to the Society of Illustrators, and that year she bought a pre–Revolutionary War four-bay house on Nantucket Island where the family spent summers.

Enright served in World War I, but, for reasons unknown, the couple divorced soon after his return in 1920. The split took a physical and emotional toll on Maginel. Anna often wrote Frank, urging him to tend to his sister when visiting New York, noting her delicate state and reminding him how much Maginel loved him. Maginel married Hyram Barney, a lawyer in international affairs; his accomplishments included formulating a plan to stabilize foreign exchange and help the United States' efforts in the postwar rehabilitation of Europe. Their life together was short; Barney died at their home on West 12th Street in July 1925 at the age of forty, after a six-month illness contracted while arranging a major bond flotation in Poland.[15]

By the time Wright and Olgivanna arrived at Maginel's home in December 1926, she was a grieving widow and a single mother, but, like her brother, she pushed through loss to pursue her art. The work flowed, and her illustrations appeared on the covers of *Woman's World* throughout the mid-1920s, while her drawings for *Downright Dencey,* a historical children's novel, would be a runner-up for the Newbery Medal in 1928.[16]

Bonded by their upbringing and drawn tightly together by the domineering Anna, Maginel remained close to her brother regardless of his notoriety. Wright turned to her for shelter from the vicissitudes of Chicago and Spring Green, and she welcomed him and his new family.

Maginel's townhouse at 41 West 12th Street, between Fifth and Sixth Avenues, was located in the heart of Greenwich Village (fig. 18). Built in 1901, the four-story building had a brick façade with muted Federal-style details. The high-ceiling second-floor *piano nobile* featured a lovely stone

Fig. 18 Barney residence at 41 West 12th Street, New York, December 9, 1914 (door on right). Photographed for Joseph P. Day by William David Hassler.

fireplace with handsome moldings. On some of the walls Maginel hung Japanese woodblock prints that her brother had given her.[17]

All around Wright, New York flaunted its architectural history through its townhouses and elegant apartment buildings. On Maginel's block alone lay a series of six identical late-Italianate-style row houses built in 1860—a paragon of elegance and a testament to the nineteenth-century architecture of Old New York. The jewel of the block, however, was the outsized Ardea apartment building. Built in 1895 and designed by John B. Snook, the building housed seven-room apartments, one per floor. The Ardea, with its stone base and a checkerboard of cast-iron balconies, had long hosted illustrious New Yorkers, socialites, and successful businesspeople. It had enough cachet to act as Marie Curie's headquarters when she visited in 1921.[18]

Maginel's townhouse lay diagonally across the street from what would become one of the first modernist building façades in New York, at the New School for Social Research. The exterior, along with the interior lobby and auditorium, would be designed and built from 1929 to 1931 by Joseph Urban. With its rhythmic, concentric bands, being in the auditorium felt like being in the belly of a whale. The Austrian-born Urban soon became one of Wright's new friends in Manhattan. He had an impressive track record: he'd made revolutionary contributions to silent films earlier in the 1920s, had founded the American branch of the Wiener Werkstätte with an exhibition space and sales rooms at 581 Fifth Avenue, and designed for the Ziegfeld Follies. Urban bridged worlds—Vienna, Art Deco, and the latest modernist developments—a feat Wright appreciated.[19]

From Maginel's doorstep, Wright entered a world of art and artists in the culturally rich and vibrant heart of Greenwich Village, a place different from Chicago and Los Angeles, and diametric to the pastoral ruralism of Taliesin. It was a comfortable spot in the vivacious heart of Manhattan, a quintessence of urban experience fused with Village life. There they met Franklin P. Adams, a witty columnist for the *New York Herald Tribune;* Julian Street, a former reporter, critic, and author; and according to Olgivanna, the conductor Leopold Stokowski, among others. Wright had no architectural work, but he continued writing. Like good New Yorkers, the Wrights went out to dinners, to the theater and films, to art galleries, and to concerts, while continually sidestepping their illegitimate status as unmarried. Wright seethed at the situation that prevented them from returning to Taliesin, but the couple still enjoyed themselves. When Maginel sailed to Europe, they had the house to themselves. One night at the Lafayette Hotel, they got drunk over a bottle of wine, and the splurge made them silly and joyful. Wright was so tipsy he forgot Maginel's address. "We walked up and down the block of 12th Street between Fifth and Sixth Avenues inhaling the night air," Olgivanna recalled. "We had a good time laughing about the drinking adventure."[20]

The year 1927 in New York began with Wright and Olgivanna managing pragmatic issues, including the forced sale of Wright's Japanese print collection to recoup on their astronomical debts. Held on January 6 and 7 at the Anderson Galleries, the auction generated a disappointing $42,000, from which a 35 percent commission was deducted.[21]

Olgivanna recalled around the time of the sale that Wright went to several museums and dealers to sell some of his print collection and amassed the goodly sum of $25,000. How the architect did this outside of the January auction is unclear. If Wright did profit, he hid it from his bankers. With this money, Olgivanna detailed, the couple secured an apartment on Ninth Street "close to the Lafayette Hotel" where they lived for three months. The new location, not far from Maginel, gave the family more autonomy and put them in the midst of the scene that revolved around a venerable New York institution. It also put them on the parade route for Charles Lindbergh's return after his triumphant flight to France, about which Olgivanna and Wright were "excited to the point of tears." The owner of the Lafayette Hotel had initiated a $25,000 prize seven years earlier for a nonstop flight from New York to Paris.[22]

The Lafayette Hotel, at 30 East Ninth Street (replaced by an apartment building in the early 1950s), consisted of three townhouses strung together in the 1880s. The hotel was a favorite meeting place of artists and literati, attracted by its French cuisine and excellent service. John Sloan, who lived in the Village, depicted the building with its double awnings in a 1927 painting, commenting: "To the passersby not looking for modern glitter, it has always had a look of cheer and comfort, particularly on a wet evening as this." Even later, E. B. White wrote in his essay "Here Is New York": "In the café of the Lafayette, the regulars sit and talk." "It is busy yet peaceful," he continued. "Nursing a drink, I stare through the west windows at the Manufacturers Trust and Company and at the red brick fronts on the north side of Ninth Street, watching the red turning slowly to purple as the light dwindles." Here was a timeless sanctuary where nothing seemed to change, from the ageless waiters to the strong coffee filled with chicory.[23]

Although Wright's family had a roof over their heads in a vibrant locale, they faced an unrelenting problem: Olgivanna was still an illegal alien and risked deportation. In mid-January, immigration officials had showed up at Maginel's townhouse, arrested Olgivanna, and threatened to deport her. Her visit to Puerto Rico and subsequent reentry constituted grounds for action. Wright bailed her out of custody with his last fifty-dollar Liberty Bond.[24]

Wright decided a face-to-face encounter with the immigration authorities in Washington would solve the problem. He asked a friend in New York, the critic and journalist Alexander Woollcott, if he had any connections in Washington who could help them. On January 16, 1927, Woollcott wrote Colonel William Joseph "Wild Bill" Donovan, whom he knew from their service in World War I, asking him to intervene. "I am attempting no word of introduction to his architecture," Woollcott told Donovan, "beyond saying that if I were allowed only one use of the word 'genius' in getting around the America of today, I would have to save it up for Frank Lloyd Wright. If that genius is more fully appreciated in Japan and Holland than in his own country, we have it on the strength of Holy Writ that such irony is no new thing in the world."[25]

Clearly Woollcott had already made an appraisal of Wright as an unsung prophet, a persecuted figure whom, he added, was being harassed by the Hearst newspapers and the Mann Act allegations in a move of pure vengeance. Woollcott wanted to set the record straight: "Indeed, this note is written in the conviction that I have no job more important in the world than being of what use I can to men like Wright."[26]

Wright and Olgivanna did meet with Donovan in Washington, and he helped them get a six-month extension to resolve her immigration problems. While in Washington they toured the U.S. Capitol Building. For his undocumented lover, Wright interpreted the great figures of American history depicted in murals and sculpture, at times even breaking into tears. Olgivanna recalled that at that moment, "America became a sacred land, opened to me through Frank's vision."[27]

"All the things I really like to do are either immoral, illegal, or fattening," Alexander Woollcott once declared (fig. 19). This was the man to whom Wright entrusted his lover's fate; the man who would become one of Wright's greatest friends and supporters. Aleck, as he was known, was born in Colt's Neck Township, New Jersey, in 1887. His mother's family helped to found the Phalanx, a utopian community in upstate New York that modeled itself on Charles Fourier's ideas of mutual collaboration and liberated gender roles. Woollcott grew up in this rambling eighteen-room inheritance, surrounded by echoes of his iconoclastic ancestors and their communitarian values. But the family experienced financial hard times as his father drifted, like Wright's, often from the home hearth. They lived in Kansas City for a while when Woollcott was a child. There, a family friend took him to the theater to see *Sinbad the Sailor*. He was so enthralled that he wanted to see every matinee in town. At the age of six, it was obvious that the theater was Woollcott's great love, and he decided to write for newspapers as his means of getting free entry tickets. Woollcott attended Hamilton College, a small liberal arts school in Clinton, New York, where, according to his biographer, he was seen as "exotic, egregious and never quite in tune." Despite being a misfit, he developed lifelong attachments to his classmates, teachers, and the school. They gave him a chance to assert his own identity, and for that he was ever grateful.[28]

Woollcott's childhood ambition took shape when, immediately after graduation, he applied for a job as a cub reporter at the *New York Times*. His first residence in Manhattan was a cheap boardinghouse, shared with his sister Julie at 34 West 12th Street—but a few doors down from Maginel. By 1914, the *Times* had named Woollcott its drama critic, an appointment that made him the youngest in the United States, and certainly the youngest of importance since, of all people, Edgar Allan Poe. His lively prose outmoded the standard moribund reviews of the 1910s, and he quickly became a formidable figure on Broadway. Cornelius Vanderbilt, who was working for the *Times* as a police reporter, described him as "a plump, good-natured cuss, rather showy and gaudy, who liked to hang around late and talk." Service in World War I interrupted Woollcott's stint as a drama critic, during which time he became part of the editorial

Fig. 19 Alexander Woollcott.

board that included several young literary newspapermen who created *Stars and Stripes,* the official government publication intended to raise troop morale. Upon returning from the war, Woollcott injected more bite into his reviews, joining the coterie of scathing critics of the 1920s that included George Jean Nathan, the "Dean of Broadway," who wrote for the *Smart Set,* Dorothy Parker, and Robert Benchley, who began at *Vanity Fair* and also wrote for the young *New Yorker,* which was launched in 1925. Among his sharp-tongued peers, Woollcott became "the most courted and best hated in the business." Woollcott left the *Times* on good terms and transferred to the *New York Herald* in 1922. From there he would move to the *Sun,* and then on to the *World,* edited by Herbert Bayard Swope.[29]

While in his twenties, Woollcott became not only successful but rich. His funds supported a lavish lifestyle, including a secretary, a valet named Junior, and a chauffeur. He grew from a plump, little cuss to a first-class celebrity of impressive girth, described by one friend as "a mountainous jelly of hips, jowls, and torso [but with] brains sinewy and athletic." He would go on to become a radio commentator, actor, and celebrity in his own right, so well known that at the end of his career he promoted brands of motor cars, whiskey, and tennis rackets. Friends, colleagues, and foes had strong emotional reactions to him, ranging from disgust and fury to adulation and adoration. Regardless, he was powerful, and at his peak as "a literary supersalesman" he could turn books into bestsellers and transform his friends into celebrities.[30]

Woollcott was also a founding member and central figure at the Algonquin Round Table. This "intellectual oasis in the arid Philistinism of Broadway," as described by Woollcott's biographer, began as a lunch gathering for authors, playwrights, illustrators, cartoonists, actors, artists, sculptors, and celebrities. Gertrude Atherton described the ensemble in her bestselling novel *Black Oxen* as the "Sophisticates." The members closest to Woollcott viewed him as talented and sentimental but also spoiled, selfish, and rude. Margaret Case Harriman said, "Much as we all admired Woollcott for his brilliance, his hidden (often too hidden) tenderness, and his talents as a storyteller, a good many of us in New York think that people who managed to get along with him at the Round Table, in one way or another, for more than a decade deserve some kind of award." Woollcott's being one of the Sophisticates and sharing the Round Table meant Wright too could become a topic of conversation. Wright even claimed to have attended one of their gatherings as Woollcott's guest, observing Aleck in action: "I have seen Aleck bubble with wit in his lair by the river and scintillate in his seat with the mutual admiration society at the Algonquin." He and Woollcott would create their own society of mutual admiration and adulation.[31]

When Woollcott first met Wright, he was still writing for the newspapers. He might have read about Wright in any of the lurid accounts of the architect's private affairs that permeated the press, or he might have heard of Wright through their mutual friend Charles MacArthur, whom Woollcott favored and had brought into the circle of the Sophisticates.

Woollcott, ever the savvy newsman, was always searching for intriguing stories and fascinating figures. A piece on the architect was right up his alley. The critic had been on a lecture tour of the Midwest, and, aware of Wright's work and finding himself in Madison, wrangled an invitation to meet the architect.[32]

Woollcott visited Wright at Taliesin at a strangely auspicious moment, on April 19, 1925, the day before fire destroyed the house for the second time. "I had not enough gift of divination to realize in advance," Woollcott wrote in his treacly but precise prose, "how inexpressibly consoling would be its every aspect, how happily would the house grow like a vine on that hill-crest, how unerringly would every window foresee and frame the landscape that was to croon to the man within, above all how pliantly the unpretentious home would meet halfway the participation of the countryside." "Why, if a lovely tree was in the way of that house," he added, "the house just doffed its cap respectfully and went around it."[33]

Despite both having immense egos, the bond between Wright and Woollcott was understandable. Woollcott's biographer described him as a Horatio Alger figure, "the poor boy who by assiduity, pluck, and self-denial . . . has surmounted all handicaps to become rich, respected, and eminent." The description could just as easily apply to Wright, by then a generation older, but Woollcott already had the wealth and status that Wright could only dream of in the 1920s. Though many of Woollcott's friends were celebrities, Wright was the only architect in the critic's coterie of stars, a privileged position, to say the least.[34]

Woollcott's New York companionship was but one factor in the city that led Wright away from turmoil. A new circle emerged of young, energetic artists and designers who, while on the cutting edge of modernism, welcomed Wright. Foremost among them was Lewis Mumford (fig. 20). They had been in touch earlier in 1926 when Wright, ever vigilant, criticized Mumford's remarks in *Wendingen,* the Dutch journal that had published a compendium of his work to date. "I had doubts as to whether I ought to write the essay at all," Mumford replied, "not because I am lukewarm in admiration; but because I have not yet been west, and have not yet seen your work. . . . What you felt in my article was, assuredly, timidity: but this was occasioned not by a failure to grasp your work but by an ingrained distrust of saying anything about buildings I had not yet seen and walked around and gotten into." Mumford, who was thirty, soon grasped Wright's work more solidly, and his ideas of it grew sounder. He and Wright would develop a close exchange and, and at least initially, a powerful mutual esteem. Mumford would stand out as the most intellectual figure in Wright's new circle and, eventually, a broadly ranging historian and the leading urban critic of his generation.[35]

Paul T. Frankl, designer of the iconic "skyscraper" furniture of the 1920s, would also play a significant role in bringing Wright back into mainstream awareness. Born in Vienna in 1886 and trained there and in Berlin, Frankl had seen Wright's *Sonderheft,* the little Wasmuth picture

Fig. 20 Lewis Mumford.

book, in 1913. In 1914, like many other European émigrés in America, he made an architectural pilgrimage to Chicago to see Wright's buildings, but he did not meet the architect. He claimed their first encounter was in 1926 when Wright parked his car in front of his gallery at 4 East 48th Street and dropped in while a cop wrote the architect a ticket. The two immediately bonded over the crusade for modern design and a shared appreciation for Japanese aesthetics. In February 1927, Frankl cited Wright in an essay for *House and Garden* as proof that America already had a spirit capable of adapting itself to "the New." Its richly creative designers, Frankl maintained, had a major advantage in producing their own version of modernism: "If possession is nine-tenths of the law, then everything is in our favor; it was an American who created the entire current of modern architecture and decorative art: Frank Lloyd Wright."[36]

Olgivanna also had friends in New York, and she returned to her old circle of Gurdjieffians for comfort and belonging, but only after a spiritual revelation. In December 1926, when she first arrived in Manhattan, she kept her infant, Iovanna, close to her but left her other daughter, Svetlana, at a boarding school in Chicago. The separation weighed on both mother and daughter. The lingering effects of postpartum depression continued until Olgivanna had a transformative vision: Gurdjieff's dead wife appeared to her as if in a dream. "It was [the] first time in my life, *my first experience*—I knew, felt, understood, that she did not die," she wrote later. "The first human being I know that did not die. . . . She stayed with me for a few days . . . and left leaving the light and life." Olgivanna had strived for years under Gurdjieff's direction to achieve some level of spiritual transcendence, and now she finally felt closer to that exalted state.[37]

Although she had been distanced from her former dance students, Olgivanna reconnected with them, and enjoyed "being in the whirle [*sic*] of social life." A world of ideas opened to her, an "intellectual life . . . through talks, conversations that sometimes lasted hours." She also began to study Yogic philosophy, the current rage among intellectuals, an interest that Maginel also developed.[38]

Wright could not avoid Olgivanna's esoteric interests. Alfred Orage, Gurdjieff's front man and promoter, was giving public lectures and readings from a manuscript of Gurdjieff's "Beelzebub's Tales." His intention was not only to raise interest in the mystic, but to amass funds. Wright was intrigued and, having previously met Orage, requested that they meet again. On March 3, 1927, the two men conversed at length on topics ranging from the work of Gurdjieff's center to Orage's theory of social credit whereby people received value for their contributions to society. Wright would incorporate a similar concept of social credit into his evolving principles for Broadacre City.

Wright's interest in the Gurdjieffian program may have also come from the continuing notion of allying Gurdjieff's new center in America with his own vision for an educational complex located at the former Hillside Home School at Taliesin, which Wright had inherited and quickly mortgaged. But any chance of Gurdjieff contributing money for the effort was null, as Orage was forwarding all cash raised back to Gurdjieff, who was desperate for funds and new members. Unaware of the financial realities in France, Wright asked about Jean Toomer's Gurdjieffian circle in Chicago as a potential ally for Wright's own project. The long meeting with Orage ended when e. e. cummings and John Dos Passos joined the pair in seeing a demonstration of sacred movements. Cummings, Dos Passos, Wright, and Orage formed an unlikely assembly, but the foursome encapsulates the typical creative crosscurrents of New York in the mid-1920s.[39]

Wright and Olgivanna were settling into New York. Olgivanna often took Iovanna through the streets of Greenwich Village in a baby carriage (fig. 21). On one outing with Wright in early February 1927 they bumped into Elizabeth Coonley Faulkner, the daughter of Queene and Avery Coonley, Wright's clients from the Oak Park days. Wright presented Olgivanna as his wife, though they weren't married, and, with mock humor, pointed to the infant in her pram as his "crime." Now their neighbor, Elizabeth invited them to dinner.[40]

A heavy burden lifted as winter moved toward spring: on March 4, charges against Wright for violating the Mann Act were finally dropped, and the event made national news. In part to celebrate Wright's liberation, Woollcott invited him to a concert on the following day. As Ferdinand Schevill described the news, "This opens a new chapter."[41]

During the winter and spring sojourn of 1927, Wright also reconnected with his old friend Guthrie. The two were neighbors, with Guthrie's residence at the rectory of St. Mark's Church on East 11th Street and Second Avenue, close to Wright's apartment on East Ninth Street. They began hatching plans that would lead to Guthrie becoming a major client, though one with limitations.[42]

Wright remained anxious and unsettled. He continued to work out his feelings about the city through writing. In late spring of 1927, he took the essay "In Bondage" that he had drafted in Hollis and reworked it, changing the title to "The Pictures We Make." "For four months I've been marking time in New York," Wright began in the revised essay, "dying a hundred deaths a day on the New York gridiron in the stop-and-go of the urban criss-cross." During the winter, he felt as if he had been "hanging above this spasmodic to-and-fro," the "in-and-out," and the "up-and-down." The city, Wright still maintained, was a disorienting fusion of motion and stasis, waiting for everything; its men had no style, and advertisements exploiting sex were pervasive. The nuance of change in his perception came from sensing the impact of visual culture and the transformative—and deflating—role of media: the city had entered "the pictorial age" where "the pictures we make for ourselves of ourselves, to each other, or of what is honestly ours" were less than

Fig. 21 Washington Arch in Greenwich Village, March 3, 1929.
Photographer: Samuel Herman Gottscho.

"honest." "So greater New York seems," he wrote, "the Triumph of the Insignificant."[43]

So "significant" was this "insignificance" that Wright couldn't even trifle over architecture—it cut to the core of American identity and the alienation of modern life. "We erect a tedious, flimsy pictorial screen," and it is "impossible for society to see itself, and, except in rare individuals, it is unlikely that men or women will ever see themselves face to face." This pictorial deluge had a psychological impact on humanity. As for his own position, the architect set himself apart as an "artist," interested in "significance only where it may be a beautiful expression of this life of our own." Of course Wright was far from ascetic; his expensive tastes indicated as much. Yet he was horrified by the gluttonous materialism of New York City. It impoverished the spirit: this superabundance that neutralized humanity to "deadly animosity" from the "sameness, the unanimity, the conformity of it." Wright tried later to publish the essay; he was unsuccessful, but the essay served its purpose to sharpen his rhetoric and to help alleviate some of his angst.[44]

In early April 1927, Wright visited the Martins' cottage site on Lake Erie. In the same month, he and Olgivanna started discussing plans to leave New York but were unsure where they could go. Finally, Philip La Follette, Wright's lawyer, worked out a potential solution that would allow Wright to return to Taliesin—but with a catch. The bank insisted that cohabitation be forbidden while the financial resolution of Wright's affairs was taking place. Wright nodded approval, but thought he could outwit the bank by at first hiding Olgivanna at Jane's house, Tan-y-deri, and then discreetly transferring her across the hill and fields to Taliesin.[45]

Wright left New York and returned to his homestead in May 1927, for the glorious months of the Wisconsin late spring and summer. Under the bank's watchful eye, he tended to the loose ends of his life. In mid-May he went to Chicago, visited one of Toomer's Gurdjieffian groups, and endured a horrific courtroom rumble with Miriam. To grant Wright a divorce, she demanded that he drop Olgivanna. Wright refused. Miriam countered by accusing Wright of physically abusing her. The press, per usual, covered the skirmish in detail, and the nasty event only continued a sad and violent marital melodrama. A month later, however, La Follette made progress in the negotiations and the two parties appeared to head toward resolution.[46]

Wright's fraught life finally turned a corner when the divorce from Miriam was decreed on August 26, 1927. Unfortunately, the saga continued in a different format, for Wright now had debilitating alimony payments. The *New York Times* reported that Miriam received a cash settlement of $6,000 with $30,000 placed in a trust for her, in addition to payments of $250 per month for the rest of her life. Not only had she squeezed Wright for cash, but she required that he promise "to lead a moral life." The costs were in addition to alimony payments Wright had already made to Catherine, his first wife. The new expenses surprised the subscribers of Wright's corporation, who became angry and resentful. In addition to the financial burden, the divorce meant by Wisconsin law that Wright was forbidden from living with or marrying Olgivanna for one year, as doing so constituted an "immoral situation."[47]

The *New York Times* account of the divorce was coupled with a recap of Mamah's tragic murder, erroneously reported as occurring in 1924, not

1914, and with the additional claim that Wright's previous divorce from Catherine Wright had been on the grounds of desertion. The spurned first wife came off as noble as she had offered to help Wright unravel the domestic troubles encompassing the second wife, Miriam. The newspaper also recounted that Wright had announced in court a year earlier "that he had loved only four women, and that 'the world knows who they were." They could only have been Catherine, the first wife; Mamah, the murdered lover; Olgivanna, the current lover; and despite the bitterness of their long divorce, Miriam. Finally, Wright was labeled as "the founder of a new school of architectural design, involving broad, low line and cubist effects," and Olgivanna was identified as a "Montenegrin dancer and mother of his child." Wright emerged as a serial adulterer with exotic tastes in women. The paper also labeled him an "internationalist" of Cubist persuasion.[48]

Guthrie read the *New York Times* article and wrote his friend. Teasing the architect about promising the court that he would "be good," Guthrie noted the comment about Wright having only loved four women and expressed sympathy for Olgivanna, the "fair dancer." "I just squirm for you," Guthrie told Wright, with respect to all the bad publicity.[49]

By the fall of 1927, a few positive developments punctuated Wright's life, and the benefits of his New York visit began to accrue. He was still working alone at Taliesin, but some design projects moved toward him. In an expansion of Wright's European connections, the director of Leerdam Glass, a Dutch company, approached Wright to produce designs for their product line. Discussion had begun earlier in the year; while Wright was in New York, Petrus Marinus Cochius asked him to design glassware for their new San Francisco showroom. Cochius saw Wright on par with, or better than, the best contemporary Dutch designers. Wright, at Taliesin, was relieved. "I have been absent from my work nearly two years," he explained to Cochius, "but I am back again and eager to do all I can in every way. I can be reached now permanently at this address as the persecution of the press from which I have suffered too much in the past years has now become no excuse [not] to continue."[50]

Known as a liberal and a progressive sponsor of modern design, Cochius had become aware of Wright's work through the network of Dutch publications that featured the architect. He saw Wright as the designer to reinvigorate Leerdam's sagging product line. This was the start of a long-term business relationship and potentially the kind of recurring income Wright needed.[51]

Wright's tone was optimistic, and there's nothing like optimism to generate sartorial need. While Wright had been in New York in the spring, he had stored his clothes with his son John. By September, Wright was desperate to find his missing items: sealskin caps, a detachable hood for his overcoats, eight pairs of expensive field hose. He sorely missed his olive-gray tie, as well as a mixed gray and several black ones. Gone astray was a shawl, a scarf, a brown vest, two pairs of spats (one white, one tan), and a ladies' striped sweater cap. Fortunately, the absent gray linen suit was too small, so Wright didn't miss it. Wright couldn't wait for John to look for the items in his attic and, though scrambling for funds, he took action. Wright wrote his tailor in Chicago that he was "badly in need of clothes" and ordered a leather coat, a brown leather suit, and white vests.[52]

In September 1927, Wright sent an upbeat summary of his activities to Darwin Martin in Buffalo. He hit all the high notes with Martin: new publishing projects, European connections, extensive networking via letters, and potential projects. Among the details, Wright gave Martin a brief sketch of life at Taliesin. "We get up at six and go to sleep at nine-thirty, working every evening," he informed Martin. "All are well. Baby has just triumphed over measles—as a princess should. Have written fifty letters. In other words the creative power is no longer idle but seeking opportunity."[53]

Wright also shared his optimism with family and friends. Even his paternal instincts reawakened. When his youngest son, Llewellyn, told him he wanted to be a lawyer, Wright advised him to become a judge. "I don't see why you should waste time being a lawyer," Wright teased. "It would have been impossible for fate to have let me off without contributing *one* lawyer to the cause of civilization. . . . I am not saying you won't make a natural 'lawyer,'" but that "I should have got one born, fed, homed and educated out of myself is one of Life's little ironies,—N'est a pas? [*sic*]."[54]

Wright also updated Aline Barnsdall, his peripatetic client from California. Though they constantly squabbled, the two cared much for each other. He complained about her money but tried to make amends for hurting her. She moaned about Wright letting her down, but always in the end expressed sympathy and support for his travails. "How is it that you are back at Taliesin?" she implored. "You belong there," she continued, "and not uprooted wandering about the world."[55]

Despite his optimism and upbeat accounts, Wright's domestic situation remained messy. He had surreptitiously defied the bank's prohibition against cohabiting with Olgivanna. La Follette and friends insisted that Olgivanna and her children temporarily leave the country to take the heat off Wright and allow her time to get a passport and visa. Wright worried, rightly so, that once Olgivanna left the country, she might not get back in, and he refused to send her away.[56]

And despite having secured a divorce in August, Wright remained a target for sensational press coverage. In November 1927, a Milwaukee newspaper carried a full-page, illustrated spread, "The School the Wright Scandals Wrecked" (fig. 22). According to the article, the decline of the Hillside Home School run by his aunts stemmed from Wright's notoriety. Although containing inaccuracies and ignoring the aging of his aunts as a factor in the school's decline, Wright came off once again as a disgrace to his family.[57]

During the fall of 1927, Wright, at Taliesin, corresponded not only with Guthrie, but with his other friends and associates that he had met in New York. Writing to Frankl as his "Usonian friend," Wright filled him in on his projects. They even had a brief but intense discussion about Wright and Lloyd working together to design a store on Fifth Avenue for one of Frankl's California clients. The project went nowhere, but Wright remained a stellar figure for Frankl as their friendship and collaboration deepened.[58]

By early December, Wright and Aleck Woollcott resumed their correspondence. Woollcott felt close enough to Wright to share that his beloved sister Julie had died of a "dreadful malady." Although he hadn't written Wright recently, he'd read about the fire at Taliesin and had followed Wright's escapades with the law in Minnesota. Working for the *World* and writing from his temporary residence at the Algonquin Hotel,

Fig. 22 Newspaper clipping from *Milwaukee Journal*, November 13, 1927.

he explained his tardiness: "I have such an accumulation of unspoken good wishes and apologies and congratulations," Woollcott wrote, "that I despair of getting them all into this letter. Toward the end of June, my life was knocked into a cocked hat and all my plans for both work and play went into the scrapbasket."[59]

"Your letter was a terrible shock to me," Wright replied immediately. "There is something noble, in the simple way you tell of terrible things. The nobility is usually in whatever, of a practical nature, you write." "I wanted to have you both here—notwithstanding everything—and now," Wright added, for mutual consolation. "More and more a stranger, in my own land—Alexander. I should love to see you again—here's hoping."[60]

At this moment in late 1927, Wright was still a subject of controversy, he and Olgivanna were unmarried, and their life lacked long-term stability. He had, however, lurched forward in some positive directions. Most importantly, his extended five-month refuge in New York allowed him to take up with a few old friends and to make new contacts, all of which integrated him further into the city's life and offered a base for attracting new projects. New York had begun to stimulate fresh directions, with dreams of new opportunities and new clients. Among them, the Reverend Guthrie emerged as the catalyst for the most daring architectural vision of Wright's career—it would be the perfect "New York" commission for Gotham City.

5

URBAN VISIONS

From his church in New York, the Reverend William Norman Guthrie provided Wright with one of the most visionary projects of the architect's career. St. Mark's Church in-the-Bowery—with its exotic pageantry and its non-Western spiritual delights—had the potential to transform a neighborhood. The church sat on the original site of a Dutch Reformed chapel on the "Bouwerie" farm of Governor Peter Stuyvesant, but when the family converted to Anglicanism in the eighteenth century, they gave the chapel grounds to the Episcopal Church. So "St. Marks-in-the-Bouwerie," a second parish, was established with extensive real estate in the Lower East Side. The new building, designed in a restrained Georgian style and dominated by its tall steeple, was consecrated in 1799 (fig. 23).[1]

A slow decline followed, as many of the fashionable parishioners moved uptown. By the time Guthrie arrived in 1911, Russian, Italian, Polish, and numerous other immigrant groups, including Eastern Orthodox, Catholics, and Jews, had replaced the gentry in the neighborhood.

Fig. 23 St. Mark's Church in-the-Bowery, 131 East 10th Street, New York.
HABS, Photographer: Arnold Moses.

Some—with leftist political bents—were hardly receptive to the Episcopal Book of Common Prayer. Guthrie set about attracting new members to the church's dwindling flock and, on a grander scale, to revise Episcopal liturgy and reform religion itself. Though sensitive to the poor conditions of his working-class neighborhood, many of these programs were aimed at the artists and literary figures who also entered the area in search of cheap rents and whose agnosticism would make them more susceptible to engaging Guthrie's new liturgy.

The rector's grand reform agenda had three major tenets: universal religion derived from diverse spiritual sources but funneled into Christian worship, eurythmic dance of Guthrie's own invention, and a modern language of architecture for these new practices. Instead of incorporating the religious rites that locals knew from the Old Country, the rector looked to other sources to lead them into religion. Guthrie's unorthodox services—a cultural amalgamation of Native American, Egyptian, and Greek mythologies; biblical storytelling; pageantry; and contemporary dance—were sensational and controversial. He had been pursuing these interests for over twenty years and had even recruited for his vestry board a devout member of the Bahá'í sect, Horace Holley, to guarantee authenticity.[2]

By 1922 Guthrie had begun to produce dances as a sound and light show with scantily clad dancers in an attempt to raise spiritual consciousness in the tradition of whirling dervishes and other Eastern religions. He considered most contemporary dancing as offensive: the foxtrot, for example, degraded the body's ability to communicate nonverbally. His dances of "eurythmic worship," he maintained, were different—and sensational.

The press covered Guthrie's exploits in detail. He had his secretary clip out a detailed account of the dances that appeared in the *New York World:*

> The doors of old St. Mark's-in-the-Bouwerie, closed by firemen and guarded by police reserves, creaked on their hinges yesterday under pressure of disappointed throngs eager to witness "the ritual dance of the Della Robbia Annunciation." . . .
>
> The dance does not burst upon one in a blaze of glory. The lights, the music, the service that precedes it, all lead up to it, aid in the creation of an atmosphere that puts the mind of the spectator in a condition of utmost receptivity. He is splendidly prepared by all that goes before to credit the dance with all the good motives claimed for it.

And so:

Picture an ancient church where lights burn dim, with stained glass windows that make a golden afternoon without seem like the twilight hour, surpliced figures in pulpit and in choir loft, minor strains of a great organ and the odor of incense all about. Then a voice, which seems to awe but does not quite subdue the organ, reading in impressive style Dante Gabriel Rossetti's "Ave." . . .

And then the lights grew dimmer and the "Hymn to the Madonna" sounded like a farewell to-day. With almost funereal strides two black-gowned men drew great curtains that shut off the church sanctuary back of the pulpit and with reverent hands carried to the front a great "Banner of the Annunciation." A harp had joined its softness to the organ's flutelike notes.

Even the twilight had faded now and a pale moon seemed to have drifted from behind a cloud. The audience was hushed. Curtains on either side of the stage in front of the sanctuary parted slowly and there entered four barefoot figures in flowing rustleless white silk robes. Their heads were bare and (despite the dim light) their faces pretty.

These four (the interpretation throughout is the author's) were Birth, Death, Pain and Pleasure. They walked silently forward, crossed, exchanged places and crossed again indicating symbolically that each understood the other's functions. . . .

Thus much of the dance had been extremely slow motion. Suddenly the white clad symbols quickened their steps, the walk increased to a run and hilarity seemed about to enter into the rhythm. A gong sounded—the Voice of the Conscience had spoken and the dancers quickly halted in their ripping pace, then resumed the slow measure once again.

Once more the curtains parted and the sixth white robed figure appeared. From her head a long veil draped its folds to the stage. . . . She was the Virgin Spirit of the Earth representing receptivity to higher things, a sixth sense, the "higher life that helps us pass from self-consciousness to God consciousness."

She was dressed as the Virgin Mary is often pictured and the other dancing figures bowed to her and made her their Queen. Then the ninefold candlestick was lighted. There were eight small candles with a large one in the centre. Birth, Death, Pain and Pleasure each lighted two candles, one representing life before and one life after consciousness came. . . .

While receiving these gifts and the homage of the other five symbolic figures, the Virgin Spirit suddenly gazes at the Banner of the Annunciation, picturing the Virgin Mother of Christ. She takes off her gifts and offers them to the Virgin Mother "who expresses to us our own virginity." Birth, Death, Pain, Pleasure and Consciousness, all turn adoring eyes upon the typical virgin and there find complete understanding. The dance has ended.[3]

Wildly popular, the dances were also the subject of controversy. In 1924, the year the review appeared, Guthrie defended his new methods as a means to rejuvenate the Episcopal Church even as the dances outraged William Thomas Manning, Guthrie's former classmate at Sewanee and now the bishop of the Diocese of New York. From his perch at St. John the Divine, Bishop Manning forced Guthrie to halt the dances.

Guthrie neither repented nor relented. His eurythmic dances, with their synesthesia of light, sound, and movement, were intended to transform experience and consciousness. In that sense they represented a psychedelic rapture that prefigured the happenings that would rock the East Village some forty years later. Guthrie, Wright's most mystical friend, was a spiritual impresario whose performances exceeded even the mystical gyrations of Olgivanna and her Gurdjieffian colleagues. In his own words, Guthrie sought to create religious services that were "a-thrill and a-throb with spiritual conviction." Guthrie was also Wright's most imaginative collaborator. For them, a modernist response to culture and religion in the 1920s needed a modern place of worship.[4]

Guthrie became the rare client who not only could articulate a grand vision that equaled or even exceeded that of his architect but could also ground that vision in architectural form. In his Easter Sunday sermon of 1925, he laid out his ideas for a radically innovative church: "The Resurrection of Our Dead Christianity: Clothed with the Body on an Impossible Cathedral," attacking the Cathedral of St. John the Divine and Bishop Manning, his enemy. He bluntly told his congregation: "New York does not want the cathedral of St. John the Divine. . . . To hold modern preaching services in the cathedral as planned would be the craziest idea imaginable." Guthrie reviewed for his congregation the history of Christian architecture, noting even that the traditionally styled St.

Mark's Church in-the-Bowery was too sectarian a building to properly serve modern worship. At the core of Guthrie's thinking was the idea that all religions must unite in "a Shrine of Worship for all People." A new form of worship was required and, with it, a new kind of sacred building, one where there were no officials, no priest, no profit, no king—only a unitary body for one God who surveyed all.[5]

Guthrie concretized his fantastical vision by appending to the manuscript of his sermon a drawing of his "futuristic cathedral." An association of various denominations and religions would cooperatively own and operate the new cathedral. It would consist of a central holy tower and twelve square chapels, each of which contained a denominational altar. Guthrie's Modern Cathedral would house 15,000 to 25,000 worshippers—though Wright's later drawings would describe a cathedral for "a Million People." They could enter each chapel from the outside and proceed through a stained-glass wall to a vast interior central space. Different religions used the chapels on a rotating basis. Guthrie imagined their form to be "a rectangular skyscraper, receding polygonally as it goes up, and at last spiraling conically." The upper floors of the cathedral served ecclesiastic functions, while secular activities took place on the lower levels. Between each of the chapels were wedge-shaped artist's studios, each of which led toward the central hall. Above the studios were assembly rooms for artists, poets, musicians, dancers, and actors, as well as meeting spaces for social workers, political reformers, and philanthropic groups. Arched bridges connected these spaces, unifying the sanctuary into a continuous expanse of fellowship.[6]

Guthrie's proposed cathedral would embody the magic of the number thirteen. In addition to the twelve chapels, a thirteenth side served as a grand entry facing east so that the rising sun could make its "triumphant entry everyday." While the number twelve had standard references to the zodiac, the tribes of Israel, and the disciples of Christ, the number thirteen, Guthrie claimed, bore particular relevance for Americans, whose thirteen stars and stripes on the original flag denoted the foundations of the country and its thirteen colonies.

Eurythmic dances would play a role in the Modern Cathedral. Processional paths allowed dancers to move along the interior toward the zenith of the central space. Appended to this soaring void were glass walls with balconies containing orchestras, choirs, and organs all illuminated from the top by the "Eye of God." Because the great "common holy space" contained no priest, conductor, or actor, it required no pulpit or altar. Instead, Guthrie located a sunken centralized orchestra pit with smaller orchestras around it as well as organs, which issued abstract resonant tones. Above the pit, Guthrie called for a drum-shaped platform on which stood a huge, translucent bowl of clear water that bubbled fresh as if it rose from Valhalla. The bowl fed a series of geysers that shot jets of water toward the central crystal dome. Above this bowl, a second circular dish with flames dancing from it, mounting upward "into free pure space, red and green, and wicked white, and skyey [sic] blue." On the next ascending tier, a cosmic sphere poured forth fragrant clouds of incense that rose in quiet billows. Interspersed through these clouds were jets of light in every imaginable hue, creating the effect of an aurora borealis.

This ensemble of light and color would be neither universal nor democratic unless it provided for "the intellectualists, the man of imagination and craft, and for the unemployed and unemployable." Below its main glass floor would lie "vast caves, for the simple hospitalities that a great city should render freely to all human beings." Here the poor and unemployed would find a refuge, a hospice, and a clinic addressing medical and mental health needs. Religion became community in this vision.

Guthrie made sketches, in a ground plan and little perspective to work out his concepts, revealing that overall form corresponded to what he described as a "star-tickler," and not a conventional skyscraper. His cathedral would soar 1,000 to 1,500 feet and take the shape of a sloping obelisk, at whose base would be tapering glass towers over each of the denomination chapels. The arched doors of the workspaces lay between them. Constructed with a steel structure, the edifice would have surfaces of stained glass.[7]

To accommodate all religions, the church and its programs would appeal to all human senses in the broadest and most universal terms, as they had been experienced in primal nature. Here, at its core, was the association to Frank Lloyd Wright's own admiration of primitivism that had emerged in the 1910s and early 1920s. Not only did Guthrie toss out priests and celebrants, but he banished all conventional sacred languages, including Hebrew, Latin, and even Coptic. In their place he called for more exotic liturgical languages such as old Slavonic or Hindi. Though the typical American audience could not understand them, their sonority alone would be transformative. The metamorphic effects that Guthrie intended transcended mere sensuality to inspire people to renounce sinful activity. As a result, the experience of his Modern Cathedral, he argued, would augment the moral well-being of the city itself. A New York united by one common experience would lead to the closing "of alcoholes," the opium dens that actually existed near St. Mark's, and the morally bankrupt theaters and dance halls. In the Modern Cathedral, the new parishioner would find "grand accessible ecstasy."[8]

Wright knew about Guthrie's concepts for the Modern Cathedral in 1925, but the architect had little time to respond immediately to his apostate vision—just eight days after Guthrie's infamous Easter sermon, the fire of April 20, 1925, devastated Taliesin.

Two and a half years passed. After all the fuss—accounts appeared almost daily on the front pages of the *New York Times*—Guthrie took a year's sabbatical from October 1925 through 1926. After the Christmas season in New York, he resumed his crusade to save his church and transform its worship practices. In February 1927 he decided to resurrect his controversial exotic dances at St. Mark's Church in-the-Bowery. Bishop Manning remained so opposed to them that in October 1927, he forbade the church to offer Holy Communion. During his sabbatical, Guthrie had written an article on his plans for the cathedral and sent the manuscript and his ideas for the building to Wright. When Guthrie raised the subject, Wright replied that during this hiatus he had developed drawings for the scheme.[9]

"I believe in the 'Cathedral' idea," he told Guthrie. "There would be some good effects as the result of broadcasting it. And we might build it before we die—who knows? I have already got it born." There were other reasons why Wright "believed" in the cathedral: it represented his first project for an American urban, public architecture since the completion of Midway Gardens in 1914.[10]

Almost a whole year passed before the discussion resumed. In November 1928, Wright told Guthrie that he had revisited the sketches and thought "them exceedingly interesting as I see them again." But, he added, it would be a large labor to develop them to the point of being illustrations. Wright invited Guthrie and his wife to work with him on the drawings. Guthrie declined the invitation but amplified his vision at the end of the year.[11]

"What we want is . . . a *meetinghouse* for a sort of ritual; color, sound and NOT verbal," the reverend told his architect. "Procession and Dance, but not indiv[idual] latent exhibitionism. It wants *vast* sacramental visions to music . . . Krakatoa in dynamic operation—erupting fragrant souls of flowers. For that who could work better than *you and I;* and couldn't we sell it too?" "That plan," he rhapsodized, "could buy me free of my little prison job here and you . . . from needing to compete with machine architects. Can we effectively confer on this?"[12]

What Wright had given birth to was the most visionary invention of his forty-year career. The Modern Cathedral—later inaccurately identified as the Steel Cathedral—was a soaring glass structure unlike anything he, or any other architect, had ever created. Working alone at Taliesin, he produced drawings—one plan and two elevations remain—that testified to the combined vision of enraptured client and enthralled architect. Wright took Guthrie's evanescent object and provided automobile access to it, as if it were solid, real, and freestanding in the urban fabric. He further multiplied the number of entries and provided the essential structural system to allow the building to stand erect. As Joseph Siry described in his brilliant analysis of the scheme, the base of the building that Wright proposed consisted of a huge hexagon that sat on an even larger platform made from two overlapping equilateral triangles (fig. 24). The structure, at its core, spoke a language of basic, primal geometry that was at once platonic and sacred in religious practice. The various thoroughfares that led into the space circulated toward parking garages located under triangular raised garden terraces. Three main entries, each of which consisted of a pair of doors, flanked hexagonal chapels. The perimeter, at the main level, consisted of halls that Wright initially called chapels, and later, cathedrals. In the spaces between them, he inserted what he labeled commercial art galleries. Taking his cue from Guthrie, Wright placed at the center of the central cathedral a pool of water, containing a "fountain of elements." A twelve-sided balcony encircled the

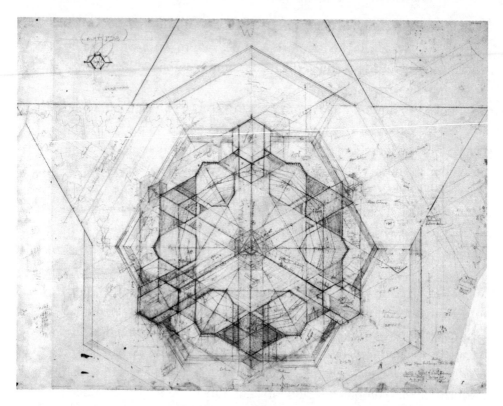

Fig. 24 Modern Cathedral, plan drawing, 1926.

vast central space. To support the sloping walls and balconies, Wright invented a structural system: a steel tripod to support the glass walls as well as secondary girders and cross bracing. From the girders, Wright suspended pendants and structural members with cables.[13]

At the base of the tripod, the cathedral spread to a width of 2,120 feet. Encompassing four-tenths of a mile, this enormous space would be "the largest known interior space of all history." In the elevation drawing, Wright included miniscule figures scaled to the building's façade (fig. 25). The architect's Modern Cathedral dwarfed the Great Pyramid at Cheops and the Eiffel Tower, both of which he sketched in the margins of his design. Wright's cathedral would have been the tallest building in the world, at a height of 2,100 feet, exceeding the 984-foot Eiffel Tower, which itself would be eclipsed by the 1,046-foot Chrysler Building, the latter of which was still under construction when Wright articulated his design.[14]

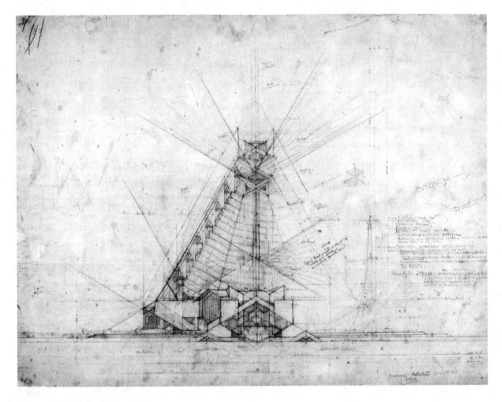

Fig. 25 Modern Cathedral, elevation/section drawing, 1926.

Wright filled his drawings with explanatory notes:

THE SPIDER'S WEB (STEEL IN TENSION) PERMANENT STEEL AND GLASS
CANOPY FOR COMMERCIAL ARTS FESTIVAL. INTERIOR AND EXTERIOR
SPIRAL ROADWAY OR RAMP FROM BOTTOM TO TOP.

    MAIN FLOOR OF CENTRAL CHAMBER STEPS DOWN TO COURT. 'FOUN-
TAIN OF ELEMENTS' TO FORM VAST AUDIENCE HALL SEATING 100,000
PEOPLE. POWER SUPPLIED FROM CENTRAL PLAN IN BASEMENT. ALL
MAJOR AND MINOR COMMERCIAL CATHEDRALS OPENING TO THIS SPACE.
550 GALLERIES 220 BALCONIES.

Inspired by Guthrie, Wright expanded every dimension of the reverend's vision with a fourfold increase in seating for the central space,
augmenting both height and width along with the expansion of galleries
and balconies. He also synthesized Guthrie's idea for a winding walkway
of torch-lit dancers with his own spiral roadway, originally envisioned for

Gordon Strong's Automobile Objective. The spiral ramp now led to gardens at the top of the Modern Cathedral. Elevators, hung from the main girders of the steel tripod, allowed visitors to access the upper balconies. The roadway wound around the face of the dome. Dramatic effects came from lighting of clear and colored glass as well as sculptures and statues for the gardens, which would shoot illuminated water a thousand feet upward into the interior.

Wright's experimental tendencies appeared in a second elevation study with variations from the preceding drawing (fig. 26). He changed the geometric forms of the main entry, and he articulated his own analogies for the building's structure as "1. Spider's Web, 2. Fish Net, 3. Passion Vine and Flower, 4. Fringe [?], 5. Pendant, Stalactite, and Stalagmite." To supplement the metaphorical resonance, Wright added spires on top of spires to the edges of the supporting tripod. He intended these to recall Guthrie's vision of "twelve churches, themselves star-ticklers, say with 600 foot spires." This colossal complex conception was subsumed into a single equilateral triangle symbolizing, in Wright's theories, structural unity.[15]

A proposal for the tallest building in the world at a height of 2,100 feet poses an obvious question: where to build it? Wright and Guthrie both ignored that question. In New York such a building would require at least a city block. But without dwelling on logistics, the vision of the Modern Cathedral satisfied the two. It was a liberating exercise, a means of working through the most altruistic of sentiments, a vehicle for ridding the creative mind of any inhibition whatsoever. "Feasible but impossible," as Herbert Muschamp described it, the physical creation of the building mattered little to Wright. Rather, the project as dream stood as "testament to his irrepressible spirit." In sum, it is just what Wright needed after the defeat of his major projects throughout the 1920s.[16]

Conceptually, this freestanding sculptural object was positioned not merely independent but in defiance of the surrounding urban fabric. It didn't fit the space; it made the space. Wright's cathedral not only embodied idealistic visions of universality of religion, but symbolized the liberation of the architect as an artist who ignored practicalities like site and cost. The Modern Cathedral signified that the architect was freed from the constraints—and responsibilities—of actual construction.

Fig. 26 Modern Cathedral, second elevation/section drawing, 1926.

A vision of urbanity, the Modern Cathedral was the kind of dense, diverse harmony that only a city, at its best, could provide. "An idea is salvation by the imagination," Wright later remarked. His and Guthrie's mutual creation, developed discontinuously in time, was just that. But the vagaries of Wright's fates and fortunes were elusive and random. Little did he know that from the seat of utopian dreaming about the city he would be thrust far away into the emptiness of the Arizona desert. While the idea of the building existed only in imagination, the city as it stood in the flesh—pockmarked, chaotic, superficial—maddened the architect to no end. The desert provided the perfect antithesis.[17]

6

DESERT DIALOGUE

The intermittent progress in Wright's partnership with the Reverend Guthrie had been interrupted by challenges for both. Guthrie had his hands full resisting the angry and disapproving Bishop Manning. And Wright was ordered out of Taliesin in January 1928 when the Bank of Wisconsin claimed he had defied their terms by cohabiting "for immoral purposes" with Olgivanna. Dispossessed of home, in winter, Wright was unsure of where to turn and how to shelter his family.[1]

Good fortune struck in the form of an invitation to Arizona. His journey there would mark the first of two protracted stays in the desert. Although he had done projects for Death Valley in California earlier in the 1920s, he found in Arizona a force of nature that would have a profound impact on him.[2]

The contrast to his urban vision couldn't have been starker. Vast tracts of land lay pure and empty. Only the ancestors of the Pima Indians had left traces in the petroglyphs scattered on the sides of mountains that had once been the cones of volcanoes. Neither developed nor polluted, the landscape altered his perception of the world, transforming his architectural vision and providing the foil against which he began his rhetorical attacks on the very idea of the city. New York, its embodiment, struggled and jousted with the effects of technology and commerce. The desert was the city's inverse: its purity, emptiness, and pristine nature forged its spirituality. From this point forward, the desert and the city became the two poles for Wright's vision of America, each enabling an appreciation and a critique of the other.

Wright's stays in Arizona intersected with his visits to New York over the next two years. He scurried across the country, often fleeing Miriam or his creditors and returning briefly to Taliesin. While the Modern Cathedral represented the most ambitious urban scheme of his career, he would soon produce an equally stunning vision for the desert as he began refining his polemics on the city and roughing out an alternate model of American life in general.

The invitation to the desert came from a little-known architect, Albert Chase McArthur, who had worked for Wright twenty years earlier. The purpose was a consulting gig for a luxury resort planned on the outskirts of Phoenix. Wright accepted. The opportunity provided temporary salvation, money that would keep a roof over his head and that of Olgivanna and the two children. Albert's brothers, Warren Jr. and Charles, commissioned Albert to design a resort called the Arizona Biltmore. Wright was hired to provide technical advice on the use of patterned concrete blocks similar to the textile blocks he had designed in Los Angeles.[3]

The project reflected the needs of a burgeoning tourist industry in the desert of the Southwest. The site consisted of two hundred acres in the foothills of Squaw Peak and included an extensive residential park. The resort complex would encompass a main building, featuring a lobby, dining room, and ballroom, surrounded by several satellite cottages—a place to enjoy all winter, as the hotel later advertised.

Wright left Wisconsin for Arizona in late January and by February 1928 had rented a house in central Phoenix for himself and his family. He immediately began collaborating with McArthur. Work initially proceeded well, with good relations between the older architect and his former employee. "Sorry for your exodus to New Mexico," Guthrie wrote from New York, mistaking New Mexico for Arizona, "and happy that it pays its way." The rector tempered his congratulations with a reminder to Wright not to offend his new clients: "you have often done your fighting very perversely and sometimes offensively, hence you made unnecessary enmities between yourself and those who ought to be your best well-wishers."[4]

As Wright pushed forward with the Biltmore resort project, good luck struck again when he crossed paths with Dr. Alexander J. Chandler over dinner at McArthur's home. A former veterinarian who had become a successful real estate developer in Arizona, Chandler was a man who built actual empires; he even had a town named after him, south of Mesa and Phoenix, where he had an 18,000-acre ranch. He, too, wanted to take advantage of the Southwest's impending tourism boom. His new hotel, San Marcos in the Desert, would replace his existing facility and compete with other resorts, such as the Arizona Biltmore. It would also boost his town's economy after a recent downturn in the local cotton industry. "He looked like the man of independent power and judgment always necessary to characterize thoroughbred undertakings—in building or anything else," Wright wrote as he sized up his new client.[5]

He was on target. From 1924 to 1926, Chandler had gradually accumulated 1,800 acres of land for the project, but only in 1928 did he select an architect. Shortly after meeting Wright, Chandler recruited him to design the hotel. In late March, Wright spent two days visiting Chandler's ranch to examine the site and to discuss the project's logistics. Unlike with the Biltmore, Wright would control the total design and ultimately create a sprawling angular complex that spanned a ravine and the desert terrain. He began drawings in the first weeks of April, and by May the concept of the scheme had "taken shape definitely," as Wright enthused to Darwin Martin.[6]

Wright's domestic life remained turbulent, however. He moved at least three times in Phoenix over three months. He still had no studio and was forced to produce the project drawings by himself. Constantly in motion, Wright was difficult to track, and as soon as his lawyers and friends found him at one address, he had already left for another. In May, the

Bank of Wisconsin further complicated his situation when it announced that it would put Taliesin up for auction. Fortunately, Wright's lawyer, Philip La Follette, cobbled together a deal: the bank would acquire the property initially, but a consortium of Wright's friends would immediately buy Taliesin back from the bank, after which the architect could return home. Meanwhile, Wright was in limbo. With his rental lease almost up, and the summer heat in lockstep, he fled to La Jolla, California, for the season with the scheme for the San Marcos resort in tow.[7]

La Jolla's setting by the ocean and within greater San Diego was ideal. The community benefited from the largesse of Ellen Browning Scripps, who had funneled money into the oceanographic and medical research facilities that would bear her name. Its temperate climate, replete with a continual sea breeze, was nearly perfect—certainly one of the most agreeable in the country.

Miriam still haunted Wright and Olgivanna, following them even to their seaside cottage. But Wright made headway with the challenges before him. In early August, the friends who had initially incorporated Wright's holdings as Frank Lloyd Wright, Inc., reorganized the corporation, which assumed its abbreviated name, Wright, Inc.[8]

Even more important, after the court-imposed wait of a year, Wright and Olgivanna married on August 25, 1928, at Rancho Santa Fe near La Jolla. Finally, Olgivanna was free of immigration difficulties, the couple was legally united, and their two young children witnessed the event. Although Chandler still needed to secure his financing, the San Marcos project seemed all but assured. Even the wire services ceased to harass Wright. To celebrate their honeymoon, Wright took his family to the elegant El Tovar Hotel near the Grand Canyon. He left without paying his bill, an oversight the hotel futilely brought to his attention several times without results.[9]

New York had not forgotten Wright during his shuttling between Arizona and California. The American Union of Decorative Artists and Craftsmen, or AUDAC, an organization that Paul Frankl and five other artists had conceived in New York to promote modern design, officially recognized Wright's work as constituting that of a major modernist and made him an honorary member. In appreciation of AUDAC's interest, Wright wrote the foreword to Frankl's book *New Dimensions: The Deco-*

rative Arts Today in Words and Pictures, published in the spring of 1928. It was a sprawling summary of the previous three years of modern design, with half the photographs of Frankl's work and the rest of that of his fellow New York modernists.[10]

Soon after the AUDAC honor, more welcome news followed: Wright could return to Taliesin. With his most pressing debts ostensibly resolved in Wisconsin, he left Phoenix on September 27, 1928, and installed his family at their Wisconsin homestead by early October. After a peripatetic ten months, Wright required the domestic stability that Taliesin provided. But the pastoral life wasn't without its own problems. The farm was derelict; the cows, horses, and pigs had been tendered for debt and needed restocking; and the old Hillside Home School lay in shambles. The tasks confronting Wright and Olgivanna were extensive, long term, and required a constant and continuous cash flow.[11]

Professionally, Wright again faced the challenge of establishing an office with a coterie of draftsmen and a secretary for support. This would be his sixth office in twenty years. In October he began assembling a team that could aid him in developing the San Marcos project and any other work that might arise. George Kastner came to Taliesin in late November of 1928. The "brave George Kastner," as Frank described him, was joined by Cy Jahnke. They were two of his fellow "Wisconsin sons" from Milwaukee. Wright started to recruit other draftsmen as well. Meanwhile, the architect himself continued developing the design for the San Marcos resort.[12]

With the holidays approaching, Wright assessed his situation, sent a detailed account of his finances to La Follette, his legal minder, and reached out to his first family. He contacted his son John, who needed a job of any sort, about working for him. He also wrote Lloyd, his eldest, about his activities and asked after Helen, Lloyd's wife. He reported having seen his other children and their spouses, John, Frances, David, and Llewellyn, the youngest, who had become a "very conservative man." "I have always had the hope that the break was coming for you," he wrote Lloyd, who was also struggling for work. "You have real ability and with the discipline and mellowing that the years are sure to bring you, personal feelings ought not to get in the way of its success." Noting that Christmas was coming, he enclosed a check for a thousand dollars. Lloyd would join his father and work on the San Marcos resort, producing the splendid perspectives of the fully developed scheme.[13]

The day after Christmas, Wright received a surprise of his own when he discovered in the basement under his studio 1,500 copies of the *Sonderheft,* in addition to about 100 sets of the large Wasmuth folios published in Germany in 1910. The former had sold for $3.50 and the latter for $36.00. Knowing they were out of print, he immediately thought there could be a market for them. He presented his plans for the trove, along with ongoing efforts to hustle his remaining Japanese prints, as proof to La Follette that he was serious about trying to raise funds. "I have a direct inquiry from the head of the Detroit Museum, the Libby-Bequest Museum having millions now to spend, asking me what I have to offer them," he boasted. "A letter of similar purport from the Philadelphia Museum." Good intentions, but without beneficial results.[14]

Wright now had regained Taliesin, his ancestral hearth. He had made progress in assembling a young team of talented assistants and an operation that would even become mobile with the seasons and as the jobs required. Having suffered badly from the flu in snow-bound Wisconsin, he now thought about returning to Arizona to complete the San Marcos resort and to work on other potential projects, including St. Mark's Church in-the-Bowery.

At the start of 1929, Wright began preparing a caravan of people and supplies that would make the trek from Wisconsin to Arizona. Chandler provided some land for Wright and his entourage to live on while they continued work on the San Marcos project. The site was fifteen miles from anything civilized, and they would have to build a desert camp with their own hands. Wright would call it "Ocatillo," a phonetic interpretation of "ocotillo," the name of a spiny desert plant with crimson flowers he described as "a tiny little hollyhock."[15]

On January 15, 1929, Wright, along with his wife and daughters, two nursemaids, a carpenter-handyman whose wife was the cook, their son, and six draftsmen, began the journey south to the desert. They included Jahnke and Kastner, the latter of whom became the great observer of Wright's Ocatillo "ephemera." Kastner's notes, photographs, and watercolors from Arizona documented the life of the camp and its creator.

"Papa," as Kastner referred to Wright, was ever the experimenter, ever the explorer, perpetually hailing, "Boys, you all follow me now!," Kastner noted in his diary.[16]

Wright had also recruited Vladimir Karfik, a young architect born in Slovenia (and destined to spend most of his career in Czechoslovakia). With technical training in drafting and construction that Wright admired, Karfik provided a link to modern architectural developments in Europe. He embarked upon several months of work under the intense American sun, his deep-set eyes constantly shadowed beneath a pair of eyebrows that, in his older years, would whiten and expand.

Another European on the San Marcos team was Heinrich Klumb, a Cologne native who had worked in Hamburg. "All this achieved with bare hands," Klumb later reflected admiringly on Ocatillo and what they built there. He took well to the heat, and his career would later blossom in Puerto Rico, where he built some of the island's most famous civic and institutional architecture. For the time being he toiled "side by side" with Wright, learning "how to rake patterns on a gravel path with a twist of the wrist." The others included Donald Walker, a draftsman from Kentucky. Cecil Tomblins and Frank Sullivan, "a sick man when he arrived," also tagged along. Sullivan's adventure would be cut short when, after checking into the Eucalyptus Sanatorium in Phoenix, he soon died of tuberculosis.[17]

By the end of January, they had all reached Arizona—Wright and his family by car, the others by the Santa Fe Railway—and immediately began building the makeshift camp. On their first night they slept on cots, and the next day they inspected a low hill overlooking the building site where they would make camp. That evening, Klumb drew up sketches for the layout of the complex. With building materials at hand, Wright would later claim that he and his team erected Ocatillo in three days, an exaggeration, as the compound comprised cabins, an office and drafting room, a dining room, a kitchen, and service quarters. By January 23 the camp's boundaries, at least, were set; work would continue through February. Kastner recorded in his diary that it took a month before they could focus fully on developing the construction drawings for the San Marcos resort.[18]

While his crew were roughing it in the desert, the architect attended the opening of the Arizona Biltmore on February 23, 1929. Wright appeared to have maintained good rapport with Albert McArthur. The *Architectural Record* published a lavish spread on the resort in which it identified Wright as a consultant and McArthur as the architect. However, Wright later criticized the design while simultaneously claiming that he deserved more credit for it, an accusation that ultimately soured relations between Wright and the McArthurs.[19]

Ocatillo was relatively complete by late March (fig. 27). Life was spartan and took place in the company of rattlesnakes, scorpions, and spiders. Wright, however, had his own quarters floored with carpets and outfitted with a baby grand piano. The children were sent to school in Phoenix.

The San Marcos in the Desert resort was to be sited at the point where the southern face of the Salt River Mountains begins to flatten into a broad valley. Wright used the triangle to generate the angular forms inspired by the desert landscape. The hotel's central core, from which two long wings extended, would bridge an arroyo that cut down the face of the mountains to the valley below. This central block, acting as a hinge in the composition, would contain a spacious lobby with a dining room above. Guest rooms would be located in the wings, which were designed to rise up from the valley floor in three terraces, mirroring the topography of the mountainous backdrop. Each room offered a fireplace and a private terrace, and some even provided private pools. The vertical ridges in Wright's textile-block system gave the building skin a texture reminiscent of the saguaro cactus. In addition, plantings along the terraced walls harmonized with the desert flora, serving to integrate the structure into the landscape. "I saw this desert resort to embody all that was worthwhile that I had learned about a natural architecture," Wright later recollected. "It was to grow up out of the desert as the Saguaro grew, and the Saguaro should be the motif that inspired its style."[20]

There was poetry and then there was pay. While discussions about projects with Guthrie at St. Mark's Church in-the-Bowery were in limbo, the San Marcos resort appeared to answer all of Wright's financial problems (fig. 28). He dreamed it would produce income for years to come. Chandler fueled Wright's fantasies by suggesting that the architect

Fig. 27 Ocatillo desert camp under construction, near Chandler, Arizona, 1929.

design, in addition to the resort, a desert motel called the San Marcos Water Gardens. Wright jumped on the idea, and soon he and his draftsmen had produced an innovative version of the standard roadside cabin court motel. Wright aligned a series of cabins along channels of water that fed flower gardens. Constructed of wood and canvas, they recalled the materials of the Ocatillo camp. Each cabin would include a bed, a sitting area, a private bath, and a covered porch. Fabric flaps could be opened to provide ventilation, another system borrowed from the camp. A large hexagonal pavilion with a faceted wood and canvas dome was also planned for the complex. Sited near the entrance road, the pavilion would have adjoining lounges surrounding an enclosed garden patio, as well as a dining room. Additional facilities within the complex included a swimming pool, tennis court, and quarters for employees. In addition to San Marcos in the Desert and the Water Gardens, Wright designed a

Fig. 28 San Marcos in the Desert Resort, perspective view, 1929.

residence for Owen D. Young, a "simple block house," and alterations to the original San Marcos resort building. None were built.[21]

Although Wright was bivouacking on the northern edge of the Sonoran Desert in the winter and spring of 1929, he still engaged his growing circle of literary and professional contacts in New York by mail and telegram. In mid-May he resumed corresponding with Lewis Mumford, deepening their connection. "What a shame that you've been to Madison near my Wisconsin home while I've been out here in Arizona with the rattlesnakes, scorpions, tarantulas, et al.," the architect wrote. Mumford replied by taking Wright into his confidence as he discussed some painful, recent criticism of his writing. "I daresay you have been through all this more than once," Mumford observed, "but literary warfare is a little more open than it is in the other professions."[22]

Another member of the architect's new circle, Paul Lester Wiener, contacted "Dear Master Wright" in the desert with an invitation to speak at an exhibition on the work of Erich Mendelsohn, the German Expressionist architect renowned for his monument to Einstein in Potsdam. Wiener, a German-born architect, was executive director of Contempora

Inc., the organizer of the event, and a colleague of Paul T. Frankl's, who in addition to his activities with AUDAC had started Contempora with Wiener to provide international services of art to industry. The invitation placed Wright as a patron among New York's architectural elite, including an A-list of players: Harvey Wiley Corbett, a designer of skyscrapers working on the one-hundred-story Metropolitan Life Building, intended to be the tallest building in the world; Hugh Ferriss, delineator of inspirational stepped-back skyscrapers; E. J. Kahn, master of massive Art Deco edifices across the city; Ralph Walker, renowned for designing the Barclay-Vesey Telephone Building; and Raymond Hood, another major Art Deco practitioner, who would soon shift toward a modernist aesthetic. Hood and Wright would become friends, and Wright would have dealings with all the others.[23]

Wright was delighted to help make Mendelsohn's exhibition a success. Not only had the famous German architect visited Wright at Taliesin in November 1924, but the two had become close. Mendelsohn had published articles about Wright in Germany and provided a major sympathetic conduit for Wright's ideas and work. By reconnecting the two, New York was calling in more ways than one.[24]

As late spring temperatures soared in the desert, Wright prepared to leave Ocatillo. Olgivanna later wrote that the heat was too much for her and the children, but that it was inconsequential for her mate. "Frank thrived on hardships and he was a master at creating them," she wrote in her account of the desert residency. "Obstacles did not exist in his psyche," she beamed, "nor did doubts or indecisions. Before leaving Chandler, he bought a second-hand open Packard, the top of which could not be put up. 'What if it rains?' I asked doubtfully." Untroubled, Wright marked the departure on May 24, 1929, by having a photograph taken of him, in goggles and a driving hat, the family in the roadster, and the Ocatillo camp in the background (fig. 29). Having packed his precious drawings, Wright and the family drove off, fearless of sun or rain.[25]

"Soon we became sun-worshippers ourselves," Wright later reflected after he and his entourage had spent six months in the desert. "One and all look back on the experience, hardships too, as something constructive in our lives." That was understatement compared with the way Wright

Fig. 29 Wright and Family leaving Ocatillo, March 24, 1929.

rhapsodized about the desert from then to end of his life. After returning to Taliesin from visiting New York in the summer of 1929, Wright started to record his impressions of the desert after two extended stays in Arizona. The city was fresh in his mind and provided its role as foil.[26]

"There could be nothing more inspiring on earth," Wright decided, "than the spot in the pure desert of Arizona, I believe." "In all this weird, colorful, wind-swept, wide-sweeping terrain nothing is so deciduous as Arizona buildings, unless it is the crows lighting on the irrigated fields only to fly away. . . . But there lie her great striated and stratified masses, too, noble and quiet. The great nature masonry rising from the mesa floor is all the noble architecture she has at present." The desert required no human intervention, or as Wright put it, paraphrasing Victor Hugo, "The desert is where God is and man is not. And that is the Arizona desert."[27]

Yet to Wright, the Sonoran Desert was also terrifying and menacing in its transformative power. It shifted from "sun-life" inevitably to "sun-death." Its world was one of self-defense, from the prickly cacti to poisonous reptiles. "The inexorable grasp of vegetation" terrified him, while "every line and the very substance of the great sweeping masses of rock and mesa speak of terrific violence." In the desert there was the daytime, and then there was the fearsome night: a cold so intense that keeping warm was impossible, while the coyote howled.[28]

Wright also knew that the desert's pristine purity was impermanent, that the human hand would intervene, and that all was at risk. In "this vast battleground of titanic natural forces," an architecture of the desert—his organic version—would be the mitigating factor. "Arizona is Architecture in tremendous sense," Wright observed, recognizing that his own work was undergoing a profound transformation. "It will make any right-minded architect sick of everything he has ever done in his life, I hope." Instead of carrying forward the traits of his rectilinear designs, he proclaimed, "The straight line and broad plane should come here—of all places—to become the dotted line, the textured, broken plane, for in all the vast desert there is not one hard undotted line!"[29]

Within this realm, all creatures of the desert were inspirations for his architecture, from the firebird of the Pima Indians and the ancestral Anasazi to the blooms of the ocotillo, and most spectacularly, to the anthropomorphic saguaro cactus. Erect and possibly six centuries old, its outstretched arms were to Wright a model of reinforced construction, "A truer skyscraper than the functioneer builds." It embodied the contradictory essences of Wright's desert experience, a powerful life force filtered through with impermanence. "In season it puts on a small chaplet of voluptuous white flowers that it may continue? The white Saguaro blossom opens with the sunrise, obeys some mysterious inner rhythm, for it closes every afternoon at four o'clock, never to open again. Each white flower in due time becomes a small apple, sought by the birds and the Indians for the same end, to carry the seed afar and return it to the earth. The Saguaro message to the future?"[30]

Desert life was fleeting. They had built Ocatillo in two months and made it a place of "transient liveliness." The settlement as a manmade object would return to the earth: "It will be gone from the hill near Chandler, perhaps tomorrow. In any event, gone, before long. Since they will be temporary, call them ephemera." The classic theme of time fleeing was evident elsewhere and underlay death itself. Nature's force of sun, wind, and defiant growth subsumes all, fragmenting even speech. "Wind ceaselessly eroding, endlessly working to quiet and harmonize all traces of violence," Wright added, "until a glorious unison is bathed in light that is eternity. . . . There seems to be no mortal escape. Even in death, from this earth-principle—or is it sun-principle—of growth.

Death being necessary to this creative creature's increase, death was invented."[31]

The desert was the antithesis of the city. New York seemed like the imposition of architecture upon a place, while the desert *was* architecture in and of itself. His rhetoric positioned the city as the desert's obverse. Claustrophobic, nose-diving toward smallness, inconsequentiality, and a slow, muted death, the city relegated humans to anonymity: "say, pigeon-hole 337611, shelf 552, block F, avenue A, street 127." "The carcass of the city," Wright maintained, "is old and *fundamentally* wrong for the future. The city has become helplessly inorganic." It lacked integrity of idea and was monotonous. "The man-eating 'Skyscrapers'—the Hollanders call them 'wolkenkrabber'—were all seeking false monumental-mass for steel skeletons," Wright declared. Buildings contradicted the logic of infusing structure with innovative ideas. Instead of using the openness and lightness offered by steel as framing or as cables in tension, city architects depended on mass, the exact opposite.[32]

City life was incarceration. Over dinner in the desert one night, Wright declared to his visitors, including his son Lloyd: "The city is a prison. There's no place to breathe. There's no sun or light. No place for a man's spirit to grow." In contrast, the desert's purity, its paradox of threatening void pulsating with subtle life represented something deeply personal for Wright. "Living in the Desert is the spiritual cathartic a great many people need. I am one of them." "For the Desert," he elaborated, "comes to the Artist as an inner experience. Like Art or Religion, it comes to some quickly. To others only after repeated experience. When it does come it comes to all as a beneficent simplifying influence."[33]

The desert played a fundamental role at this turning point of Wright's career, coinciding with the closure of the turmoil of his wider wilderness. As Reyner Banham observed, Wright was using the vision that he found in the wilderness to open out "confidently into the new career." The architect needed both desert and city to "square his self with life," as he once said. Despite its transformative power, the desert could not make his future—only New York could do that. The question is whether he could "square them." Could Wright succeed in reconciling the organic desert with the inorganic city?[34]

7

SPINNING TOWER

The city had been the locus for Wright's organic vision of the Modern Cathedral, but the discussion receded while a second project with greater likelihood for realization emerged: a skyscraper on the grounds of St. Mark's Church in-the-Bowery, a scheme intended both to revitalize the church and to generate an urban renewal of the entire Lower East Side neighborhood. This was a real New York project—not a pan-religious fantasy—that if it happened would allow Wright to rise to prominence among the most celebrated coterie of modern architects and Guthrie to secure the future of his iconoclastic mission. The efforts would bind them inextricably closer as they devised their scheme to revolutionize skyscrapers. By the time Wright finished, the floor plans of his tower called for it to pinwheel around a concrete core. Though the building was stationary, the rotation around the core and the differences from one façade to the other made the building appear to spin. It would be unlike any other building New York, in the midst of its Art Deco boom, had ever seen.

Because so many developments occurred simultaneously in Wright's life and work, we need to retrace a few steps to get at the story of the St. Mark's tower. Discussion of the tower had begun in the spring of 1927, when Guthrie took advantage of Wright's presence in New York to discuss the project. Like most clients, Guthrie wanted to know what such a building would cost. In early May, Wright supplied details. The architect had recently conceived of a new structural system that would make the building both economical and durable. While other architects might stress beauty or function, Wright emphasized how his new system would allow the building to resist the depredations of time. Proof of his earlier success could be seen, he claimed, in the survival of the Imperial Hotel, which Wright attributed (not quite accurately) to its structural system. He had pushed ahead with his "simplification of the modern building problem" focused on the skyscraper that had interested him for decades. He had kernels of a new approach in his design for the *San Francisco Call* building in 1913/14, which shifted the loads of the floor to their edges. In 1925, his plans for the National Life Insurance Company building in Chicago moved the loads on the rectangular floors toward a central shaft. But neither had been built. With the technique he was proposing for the St. Mark's tower, the building's floors would be cantilevered from a central core. This allowed for material savings and created a building that was, as he put it, "1/3 lighter, 3 times stronger than anything yet built." Replacing the outside walls with glass and panel sheets would not only supply more circulation space on the interior but reduce costs. The overall approach would offer economic benefits in construction and, as Wright told Guthrie, "value, too, of greater integrity and simplicity made evident in the beauty of the whole."[1]

Wright initially proposed a twelve-story building on East 11th Street that would cost between $500,000 and $600,000, figures that would equal $7 million and $8 million today. He calculated the price at about eight cents per cubic foot instead of the conventional estimate of dollars per square foot. A building like this—tall and thin and with a small footprint—would cost less per square foot than buildings that were more broad and wide. At this stage, Wright suggested a single structure but noted that several towers could be connected in a series as the property was further developed. Wright asked for a down payment to develop the scheme and to get firmer cost estimates. He also made two stipulations: that Guthrie and his people not show the design to anyone—Wright was afraid of its being ripped off—and that *he* would select an associate architect in New York whom Guthrie's board could approve.

Guthrie now had a clear picture of costs and Wright's general approach. His next task involved convincing his vestry board and then confronting the fundraising requirements for the project. Like most architectural ventures, however, moving from plans to reality took time.

Convincing the vestry board was the first challenge. "I can get my project through properly without friction provided I give you up," Guthrie wrote the architect fretfully. He was worried in the fall of 1927 about Wright's temperament. "You are not 'persona grata' and I have got a nice job now to tell you why without losing your friendship. . . . You blow in breezily, assume everybody knows you are the greatest architect in the world." Wright's reputation, for good or ill, preceded him. "You are from Chicago and you have a newspaper record and you have built a hotel in Tokyo that most architects cordially dislike," Guthrie clarified. "You appear to them egotistic, overbearing, arrogant." He worried that the board would be skeptical about Wright's building a skyscraper when he had never built one. What guarantees were there that he could pull it off?[2]

Despite his tendency toward theatricality, Guthrie had practical advice for Wright: "In New York architects get their business by proposing a design, not too technical, that shows the exterior and has an elastic proportion as to the interior and doesn't present to the layman the technical problems of construction." They were paid about $150 for such a presentation, and if the client loved it, he would commission the architect to move forward with developing the design. Of course, it didn't help that Wright was from Chicago, a city and "all that comes out of it" that every New Yorker "despises." And Wright's "flamboyance" would rub conservative New York businessmen the wrong way.[3]

Guthrie went on to explain the internal politics that affected money and the dynamics among members of his vestry board. Wright knew only one player, Horace Holley. It's unclear when they first met—Miriam had known the Holleys in Paris—but it could have been through Guthrie. A Connecticut Yankee born in 1887, Holley had attended Williams College and later became a devotee of the Bahá'í faith while traveling in Europe in the early 1910s (fig. 30). A friend and colleague of Guthrie's, Holley served as junior warden on the St. Mark's vestry. From his office at 4 East 12th Street near St. Mark's, he also published tracts that promoted wisdom and universality in what would later pass as New Age literature. A fellow Bahá'í described him as "a tall, spare man with a pleasant, intellectual face and singularly luminous light blue-green eyes that regarded the world and his fellow man shrewdly and openly." He combined an analytical mind with the openness of a dreamer, an idealist, and a mystic. He was a member of a generation that explored new social concepts and "questing ideas," as the Bahá'í literature had it, moving through "a circle of artists and writers, progressive, independent, often Bohemian."[4]

Holley became Wright's devoted supporter, but Guthrie cautioned Wright about another figure on the vestry board, Warren Shepard Matthews, who was, significantly, an architect and therefore charged with special responsibility for any commissions. Matthews had graduated from Princeton in 1912 after studying architectural engineering and worked out of an office on East 56th Street in Manhattan. He was eventually foisted onto Wright as the associate architect for the St. Mark's tower. Wright objected but had no other recourse than to accept the arrangement. A young practitioner oriented to the tastes of gentry, Matthews's stance on architectural design differed sharply from Wright's radicalism. Their inevitable conflict would run through the duration of the project.[5]

Guthrie realized that if he pushed too hard for Wright's commission, he would ultimately fail. It was Wright, not the rector, who needed to woo the vestry. "Take my letter, now, my dear fellow," Guthrie pleaded, "and read it the second time if it provokes you to wrath, and realize it is a good friend's letter." He wanted Wright to be his architect, but he was even more committed to getting the project off the ground. "You must do something to extricate me from my difficulty."[6]

Wright answered Guthrie a week later, acknowledging his "handicaps"—his being arrogant and overbearing, and his having "ideas." "The last is my ruination—as things are with you now. . . . It would be foolish indeed to argue my case," he reasoned. "And I have no wish to be architect of St. Marks Apartments at the expense to your ambitions. You have load enough to carry without me."[7]

Fig. 30 Horace Holley (right) with fellow Bahá'í Ali Kuli Khan, 1926.

Guthrie had wanted to start with a few sketches paid by the sheet. Wright, who envisioned every project as a total design, would not have it, and he asked to be paid accordingly. It was not about "professional dignity" but about making the circumstances in which "a fine building may successfully issue." If the issue came down to his "personal misfortunes," he wondered whether New York was as "provincial as a village."

Ignoring the political dynamics between Guthrie and his vestry board, Wright claimed that he should pick the superintendent for the project. Guthrie and the board—his clients—were welcome to approve, but Wright made his feelings clear. "So why cast my pearls before swine? Just to get you the humiliation of defeat? And you would be defeated, by your own confession." Still, Wright concluded, he would gladly meet at any time with the committee, show them the drawings he had already made, and explain the details, patiently and humbly. All he needed was an invitation to do so.[8]

Guthrie launched into high gear. He composed a succinct statement, ticking off the details, numbered point by point, as they lay at the end of October 1927, and sent it off to Wright:

My dear Frank Lloyd Wright:

Got your letter and will think it over carefully and see what I can do. Evidently there has been some confusion in our "connections." I will try to find out "what's what."

The facts are:

1. I want to have you for our architect.
2. I want you engaged as that.
3. I have got to try to persuade my present Vestry to do that.
4. For this purpose you have to assist me by putting on a due appearance of humility, which is hard for you to do.
5. If necessary I can get a new Vestry after Easter, but this involves delay, and a certain amount of "wear and tear" for the organization as well as myself.
6. I shall resort to this only if absolutely necessary.

Now you understand me, don't you? Help.[9]

Guthrie then called on Holley to get Wright in line; Holley dutifully and tactfully wrote the architect. Both Holley and Guthrie said Wright needed to appear humble to convince the board that he deserved the commission.[10]

Wright composed his rejoinder from Taliesin. Blatantly flaunting requests for humility, even after promising to provide it, Wright parroted Guthrie's numbering mode when he replied to Holley:

I think I ought to build your St-Marks building for you.

1. Because although it is extremely rare as yet, engineering-architecture is the only permanent profitable kind—today and I am an engineering architect as distinguished from the kind that merely puts the architecture on the outside of the structure—which is what most New York architects are doing today.
   (I apologize to them.)
2. The thought-built buildings of which I have been the author have attracted the admiration and emulation of the entire old-world— as many publications and European authorities attest in increasing degree in their own and in our country.
3. I have—with the experience of the past thirty years devoted to 177 various buildings in this spirit—recently, at the request of one

of our National insurance companies, given the tall building especial study. . . .

4. The best of architectural talent to be had in the world is none too good for any building—and for St. Marks land-mark you should not be governed by expedients or prejudice—but should select your man for his abilities—regardless of all other considerations. . . .

5. Were a vote to be taken by you among architects of Europe whose work our American Architects emulate—as to whom they would nominate as best qualified to build your building for you—they would give you my name.

6. No building I have erected among the 177 to date has any record of unfaithfulness or scandal connected with its handling by me. . . .

7. My fame should determine my fitness to build for you not such notoriety as has been forced upon me, because of it, to make provincial holiday.

8. I believe St. Marks needs a modern expression of this vital-spirit in architecture to justify its expenditure of trust-funds devoted to religious purpose. . . .

9. I offer myself, with all the modest assurances of conscious worth, as a candidate for your favor—and, as I am unaccustomed to making sketches "free" or in competition . . . I suggest that your committee pay my expenses to you to explain and illustrate by drawings of what has been done . . . why not come out here to me?

10. Finally Art—and architecture is a scientific art—knows no sectional boundaries. The idea I stand for is that relation is of the whole civilized world. I hail from no limited area nor specified region as an architect.[11]

The bluster left his friends and clients temporarily speechless. Having heard nothing from them in response, Wright contacted Guthrie the day after Thanksgiving of 1927. "We seemed doom to disappointment."[12]

Wright's fatalism was well founded. Still working at that time without help, he drew all day and wrote at night, so much so that his arm pained him continually. Any sense of security was illusory. Getting appointed as architect for the St. Mark's project remained a distant prospect. Olgivanna remained at risk for deportation, as she and Wright were still not married. Wright had no income from his architectural practice. The corporation formed to save him financially was struggling. The year 1928 began with his expulsion from Taliesin and his trip to Arizona, which, whatever its salutary effects, slowed progress on the St. Mark's project, though he and Guthrie remained in touch.[13]

By early April 1928, Wright was not only involved with consulting on the Arizona Biltmore Hotel but had started the designs for Chandler's San Marcos in the Desert resort. He continued moving from house to house in Phoenix. Meanwhile, Guthrie had his own problems in New York as the tension between him and Bishop William Manning continued; Guthrie claimed Manning was motived by personal animosity. Discussions about the St. Mark's tower went on hold until Wright's return to Taliesin in October 1928. Guthrie congratulated Wright on regaining his "ideal home" and seized upon Wright's return as a chance to move the tower project forward.[14]

Much was at stake as the next phase began. Although Wright was working on the design for the San Marcos resort, the future of that project—and his paycheck—depended on Chandler's raising millions of dollars. Having endured years of personal and professional struggle, Wright was still broke. If the San Marcos project fell through, then the St. Mark's tower in New York would be the source of income on which he would depend. But beyond financial necessity, he saw this project as an opportunity to create a new vision of the skyscraper that would transform urban life.

The moment was also critical for Guthrie. His church lived hand to mouth, its neighborhood agitated with newly settled Poles, Lithuanians, and Slavs. Many of its deep-pocketed parisioners were either dead or alienated by Guthrie's radical programs. He invited Native American chiefs to hold ceremonies in his church and commissioned scantily clad women to perform eurythmic dances. He wanted to overturn the foundations of church liturgy and replace them with rites of universal worship. He surrounded himself with mystics, poets, and performers. Finding a steady source of revenue, though essential for his agenda, was no small task. Failure would jeopardize Wright, Guthrie, and the oldest running church practice in Manhattan. Hoping to ease Guthrie's angst, Wright suggested that the San Marcos resort and his various publications were compelling accomplishments. "Now if we can put St. Mark's on the map with a successful solution to a hackneyed problem, put fresh feeling into a new form, that will be another," he told Guthrie. Their friendship thrived on their shared goal. "The brother-feeling I have had for you all these years may suffer neglect and some abuse and be guilty of both," Wright said, "but it does not diminish, and I count it one of the best things I have."[15]

For Wright, this "hackneyed problem" was nothing less than the entire standard of skyscraper design. The current crop of skyscrapers, he felt, blocked light from their lower floors, clogged the city with traffic, and were uneconomical and impermanent. For Guthrie, two options lay before him: his vestry board could choose to either launch a million-dollar endowment campaign or pursue a real estate development for a new, income-producing building. They had both a precedent and competition: the Baptists across the street on Second Avenue, north of East 10th Street, were converting their former church quarters into a fourteen-story apartment hotel. It was adjacent Warren Hall, an apartment building they'd already built, with both designed by the Art Deco firm Emery Roth and Sons.[16]

If the board went with the endowment, Guthrie would have to raise money privately. He remained at war with Bishop Manning, who hoarded funds for his pulpit and residence, St. John the Divine. But if the board opted for a new building to generate rental income, Guthrie had other issues. One problem was that New York appeared overbuilt with apartments, and the only way to attract renters who were shopping in this glut was to create "prestige." The area on East 10th Street between Third and Fourth Avenues, in deplorable shape, would turn off prospective renters (fig. 31). Another issue was selecting the architect. Wright assumed the job was his, but Guthrie explained the decision was still up in the air.[17]

"Now our New York people are scared of an out of town architect," Guthrie told Wright. Furthermore, according to him, New York tenants were finicky, particularly about the functionality of their abodes. Even Number One Fifth Avenue (designed by New York firm Helmle &

Fig. 31 Hard Luck Town, East Ninth Street and the East River, September 9, 1932.

Corbett in 1927) was heading for bankruptcy because tenants found the apartments impractical. In any case, the real power behind selecting an architect, he insisted, lay elsewhere. "Financing people usually dictate the architect. Do you apprehend?" he asked Wright. "That is why so many Jews get rich as so called architects & so many building corporations hire small architects & wax fat."[18]

"Manhattan is no mystery," Wright claimed, attempting to justify himself and prove his worldliness. "It is more obviously commercialized than its brother and sister cities in the United States,—that is all. I am no stranger to its demands, its habits of thought, its desires, its fears." To make the case for hiring a Midwesterner who had never built a skyscraper, however, Guthrie needed Wright's drawings. With them in hand, he could show the vestry board a distinctive and inspiring scheme that would convince them to hire the architect. Raising that positive enthusiasm was crucial. As Guthrie again reminded Wright, the tag he was known by, Architect of the Imperial Hotel, carried baggage: "Don't forget the Japanese hotel is by many architects called hideous & wholly inexcusable—although apparently a good piece of engineering."[19]

Despite having Guthrie's and Horace Holley's goodwill, Wright had to find other means to reassure the financiers and skeptics in Gotham. Throughout his career, Wright relied on the salesmanship of his own designs to get commissions. He was the singular star in his firmament. But this job was so important to him that he made the unprecedented suggestion to bring in a famous New York architect as his associate on the project. "Say Otto Kahn or Wiley Corbett," he proposed to Guthrie, "or perhaps lesser men in the architectural field in New York. Even these men would be, I think, both proud and glad to work with me, and I should share my fee with them." Despite confusing Otto Kahn, the Wall Street financier and opera patron, with E. J. Kahn, Art Deco practitioner, Wright had identified two major innovators in skyscraper design, a pair of the most prominent architects in New York.[20]

Wright still refused to send drawings of his designs before the commission was fixed, claiming that when he had done this in the past his designs had been bootlegged or stolen. They jousted; Wright worried Guthrie was getting cold feet, while Guthrie reminded him of reality. Wright insisted, contrarily, that that the new building "would put St. Mark's in-the-Bouwerie into working order with a new lease of life, rendered independent, and put it in fighting trim." Guthrie was unconvinced. In early January 1929, Guthrie grew more positive. The vestry board very much wanted to see Wright. "If you just 'speak softly' & hide 'your big stick'—it looks as if we should really do something," Guthrie wrote. "It is a great relief to me for I crave to see a building by you on this property & the pride of showing this great crazy metropolis that a westerner can have genius which is worth all the talent & the acumen & the pull & then 'some.'"[21]

In January 1929, Wright's return to Arizona for a four-month stay again interrupted the St. Mark's project. He initially neglected Guthrie in the frenzy of constructing his desert camp. When he caught his breath in early March, he wrote the reverend that he was eager to follow up on the St. Mark's tower project. Soon from Ocatillo's canvas-roofed sheds came not only designs for the San Marcos resort and related projects, but also the first drawings for the St. Mark's tower. The two projects, both named for the same Christian saint, were wildly different—one low and sprawling, the other tall and projecting.[22]

In fact, Wright had already started on the early phases of St. Mark's across dozens of sketches. He recalled the site in New York well—the odd shape of the lot, the church rotated at an angle, the weathered tombstones, and of course the bustling neighborhood. In one of the very first sketches, Wright took the site plan and crossed out a series of row houses west of the church that would be torn down to provide space for up to four towers (fig. 32). On the reverse side of the site plan, he made a rudimentary calculation of a building footprint. Wright's general procedure was to make sketches and then turn them over to his draftsmen, who were then living and working in the tents of Ocatillo. Since the drawings were not signed or initialed, it is difficult to tell who did what, and when. But the project was crucial for Wright, and he oversaw every drawing with eagle-eyed attention, making changes or corrections as the design evolved.[23]

While still in Arizona, Wright informed Guthrie that he planned to bring the sketches to New York by May. Although the vestry board now had enough documentation to make the decision to appoint Wright as architect for their new apartment building, they still wanted to see him in person before they did so. By the end of the month, Wright had left Arizona, but before heading to New York, he made a detour north to Taliesin. After checking on the condition of the compound and farm, the architect and his family resumed the journey east. En route, he telegrammed Donald Walker, Wright's draftsman at Taliesin, that he would arrive in New York by June 19. Wright planned to check on the construction of the summer home he had designed for Darwin Martin and his wife, just south of Buffalo.[24]

Wright described his momentous return to New York in June 1929: "We drove through the new Holland Tunnel into scenes of indescribable confusion." There was construction everywhere, but he found the "same architectural insignificance except bigger and better in every way than the insignificance we had seen all the way along." Typically, he prolonged his rant, concluding with a comment on freedom and reprising remarks he'd made in the desert: "In this prison-house for the soul, the city, we shall not find much of it."[25]

Despite his broadsides against the city, Wright would continue to enjoy its offerings. He could see his sister Maginel, visit an expanding

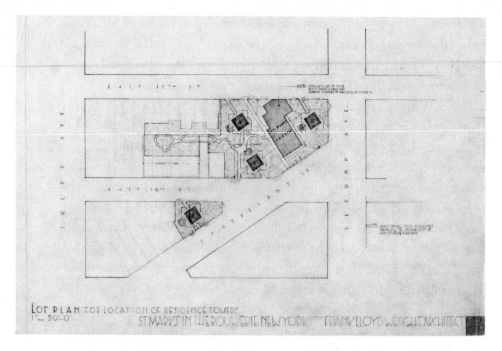

Fig. 32 St. Mark's Church in-the-Bowery, site plan, with multiple towers, 1929.

cluster of new friends and colleagues, and find a counterpoint to the bucolic life of the Wisconsin countryside and the solitude of the desert. But if Wright saw his visit to New York as potentially a temperate break from the heat of Arizona, he would be disappointed: New York and the region were suffering an intense heat wave. Newspapers reported that the weak and infirm were dying of hyperthermia. Crowds took refuge at the local beaches, and a contingent of people at Far Rockaway on Long Island gathered to watch former governor Alfred E. Smith take his first dip of the season. Stylish women had shifted their fashions to lightweight midsummer frocks and white ensembles.[26]

Yet the city's construction boom continued, with new office buildings advertising modern and open floor spaces in prime locations. Gotham rocked between nights pulsating with lively rhythms and hot, languorous days when people either fled the city or just moved at a slow pace. The city could be lively and languid.

Wright arrived just in time for the June 18 opening of the *Contempora Exhibition of Art and Industry*. Organized by Paul T. Frankl and Paul Lester Wiener, it debuted at the Art Center at 65 East 56th Street. Intended to promote modern design in America, the exhibition pooled avant-garde designers, socialite patrons, an art committee, as well as an architectural committee, with Wright as its chairman. With its emphasis on home furnishings, Wanamaker's department store was its logical host. The event, which honored Wright's friend, the German architect Erich Mendelsohn, further exposed Wright to New York's cultural elite. As Wiener reported to Wright, "I must say that we were all very happy to have the privilege of hearing more of your side."[27]

Four days later, Wright took part in a radio interview along with the brilliant architectural renderer Hugh Ferriss, whose dramatic graphic designs embodied the swaying, stepped-back skyscraper. The broadcast, intended to promote the Contempora exhibition and on view at Wanamaker's, had "Modern Architecture" as its theme. Wright was billed as "among the world's most famous modern architects," while Ferriss was "of the younger school." Wright was shifting from his former crisis mode toward a more curated and crafted new identity. "Architecture is really the humanizing of buildings," he began, "something which, perhaps, is more important to us, where we live, than anything else in the world. A real expression of ourselves is bound to appear in our architecture eventually." He talked about the "145 towns" he'd driven through on his way from Chandler, Arizona, to New York. All of them seemed to be premonitions that something new was coming, something with "astonishing—yes with alarming rapidity for the cornice is dead!"[28]

Wright then addressed his nemesis: "I would like to have everybody think of the so-called 'new movement' and even of 'Modernism'—that rather awful aspect of the thing—not as a freakish effort to realize something peculiar for some peculiar people, but the sign and often the substance of a very real awakening to what is intensely valuable in human power, that is, simple, love of Life."

Ferriss took a humbler stance. "The real tradition of architecture is that a building must express the material of which it is made and the purpose for which it is built." From his point of view, architects weren't "really engaged in a really new movement." Instead, like Wright, the "new architects" were "carrying on that tradition."

Wright replied, somewhat cryptically, that the "'New' architects" were new because they were "more true to tradition almost than [any] other tradition can be true to itself."

Ferriss then asked Wright about artistic intent, wondering if the houses he designed were expressions of himself, or if he "calculated the impression [they were] going to make on the beholder." "Usually every man who truly builds is true to himself," Wright answered. Catering to "'popular opinion' or 'society' or what you please—we fall into its power and lose our own and we cease really to be the artist." When Wright received a copy of the interview transcript, he carefully edited it to conform with his ideas and retained it in his files.

Wright was making the most of his time in New York, popping into galleries and museums, conducting business, and collecting accolades before heading back to Taliesin. His foremost professional obligation was, however, to provide an update on the St. Mark's tower, which he duly gave, but only to Horace Holley. Guthrie had already left for an extensive vacation in Europe. Missing him had been poor planning on Wright's part. Excited by the social event of the Frankl opening, Wright laid out the studies he brought at a brief meeting held at Holley's offices at *World Unity* on East 12th. Holley gave tacit approval, which Wright interpreted as the sign to proceed. Without Guthrie present, however, little more could be accomplished.[29]

Rather than driving straight back to Taliesin, Wright drove through Philadelphia, Baltimore, and towns in Maryland and Ohio, prompting him to write Chandler in early July that he had "learned a good deal" and "more about my country than I ever knew before." Combined with his increasingly intimate knowledge of the desert of the Southwest, driving through rural America provided the foil for the freneticism of New York. From Zanesville, Ohio, Wright telegrammed Donald Walker that, after a weather delay, he planned to return to Taliesin on June 26.[30]

Meanwhile, Guthrie, on holiday and enjoying the absence of responsibility and inspiration of new sites, became even more long-winded and poetic than usual. From Paris, on July 4, 1929, he sent Wright, his "old lion," a rhapsodic account of topics ranging from Japanese art to Monet's water lily paintings at the Orangery to Buddhist art. He confirmed his affection for Wright and warned him not to take too much of the life out of his young wife, as he was "a natural volcano & can't always realize how your lava may burn & not just warm the little dells into which it flows."[31]

Back at Taliesin, Wright continued getting the sketches for the St. Mark's tower into presentable form. Parceling the work among the "boys," Wright wrote Guthrie that he would have something substantive—"a really great project in every sense"—for him when he returned to America in early fall. Any further discussion about the project would be put on hold until Guthrie's return, but Wright again invited Guthrie and his wife to visit Taliesin: "It is," he told him, "a rough old place but there is something about it, it has character by no means common." Wright honored their friendship with the familiarity of knowing each other's character well, even how each suffered from "dreaded publicity" but would feel "a sad hole" without it. "Also," Wright concluded, "we are interested in you, count you our friends, depend upon you."[32]

Wright also tended to quotidian matters in anticipation of returning to New York. He ordered shirts from Brooks Brothers. "Gentlemen: Shirts duly arrived and are entirely satisfactory," he advised the store. "Kindly make three more with the collar attached and one of the same material as those sent—white linen. Also make three more of the finer linen, lighter in weight, and stiffen the collar band so that the collar will stand up when the shirt is unbuttoned."[33]

As the summer of 1929 concluded, Wright continued planning to return to New York. Holley wrote that he was excited at the prospect, noting that with the resolution of Wright's domestic life, great things were on the horizon for the architect. Wright replied that he had a big surprise for Holley: four-fifths of the preliminary drawings for the St. Mark's tower were done, and the vestry would have them in a week or two.[34]

These drawings, which Wright and his draftsmen had developed at Taliesin that summer, revealed what made his concept so revolutionary (fig. 33). Instead of being supported by a forest of columns set in a grid, the building would be organized around a concrete pylon that ran its en-

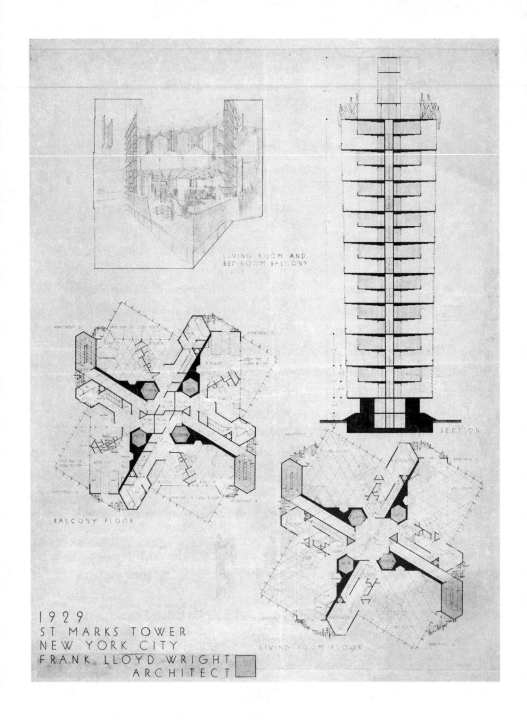

Fig. 33 St. Mark's tower, section, two plans, interior view, 1929.

tire length and contained the elevators and mechanical shafts. The shaft penetrated deep into the earth, like the taproot of a great tree. Each floor would be cantilevered from the pylon, like branches extending laterally from the trunk. Not only would the floors be hung from the core and spun around it, but their undersides thinned toward their unsupported edges, saving both in material and in overall weight. With the St. Mark's tower, Wright could develop and perfect what he had started with his earlier skyscraper designs.

Not only was the scheme central to Wright's own work, but it represented his attempt to create a skyscraper prototype that challenged conventional methods of construction in America and Europe. A functional, income-generating structure, the tower would also be a technological marvel.

In early October, Wright informed Guthrie—back from his travels—that he had ready an "exhibit from A to Z" on the St. Mark's project and that he would soon "invade" New York to attend an event organized by AUDAC. "I shall be awfully glad to see you all again and hope I can please you all with what I have done," he added.[35]

Frankl had facilitated Wright's visit by inviting him to be the first speaker in AUDAC's new series of events. Wright accepted, and AUDAC's organizers were thrilled. Wright wrote Maginel, inviting her to the event, and asked if he and Olgivanna could stay with her on West 12th Street for a couple of nights. Wright also boasted to Holley about the "swell dinner" organized by AUDAC where he would "take the spotlight." AUDAC's gala dinner on October 11 took place at the Central Park Casino, which had been decorated by Joseph Urban. The *New York Times* mentioned the event briefly in the "City Brevities" column, noting Wright as the "guest of honor."[36]

That Friday, the city was pulsating. New York was giddy with the return of J. Ramsay MacDonald, the Labor prime minister of Great Britain. He repaid the affection, claiming Gotham was the "city of his adoption." Manhattan was moving forward with new developments: the Board of Estimate recommended construction of an East Side drive, extending from the Battery to 125th Street, where it would connect to the Triborough Bridge. The project would parallel the West Side express highway that was already under construction. Meanwhile, William Fox of Fox Theatres celebrated twenty-five years in the motion picture business, having grown the company from a mere nickelodeon to a gigantic enterprise, featuring 102 cinemas in metropolitan New York alone.[37]

"They gave us a dinner at the Central Park Casino, 200 people there," Wright later wrote his son Lloyd. "I found my feet and delivered myself of what everybody enthusiastically regarded as, more or less, a speech." He noted the "many important people" in attendance, such as the architects Raymond Hood, who introduced Wright, and Joseph Urban, who sat near Mrs. Harry Payne Whitney, formerly Gertrude Vanderbilt Whitney, art patron, collector, sculptor, and future founder (in 1931) of the Whitney Museum of American Art. The authors Sheldon Cheney and Richardson Wright attended, as did "the editors of various magazines in New York city—well, really, quite a distinguished company." Wright summed it up for his son: "For once in a way, New York took its hat off to your Dad."[38]

Encompassing a broad swath of progressive artists and designers, both European transplants and Americans, the gala signaled that New York had publicly begun to recognize Wright. This was the first of a series of events in which he would take the spotlight. Once vilified, primarily for the mess he had made of his personal life, he was now honored and engaged. It was one more sign that Wright's life was moving forward. His new status could only be an asset when the St. Mark's vestry got around to announcing plans for its tower.

Thus, Wright's spirits were soaring when he went to present the St. Mark's drawings to Guthrie, Matthews, Holley, and Justin L. Miner, a lawyer on the vestry board with a keen business sense and experience in real estate. Wright intended this to be a preview of what he would show later to the full vestry board.

After the preview presentation, Guthrie began formulating questions for Wright, whom he hoped to meet in private on the following day. Although Wright remained a few days longer in the city to speak with his editor at the *Architectural Record,* he missed the meeting with Guthrie—distracted by a turn in the weather and meetings about a new book proposal—and left to return to Taliesin. Guthrie immediately sent a letter to Wright and raised issues ranging from the strategy of having four towers, to fully furnishing the flats, to the nature of the towers' tops and whether they were extensions of the core, smokestacks, or water towers. For someone who basked in long-winded prose, Guthrie turned a surprisingly rational eye on what Wright had presented. He saw that the price of the St. Mark's project was lower than comparable buildings nearby, and he wondered if Wright's standardized plan for the eighteen-story building could reduce the costs further. Perhaps if four towers were built, the church could find an economy of scale for construction costs even if at present it had the resources to build only one tower. "Doubtless one could at first fill the houses with people who desired novelty; secure tenants before we begin to work—I should not be at all surprised."[39]

The fundamental question was whether the real estate investment was safe and remunerative enough to provide the financial security that the church needed. At this moment in 1929, the church assumed the general economic boom would continue—its vestry even began planning a massive fundraising campaign. No sense of ominous subterranean tremors registered with the church or the city at large. The stock market would soon experience some occasional sudden drops, but the major financiers and their institutions took out ads in the *New York Times* reassuring the public their funds were safe. No one seemed to pay attention to the rumblings that preceded the Great Crash. The last moments of the Jazz Age were transpiring in oblivion and denial. Just as New Yorkers ignored the hints of their precarious economic situation, so followed the rest of the country, and the world.

At least Guthrie felt cautionary where his interests were crucial, and he had doubts that the location of the project would provide the revenue to cover expenses, as Wright claimed. "We must remember that in New York people will accept cubbies, if the address tickles their fancy," he told Wright. "'15 East' or 'West' sounds gorgeous. To be on or at the first decade of numbers from Park Avenue is an ability. Only sometimes do people get a fancy for a peculiar address, as in the case of these Vanderbilt-promoted settlements on the East River. It is the psychology of renters that puzzles us to a great extent."[40]

Despite the lingering questions, Wright, with a nearly completed set of drawings in hand, could not refrain from telling the world about St. Mark's. En route to Taliesin, he stopped in Chicago to announce his plans for a radical new version of the skyscraper. Although he hadn't presented the full scheme to the vestry board, he leaked the project to the press. Partly this was shameless self-promotion to stir up interest in the Midwest, apparently with the hope that competition would pressure the New Yorkers to produce the biggest, best, and newest skyscraper before Chicago could. But the competition between the cities was no longer what it had been in the past. Moreover, Wright was promoting a private project—one not yet approved by its clients and without their permission. Fully aware of the power of the press and adept at satisfying and manipulating the media, Wright was seeding the ground prior to his forthcoming sales event.

News reports spread quickly from Chicago. Just as the hinterlands had followed Wright's scandalous private life throughout the mid-1920s, they now heard, courtesy of the Associated Press, of a new type of apartment building built around a concrete core. Local papers from Chicago to Ogden, Utah, from Lubbock, Texas, to Kokomo, Indiana, carried at least a small notice. Many reports focused on the idea of the building having an inverted cone shape. The description exaggerated the building's form, creating the impression of something alien.[41]

In his accounts to the press, Wright emphasized how the tower would revolutionize skyscraper design. He made sure that notices appeared in weekly magazines. *Outlook and Independent* carried articles, while *Time* magazine reported on Wright's efforts as the first demonstration of ideas he had been mulling over for thirty years, though also describing it as "a new and puzzling project." *Time* gave the impression that the building was an upside-down pyramid, a configuration that would cast shadows at its bottom. New York's zoning code required skyscrapers to step back as they rose, to allow for light to hit the lower floors and ground level. According to these reports, Wright had turned the skyscraper on its head.[42]

Warren Matthews, the architect on the vestry board and Wright's putative professional associate for the project, interpreted the announcement as a positive development. "Your second story from Chicago on the towers for St. Marks has stirred up real interest," he informed Wright. "I have told people looking for stories that we expected sufficient plans from you in about two weeks to take to the building department for analysis." The *New York Times* report on the St. Mark's project said that four "Odd-Type" buildings, in the shape of a "novel inverted cone" would overlook the church, and each tower, rising sixteen to eighteen stories, consisting of duplex suites, would cost an estimated $400,000 to build.[43]

"We are interested in surrounding our church," Matthews told reporters, "with as much beauty and charm as possible." Instead of replacing the church itself with a skyscraper and putting the church within it on the lower floors as had been done elsewhere in the city, St. Mark's was building separate towers to produce rental income. Matthews added, "We consider Mr. Wright's design a happy one for this purpose."[44]

But the premature announcements annoyed Guthrie and Holley. It was bad enough that they had had to grapple with the newspaper reports in late September that Wright's friends had made a corporation to "save him from himself." Now Wright had appeared to announce that the building was a done deal and would go up in the next year though it still lacked the full vestry board's approval. Wright had also inadvertently tipped off adjacent property owners about the church's plans. They now could jack up the price for any additional properties the church might need for its project. Furthermore, while this was happening in public, the vestry's members were privately trying to digest a major report on raising a million dollars that a subcommittee had just presented.[45]

Wright tried to relieve Guthrie's annoyance. Matthews and Miner had favorable reactions, Wright reported, and the project was the "real solution of your economic difficulties and the emergence of St. Mark's into real economic glory." Guthrie simply needed to keep a level head. According to Wright, all looked good, as confirmed by local reaction. "There is immense interest here in Chicago in the idea," Wright claimed. "I have held back as well as I could but they are gradually getting it. All this shows the time is ripe for an enterprise of this type."[46]

Guthrie's reply was still petulant. "Do you realize you have just flashed before us, wizard-like, a beautiful vision, and fled incontinently?" he asked, referring to the fact that Wright had left New York without meeting with him. "You seem to think you can shoot through this town like a gorgeous coruscating celestial explosion, and take effect; but really

I cannot manage to get a quote for a Vestry meeting in less than a week's time, and that is hard work."[47]

Wright realized that he had crossed a line with his friends and began to step back. He tried to set matters straight with Guthrie by claiming he'd said nothing to the New York newspapers, in fact given only a cursory interview to the *Chicago Tribune,* and believed that the press was a good thing. "I have a feeling that any notice made about this subject would not be harmful," he claimed, "and it could be charged up, as in fact it is the truth, to the eagerness of the press of the country to know what is going on wherever I happen to be working."[48]

The leak had certainly reached a wide audience, including members of New York's literary world. Bruce Bliven, editor at the *New Republic,* asked Wright to send him sketches of the St. Mark's towers. A journalist and previously managing editor of the *New York Globe,* he not only edited at the *New Republic* but freelanced for a variety of publications. Writing from the *New Republic*'s office at 421 West 21st Street, Bliven wanted the sketches for a piece he was writing for the *Manchester Guardian.*[49]

Bliven also challenged Wright's inverted pyramid idea, saying that it would block light and air and make things worse than in the days of the "packing-box skyscrapers." Sobered by the criticism, Wright uncharacteristically replied that the sketches weren't ready for publication. His towers, he explained, would not block light and air like many setback skyscrapers in New York. Instead, each would sit in the verdant center of its own property, thereby giving more light and air, not less. His tower was not really an "inverted cone" or "inverted pyramid" but a building with a beautiful silhouette resulting from the windows slightly stepping forward as the building rose. The cantilever construction would reduce wall thickness, produce a lighter building, and ultimately provide a more delightful living experience. The whole concept rebutted the standard practices in New York. "I must say," Wright continued, "I am tired of the eternal repetition ad libitum, ad nauseam, of the fountain-pen motif. And the city is becoming undesirable below the tenth floor notwithstanding the step-back relief."[50]

By late October 1929, in the midst of the chaos over the leak, Wright reviewed what he had accomplished and what lay ahead. In a long letter to his son Lloyd, Wright mentioned two highlights. One was his recent essay "The City," in which he proposed an antidote to the *urbanisme* of Le Corbusier, the young Franco-Swiss architect and star of modern architecture in Europe. This essay, which Wright considered one of his most important, was one of a series of writings, some published, others not, in which he was working out his rebuttal to European modernists and formulating his thoughts on the challenge of urban life. They formed a plank in the platform in Wright's incipient battle for the soul of American architecture. The other highlight was his recent visit to New York, which he described to Lloyd as "quite a revelation." Wright had relished the honor of the gala in New York. "But better than all that, the drawings for St. Mark's in-the-Bouwerie which are now complete in sketch form, made a great impression where they intended to be impressive. It looks as though by spring we would have this project in good working order."[51]

The pace for finishing the tower scheme in New York accelerated daily leading up to the presentation to the vestry board on November 4, 1929. Wright wrote Warren Matthews to finalize fussy practical matters and assure him that he'd see the plans soon. "Also," Wright added, "I believe the relationship between the old church and the modern prismatic building would be extremely agreeable." A sketch plan of three towers was included to make his point.[52]

Meanwhile, Guthrie had a clever idea to clarify the confusing publicity over the tower: hold a public symposium with Wright and other New York architectural luminaries to expound on the topic "The New York We Are Making." Though he outlined its participants—and Wright liked the idea—it went nowhere. Wright continued to express regrets about the premature publicity and to work on a complete set of studies of the project that, he hoped, would satisfy everyone, particularly Guthrie. Convincing all about his "modern prismatic building" would require Wright's most powerful performance.[53]

8

COMMAND PERFORMANCE

When Wright stepped off the train in New York on November 4, 1929, the city's political machine was firing on all cylinders. Tammany Hall buzzed with confidence over the next day's municipal elections. Democratic mayor Jimmy Walker was expected to triumph in spite of Republican representative Fiorello La Guardia's success at swaying swathes of Italian, Jewish, and black voters from the usual Tammany ticket. An editorial in the *Brooklyn Standard Union* enthusiastically supported Walker's reelection as "a rebuke to this man La Guardia for his mud-slinging campaign." La Guardia's plans to end corruption would be thwarted; he would lose the election, and his goals remained a dream for the future.[1]

Wright, willfully oblivious to politics and economics, walked into the heart of imminent global financial chaos. Later known as "Black Tuesday," October 29, 1929, had come and gone less than a week before. While markets rumbled for several days, not even Wall Street's most experienced financiers could grasp what lay ahead. Brokerage houses were inundated with orders from around the world, but brokers saw little strength in buying amid a continuing deluge in selling. Pundits claimed that the panic was successfully stymied. The Commercial National Bank and Trust Company took out a large ad in the *New York Times* to announce that the economic condition of the country was fundamentally sound and unimpaired, that progress in America would be steady, and business and industry would proceed with banking's cooperation. Thirty-two directors of the bank signed the statement, representing all aspects of American commerce, from Walter P. Chrysler and William H. Vanderbilt in New York to William Wrigley Jr. in Chicago. Some financiers called the situation an opportunity for bargain buying. Brokers tried to calm investors, claiming that despite violent market fluctuations, the intrinsic value of common stocks had not been affected. Niche markets still held promise: insurance companies took out ads to recommend specific stocks of well-managed companies.

Still, the quotidian perils and delights of the city persisted. An elevated train on the B.M.T. line stopped for a stray dog on its tracks, causing a collision with another train that injured eight people. Walking sticks remained fashionable for men. Lightweight models made of half-bark Malacca were easy to swing and reasonably priced at $2.74. The *20th Century Limited,* the luxury train Wright took from Chicago to New York, was about to make its ten thousandth run between the two cities. It was hailed as "a national institution, typifying the spirit of American achievement."[2]

Upon his arrival, Wright found the city enjoying itself. Warner Brothers had ushered in talking movies as a permanent feature of the world's entertainment. The Fifty-Sixth Street Galleries opened an exhibition of the work of over one hundred modern sculptors alongside classic American paintings, with a thousand guests attending the reception. "Modern" still implied considerable breadth, as the artists ranged from Daniel Chester French, A. Stirling Calder (figural sculptor and father of Alexander Calder), and Augustus Saint-Gaudens, to Paul Manship, Alexander Archipenko, and the twenty-five-year-old Isamu Noguchi.[3]

In terms of new construction, London Terrace, a mammoth rental complex, was in the excavation phase of its construction in Chelsea. Replacing picturesque mansions on the former estate of Bishop Benjamin Moore, the complex occupied an entire city block from Ninth to Tenth Avenues between West 23rd and 24th Streets. It would encompass a thousand homes and the biggest gardens in town. Marketed as airy, stylish, charming, and modern, it would be available for tenants by the summer of 1930. When Wright passed the site on the West Side, he could not help but compare his slim St. Mark's tower to this megalith of continuous step-backed masses.

By the early evening of November 4, Wright presented with the full power of his charm and eloquence the scheme that had the most potential to lift his practice—and his life—out of uncertainty. He had brought two sets of drawings, each composed of ten carefully delineated sheets, rendered with colored pencil, to show the project in all of its aspects— from floor plans, to interior views, to exterior perspectives that put the towers in place on their site. Unfurling a set of the rolled drawings, he took one sheet after another of the carefully organized material and explained their purpose. The drawings represented both concept and detail for the building.

They revealed that Wright had created an eighteen-story tower (a boost from the original twelve floors) with four duplex apartments on each floor above the entry level. The tower's walls were mostly glass screens with small balconies protruding like open-air bays (fig. 34). Bands of sheet copper formed into patterns punctuated the glass screens horizontally. Each floor spun around a central core that protruded from the top of the structure; the layout was a pinwheel. The spinning would make each building side dynamic, shifting with the changing light of day. The floors were concrete slabs cantilevered from a central, concrete pylon, the design's major structural innovation. Furnishing and utilities were integral features of the whole.[4]

On the exterior, the glass skin shifted slightly outward as the building rose. Wright claimed that this sawtooth treatment would prevent rainwater from cascading down the entire building face in torrents. The gesture made the building appear slightly larger at the top than at the bottom, the treatment that had caused some critics to see it as an upside-down

Fig. 34 St. Mark's tower, perspective view, 1929.

pyramid. Even at eighteen stories, the stepping effect was negligible, and without mentioning it, Wright had refined the presentation drawings to make them appear even less pyramidal. The façade was ingenious and practical: the windows pivoted vertically and had screens in alternate rows so that the entire glass surface could be washed from the interior. Vertical blades could be extended or contracted to control light, so the glass would appear more or less brilliant.

Moving from a perspective drawing to plan, the entry level of the tower took the form of a pedestal (fig. 35). From 10th Street, a resident could ascend steps to the building's vestibule with its four hexagonally shaped elevators. At their center lay an embedded icon of four triangles, touching and rotating around a common point. Forming a pinwheel, they embodied, like an abstract monogram, the core design concept of the building itself. A visitor could take an elevator or move straight through the vestibule up additional steps and enter an outside garden park, protected from the street in the center of the site. Adjacent the interior elevators sat four storage units, addressing the bane of all New York apartment dwellers, the need for more space. Showing his attention to detail and operational pragmatics, Wright added an office at the right side of the vestibule in addition to a housekeeper's residence.

In the typical room layout a hexagonal foyer opened onto a duplex. A kitchenette with storage lay to the right of the entry. An open living room emerged on the left. It included a metal dining table, hinged to a built-in sideboard, so that the table could be swung up to provide more open space when not in use. The living room included a hearth. An internal stair led to the bedroom level and master bathroom of the duplex. The bedroom floor of the duplex would also spin, again like a pinwheel, forty-five degrees around the central core, exposing the living room below it and giving a dramatic double-height space. As Wright described it, the "space carried" through both floors. The rotation of the upper floor plan also allowed Wright to insert a small outside terrace on both living and bedroom levels.[5]

Many of the finer details of the scheme had been developed. The facing of the bedroom floor slab that overhung the living room continued the copper ornament of the exterior; inside and outside were literally continuous (fig. 36). The horizontal bands of formed copper were in a diagonal pattern that had become a standard motif in his ornament. They came from the lessons in diagonal geometry that Wright had begun developing fifteen years earlier at Midway Gardens in Chicago and the Imperial Hotel in Tokyo, and which he had perfected with his textile-block houses in California. Because these patterns were rotations of simple geometric shapes, like the floor plans themselves, they contributed to the overall harmony of the tower design. This patterning for the St. Mark's

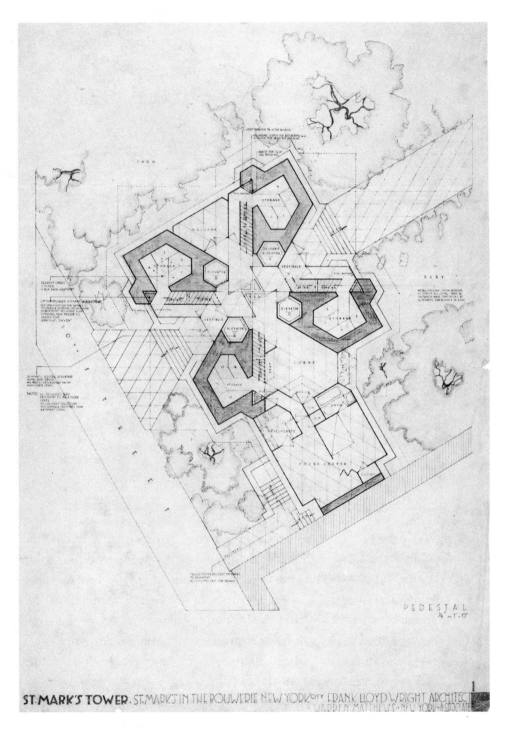

Fig. 35 St. Mark's tower, pedestal plan, 1929.

Fig. 36 St. Mark's tower, cutaway perspective view of typical interior apartment, 1929.

tower provided a powerful, if subtle, icon; the ornament was essential, not an extravagant irrelevance. By bringing the outside pattern into the interior, Wright was making a harmonic, unified whole. This feeling of totality and integration lay at the heart of his organic architecture. His approach veered vastly from the bare and planar aesthetics of Functionalism. In line with his efforts to create a harmonious whole, Wright elaborated the furnishings of the apartments in extensive detail: furniture, fabrics, cushions, and as always—a baby grand piano.

Although he acknowledged Guthrie's original request for a single tower, Wright had gone ahead and provided the option for three more towers surrounding the church, and a fourth one replacing townhouses

Fig. 37 St. Mark's towers, perspective view, 1929.

at the corner of East 10th and Stuyvesant Streets as the optimal solution for the church's conjoined properties (fig. 37). With a series of towers, the park between them would become continuous, forming an extended green zone at ground level for light and air. Each tower would sit in the garden park and could vary in height, with the shortest one closest to the corner. Guthrie and the vestry, however, still counted on building only a single tower.

Wright supplied no specifics of construction costs: the numbers seemed undignified as his work of art took its first public bow. After all, his creation would do much *more* than merely provide rental income—it would save the church for the future, it would transform the neighborhood, and it would alter how New York—and the world—perceived the skyscraper, the symbol of modernity itself.

Was Wright's St. Mark's tower as revolutionary as he claimed? The structure was certainly unlike his earlier efforts to design a tall building. Though the Chrysler Building, still under construction at that moment (it was completed in 1930), featured an amazingly tall and narrow spire, it was, as Wright ruefully observed, an elegant, elongated ink pen. *His* glass curtain wall, however, was alive with movement. In Europe, thirty-six-year-old Mies van der Rohe had proposed a glass skyscraper for Berlin in 1922 that emphasized the reflection of light. Visionary in its own way, this curtain-wall concept would transform the experience of the building. But Mies's idea was mere utopian dreaming at the time and had no potential for actually being built. Wright's tower, however, was poised for construction. A light, airy spinning top, his skyscraper pulled itself up from the earth and into an elongated crystal, twisting dynamically and expanding subtly from bottom to top.

At the conclusion of the presentation, Guthrie, Holley, Matthews, Miner, and the other members of the vestry had two questions: could they afford Wright's tower, and would it ever get built?

At first it seemed the tower at St. Mark's could be built. In Wright's mind it was merely a matter of tending to a few details. He stayed in New York a day after the presentation, and he and Guthrie worked to handle those details, which involved the site plan and buying out a nearby property owner who was worried about having an "inverted cone building" as a neighbor. Instead of a quick resolution, final approval remained unsettled. The arguments among the vestry, pro and con, continued with increasing frustration for all involved—for over two years. Verbal skirmish followed by periods of silence became the norm. Immediately after Wright's return to Taliesin in early November 1929, more tedious matters, like having fire stairs, cropped up, foreshadowing persistent issues with Warren Matthews.[6]

A month after the grand unveiling of the scheme, Wright had little word from New York while the church examined costs for the project. Growing anxious, he tried to pressure St. Mark's in mid-December by claiming to Holley that a "lively interest on the part of some substantial interests in Chicago" reflected an enthusiastic reception there for the scheme. For the alleged Chicago enthusiasts, Wright had quickly drawn up a scheme involving a series of linked towers. To get St. Mark's moving forward, Wright suggested that he might return to New York either before or just after Christmas. As the holidays approached, Wright, Guthrie, and Holley tried to stay optimistic about the tower's chances: Wright sent Guthrie a little layout drawing of his towers grouped together, and to Holley, a Christmas telegram of good cheer.[7]

Although the fate of the St. Mark's tower was in limbo, Wright had no hesitation about publicizing the project, again without informing his clients. Perhaps he saw the continuing publicity as a means of pressuring the church. Or, perhaps he was simply keen on keeping his name in the press. He was, after all, designing for the country's greatest metropolis. Only a month after the presentation to Guthrie and his vestry, notice of the project appeared in the December 1929 issue of *American Architect*. Unillustrated, the article repeated previously circulated material, including the confusing descriptions of the building as an inverted pyramid. Wright appeared like a rhapsodic and visionary *artiste* in the article, inveighing against his two current architectural targets, American *moderne* and European Functionalism. The former was a variant of Art Deco as it became more streamlined, and the latter represented the search for efficiency and economy over beauty. To Wright, they were combatants in the struggle for the true American modern architecture. Wright claimed that the others had missed seeing a "beauty in steel" that symbolized the times, and thus they failed to capture the real spirit of the Machine Age. Wright offered his "towers of glass and steel with copper floors" with their provision of light and air as the successful alternatives. "My building will be modern," Wright added, referring to Art Deco, "not modernistic."[8]

Wright's plans echoed Henry Ford's innovations, as buildings would "be constructed in parts, as an automobile is manufactured, and then assembled." These pieces would be carted to the site and "fitted together without the bother of lengthy construction work." European Functionalist architects continually looked to standardization and factory mass production to solve their housing crises, but desperate economic conditions after the war thwarted them. "It's a big step ahead, we think," Wright added, "and truly representatively American. As for the 'inferior

ST. MARK'S TOWER· ST. MARK'S IN THE BOUWERIE· NEW YORK CITY.

Fig. 38 St. Mark's towers, aerial perspective view, *Architectural Record*, January 1930.

decorators,' they won't get a chance at the buildings. Our furniture will be designed by myself, made of steel in truly modern patterns (not Grand Rapids modern)."[9]

Wright next had the project published in the January 1930 *Architectural Record,* this time with four-color renderings (figs. 38, 39). The journal provided a brief synopsis of his intentions to counter the inroads Functionalist architects had made: the St. Mark's project would realize "some of the most advanced aims professed by European architects, without attendant anomalies." Those "anomalies" involved the use of space and the amount of privacy—Europeans sought the minimum dimen-

Fig. 39 St. Mark's tower, perspective view, *Architectural Record*, January 1930.

sions possible for economical housing, and the contraction of units' sizes affected privacy as people were piled up on top of each other in slab buildings. Wright's towers would have "a high degree of privacy, plenty of daylight and utilizable space." "Located in a park on church property," the article concluded, "these towers will always stand free."[10]

The *Architectural Record*'s article about the St. Mark's tower appealed, with wire services picking up the story and reprinting the pictures without permission. Wright claimed, with typical exaggeration, that a thousand newspapers had taken the design from its pages. The story was widespread. Responding to a United Press report calling the tower "just one big window pane after another," James Ford, then executive director of Better Homes in America, wrote Wright from the Department of Social Ethics at Harvard University, requesting articles or prospectuses that he could distribute. His organization was at the forefront of a movement to provide Americans with ownership of modern and beautiful homes: Wright's project appealed with its "special glass" that would allow more sunlight into interiors.[11]

Nevertheless, a publicity campaign alone could not make the St. Mark's project move forward. Wright continued to press for it throughout 1930. An editor at the *Architectural Record* telegrammed Wright to send pictures of the renderings of the St. Mark's towers for publication in the *New York Sun*'s Real Estate section. At least this time Wright mentioned the potential publication to Horace Holley, and reiterated his anxiety about proceeding without a formal job contract: "There is, of course, a limit to which an indigent architect like myself can drag himself over the ground in the mere anticipation, hamstrung." Wright followed up the next month with Holley: "How is our skyscraper garden growing? . . . Hell is paved with such good intentions as mine." Meanwhile, Guthrie wrote Wright in February to quell his twitchiness. "Your letter great disappointment," Wright thundered back in a telegram. "Do you realize that if contract with architect is delayed until May St. Mark's loses a year of profit from the construction program? This means financial embarrassment for me and probably defeat for you."[12]

The following day, Wright wrote Guthrie a calmer note, recasting his claims to sound sympathetic to his friend's predicament. Though he continued to make excuses for the publicity he had generated for the project,

Wright claimed that it was a boon, for it would help city development lift the St. Mark's neighborhood: "I should think you could easily see that it is just as apparent to others as to yourselves that New York, having gone recklessly so far Up Town, is now right about face, and coming back by way of your side of the city." Wright went so far as to propose resurrecting their fantastical Modern Cathedral to focus attention on St. Mark's: "I think it would draw tremendous interest." Although he could not proceed with plans for the cathedral until he was paid for the work he had already done on St. Mark's, he insisted that he had not lost his enthusiasm for it. On the contrary, he would "get to it some day with a result that will gratify you, and probably do you no end of good."[13]

Wright's desperation soon returned. He wrote Guthrie in March that if it would help, he would work with other notable New York architects, like Harvey Wiley Corbett, Ray Hood, or Ralph Walker of the firm McKenzie, Voorhees, & Gmelin, Art Deco designer of both the Barclay-Vesey Telephone Building and the Irving Trust Building, then under construction. He even offered to make Guthrie "another and better design if the first one has gone off." Guthrie answered, this time balking at the cost of the towers, which was estimated at $700,000. He had grown pessimistic. "We aren't miracle workers," he told Wright.[14]

Wright and Guthrie continued to spar over the project's fate throughout the year even though it was clear it was doomed. Both drew on a propensity for flowery bluster and outrage, and also on mutual affection. The dialogue was heated, at times full of frustration and even anger, and tested their friendship. When Guthrie finally got the definitively bad news in May 1930 from Justin Miner, the real estate expert on the vestry board, he lamented to Wright that it came as a shock. "When I first started my day-dreaming it was because I believed so deeply in beauty, but I was not prepared, of course, for the terrible factual revelations." Still, he had already begun to reconcile himself to it. Perhaps the towers did not belong in a city "but in a grove of trees full of brown thrashers or mockingbird." Living in New York meant seeking not openness but refuge. "You ridicule the cave, but I suspect that in Manhattan each has to have a cave in which he can escape."[15]

Wright was not convinced. He thought his friend had been "poisoned by the New York atmosphere." He was disappointed that Guthrie was "passing the buck" and that he had "gone weak." The St. Mark's project would have done miracles for the city, more "than any World's Fair *could* do." Guthrie should stand his ground. "But you just don't know what all this is about," Wright lashed out. "You are afraid to know, I am afraid—but why?" "I did not answer your irate letter, as you know," Guthrie replied, "because it would have merely made bad blood to take it seriously, and friends should have patience." He then refuted Wright's dogmas point by point. Guthrie told his friend that economic reality had doomed them, and that moreover his ongoing support of Wright and the project had begun to undermine his stature with his own vestry. In late February 1931, he wrote that he was now convinced that "this particular project" would never work in lower Manhattan, "except on some quiet square like Gramercy Park, or, just possibly, Washington Square."[16]

For Guthrie, the project was dead. Yet Wright was relentless. Elaborating on multiple reasons why it could be built and mentioning his whipping boy, Matthews, who had "poisoned the situation," Wright pointed to himself and his value: "I've done great work—and doing greater and better work every year." And after all the controversy Wright had created, he had the audacity to lament to Guthrie, "I shall never be popular. . . . I am not hard to work with because I never ask an unreasonable thing of anyone. If I can't show my client his best interest by patiently educating him along one line—I try another. So it will be with you and your people. But so far you've been so afraid of committing yourself. . . . The matter has never come squarely up . . . Why?—I don't know why—. Ask yourself why?"[17]

Wright's protracted battle for building the St. Mark's towers was ultimately undone by disastrous timing. He originally unveiled the project on November 4, six days after Black Tuesday. The full impact of the impending financial catastrophe was not graspable at that time, but Guthrie, for one, certainly took note. Wright ignored how the Depression doomed the St. Mark's skyscraper. Instilled with fresh confidence from his New York ventures, Wright assumed that by the sheer force of his will, money would materialize to build the project. While will alone couldn't build the St. Mark's project, it had provided Wright with a brilliant idea—a revolutionary model for the American skyscraper—that he would never relinquish.

9

PIVOT POINT

The project for St. Mark's Church in-the-Bowery had resulted in acrimony and failure, but the designs brought Wright some real measure of success. Part of it was, again, timing. He was no longer at the mercy of divorce attorneys, bankruptcy judges, or the yellow press; his stature as a player on the modern architecture scene was rising. Soaring, he felt justified in insisting that his work be realized. He could never take that attitude when Gordon Strong bluntly rejected his designs for an "Automobile Objective" as "inorganic," or when Albert M. Johnson abandoned the design for the National Life Insurance Company. Wright would now begin to demand much of the world, and expect more from it.

Miriam's death in January of 1930 also played a liberating role in Wright's life. Though she had tormented him for years, he described her passing without bitterness. "What was left of a remarkably vital high-spirited woman, who for fifteen years—psychopathic—had been going up in flame, seldom knowing real rest unless by some artificial means, had found it," he wrote. Her death was a "mercy to herself and to all who had ever cared for her." It also brought with it financial release, ending his alimony payments and releasing Miriam's trust fund. With $15,000 in hand, he paid off his mortgage on the Hillside Home School.[1]

Wright's rising stature couldn't revive the St. Mark's tower, which was never erected. Had it been built, it would not only have been Wright's first skyscraper, but the city's first all-glass curtain-wall high-rise. But the project's defeat merely seemed a temporary stumbling block in Wright's relentless quest, a pivot point around which Wright's life and work spun upward. As the Depression permeated American life, and most architects' prospects evaporated, Wright's professional career began a rapid ascent.[2]

In February 1930, professor E. Baldwin Smith invited Wright to give a series of talks at Princeton University. Smith proposed eight presentations over ten days, but Wright suggested instead six lectures, as well as an exhibition of his work, one that he was already preparing for New York. The exhibition would represent the first phase of a show that would travel domestically and then head to international venues. Princeton would publish the lectures as a book the following year.

Lecturing at Princeton meant a great deal to Wright, an autodidact who had never graduated from college. The invitation confirmed Wright's status as a major American architect. It seemed almost impossible that barely four years earlier he had been dragged bleary-eyed into the Hennepin County courthouse in Minneapolis and charged with violating the Mann Act. Wright mentioned the Princeton invitation to almost everyone he wrote, from his son Lloyd to Darwin Martin to Guthrie, and even to whatever neophyte architect requested an interview to work for him.[3]

"I am glad you are going to Princeton," Lewis Mumford wrote after Wright informed him. "Someone must be trying to break loose there, and you can at least saw off the ball + chain for him." Wright had sent Mumford an essay by Erich Mendelsohn, and Mumford returned a précis of it. "The gist of it is that you are the father of modern form," he told Wright. "In creating modern architecture, Olbrich worked from steel construction: you used the static compositions of old materials, wood +

stone, + the new pressed concrete. Both processes were revolutionary + both were necessary. Today both are being united in a common platform, as the foundation for modern architecture." "As for your exhibition, you ought to deposit it in our midst at least half a year before letting it go on tour."[4]

Throughout the spring of 1930, Wright worked on his lectures for Princeton. His writing was interrupted in mid-March when he went back east for a few days. Meanwhile, Wright and Baldwin Smith were in frequent contact. "The lectures are now finished," Wright wrote Smith on April 1. "I must say I have enjoyed writing them." The six lectures didn't need images, he added. "Personally, I have never cared much for illustrated lectures. If we might have some good music to begin with and end with—that might help."[5]

With the lectures written, Wright moved on to refining the event, which he saw as an opportunity to launch a long-standing ambition: the creation of his own school. "I should like to meet some people," he wrote Smith, "interested as we are in Art and Architecture, especially in the establishment of a new kind of school wherein Art might take the lead in Education and Industry." He would leave the details to Smith, adding, "While not adverse to playing the role of guest occasionally it is my feeling that I am too ego-centric by nature to be a very successful guest—however, this is all up to you."[6]

Ever his own publicist, Wright sent an advance excerpt of his lectures to Mumford at his home in Long Island City. "As you will see by this," he wrote, "our hat is 'in the ring.'"

"Thanks for your brave and beautiful manifesto," Mumford replied, adding that he'd be happy to make the "pilgrimage" to Princeton to hear them in person—a trip he did not take.[7]

Scheduled to give his first lecture on May 6, Wright planned to stop in New York on his way to Princeton. He brought with him texts of the lectures: "Machinery, Materials and Men," "Style in Industry," "The Passing of the Cornice," "The Cardboard House," "The Tyranny of the Skyscraper," and "The City." Sometimes, as in "The Passing of the Cornice," his argument reads like a series of soundbites, featuring pithy statements about architecture with attacks on the avant-garde: "Form is organic only when it is natural to materials and to function. . . . Chewing-gum, the rocking-chair and picturizing. Are all habits equally valuable to modern art." But generally the lectures allowed Wright to deal with the current topics in the modernist debates, including the expression of materials, the representation of technology, the irrelevance of historical imitation, the density of skyscrapers, and what might be called the "urban dilemma."[8]

Wright presented the six lectures from May 6 to 14. They provided an ideal opportunity to push forward with his definition of Usonia. He took further issue with Le Corbusier's image of the "Machine-city of Machine-prophecy," rejecting the concept, however reduced, that the city should resemble a machine. For Wright, the "Machine Age"—a quintessential modernist concept developed in the nineteenth century—was still the prevailing "Zeitgeist," but the Machine Age had brought not a machine city but the end of the city in its traditional role as a meeting place of trade and culture. Combining an attack on skyscrapers with a notion of the city as outmoded, Wright stated that the city was tyrannized by the skyscraper because it exacerbated traffic and because it brought serious overcrowding and exploitation of the citizenry, now reduced to a mob of huddled masses, or a "mobocracy," as Wright called it. Wright added an issue that followed from urban crowding, the question of optimum density, and placed it in the Jeffersonian context fundamental to his philosophy: "Even the small town is too large. . . . Ruralism as distinguished from Urbanism is American and truly Democratic." The evolving ideology of Broadacre City took greater shape as Wright identified the central problems of congestion, property ownership, density, and national identity itself. Absorbing the ideas of other commentators, Wright further identified the prime factors in the current dispersal of the population as mass transportation, technology of production, and electronic communication, all of which were having inevitable dislocating effects on the city.[9]

Attendance, mostly from the academic community, was strong throughout the series. The *Daily Princetonian* summarized the lectures, quoting from them and reporting twice on the exhibition, which opened May 12, during the lecture series. The two-week period provided Wright with something he had not yet experienced: protracted dialogue with students and faculty. Wright's lectures were such a hit with the architecture students at Princeton that two of them who won prizes at commencement requested copies of Wright's little Wasmuth picture book as their awards.[10]

Entitled *The Work of Frank Lloyd Wright, 1893–1930,* the exhibition accompanying the Princeton lectures was the first major presentation of his work since 1918, when the Art Institute of Chicago featured his drawings. Though short in duration—it closed on May 22—it was the largest assembly of both Wright's built and unbuilt projects to date, and the first of many traveling exhibitions.[11]

Even before Wright lectured at Princeton, he was the object of considerable interest in the New York architectural scene. Paul Frankl picked up on it and sent his book *Form and Re-Form* for the architect to review. George Howe, a leading figure in moving from American Art Deco toward European International Style, took an interest. He had written an article on modern architecture for a new magazine, *USA,* and had his partner William Lescaze contact Wright for illustrations for a second article on some of "the best examples of modern architecture in America."[12]

For a symposium on the "Vitality of Tradition," Parker Hooper, the editor of *Architectural Forum,* asked Wright to write a rebuttal to Royal Cortissoz, a traditionalist and opponent of modernism who was an art critic for the *New York Herald Tribune.* Located at 521 Fifth Avenue, the *Forum* was attempting to compete with the *Architectural Record* and wanted to recruit Wright as a spokesman of American modernism. Hooper wanted the architect to comment on "The Logic of Contemporary Architecture as an Expression of this Age" and told Wright that this very subject would be debated in the May meeting in Washington of the American Institute of Architects. Wright replied enthusiastically to the *Forum's* request, stating that he was just finishing his lectures for Princeton, and that he had written the requested essay for Hooper. But Wright had a stipulation: "I trust you will use the 'piece' as written and allow me to correct the galley proofs if possible. Controversial articles at this time are too important to be left to shift for themselves."[13]

Interest in Wright began coming from unexpected sources. Riis and Bonner, a fledgling public relations agency, solicited Wright's review of Norman Bel Geddes's designs for their client the Toledo Scale Company.

Wright and Geddes had met in New York in 1929; they even had planned to have dinner together in early December, but Wright stood Geddes up. In reply to the agency's inquiry, Wright said he thought Geddes, a leading practitioner of streamlined *moderne* design, had "caught the look of Modern Architecture and each building itself a fine example in effect of the Simplicity that should distinguish the movement; and each taken by itself is quite the finest thing of its kind I have seen." Wright further commended Geddes, a fellow Midwesterner, for affirming "that our industrial buildings are our genuine Architectural opportunity and might be great Architecture if only the industrialists themselves would want them to work out that way." In sum, Wright's remarks suggested that the industrial buildings of America could dominate any competing efforts in Europe in directing the future trends of modern architecture. Geddes indeed took on the task: he would design the Futurama exhibit for the 1939 New York World's Fair.[14]

The Princeton exhibition itself had come about from New York buzz. A trio of New York's most prominent architects, Raymond Hood, Ralph Walker, and E. J. Kahn—known as the "Three Little Napoleons of Architecture"—came up with the idea of inviting Wright to put on an exhibition at the Architectural League of New York. They delegated A. Lawrence Kocher, managing editor of the *Architectural Record,* to ask if he would exhibit his work in the series they were planning, which would also travel. Wright accepted with delight in October 1929.[15]

The League had outgrown its spaces in the Art Students League Building on West 57th Street, and had found new accommodations at 115 East 40th, near Grand Central Station and the Architects Building on Park Avenue. The renovated five-story townhouse included a bar, restaurant, galleries, studios, and apartments.[16]

In spring of 1930, planning for the exhibition and a grand fete to honor the architect began. In mid-April, Raymond Hood, president of the Architectural League of New York, sent out an elegantly engraved invitation for a gala celebration of Wright to be held on May 28, 1930. Hood, the designer of the American Radiator Building, was one of New York's most prominent architects. Though a graduate of the École des Beaux-Arts and an Art Deco practitioner, he appreciated the practical dimensions of architecture. He would soon become chief designer of Rockefeller Center and the McGraw-Hill Building, the first Functionalist building of the early 1930s. Reminding invitees that the League planned an exhibition of Wright's work, he also requested a check for five dollars to reserve a place at dinner—space was limited to 120 guests.[17]

Wright intended to arrive in New York a couple of days before the event. He sent his assistant Donald Walker, who'd help set up the exhibition in Princeton, ahead to oversee the installation at the Architectural League. *The Architecture of Frank Lloyd Wright, 1893–1930* would open to the public on May 29 and continue until June 12, 1930. With an "approach and setting" designed by Wright's friend Joseph Urban, the show was the third in a series featuring living American architects, "decorative" sculptors, and painters. The series highlighted trends in Europe and America, and some of the drawings in Wright's exhibition would specifically express what its organizers called his "organic architectural philosophy." The exhibition encompassed 204 drawings, 448 photographs, and at least 5 models, including what Wright described as a "beautiful scale model" of the St. Mark's tower (fig. 40).[18]

The day of the League's testimonial for Wright coincided with the opening of the Chrysler Building. The *New York Times* reported that the building, briefly the city's tallest (it was superseded in 1931 by the Empire State Building), was celebrated the day before with visits and events. Many attendees viewed the city from the sixty-second floor of the sixty-seven-story building. Edward Trumbull's epic murals—intended "to express the spirit of the mechanical age and man's use of energy"—captivated visitors. After the inspection, the Forty-Second Street Property Owners and Merchants' Association honored Walter P. Chrysler at a luncheon at the Commodore Hotel. His fellow businessmen lauded him, presenting him with a bronze plaque. Former governor Alfred E. Smith commented on how in only a few short years 42nd Street had shifted from horse carts and small buildings to the grand pinnacle of growth with buildings like the Chrysler. Land and lease values soared accordingly.[19]

The opening of the Chrysler Building reverberated throughout the New York architectural scene as a near-miracle under the current economic conditions. If the irony of its opening as the Art Deco antithesis

Fig. 40 Typical installation of traveling exhibition, *The Architecture of Frank Lloyd Wright, 1893–1930*. The St. Mark's tower model is at the left. Art Institute of Chicago, September 25–October 12, 1930.

to Wright's organically modern St. Mark's tower occurred to him, Wright made no mention of it. In any case, he was savoring his success at the Architectural League's dinner, an event noted in the *New York Times*. Hood moderated and at least seven speakers made remarks, including Lewis Mumford, Bruce Bliven, Ralph Walker, and Harvey Wiley Corbett.[20]

No doubt some had reservations about Wright, but the atmosphere was one of appreciation. Henry H. Saylor, an author of books on domestic architecture and editor at *Architecture,* a monthly journal published by Charles Scribner & Sons, wrote the event held "a distinct note of sadness . . . due to the extreme tardiness of recognition on the part of his brother practitioners." Wright, he added, commented that "for the past twenty years he had been a lonely man, and now suddenly finds that he . . . is surrounded by friends."[21]

Wright was recognized by New York's architectural elite as well as a segment of its literati. He was certainly proud and thrilled: on May 30, just after the event, he sent Olgivanna a telegram in Spring Green: "PARTY A WONDERFUL SUCCESS. LEAVING ON CENTURY TODAY. WILL CALL FROM CHICAGO TOMORROW MORNING. FRANK"[22] To his son Lloyd he sent a note: "That hard-boiled New York outfit simply plastered me [with compliments], sincerely I believe."[23]

The League's testimonial strengthened Wright's connections to major players in New York's architectural world and generated a wide range of responses. He immediately sent a warm note to Raymond Hood: "I am so glad to have found comradeship in my own profession at last—with you at the head of the procession." "There will not be many occasions like that one, we'll be talking about it once in a while all our lives, won't we?" The exhibition "started some of our minds revolving in a new way," Hood replied, as if responding to the design of Wright's spinning towers. He added that "a lot of people here have found out that they were your friends without knowing it." Wright's friends, led by Frankl and Joseph Urban, even made an effort to offset Wright's costs in setting up the show. By the end of June, several had contributed, including some of the city's most prominent architects, such as Urban, E. J. Kahn, Ralph Walker, Chrysler Building designer William Van Alen, and architect and furniture designer Eugene Schoen. To Hood, the contributions were a confirmation. "I am pleased, in one fashion," he informed Wright, "because it certainly includes some of the fellows that you probably had in mind when you spoke of shooting at them from ambush, without knowing that they were in reality your friends. I can assure you that they were just as glad to have gotten to know you as you could be to have gotten to know them." Hood wrote him in early July with the final accounting: "You can write in your memoirs that at your New York appearance, after all expenses were deducted from the total box office receipts, you netted $19.70." For Wright, the effort is what mattered.[24]

Wright followed up with a number of New York architects who expressed their appreciation. He flattered some of them but hid, for the moment, his reservations about their work. He visited William Lescaze, who hoped he would "have the pleasure of continuing our interesting talk some other time," and expressed his "best wishes for the progress on your glass houses in the Bouwerie." Wright sent E. J. Kahn a signed copy of one of his publications. "I so enjoyed meeting you when you were in New York," Kahn replied, "and I trust on some other occasion when you have leisure and can be here we can spend a little more time together, giving me the opportunity of seeing more of the man whom I have so much admired for a long time." Wright had come to the attention of Ralph Walker. He later asked Wright for pictures of his work to use in a lecture he was preparing for the Brooklyn Institute of Arts and Sciences. His topic was modern architecture and its relationship to social problems.[25]

Several of Wright's other friends and colleagues congratulated him on the New York events. Emil Lorch, a friend and the progressive dean of the College of Architecture at the University of Michigan, sent a note to congratulate Wright and the Architectural League for having the good sense to put on the exhibition. "It has taken a long, long time for some to recognize what has been accomplished by you and others," he told Wright, "and I for one am very happy that this recognition comes to you while you are still with us."[26]

In the midst of savoring these responses, Wright regretted that after the dinner he missed seeing Mumford. Wright considered him to be "'the most valuable critic our country has—a mind of Emersonian quality— with true creative power.'" Mumford stood out because, as Wright put it, "Every innovation brings a flood of incompetent criticism." Still, he told Mumford, he was grateful that the "New York boys" had paid for his visit and the exhibition. "But please understand my dear Lewis, I am really uncomfortable with this 'recognition.' Am I really losing my power and so they are no longer afraid of me?"[27]

Mumford was less charitable about the New York crowd. The memory of the dinner "makes me grit my teeth and cuss," he replied. "These boys all meant to do the right thing, I have no doubt: they knew they owed you a debt and that the world owed you a debt, too: at bottom, they realized that they were honoring themselves." To Mumford, they were "jackals with a lion in their midst!" Mumford assured Wright, however, that some of the younger men, like Henry Churchill, were more sympathetic. "The day of your power is just beginning," he told Wright, echoing Emerson's famous letter to Walt Whitman. "I salute you at the beginning of a great career!!!"[28]

The irony of the sixty-three-year-old architect's "new career" was not lost on Wright, but the prospect of a national and potentially international exhibition of his work did suggest new professional waters. After the exhibition's debut in Gotham, Wright doubled its size and began planning a triumphal procession for *The Architecture of Frank Lloyd Wright, 1893–1930* (fig. 41). For its second phase, Wright planned venues in Chicago, Madison, and Milwaukee. In searching for additional locations, he hoped that other Ivy League schools would be as receptive as Princeton had been. In July he contacted Everett V. Meeks, chairman of the architecture department and dean of the School of Fine Arts at Yale. Wright suggested that Yale, Harvard, Cornell, and MIT might split shipping costs and show the exhibition over a six-week period. The expense, however, was too much for Yale, and Meeks passed on the opportunity. The rejection of the Ivy League, as practical as it may have been, became a slight Wright would not forget.[29]

Fig. 41 The Architecture of Frank Lloyd Wright, 1893–1930, exhibition. St. Mark's model, rear right. Art Institute of Chicago, September 25–October 12, 1930.

The show would travel to Salem, Oregon, and Seattle, Washington, for its final domestic leg in early 1931. Wright ventured to the Northwest for the opening, a trip he found refreshing. "How beautiful out there, and what a reception!" he wrote to Guthrie. "There is no longer a doubt about the way the country is waking to Modern in Architecture—and properly wary of the 'modernistic.'"[30]

In its third and final phase, the exhibition would transfer to Europe, where Wright hoped to show it in Holland, Germany, and Belgium, as well as Vienna, Prague, Munich, and Paris. Ultimately its venues were Amsterdam, Berlin, Stuttgart, Antwerp, Brussels, and Rotterdam (figs. 42, 43). Although his work and ideas had been known in Europe for twenty years, this was the first major European exhibition of his work. It refocused attention on Wright, who had been critically discussed within Europe throughout the 1920s, and set him up for an unprecedented round of honors. It also reconnected him to some important friends. Erich Mendelsohn's wife Louise sent Wright a note to acknowledge the long rapport and mutual respect between him and her husband. To reciprocate the hospitality Wright had shown the German architect, she invited him to stay at their new house in Berlin. "We are so happy that the exhibition of your work is settled now for Berlin, Wien and Prague. . . . You will live here like in Taliesin on the top of a hill." Wright thanked the Mendelsohns for their invitation, but any immediate visit to Berlin was impossible.[31]

Wright had emerged from the New York testimonial not only with a major traveling exhibition but with a new outlet for his ideas: the public lecture circuit. Sometimes he lectured in conjunction with the domestic run of his exhibition, and at other times by invitation. No longer a pariah, he had already appeared in Chicago in September 1929, alongside Francis Barry Byrne, a colleague and fellow Prairie School practitioner, at the local chapter of the American Institute of Architects. The Art Institute of Chicago also welcomed Wright back into the fold by inviting him to give two lectures on October 1–2, 1930. Titled "In the Realm of Ideas" and "To the Young Man in Architecture," the lectures allowed Wright to sound his clarion call for others to pursue his vision of organic architecture.[32]

Wright enjoyed performing. After lecturing to 1,200 people at the Minneapolis Institute of Art, the director, Harold Stark, wrote him to say he found it "difficult to express the deep impression your visit made upon me." He was clearly not alone in feeling that Wright had shown them "what architecture can be," and that henceforth they would look "forward instead of backward." The Minneapolis lecture was one of several Wright gave at various venues, from women's clubs in Brooklyn to the University of Oregon in Eugene. Crisscrossing the country by train, he was so much in demand that he engaged a lecture bureau to book his events. Wright's lecturing not only generated income, modest though it may have been, but also propagated his ideas and gave him the opportunity to engage the public. He could feel the pulse of America as it listened to him.[33]

The general acknowledgment of Wright's rising stature continued to swell in the aftermath of the New York events. The *New York Times* had published a short notice of the Architectural League's gala, but at the end of June 1930 it gave him the fullest positive coverage he'd yet received in a newspaper. The architectural critic H. I. Brock's feature "A Pioneer in Architecture That Is Called Modern" allowed Wright a platform from which to expound on his theories. It included three key illustrations: a three-quarter-page-long rendering of the St. Mark's tower (described as "the House Built Like a Tree—Projected Glass, Steel, and Concrete Tower Near St. Marks-in-the-Bouwerie") as well as Wright's Hollyhock House ("A Striking Example of the Wright Method of Bands of Decoration Applied to the plain surface of a Hollywood Estate"), and lastly, a photograph of Wright, looking youthful for his age. Sympathetic and thorough, the piece pointed out the "ill luck that his consequences over took him," stating that only when "a certain type of 'modernism' in building of which he was a pioneer returned to America with a European stamp of approval" did Wright start getting his due recognition.[34]

"The Wright doctrine is that the machine has got us," the *New York Times* essay explained. "Since it is 'irrevocably fastened upon us,' we are to make a blessing instead of a curse." Implicitly, the European modernist fixation on standardization and mechanization can be in America "realized and beautified as the service of the machine to civilization."

The *Times* reporter sought out Lewis Mumford to confirm Wright's status. The critic called Wright "our most distinguished outcast" and

Fig. 42 Students from art school and assistants help with installation of *The Architecture of Frank Lloyd Wright, 1893–1930*, Amsterdam, May 1931. Heinrich Klumb (left) and Oscar Seyferth holding model of St. Mark's tower. From the scrapbook of H. Th. Wijdeveld, Avery.

recounted a story that when E. J. Kahn, "builder on the slopes of Murray Hill itself of great masses full of acres of loft space for the silk trade," traveled to Germany to see its latest developments, German architects said, "Go back across the Atlantic and get the stuff from the man who gave it to us."

All in all, the account in the *New York Times* was another confirmation not only of Wright's status but of his rebirth. Horace Holley sent a touching congratulation. Realizing that their dream for St. Mark's would never be realized, Holley saw a silver lining. However "put out" Wright might have been about its failure, "the design of the tower is already famous and copyrighted by the power of publication, so you have apparently used us as the stepping stone to greater things."[35]

Wright sent a copy of the *New York Times* piece to Chandler, who'd recently been in New York and seen Wright's exhibition, which he liked. But Chandler's reply was also a downer about their venture in Arizona.

Fig. 43 The Architecture of Frank Lloyd Wright, 1893–1930, exhibition entry. St. Mark's tower model, center. Prussian Academy of Art, Berlin, June 1931.

"Some things look quite encouraging here at this time," Chandler reported to Wright, "but in the East everyone I saw was talking hard times and the possibility of starting something new at this time is out of the question, so I expect we will have to be more patient—but hope to do something at later date." So ended Wright's prospects for San Marcos in the Desert, the project on which he had spent many years and devoted immense creative energy. The meteoric soaring of his reputation mitigated the setback.[36]

Aleck Woollcott continued to be both a player in and a producer of Wright's New York exploits—and would augment Wright's career to dimensions the architect had never known. While Wright was busy politicking for the St. Mark's commission, Woollcott had made a few changes in his career. Tired of writing about the theater for newspapers, he shifted into the lifestyle of a lucrative freelancer. In the fall of 1928 he had moved to a luxurious new apartment in "The Campanile" at 450 East 52nd Street. Finished only a year before, the building was so far east that his Round Table friends called his place "Wit's End." It overlooked the East River and lay opposite the River House, whose tenants originally moored their yachts on the East River before the East River Drive went under construction. The location befitted Woollcott, an entertainer of stars of the screen, stage, and literary worlds; it later sheltered Greta Garbo. Irving Berlin, one of the figures Woollcott's encomia had made famous, would also live in an elegant brick townhouse nearby on Beekman Place.

In 1929 Woollcott had accepted a staff position at the *New Yorker*. He was on intimate terms with the magazine's founders, Harold Ross and Jane Grant; he even lived with the couple until they found his late-night verbal ramblings unbearable. Having followed the magazine since its inception in 1925, he contributed a regular column called "Shouts and Murmurs." From here he gained his infamous sobriquet, "The Town Crier." He also contributed "Profiles," a *New Yorker* standard that he often used to showcase his friends, including Ruth Draper, Noel Coward, Harpo Marx, Wright, and others.[37]

Woollcott's profile of Wright appeared in the *New Yorker* on July 19, 1930. Titled "The Prodigal Father," it reads like the testimonial of a witness and a convert. The piece was framed alongside a shadowed illustration of a stoic-looking Wright, his head floating between the ornamental outcropping of his own Hollyhock House. In this profile, which would establish a perception of Wright that endured for decades, Woollcott presented the "three standard myths" about Wright and added a fourth. "In Europe and the Far East," Woollcott declared about the first myth, "there has been for some time past a disposition to refer to Frank Lloyd Wright as the Father of Modern Architecture, and of late this salutation has been caught up and echoed in this, his native land." His impact in Europe was so pervasive that every student studied his drawings. But appreciation in his native land was new.[38]

"Today there is less, it seems to me," Woollcott continued, "of the old disparity between the high honor in which Wright has long been held abroad and the position which he was permitted—or let us say encouraged—to occupy here at home." Woollcott explained that Wright's eclipse after the Prairie period's closure around 1910 came about because Wright did almost no work (Midway Gardens being omitted) in the United States for ten years. But this period of anonymity in the United States was still "magnificently fertile," as his work on the Imperial Hotel in Tokyo attested. "A beautiful and spacious palace," the hotel would "modestly take its cue from all the folkways and traditions of Japan," but with one exception: "It must discover and express the secret of withstanding an earthquake."[39]

Woollcott thus invoked the second standard myth: Wright's Imperial Hotel had resisted the devastations of Mother Nature, a claim no other architect could make. "It was a scheme to outwit rather than to defy the temblors," Woollcott concluded in blushing praise. Of course, a few other buildings withstood the quake, and it was later determined that the survival of the hotel was not as dependent on its structural system as Wright maintained. But the label of "the architect who outwitted Tokyo quakes" stuck, and Wright himself exploited it.

Wright's accomplishments, however, receded in the 1920s. "Most of the remaining time," Woollcott explained, "was taken up by sleazy scandals and the ignominious procedure which our ugly divorce laws enforce, taken up by witless and vindictive indictments and all the ugly hoodlumism which the yellow newspapers can invoke." These events, along with perceptions of Wright as an eccentric artist, had impeded his opportunities to work with those who call the shots for the big jobs.

Woollcott recounted his own first visit to Taliesin in April 1925 (fig. 44), alighting on the third myth of Wright's legacy: the horrific tragedy of 1914, when Mamah Borthwick, her children, and others were murdered. Woollcott revived that "old wives' tale of blasting disaster" by reliving the "holocaust." Inevitably drawing on the kind of newspaper accounts he dismissed as yellow journalism, Woollcott reiterated the claim that the "Negro butler" exacted divine vengeance on the sinning couple, further embedding the moral dimension to the Taliesin murders. However, Woollcott provided something more original for his readers when he described his own reactions to Taliesin. Having studied Wright's pronouncements on organic architecture, Woollcott had been expecting that the house would match its surroundings, "that indeed it would not be so much *on* the hill as *of* it." The structure's "Sweet reasonableness" was

Fig. 44 Alexander Woollcott (right), Olgivanna, and Frank Lloyd Wright, at Taliesin, April 19, 1925.

nothing short of transcendent. "Inexpressively consoling," he wrote, "the house grew along the hillcrest, framed every view of the landscape, and ultimately presented itself as utterly unpretentious."[40]

Woollcott's description of Taliesin was as insightful as any ever written. He discerned that Taliesin, the home, with its respectful modest deference to nature and site, was the inversion of its author, who thumbed his nose at the world. Inevitably the conflict in Wright between man and nature would not abate. As if a mythic battle between the Titans and the Gods were continuing, within an hour of Woollcott's departure, the writer reported, lightning struck Wright's house and burned it to the ground. "You can see for yourself how malignant circumstances have buffeted this man. This giant. This ingenious giant," Woollcott declared.

Woollcott's portrait of Wright stressed his endurance. However, "it would take more than a few murders, some bolts from the blue, and the ugly lynching cry of the mob to repress for any length of time a fellow with so rich a gift for life." Domestic life was sunny again, with a new marriage and young children. The spin was positive even if it mischaracterized reality: Woollcott claimed prospects appeared good for the proposed glass towers at St. Mark's Church in-the-Bowery. Even Wright's work on the "vast Arizona caravansary" for San Marcos in the Desert had resumed. While Wright often tended to "upset the very apple cart he is hungrily approaching," Woollcott, for one, remained certain that "no one in the modern world has brought to architecture so good a mind, so leaping an imagination, or so fresh a sense of beauty." "Indeed, if the editor of this journal were so to ration me that I were suffered to apply the word 'genius' to only one living American," Woollcott mused, "I would save it up for Frank Lloyd Wright." Thus was born a fourth myth: Wright the genius. The term had been used casually before, but from this point forward the moniker would be Wright's blessing and his curse for the rest of his life—and posterity. Blessed, he was utterly special and unique. Cursed, he was inscrutable and incomprehensible.[41]

The applause poured forth. Ferdinand Schevill, Wright's stalwart supporter in Chicago, described the *New Yorker's* appraisal as "the finest you have yet received. It couldn't be handled in better spirit and puts your problem before our public in a generous and human way." He hoped that "every prospective building and actual captain of industry in these broad United States" would read it. Writing from a rejuvenating summer holiday at the El Tovar hotel in the Grand Canyon, Guthrie saluted his dear friend for the piece: "It surely does you justice & thank God is no *Obituary!!!*" Mumford likewise approved: "I liked Woollcott's article on you, and if I hadn't accidentally done a series of obituaries in the *New Republic*, I'd be tempted to echo it there." Even the Midwestern press, which had often vilified Wright, began to soften. The editor of the *Wisconsin State Journal* republished Woollcott's article and added an editorial comment. "Believe me," the editor wrote Wright, "it is gratifying to all of your friends to see this belated appreciation in this country for the things you have done."[42]

Wright telegrammed Woollcott he was pleased. Woollcott replied: "I am delighted beyond measure that you liked the Profile, and that is that."[43]

By means of its quintessential magazine, New York once again intervened in Wright's career, propelling him to new heights—and to even greater excesses. Wright was no stranger to self-promotion, but the architect suddenly became acutely aware of his own internal transformation. He wrote to the son of Baron Okura, his patron at the Imperial Hotel in Tokyo, on his changes since leaving Japan. "I believe I have grown a good deal since we last met," he informed his Japanese acquaintance, "surely deep and richer in Experience, and a better Architect. . . . The world has given me the best and worst of everything and I ought to be able to profit by such prodigality."

Woollcott's profile had reinforced Wright's belief in his own genius, and he felt emboldened to approach others whom he saw as possessing equal intelligence. When Wright read that Albert Einstein was sailing to the United States in early March, he asked Erich Mendelsohn if he could persuade Einstein to visit Taliesin. (Though Mendelsohn had designed the celebrated monument to the physicist in Potsdam, they were not close friends.) The meeting did not take place. He wrote the conductor Leopold Stokowski, fishing for a job to design "a new home for your work in Philadelphia." He also wanted to contact Henry Ford in Detroit about building a version of the St. Mark's tower through one of Guthrie's friends. Wright saw no one as outside his reach.[44]

The possibilities seemed endless. The Pan-American Union of Architects invited Wright to Brazil to be the North American judge of the international competition entries for a memorial lighthouse dedicated to Christopher Columbus; Wright and Olgivanna sailed from New York for Rio de Janeiro on September 19, 1931. Wright not only judged the competition but received honors during their twenty-three-day stay in Rio. It was another sign of Wright's new legitimacy, recognition of him as a leader in American modern architecture, and a hint of international recognition that would follow. His talent was multidimensional, and his work spread from design to exhibitions to public lectures and, importantly, to a newfound role as a professional author. Courted by publishers, Wright began to reach audiences nationally and internationally. Writing not only allowed him to develop his ideas, but also generated the income he desperately needed. Writing became a critical vehicle for him, setting him within circles of engaged artists, critics, and essayists. Their center: New York, the crucible of modernism.[45]

10

WRIGHT AS WRITER

Frank Lloyd Wright was the most prolific author on architecture in the twentieth century. "Self-cultivation" is the term Kenneth Frampton used to describe his purpose. "From this surely came his extensive vocabulary, his sense of rhythm, and his remarkable command of metaphor and simile that accorded his texts a rich, if ornate, precision." Only Le Corbusier, an architect a generation younger, offered competition. Writing was a means of crafting self-knowledge and self-experience; writing defined Wright and compensated for his lack of formal education. It was also a vehicle to sort out and through his ideas, to establish his manifestos, and to promote his vision for a democratic organic architecture in America.

As the publishing capital of America, New York gave Wright the imprimatur of a writer. On one level, Wright "wrote" his own identity by influencing what appeared in print about him. On another level, Wright wrote to complement the visual dimension of his drawings and designs.

By using words to complement his buildings, Wright joined a few other major figures in modern architecture whose importance rests not only upon their designs, but also upon their language and ideas. Books and articles could circulate; buildings rested in place.[1]

Wright's writing was interwoven with the commentary of others about his work: the more he wrote, the more others wrote about him. One critic reviewing his writings spurred on others. He followed articles—in books, magazines, scholarly journals—about himself, nurtured collaborations to get his work out, and scrutinized the ensuing critical reception. All this occurred at a time of intense competition for architectural ascendancy between America, with its rainbow of styles and New York its center, and Europe, with a multinational avant-garde.

Wright learned his way around the publishing world and its system of public relations, driven by a relentless desire to get his thoughts into print. From the mid-1920s, writing took on a new urgency for Wright. Between 1927 and 1932, he produced over one hundred manuscripts. How Wright achieved authorial status in this time span, and what role New York played in it, is an account of one story embedded into another, with Europe playing an important role.[2]

Wright had begun writing on architecture from the first innovations of his Prairie period. As we've seen in chapter 1, his essay "In the Cause of Architecture," published in the *Architectural Record* in 1908, had presented his initial theory of organic architecture along with a grainy spread documenting his buildings. In the 1910s and early 1920s, his writing was limited, but publications of his work moved through Europe—particularly Holland, Germany, and Switzerland—and would in turn affect what Wright wrote and how he presented his ideas. Commentary on Wright and illustrations of his work appeared most frequently and most beautifully in seven issues of the Dutch journal *Wendingen*. Produced like a handmade artifact, bound with raffia and filled with sumptuous graphics, the publication's title meant "Turnings." It represented the progressive values of artists and architects associated with the Expressionist wing of Dutch modernism who, with emotion and feeling, wanted to "turn" architecture toward the benefit of society. Hendrikus Theodorus Wijdeveld, *Wendingen*'s editor, became a major promotor of Wright's work. A visionary idealist, he believed that collaboration through art and friendship (*Ars et Amicitiae* was the common slogan) could create the New Jerusalem. Wright, to Wijdeveld, was a kind of spiritual guide.[3]

By the mid-1920s, Wright became a subject of contentious debate in Europe regarding the future of modernism. Aware that the Dutch and even the Czechs were publishing works on and about his work, German architects and critics began to focus on him. It was at this moment that the German Expressionist architect Erich Mendelsohn sought out Wright, visited him at Taliesin, and then wrote about him in a number of periodicals and daily newspapers in Germany.[4]

Other architects published studies of Wright in the mid-1920s as well. The most enterprising was Heinrich De Fries, an architect, critic, and editor who had produced books on housing, modern design, and villas. Seizing on the interest in Wright, he proposed to the architect a book on his work.[5]

While De Fries was preparing his plates and text, Wijdeveld decided to pull together *Wendingen*'s seven issues on Wright into a complete monograph. A tug of war ensued between the Dutch Wijdeveld and the German De Fries as to who would publish Wright first. Though then mired in personal chaos in America, Wright could see their competition for his work, and he pitted one against the other. He gave Wijdeveld detailed instructions about how to produce the book, and praised the effort. Simultaneously, Wright was funneling to De Fries a choice selection of projects. De Fries was a packager, someone who assembled images, provided supportive but minimal text, and sold the ensemble to a publisher, hoping for maximum distribution and financial gain. Wijdeveld was a visionary who saw architecture and his publications as tools of spiritual enlightenment in the evolution of social consciousness. For him, monetary gain was nearly irrelevant.

In 1925 De Fries won the race to publish first with his monograph *Frank Lloyd Wright: Aus dem Lebenswerke eines Architecten* (From the Lifework of an Architect). It was the first book on the architect in any language. De Fries presented Wright's organic architecture as a "liberating force"—driven by the powers of sun and light. Critics were split between advocating an "organic approach" that emphasized nature and an approach that favored mass production and standardization. The organicists saw Wright's work as poetic and transcendent, while the rationalists saw it as decadent, a plaything for the rich and powerful.[6]

Wijdeveld's book followed, *The Life Work of the American Architect Frank Lloyd Wright*. His publication, however, was a *Gesamtkunstwerk* ("a total work of art"), featuring graphics, images, type fonts, and book covers all designed with attentiveness toward a harmonic whole. The contents included the seven issues of *Wendingen* with critical essays ranging from the leading figures like Mendelsohn, the late Louis Sullivan, and Lewis Mumford as well as Wright's own comments. It was an "organic" and integrated creation. Wright loved the compilation and said later that it was his favorite publication of his work. "The first Heft of Wendingen came at last," he wrote Wijdeveld, "and was a pleasant thing to see." He sent copies of it to his most important friends and supporters. Wijdeveld in turn felt honored at the prospect of being the first to produce Wright's magnum opus. "The Old World printed your work in thousands of books, has bound your mastermind in parchment, and has promised your genius an everlasting life," the Dutch editor wrote Wright. "If I have done just a little to fulfill this promise, I will be rewarded enough." However, when Wijdeveld realized Wright had also sent work to the German De Fries, he was hurt and disappointed. Although Wright had exploited his "Dutchman," Wijdeveld remained blindly devoted to the American and would play a major role in organizing Wright's European exhibitions.[7]

Interest in Wright continually crisscrossed borders and boomeranged between Europe and New York. He was a hot topic, partly for who he was and partly for his role in the ideological debate at a particularly dramatic moment for the future of modern architecture. An example of this interplay can be seen in the previously unexplored story of Wright and his French connection. France had been on the periphery while Holland, Germany, Austria, and the Czech lands considered Wright and his work. Jean Badovici had begun addressing this void in 1924 when he first published on Wright in *L'Architecture Vivante*, which he founded with the support of the publisher Albert Morancé. The journal became a major promoter of Functionalist architecture, though Badovici also had ties to the Dutch *Wendingen,* with its Expressionist leanings. *L'Architecture Vivante* usually featured several architects, though some issues focused on single individuals like Le Corbusier and Wright. Badovici saw Wright as a force of modernism, and would publish more of his work.[8]

Badovici also introduced Wright's work to the readers of *Cahiers d'Art,* which Christian Zervos had started in 1926 to publish a broad spectrum of art and criticism with work from European and non-Western sources. A major force in the world of modern art, Zervos would become famous in pursuing a lifelong ambition, a monumental catalogue of the work of Pablo Picasso. Prepared in partnership with Picasso himself, this volume would ultimately become one of the twentieth century's most important works of art scholarship.[9]

On behalf of Zervos, the architect André Lurçat wrote Wright that *Cahiers d'Art* was preparing a series of special issues on a select group of architects. Lurçat, a young French modernist concerned with issues of social housing during the 1920s, flattered the American architect. "Your work is of course amongst the first which has entered our plans," he gushed. "We should consider it a great honor to have the privilege of devoting one of these special numbers to it." Lurçat asked Wright for thirty to forty photographs of his work from the "Occident" and the "Orient," from which they would make a selection, and plans of three or four buildings of Wright's choice. The French connection thrilled Wright. In September 1927, he wrote Darwin Martin that he had sent one hundred views of his work for publication in *Cahiers d'Art.* To reinforce the upward momentum, he added that he'd also sent articles to the *Architectural Record* and that the Germans were still seeking his work and his opinions: "Meanwhile I have sent to Frankfort on Main, Germany, five designs—including color perspectives," he told Martin. "I made the response to cablegram from city inviting me to send on help in adjusting old Traditional pointed roofs to concrete flat roof construction." Wright also couldn't resist telling Paul Frankl in New York that *Cahiers d'Art* planned a big spread devoted "to your Usonian friend."[10]

Despite his enthusiasm, Wright needed prodding to follow through with his submissions. That October, Lurçat reminded Wright, "The

Cahiers d'Art are preparing their monograph on your architecture," and requested photographs of the architect, his studio, and any images of recent work. Determined to bring Wright into their fold, Zervos followed up. That Zervos saw Wright as a player on the international scene of modernism is one more confirmation of Wright's ascension in the late 1920s. Writing from his office at 30 rue Bonaparte in Paris in November 1927, Zervos sent Wright a five-page handwritten letter situating the Midwesterner in the pantheon of modern European architects and encouraging him to contribute an article for a forthcoming issue of *Cahiers d'Art*.[11]

Zervos had two pressing subjects in mind. The first concerned a crisis for modern architects in Europe: the recent competition for the new League of Nations building intended for Geneva whose results had outraged the avant-garde. Although prizes were announced, no single winner had been selected, and they saw it as a defeat for their promotion of modern architecture and a failure to provide "a testimonial to the true spirit of the 20th century." Having sent Wright an issue of his *Cahiers d'Art* that discussed the competition, Zervos lamented that the results were meaningless because politicians had made the final decision. "Amongst the designs which have garnered first prizes," Zervos informed Wright, "only those of Corbusier and Pierre Jeanneret are suitable for modern conditions." To counter this setback for what was beginning to be defined as the Modern Movement, Zervos enlisted Wright's aid. Zervos explained to Wright that he needed him to make the case in an article that would insist upon the "necessity of executing a palace for the League of Nations which will be a lasting testimonial to the true spirit of the 20th century."[12]

Zervos then turned to the next pressing issue: the book on Wright that he was planning in collaboration with the architect himself. All of Wright's publications in Europe were either sold out or too expensive, so Zervos felt obliged to fill the gap. "With the articles that you have been kind enough to send me, I am preparing a book on your work which will be sold at as low a price as possible so as to enable a younger generation to know your work," he told Wright. "If by chance, you have any recent articles since the last you sent me, I would be grateful if you would send them to me at once."[13]

Using the material it had, *Cahiers d'Art* published Wright's work in two issues. It then brought in a young American critic, Henry-Russell Hitchcock, to introduce a compilation of Wright's work that they planned to publish under the title of *Frank Lloyd Wright* as part of their Masters of Contemporary Architecture series. Hitchcock, brilliant and enterprising, had just graduated the previous year from Harvard (fig. 45). While traveling in Europe, he and his college friend Philip Johnson had plunged into its latest developments of modern architecture, and Hitchcock had already sided with Functionalists. Though he had never seen any of Wright's buildings, he proceeded to provide the first critique of Wright by an American for a French audience. Wright later sized up both Hitchcock and Johnson by saying, "Harvard takes perfectly good plums as students and makes prunes of them."[14]

In his introduction, published in 1928, the twenty-five-year-old Hitchcock attempted to bury Wright. Because Wright had been born in the middle of the nineteenth century, Hitchcock claimed that he was antiquated and out of touch with contemporary developments: "His architecture," Hitchcock declared, "belongs rather to the first quarter of the twentieth century more than the second which has just recently but brilliantly opened in France, Holland, and Germany." Hitchcock admitted that Wright had followers in Europe and had found some success: "Despite the absurdity of and provincialism of the '*nom de guerre*' 'prairie architecture' which is applied to the work, this was an original debut and full of promise." But the promise was marred, he claimed, and Wright's architecture never achieved the quality of H. H. Richardson's best work. His buildings showed a free play of mass, but the roofs were "mannered." And the greatest defect? Wright's use of ornament, for, as Hitchcock said, "it disintegrated, at least in part, the pure qualities of his architecture in which he showed unequalled mastery."[15]

Hitchcock suggested that rich patrons, coupled with Louis Sullivan's bad influence, had led Wright to use ornament and thereby damaged the purity of the exteriors and ruined the interiors. Ornament was a sin in European modernist orthodoxy. Wright's own home, Taliesin, reflected the "ancient Far East and a retardataire Japanisme," making it "a triumph

Fig. 45 Henry-Russell Hitchcock.

of the picturesque, the most anti-architectural of qualities," a fault applied to Wright's Midway Gardens and the Imperial Hotel. Hitchcock had never seen Wright's buildings in person, yet he lambasted them. Even those who appreciated Wright's art regretted that the hotel withstood the earthquake, the critic claimed. "No conventional architecture has ever produced reception rooms more mediocre that those of the Imperial Hotel," he added. Spoiled by rich clients, Wright simply did not have the necessary taste or refinement to curtail his vice.

Wright's positive attributes, Hitchcock maintained, were only those associated with the Modern Movement, which focused on the architect as engineer, the aesthetics of the Machine Age, materials—steel, concrete, and glass—and technology. It was Wright the "technician" who mattered most, best exemplified in the standardized double-wall construction of the textile-block houses in California.

Hitchcock knew the recent publications on Wright and his significance as a writer. To him Wright was "Architect and engineer—for that is the true order in spite of the training he received—without equal, among those, in America, who write about architecture." To Americans, Wright's writing style would recall Whitman, but to the French, Hitchcock claimed, it would resemble that of Le Corbusier in *Vers une Architecture*. Hitchcock also declared that Wright had missed out entirely on mass production and proposed that if Wright weren't so old, he could redeem himself by following the machine aesthetic and the rationalist dictates of Functionalism. If he could only renounce his dangerous use of ornament, he would be more acceptable to "the contemporary spirit." The young critic concluded with a death blow wrapped in a compliment: "Wright remains, it is time to say without restriction the greatest architect and perhaps the greatest American of the first quarter of the twentieth century. . . . Although he be a prophet, the work that should speak for him is the work that has already taken place among the great monuments of the past."[16]

The essence of Hitchcock's criticism reverberated in the words of some of Wright's other critics, particularly in Germany, and among other proponents of the Machine Age aesthetic. But Wright was not the only figure to be marginalized by such rhetoric. A single line of the Modern Movement was emerging as valid—all else, from the work of Wright to the Vienna Secessionists to a broad swath of Central European modernists, was rejected. Ornament and the pitched roof were the telltale signs of misfits.

Wright's reply to Hitchcock showed relative restraint. "Since I have no power to have you taken out and shot at sunrise as a traitor to your country, I might as well make the best of it and try to make a friend of you by being one." Wright enclosed with this reply a peace offering of plates from the old Wasmuth folios that he had retrieved, water stained, from his basement. Wright called them "the original impetus" and offered them so Hitchcock could reconsider his assessment. Claiming a revision was necessary as the French architects were fashion mongers and "out of their depth," he concluded by inviting Hitchcock to visit. "Sometime, I hope," Wright wrote, "you may journey to this neck of the woods, spend a day or two with me digging up the matter that so vitally interests us both,—by the roots. I should be very glad, indeed, to have you. Meantime, believe me your friend nevertheless."[17]

The review in *Cahiers d'Art* had brought Wright into contact with not only Hitchcock but also Douglas Haskell, who would also play a significant role in the reception of Wright in New York. Haskell promoted an inclusive view of modern architecture, one that synthesized the seemingly conflicted formal currents of figures such as Wright and Le Corbusier (fig. 46). Born in Yugoslavia in 1899 to missionary parents, Haskell moved to the United States for high school, graduating from Oberlin College in 1923 with a degree in political science and a minor in art. During a post-college tour of Germany, he visited the Bauhaus, where he met Walter Gropius. This encounter was formative, and the young writer returned to New York in 1923 to begin an editorship at *The New Student*. From there he went to *Creative Arts* magazine. During the 1920s, Haskell, through the support of Lewis Mumford, would meet and build a relationship with Wright. Haskell's outsider status supplied him with a sense of openness and perspective that, in Wright's view, many of his peers lacked. The connection began when Haskell contacted Wright's son Lloyd for pictures for an article in *Creative Arts* that he hoped would counter some of Hitchcock's negativity. Their association would prove mutually beneficial, at once launching the fledgling writer while buttressing the architect's work and helping to lay the foundations for his ascendency.[18]

To counter Hitchcock further, Haskell wrote another essay, "Building or Sculpture," that appeared in the *Architectural Record*. Haskell's writing criticized the disconnect between the internal workings of modern buildings and the trend to express them as massive sculptural effects that said nothing about their function—the scenographic drawings of Hugh Ferriss typified the problem. Why not have an architecture of light and glass consistent with modern technology? Haskell asked. "Is this not the age of the airplane and the suspension bridge?" The sentiments reverberated with Wright and suggested that his St. Mark's tower was the way to go. He telegrammed Haskell in New York, derisively defaming the opposition, American Art Deco stylists: "Good Boy Douglas. The right work. Hit em again. They are all wops. Criticism at last." Haskell telegrammed back: "Your wire was generous and came just when needed." Wright even followed up with a telegram to Haskell's editor, Dr. M. A. Mikkelsen, praising Haskell's work.[19]

European publications on Wright and the international dialogue they generated, and Wright's frequent presence in New York, set the stage for

Fig. 46 Helen and Douglas Haskell at Camp Treetops, Lake Placid, New York.

the reception and promotion of his work, and his emergence as a writer and a subject of interest. From 1927 onward, an onslaught of publications by and about Wright was unleashed. Woollcott, already a devoted friend, gave Wright a leg up in pursuing his career as a professional writer when he suggested that his own literary agent, George T. Bye, represent Wright. Bye, who commuted from New Canaan, Connecticut, to his office at 535 Fifth Avenue and was doing well from Woollcott's success, was glad to take on Wright. In March 1927 he offered his services to the architect. Wright accepted.[20]

After only a month, Bye negotiated a deal with *Liberty* magazine to commission Wright for an article on the miraculous survival of the Imperial Hotel. *Liberty,* "A Weekly for Everybody" which cost only a nickel, had a vast mass-market readership and provided Wright with the largest audience yet. The essay provided not only publicity but income; the magazine paid him the head-spinning sum of $1,000 for his article. Reader response to the essay was strong. Wright would publish another essay with *Liberty,* "Taliesin: The Chronicle of a House with a Heart," a lyrical description of his Wisconsin homestead. He also designed covers for the magazine; none were used.[21]

The initial *Liberty* article also piqued the interest of the editors at the *Architectural Record,* who, as we've seen, had a long history with Wright. The publication had offices in the Philip Lewisohn Building at 119 West 40th Street. Built in 1913, the building was the largest commercial edifice north of 23rd Street and covered 28,000 square feet (fig. 47). A splash of Gothic detailing coated the upper and lower floors. The Lewisohn façade included five life-size allegorical figures in glazed terra-cotta, most sitting cross-legged and holding the attributes of some trade that could be found within. A hodgepodge of businesses was located in the Philip Lewisohn Building, from the Rudolph Wurlitzer Company, manufacturer of pianos and organs, to Manny, Maxwell & Moor, seller of contractors' supplies and building machinery, to the United Cigar Manufacturers Company, the first of many tobacco firms that would rent space. In addition, the building appealed to printers and publishers, including International Magazine Company, owned by William Randolph Hearst, whose newspapers had harassed Wright. The architect would walk through the building's doors on almost every trip he made to New York.

In May, M. A. Mikkelsen, editor of the *Architectural Record,* proposed a couple of articles by Wright that would reprise the title "In the Cause of Architecture." Mikkelsen was a generation older than the young men in his office and fairly scholarly; he had received a doctorate in history from Johns Hopkins. His writing gig at the *Real Estate Record and Guide of New York* had led to his being named editor of the *Record.* For each essay, Mikkelsen informed Wright, he would receive $500, another financial boon.[22]

The essays generated so much reader interest, "both favorable and unfavorable, mainly favorable," that Mikkelsen commissioned Wright for a series of twelve illustrated articles, nine of which would be published in 1928. The *Architectural Record* would go on to publish fourteen articles by the architect between May 1927 and December 1928—during Wright's personal crisis—covering a range of themes from concrete to glass, from the machine to composition—ultimately netting him $7,500 (fig. 48). In one essay, Wright insisted that a structure's ground plan must convey the character and constructive logic of the whole. "A good plan is the beginning and the end," he wrote, "because every good plan is organic." In another, he emphasized the need to master the "machine," the symbol of technology, to construct forms in response to nature's laws, and to express the qualities of materials. Several of the essays discussed a single material: "stone," "wood," "glass," "concrete," and "sheet metal."

Fig. 47 Offices of the *Architectural Record*, Lewisohn Building, 119 West 40th Street, New York.

Fig. 48 Textile-block house, from "In the Cause of Architecture: VII. The Meaning of Materials—Concrete," *Architectural Record,* August 1928.

Each received its own discussion. In his essays, Wright gave particular attention to processes and material combinations, such as wood veneer, electro glazed plate-glass, and sheet metal.[23]

In September 1927, with the series under way and reader response at an all-time high, Wright told Mikkelsen to send subscriptions to Guthrie and other friends and colleagues to show that despite the chaos of the previous year, he was still in print.[24]

When the "In the Cause of Architecture" series started to wrap, Wright proposed to the *Record* that they publish the collected essays as a book. He would design it largely along the lines of the art book that *Wendingen* had published, mirroring the beautiful European publication.

Douglas Haskell had moved from *Decorative Arts* magazine to become an assistant editor at the *Record,* and he took on the task of producing Wright's collection. Wright would press Haskell and his colleagues—for two years—to realize the project. Haskell selected special paper stock and obtained printing quotes.[25]

Although Wright had been well paid, he tried to squeeze an extra $1,000 out of the *Architectural Record* for two additional essays. The request fell to A. Lawrence Kocher, managing editor at the *Record,* who knew Wright. "No provision was made in our budget for this year that would enable us to add to our expenditures for outside articles," Kocher informed Wright. The magazine was under financial stress; even Douglas Haskell was not immune—he was laid off at the *Record* by the summer.[26]

In the end, the *Record* passed the project on to Henry H. Saylor, who'd attended the Architectural League testimonial for Wright. "[Wright] has proved himself to be an interesting and stimulating writer," Mikkelsen counseled Saylor. "He has been encouraged by his experience in magazine writing to feel that he can, and should, set forth his matured views in a book of his own, based on the articles, prepared for *The Record.*" Ultimately, the book as Wright conceived it was never published.[27]

While publishing his series with the *Record,* Wright had begun writing for a variety of literary magazines, beyond *Liberty,* and had input in new publications. In addition to being Wright's supporter for the St. Mark's tower, Horace Holley had become the managing editor of *World Unity Magazine: Interpreting the Spirit of the New Age,* which he ran out of his office at 4 East 12th Street. For its inaugural issue in 1927, he turned to Wright as a representative of modern architecture's new age and commissioned him to write a review of the translation of Le Corbusier's *Vers une Architecture.* By the second issue, Wright was listed as a "contributing editor." Holley even asked Wright to design covers for the magazine.[28]

The commission to review Le Corbusier's book gave Wright a chance to assess his chief rival. By this point, the young Franco-Swiss architect, painter, and theorist was *the* leading figure in the Modern Movement. In his stinging polemic, Le Corbusier stated that America's contributions were in civil engineering, not architecture. In Wright's review, which appeared in September 1928, Wright applauded Le Corbusier's aesthetic but claimed he had himself made discoveries attributed to Le Corbusier decades earlier: "The fact that all Le Corbusier says or means was at home here in architecture in America in the work of Louis Sullivan and myself—more than twenty-five years ago and is fully on record in both building and writing here and abroad—has no meaning for him in this connection."[29]

In September 1927, Robert Morss Lovett, a member of the editorial board of the *New Republic*, asked Wright to consider writing for them. Noting the architect's recent stay in New York and aware of Wright's activity in the architectural press, he sent his letter care of Maginel on West 12th Street. Lovett was friends with Ferdinand Schevill and his wife Clara, who had recently visited the Lovetts in New York, and no doubt Ferdinand had talked up his dear architect friend, who was residing at Taliesin for the moment. Wright had his hands full and didn't reply to Lovett.[30]

Two years later, in 1929, after Wright had declined to send the St. Mark's drawings to Bruce Bliven, editor of the *New Republic*, he forwarded Bliven an article for consideration—likely a version of "The Passing of the Cornice," one of his Princeton lectures. For Wright, the cornice was the symbol of a dead culture, an extraneous horizontal projection from history and dead traditions. It was passing out of use not only in buildings but in culture in general, so that cars, clothing, hairstyles, and even jazz, Wright claimed, were beginning to express the new, clean lines of sculptural contours. Bliven answered that he could wait for the St. Mark's tower images but gave Wright some discouraging news. He had shown Wright's article to his staff, and the "unanimous feeling" was not to publish the architect's essay because he'd misjudged current taste: fashionable women were actually adding headdresses that resembled "cornices" in their apparel.[31]

Despite Bliven's rebuff, the interplay of Wright's European and American publications was building. Jean Badovici capitalized on the international interest in Wright and eventually released *Frank Lloyd Wright: Architecte américain*, his own compilation of Wright's work derived from the pages of *L'Architecture Vivant*. It contained an extensive twenty-seven-page spread with twenty-five plates. Wright found the book, from the publisher Albert Morancé, so appealing that after getting his complimentary copies, he ordered an additional thirty. Heinrich De Fries scored another coup with coverage of San Marcos in the Desert, Ocatillo, and the St. Mark's tower in the journal *Die Form.* Edited in Berlin, the publication was the bimonthly journal of the Deutscher Werkbund, a precursor of the Bauhaus. Aside from the tower, Europeans saw Wright's latest designs before they reached an American audience (figs. 49, 50). The article combined Wright's ideas and recent projects and exemplified his control over their presentation and factual detail. De Fries provided the text; Wright had his German draftsman Heinrich Klumb send the illustrations, drawings, and photographs. The architect also added a long extract from his recent Princeton lectures entitled "Modern Concepts Concerning an Organic Architecture." De Fries had it translated into German as a manifesto. The captions for the illustrations give the impression that Wright designed buildings with unfathomable budgets despite the current economic climate and claimed, falsely, that the St. Mark's tower would start construction in May. The hype notwithstanding, the images were stunning.[32]

The coverage in *Die Form* had a domino effect in New York. Members of AUDAC immediately took note of De Fries's article and in particular Wright's manifesto, "Modern Concepts." "These sentences are so thoroughly true," the editorial committee of AUDAC commented, "that we feel them equally applicable to design or decoration of every description as well as to architecture." They wanted to include it in their *Annual of American Design,* but as the annual covered everything from business interiors, fabrics, and graphics to industrial design, the editors wanted Wright to expand further. He promised to prepare new plans and perspectives for the version of St. Mark's intended for Chicago—and he asked one of the editors to send him additional copies of *Die Form.*[33]

Requests for illustrations of Wright's buildings and projects were now pouring in from everywhere. A Chicago newspaper editor made a typical request: he wanted photos of the San Marcos resort and the National Life Insurance Building. Sympathetic to Wright and the plight of his building, the newspaperman insisted that the National Life building piece

DIE FORM

ZEITSCHRIFT FÜR GESTALTENDE ARBEIT

5. JAHR
HEFT 1
1. JANUAR
1930

Für den Deutschen Werkbund herausgegeben von
Dr. W. Riezler / Verantwortlich für den Inhalt Dr. W. Lotz / Verlag Hermann Reckendorf G. m. b. H., Berlin SW 48, Reckendorfhaus, Hedemannstr. 24
Telegrammadresse: Reckendorfhaus Berlin

»DIE FORM« ERSCHEINT AM
1. UND AM 15. JEDES MONATS

BEZUGSBEDINGUNGEN:

Vom Verlag oder durch den Buchhandel bezogen: Einzelheft
75 Pfg., halbjährlich (12 Hefte) 8.— RM, jährlich (24 Hefte)
15.— RM. Durch die Post bezogen: Vierteljährlich (6 Hefte)
4.— RM. Jeder Briefträger nimmt Bestellungen entgegen

Mitteilungen redaktioneller Art sowie Manuskriptsendungen
und Besprechungsexemplare bitten wir zu richten an: Die
Schriftleitung der Form, Berlin SW 48, Hedemannstraße 24
Fernsprech-Anschluß: Sammelnummer F 5 Bergmann 84 00

Fig. 49 Title page, *Die Form*, January 1, 1930.

und öffnet sich dem „Menschenlicht" oder der menschlichen Vorstellung, wie die im Samen eingeschlossene Form sich dem Sonnenlicht öffnet und ihm entspricht.
Ein Innenleben ist jedem Samenkorn gegeben. Ebenso notwendig ist ein Innenleben für jede Idee eines guten Bauwerks.
Einfachheit, wenn sie organisch ist, tritt als unmittelbares Ergebnis von selbst ein.
Einfachheit und Stil sind beides Wirkungen, niemals Ursachen.
Bauwerke sind wie Bäume, wenn beide .... sich selbst überlassen bleiben.
Wer möchte sagen, die Eiche ist mächtiger als die Ulme,
die Weide der Birke überlegen,
die Buche edler denn die Fichte,
der Apfelbaum ihnen allen überlegen, — ausgenommen für besondere Zwecke.
Alles Erschaffene ist für einen Sonderzweck gedacht.
Natur gilt nur als Sonderfall. Die Gattung ist Verallgemeinerung, aber jedes Sonderwesen, das geboren wird, ist individueller Ausdruck der Gattung .... alle sind einander ähnlich, aber nicht zwei gleich, bis in Ewigkeit.

Blick aus dem Schlafraum Mr. Wrights
Vue du pièce à coucher de Mr. Wright
View from the sleeping-room of Mr. Wright

The Chinese sought qualities in colors and materials, with greater sense of depth than any other race. Their glazes produced in little all great qualities seen at large in external nature. Their textures were as soft skin to the touch, as flowers in sun or mosses in rain for color .... their sense of form found joy in the pendant .... only a very old civilization subtle and profound could have reached the last word in refinement of form. Such are the sensibilities of organic architecture.
All the color and texture the eye has seen, all the rythms the ear has heard, all the grace of form the mind may grasp ....
.... are properties of architecture.
Great art is great life.
From Princeton Lectures. Series Art. Archeology and Architecture. May 1930.

Übersetzung
des Manifestes von Frank Lloyd Wright

Der Grundsatz ist die maßgebende Richtschnur. Der Ausbau eines Grundsatzes ist die einzig sichere Überlieferung.
Menschliche Überlieferungen wie die Stilarten sind Kleidungsstücke, die man an- und ausziehen kann. Form ist nur dann organisch, wenn sie in natürlichem Verhältnis zum Material und zur Funktion steht.
Eine organische Form wächst unter denselben Bedingungen zu ihrer Struktur auf, unter denen die Pflanze aus dem Erdreich aufwächst ....
Beide entfalten sich gleichermaßen aus dem Inneren.
Alle Form einer organischen Baukunst entspricht

Eingang zum Wohnzelt Mr. Wrights
Entrée de la tente servant de pièce d'habitation à Mr. Wright
Entrance to Mr. Wright's living-tent

Fig. 50 Illustrations of Ocatillo desert camp, from *Die Form*, January 1, 1930. German text by Heinrich De Fries.

should have no title in the hopes that someone might pick up on what he renamed "a study for a Chicago building."[34]

Sheldon Cheney, who would later produce a major book on Machine Age art, was preparing one of the first highly illustrated books on modern architecture. He had met Wright in New York, and wrote him in January 1930 to arrange a meeting and to request illustrations: "I find that I want at least twenty of yours, if you are willing." The years spanned the California textile-block houses, Barnsdall's Olive Hill, and, of course, Wright's early work in the Chicago area. Cheney and his wife Maude detoured while traveling in the Midwest to visit Wright and Olgivanna at Taliesin in early February, sparking a friendship with the Wrights. Cheney's book, *The New World Architecture,* was published later in 1930 by Longmans, Green & Co., which would eventually publish Wright's *Autobiography.*[35]

Wright's new popularity extended to interviews, and for those he exercised tight editorial control. When John Taylor Boyd Jr. interviewed Wright in New York for *Arts and Decoration* magazine, the editor, Mary Fanton Roberts, naïvely sent Wright a draft of the interview. Wright edited it, taking some "small liberties," and insisted that it "be printed *exactly as it now stands without interpolation or alteration of any kind.*" Further, Wright wanted compensation in the form of free subscriptions for a year for his friends and twenty-five copies for himself. Roberts apparently acquiesced, as the interview was published that spring.[36]

This demand for images and interviews reveals in microcosm the route that modern architecture had traveled over the previous twenty years. Myriad interconnections now operated between America and Europe. Once again Wright was at the center. His position was exemplified when Julius Hoffmann, a German editor in Stuttgart whose review *Moderne Bauformen* had published Wright's work, asked Wright for pictures of his latest interiors. He was planning a book with Emanuel Josef Margold, a *Jugendstil* designer and graphicist who had studied in Vienna. Margold had even worked as an artist at the Darmstadt Artists' Colony, which Wright and Mamah had visited. He was a connection, if indirect, to Wright's relationship with the Vienna Secession of twenty years earlier. Margold had moved to Berlin in 1929, however, and was pursuing German

Functionalism. He had transited, as had many European contemporaries, from the old aesthetics of the Secession to the search for a "New Objectivity" defined by rationality, economy, and minimalism. Obviously, Margold's proposal appealed to Hoffmann, who envisioned that their book would be the counterpart to a publication by Bruno Taut, a former Expressionist who'd published *New Architecture in Europe and America*.[37]

Significantly, Margold and Hoffmann chose Wright as their lone American example. They wanted to include all building types, from sporting rooms to private houses, from cafes to shops. Their main requirement, they told Wright, was that the designs should "correspond to modern ideas of clearness and that they are free of historical reminiscences." Wright would get no money from the deal—the book was apparently not published—but the effort signified how Wright was seen as the representative of American modern architecture and reinforced his position on an international platform.

Back in America, Princeton University Press brought out *Modern Architecture: Being the Kahn Lectures for 1930*. The book was widely reviewed not only in professional journals but in literary magazines, including *Parnassus,* the *New York Times Book Review,* and the *New Republic*. And from the Art Institute of Chicago came, as promised, *Two Lectures on Architecture*, which featured Wright's speeches "In the Realm of Ideas" and "To the Young Man in Architecture."[38]

As a writer, Wright was creative, stylistically innovative, and often playful. He experimented with a new genre in an unpublished essay, "One Day in New York," written around 1930 while he was struggling to get approval for the St. Mark's tower. In fifteen pages of invented dialogue, Wright has an engineer, "Horace," and himself walking through the streets of New York, arguing about traffic, taxis, and, particularly, safety. It is one more version of his attack on the city and the promotion of his version of the skyscraper as its antidote.[39]

The architect and the engineer muse on the nature of death in the past and the threat of "accidents" in the contemporary world. Modern life is an existence of peril, they seem to hint, as they stroll down Fifth Avenue. "To live today," Wright rattles on, "is to be more continuously in greater danger than ever." The architect and Horace chat about a "Hollywood star-of-stars" accidently electrocuted in a bathtub, and about the collapse of a four-story building of reinforced concrete. Most of all, the architect and engineer bemoan the fallibility of technology, the "mechanical factors of the device," and the endless stream of taxis and overloaded subway trains. The pair stand at a skyscraper's entrance to watch the "metal jaws" of the revolving door and enter an elevator car that is hanging "in mid-air" at the mercy of "a mechanical lever in the hands of a boy or girl."[40]

The "modern miracle of our safety" was just that—a miracle, and too tenuously assured. Horace and Wright conclude their chat by vowing to leave the city. "Horace," Wright says, "let us go back to the farm." Horace agrees: "let's take our cars with us, our modern plumbing, electricity, and refrigeration, the radio, the cinema."

While he continued his attacks on the city, the country was on Wright's mind. In 1931, he finished the first part of a new tract on his ideas for a decentralized society. The ninety-page text, with five illustrations, appeared under the title *The Disappearing City* the following year. It was the first book-length statement of Wright's ideas, synthesizing his urban critique and proposing its theoretical antidote. Now refined, it became the core document for the anti-urban concepts he could develop in the future. A series of editions and rewrites would appear over the next thirty years.[41]

Of all his works, *Frank Lloyd Wright: An Autobiography* would be the architect's longest and most important endeavor of his writing career. Wright had begun the text while lying low during the fall of 1925, and he had written the bulk of it over the next five years. In addition to Olgivanna's encouragement, Wright's sister Jane provided advice and support after he sent her portions of the manuscript. She urged him to be generous to others. "Even Aunt Laura in her hardness should have some encomium for her devotion to her children—and her ability to accomplish the hard daily tasks."[42]

The *Autobiography* operated as not only a recollection of Wright's life but a loosely structured diary of the tumultuous events he had experienced. The text was organized as a series of "books" instead of conventional chapters, a notion that confounded his editors and his agent George Bye, who often misinterpreted the single book as a multibook contract.

The commission began when Bye connected Wright to the New York offices of Longmans, Green & Co., a London-based house with a distinguished list of authors. Founded in 1724, Longmans spanned at least six generations of the Longman family, publishing William Wordsworth, Arthur Conan Doyle, Robert Louis Stevenson, and even Winston Churchill. This list of authors, stellar as it was, did not feature architects—the closest figures included the horticulturist and garden designer Gertrude Jekyll, and Sheldon Cheney, author of *New World Architecture.* The company, which ran international operations from its headquarters on Paternoster Row in London, had opened an office to distribute their books in New York in 1887, and two years later Charles J. Mills was sent from England to manage the New York branch. Creating a micro-dynasty within the larger Longmans enterprise, he was succeeded by his sons and grandsons, who not only distributed titles from London but produced their own books. The company eventually had branches in Chicago, Boston, and Toronto. When Wright dealt with the firm, Edward S. Mills was the scion and owner. Bye handled all the negotiations, and, as with all business matters related to Wright, they were long and complicated.[43]

When the New York office took on Wright, it was located at 55 Fifth Avenue. Coinciding with the acceptance of Wright's *Autobiography,* Longmans had begun to feel the bitter pinch of the Depression and in 1932 downsized by partnering with a young firm, Coward-McCann, at their Fifth Avenue location. Undertaking a book by the iconoclastic Wright in the midst of financial chaos was a risk for the venerable firm.[44]

Wright submitted the manuscript with the first three sections, or "Books," to his designated editor, Frank E. Hill, in early January 1931. Over the next year, Wright sent additional sections and dickered over contract terms, royalties, and advances. Hill and his marketing department disapproved of the working title, *Generation upon Generation.* Olgivanna suggested simply *Frank Lloyd Wright: An Autobiography,* to which all agreed.

By the end of 1931, the text for the *Autobiography* was complete. Consistent with his desire for control of everything he created, Wright designed the format and layout of the text with headings to illustrate the separate "Books." He intended the first illustration to be an abstracted image of himself as a child walking hand in hand with his Uncle John. It would also appear on the dust jacket (fig. 51). The image was so abstract—a heavy black, angled line intersected with geometric motifs and ending with his red signature square—that the figures were unrecognizable. "You won't like this design at first," he wrote to Hill. "But you will like it much when you see it on the bookstands in contrast to other books. Where every cover is barking loud (like the samples you sent) no one hears (or sees) anything in particular. It is contrast that catches the eye or the ear—I am sure of this and I ought to know!"[45]

The confessional and iconoclastic nature of the *Autobiography* would resonate well with critics and the public, particularly young people, or Wright's "Young Man in Architecture." "As a text of 'life,' autobiography equivalently makes an affirmation by the writer: 'I was not always as I now am,'" the literary theorist Carolyn Barros observes about the genre. "It presents the 'before' and 'after' of individuals who have undergone transformations of some kind." True autobiography is a testament of metamorphosis "framed by its language and inscribed in its configurations of words and images. Change is then the operative motive for auto-biographical discourse." The *Autobiography* was Wright's own attempt to catalogue that change.[46]

The structure of the books initially seems random, but it is carefully crafted with deliberate points built up by the choice and sequence of sections. Poetry punctuates the text at key moments, leading the reader to unexpected juxtapositions. The *Autobiography* was also modern in the sense of being self-reflexive and aware of the deceptions of any historical or biographical fixed points.

Not all of Wright's later biographers loved his writing. "It is an odd fact," wrote the influential *New Yorker* critic Brendan Gill, "that while he took great pride in the book and from time to time fussed over corrections and emendations to be incorporated into later editions, he appears never to have read the text line for line, leaving untouched scores of conspicuous blunders."[47]

A general reader could legitimately complain that the book omits a discussion about many of Wright's buildings—the ones he chose were

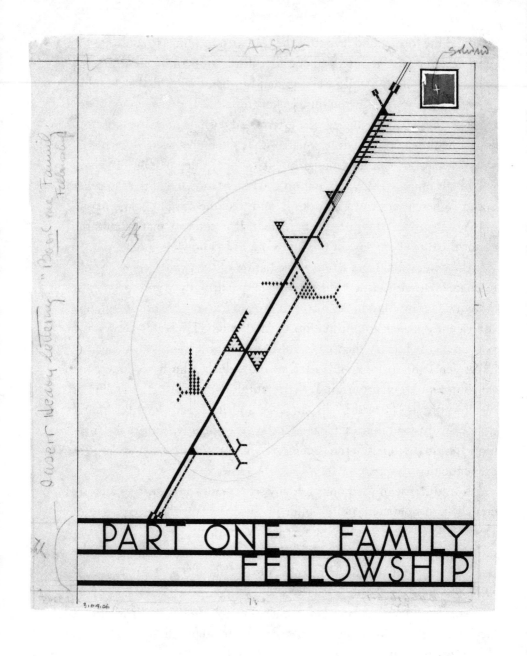

Fig. 51 Frank Lloyd Wright's graphic design for Book One of his *Autobiography*, 1931.

carefully selected—so no comprehensive picture of his architecture emerges. In practical terms, the lack of an index frustrates readers who look for specific subjects.

The first edition of the *Autobiography* came out in March 1932. Reviews appeared immediately in major newspapers across the country and in major periodicals. The *San Francisco Chronicle* opined, "Wright is concrete, intensely personal, but he is an intelligent and virile critic of the American scene. His book proves it. . . . Get hold of this book and digest it." The *New York Times Book Review* compared Wright to the Renaissance master Benvenuto Cellini, each being an artist who is "passionate, combative, impatient of control, completely single-minded in his art." The reviewer described Wright's "intense moral conviction" and noted the honesty and humility of the architect's self-revelations of his personal life: "The domestic story he has told simply and unequivocally, so that no open-minded person will fail to understand. It has been unfortunate and tragic. But the passion of the man was needed to support the passion of the architect and the end, architecturally, and humanly, has been happy." The *Saturday Review of Literature*'s assessment was euphoric: "Today he is one of the happiest men in America. We must judge him also one of the wisest and the greatest, his 'Autobiography' is one the most trenchant and beautiful books of our time."[48]

As Wright hoped and expected, the *Autobiography* quickly established a following among younger readers. His prose appealed to both college students and young professionals, and many sought him out when he announced the forthcoming opening of the Taliesin Fellowship—his communal school and training ground—in the same year. The book's attraction lay in the searching nature of Wright's voice—its resonance with those who challenge authority. "I believe that a teenager is a teenager, and I think that with him lies the hope of the future," he later told the TV journalist Mike Wallace in an interview. Wright presented an uninhibited account of an adult, showing vulnerability, noble intentions, and the ability to overcome tragic circumstances.[49]

To his credit (and the forbearance of Olgivanna), he wrote with honest grace about his life with Mamah Borthwick, the love of his early life, and her death. Its "confessional character" contributed to its ongoing fascination. Wright was a rebel who said what every youth wants at some point to say to the world of parental domination: drop dead. A misfit himself, Wright appealed to those who felt they didn't fit into conventional society.[50]

The reception of the *Autobiography* not only vindicated Wright's struggles of the previous decade but made him seem a model of courage for anyone else struggling to break the bonds of social conformity. His writing allowed him to fulfill his destiny as the champion of American architecture. New York had again provided a platform to continue his battle.

11

PHOENIX RISING

While his *Autobiography* was in its final edits, Wright continued his crusade as the prophet of American modern architecture. Sometimes he met with friction and resistance. The self-described "journeyman preacher" met just such opposition during a weeklong lecture tour of New York in February 1931. At a meeting of the Twentieth Century Club at the Pratt Mansion in Brooklyn, before the "very dignified and beautifully dressed people with old New York names," Wright wrangled with a Yale professor who claimed the present had a "right to 'the Past.'"[1]

A few days later, at a dinner dedicated to "Modern Architecture" at the Women's University Club, Wright, with Olgivanna and Maginel at his side, contended with an audience that included "prominent skyscraperites"; New York city planners; the artist, activist, and patron of modern art Katherine Dreier; and Buckminster Fuller, the thirty-five-year-old designer of the dome-like Dymaxion house, a factory-manufactured kit that could fit any site. Fuller had been living in Greenwich Village and also designed an aerodynamic Dymaxion car. "I was a minority report likely to spoil that party so I asked to speak last," Wright recorded in his *Autobiography.* Although he found Fuller to be "a dripping rag," Wright tolerated him until Fuller described the 1933 Chicago World's Fair "as the last word in modern architecture."[2]

It was a sore subject. Deeming him too much of an "individualist," the organizers of the Fair had excluded Wright from its celebration of "The Century of Progress." The international World's Fair was intended to celebrate both Chicago's centennial and the marvels of American technology. Moreover, it would become a demonstration of America's latest definition of modern architecture, buildings that followed the stylistic trends of the *moderne,* with its wavy curves that had evolved from Art Deco. It was also America's best reply to date to the European modernists—the Functionalists in particular—who loomed in the background. Unlike both the Chicago World's Columbian Exposition of 1893, which had a creative, pastry-like White City, and unlike the Functionalism that had become increasingly austere and monochromatic, the multicolored buildings of the Century of Progress created a "Rainbow City." Planned on a massive scale, the Fair was occurring in Wright's old stomping grounds near the South Side of Chicago—and he had no role in its buildings.[3]

Wright's exclusion annoyed his supporters in New York, who championed him as both figurehead and leader. With the architect's blessing, they planned a two-part event—private dinner and public lecture—on February 26, 1931, to protest the situation and to honor Wright. Led by Paul Frankl and Lee Simonson, an architect and stage set designer from AUDAC, along with Woollcott, Haskell, and Mumford, the organization sent invitations for a roundtable dinner at the Restaurant Crillon on Park Avenue. Wright's discussion, "Why a World's Fair?," would follow at the Town Hall Club at 113 West 43rd Street. *Time* magazine reported that two additional meetings were planned to protest Wright's exclusions from the Century of Progress exhibition.[4]

After the dinner, Wright and his coterie transferred to a packed auditorium for the public event. Woollcott chaired the proceedings. "I have seen Alex bubble," Wright observed afterward, obviously very pleased with the treatment being given him, "with wit in his lair by the river and his seat at the Algonquin but that night he was effervescence itself. At least living in New York City does keen the rapier and polish the thrust."[5]

After Mumford and Haskell spoke, Wright held forth. Aware that he could appear as a rejected suitor, he claimed he had only wanted to avoid a "catastrophe" similar to the Chicago World's Columbian Exposition of 1893, which had allegedly set back the cause of developing an American architecture free from European precedents. Wright did, however, propose alternatives: a skyscraper more than twice the height of the Eiffel Tower; huge, "noble pylons" supporting steel cables and a canopy for vast exhibition spaces; and a "pontoon fair" of floating vessels fabricated of pulp to create a "festival" for the eyes. To these Wright added floating gardens, colored light piped in tubing, and illuminated glass with airiness to provide "a charm of New York."[6]

Wright paired his words with drawings—quick sketches, some of them—intended to dazzle the attendees with his creativity. The protests didn't change the Fair committee's position, but the event further confirmed Wright's stature among his New York friends. After he returned to Taliesin, he elaborated his ideas for the Fair in his *Autobiography*. But the Century of Progress would go on without him. Meanwhile, Wright had another crisis looming: his debut at the Museum of Modern Art.[7]

Modern Architecture, as *Exhibition 15* was eventually entitled, brought to a head the conflict that had long preoccupied Wright: Would America heed his pleas for a national modernism defined in his organic terms? Or would it follow the currents of European modernism? Wright had been waging this battle for years, and a decisive moment had finally arrived. For Wright, at stake was not only his role in American architecture, but also the battle for the future of modern architecture, and with it the soul of America.

Alfred Barr Jr., director of the new museum (it had been founded two years earlier), engaged the twenty-four-year-old Philip Johnson to organize its first architectural exhibition for the following year. Henry-Russell Hitchcock was asked to co-curate. Barr believed that architecture, art, and design should all have a place in the museum. His views were fed by publications from the Bauhaus in Dessau, which he visited in 1928, meeting Walter Gropius, Paul Klee, and László Moholy-Nagy and loving their spare residences and industrial aesthetics.[8]

In preparing the exhibition, Hitchcock complemented Johnson's curatorial work by drawing on his book *Modern Architecture: Romanticism and Reintegration,* published in 1929. In the summer of 1930, Barr, Johnson, and Hitchcock began conceptualizing an "International Style" to promote the avant-garde European architecture they had seen during their travels in the late 1920s. Their goal was to replace the Beaux-Arts traditions as well as the efflorescence of Art Deco with an aesthetic that spoke to the spirit of the Machine Age.[9]

The collaboration was natural among friends who, in their twenties, saw the potential for overturning the architectural status quo. Barr and Johnson were neighbors in an Art Deco building at 424 East 52nd Street, only a few doors down from Aleck Woollcott. Part of the Southgate complex designed by Emery Roth, their building lay in a neighborhood that was taking on a sophisticated artsy, modernist sheen. Artists, literary figures, actors, composers, and architects found the location east of Midtown appealing. In 1933, Wiliiam Lescaze would design his own residence and studio at 211 East 48th Street, one of the first modernist residences in the city.

Barr and Johnson, whose apartments were stacked one on top of the other, were remodeling the interiors of their homes to emphatically push the "radically austere" aesthetic of modernism. Johnson was explicit in creating "a show apartment to counteract the terrible wave of modernistic [i.e., Art Deco] apartments that we now have." To achieve that impact, he hired Mies van der Rohe for his first American commission; Lilly Reich, his partner, did most of the work. Barr's intention was similarly specific: every object and design decision would reflect the aesthetic embodied in the fledgling Museum of Modern Art.[10]

Enamored of the avant-garde developments in Europe that they had seen firsthand, and interested in discovering young adherents in America, Johnson and Hitchcock intended for *Exhibition 15* to present Wright as ascendant—the American lion in the international arena—but as a man whose work had peaked decades earlier. Newly energized and emergent, Wright wanted to be seen as a primogenitor, a current player, and a leader among equals. As America's only living architectural genius, he was hardly going to let a pair of young Harvard snobs shunt him to the sidelines.[11]

Wright realized that the exhibition was more inclusive than he imagined. In January 1932, furious that his impact would be diluted, he vented about his former employees, like Richard Neutra, who had gone independent with some success. He also trashed some of the very architects—Ray Hood and William Lescaze—who had graciously welcomed him to New York. "I consented, to join the affair," he wrote Mumford, "thinking I would be among my peers: I heard only of Corbusier, Mies, et al. I found a hand-picked selected group including Hood and Neutra." They were not in his league, he claimed. "Neutra is the eclectic 'up to date,' copying the living. Hood is the eclectic copying the dead."[12]

Wright dogged Johnson, dictating how he wished to be presented and how much he objected to the "eclecticism" of many of the included architects. "I distinctly do not only disapprove but positively condemn them," he wrote Johnson. "Howe is respectable, and Lescaze, as far as I know, though a fledgling." Wright was comfortable exhibiting with younger architects trying "to build noble and beautiful buildings." "But," he added, "I am sick and tired of the pretense of men who will elect a style, old or new, and get a building badly built by the help of some contractor and then publicize it as a notable achievement." In a huff, Wright withdrew from the exhibition.[13]

Wright's decision appalled Mumford, who was organizing the housing section of the exhibition. "Your absence from Modern Museum's show would be a calamity." He begged Wright to reconsider. "As for company, there is no more honorable position than to be crucified between two thieves." With Mumford stroking his hurt pride, Wright relented.[14]

The 1932 MoMA exhibition would be a cultural milestone, a culminating moment in what became known as the "International Style," which had begun in Europe after World War I within the rubric of Functionalism and started to infiltrate the American scene by the mid-1920s. Though Wright himself had used the term earlier, it became widespread after the show as a style of simple surfaces; flat, thin planes; and flat roofs in which ornament was decadent and forbidden. The style was supposedly versatile enough to be applied globally and was therefore international. By 1932, many of its innovators in Europe were moving on to other developments as they dealt with growing crisis. Yet MoMA still presented the International Style as the cutting edge of modern aesthetics. Ironically, the exhibition was held in MoMA's temporary galleries in the Heckscher Building, a neo-Renaissance Beaux-Arts confection at Fifth Avenue and 57th Street (now the Crown Building) rather than in its iconic edifice on West 53rd Street, which Goodwin and Stone designed later, in 1939.[15]

The International Style show, as it came to be known, provided a cultural marker for the twentieth century. Wright selected a limited number of designs that were displayed in large photo murals, each reflecting a phase of his work: the Isabel Roberts house as an exemplar of the Prairie period; the Robie house as culmination of the era; Taliesin; a selection of textile- block houses, representing Wright's use of cast concrete blocks, with ornamented surfaces as an efficient construction system; the Millard house, another representative of the California textile-block model; and the Richard Lloyd Jones house—also of textile blocks and Wright's largest house to date—recently completed for his cousin in Tulsa, Oklahoma.

Wright also prepared three models, which he felt made architecture accessible to the public. Of the three, Wright exhibited only "The House on the Mesa" (fig. 52). To some it seemed odd to present a sprawling, extravagant house with a five-car garage and a swimming pool while America was in the depths of the Depression. Wright thought he was proposing a new model home for a certain kind of client: the upper-middle-class American, rather than the middle-income people he usually targeted as his "ideal American family." In this case it was George Cranmer, a well-off client in Denver. To lessen the shock to Cranmer that his project was on view in New York, Wright wrote him to explain that he had "merely wanted to show how Machine-age luxury might compare with that of former ages." "Former ages" was Wright's euphemism for the luxury status of historic styles, and, according to him, anyone interested more in the "character" of his proposed house than its cost or status would find it appealing. And with no hint of modesty, Wright added it had "a greater

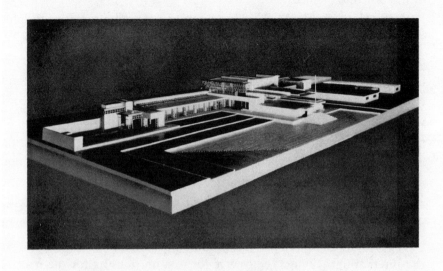

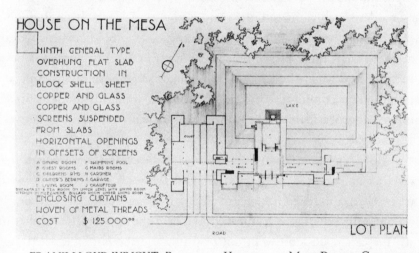

HOUSE ON THE MESA

NINTH GENERAL TYPE
OVERHUNG FLAT SLAB
CONSTRUCTION IN
BLOCK SHELL SHEET
COPPER AND GLASS
COPPER AND GLASS
SCREENS SUSPENDED
FROM SLABS
HORIZONTAL OPENINGS
IN OFFSETS OF SCREENS

A DINING ROOM   F SWIMMING POOL
B GUEST ROOMS   G MAIDS ROOMS
C CHILDRENS RMS H GARDNER
D OWNER'S BEDRMS I GARAGE
E LIVING ROOM   J CHAUFFEUR
BREAKFAST & TEA ROOM ON UPPER LEVEL WITH LIVING ROOM
KITCHEN IN MEZZANINE BILLARD ROOM UNDER LIVING ROOM

ENCLOSING CURTAINS
WOVEN OF METAL THREADS
COST $ 125 000°°

LAKE

COURT

ROAD

LOT PLAN

FRANK LLOYD WRIGHT: Project for House on the Mesa, Denver, Colorado

55

Fig. 52 "The House on the Mesa," model and plan drawing, from Alfred H. Barr, Jr., Henry-Russell Hitchcock, Jr., Philip Johnson, and Lewis Mumford, eds., *Modern Architects* (New York: Museum of Modern Art, 1932), 44.

integrity as organic I believe than ever existed in the world. And a greater beauty in consequence."[16]

"The House on the Mesa" was more than a mere showpiece to Wright, as he wrote about it in three versions of an unpublished manuscript. "A house," Wright announced, "for a moderately wealthy American family of considerable culture—master, mistress and four children, cook and two maids, chauffeur and gardener." Light and open, it would be a "conventional house," one that would do "no violence to the 'conservative' tastes" of those who preferred traditional styles. In sum, he was offering an alternative for those who could afford it, meaning able to pay $12,000 to $15,000. For the upscale who liked a neocolonial model, this house could provide everything they wanted from an old style—and more.[17]

Wright was purposefully focusing on the upper middle class, even at a moment of national economic disaster and homelessness, to counter the International Stylists, who were focused on housing for the masses. Why should the moderately prosperous be excluded from the benefits of modern architecture? Furthermore, the model, which photographed handsomely, visually communicated the differences between Wright's aesthetics and those of the Functionalists. But Wright ignored issues of identity and taste: the traditional pitched roof house offered one very popular and comfortable image of America, while his modern organic offered another. Habit and conformity were realities Wright neglected in his campaign to transform American housing.

MoMA produced two publications for the exhibition: *Modern Architects,* a catalogue for the show itself, and *International Style: Architecture Since 1922,* a more comprehensive book by Hitchcock and Johnson that accompanied the show as it traveled around the country. In another irony, the catalogue soon went out of print, and the public learned much of what it knew about the International Style from the book, which was more polemical and didn't reflect what was actually in the exhibition. The larger agenda was to promote the International Style as the only valid expression of modern architecture for Depression-era America. All else was trivia—the dramatic buildings of Art Deco, the streamlined wonders of *moderne,* and of course any references to history or traditional styles. Wright had pride of place in the exhibition catalogue; in the book he barely figured at all. In its modernist agenda he remained a relic.

The International Style exhibition took place nearly simultaneously with Wright's battle against European modernists. The conflict was about not only the house as a machine for living but the planning of the city itself, subsumed in European *urbanisme,* the rational arrangement of public space, embodied by Le Corbusier. In 1932, the *New York Times Magazine* published an article by Le Corbusier on his city of the future. His "Green City of abundant space and light" would be "a majestic array of prisms, perfect in form and aspect," and built on the cleared ground of the inefficient city. In other words, he advocated tearing down the medieval core of Paris and building a rational, modern city on top of the ruins. Well aware of Le Corbusier as his major European competitor, Wright countered in the March *New York Times Magazine* with Broadacre City. Rather than building on the carcass of a decrepit city, Broadacre City would be erected in the pristine landscape. Wright's proposal was, however, still only conception—he had no physical solution at this time—and to represent the future thrust of its architecture, he published an image of the St. Mark's tower.[18]

The debate between Wright and Le Corbusier also coincided with a public presentation of Wright's ideas for Broadacre City to an overflow audience at the Chicago City Club. Wright was hardly forgotten in Chicago: over three hundred people attended the event, the biggest crowd to attend a City Club event since World War I. Here, his concept of Broadacre City appeared as the words of an "apostle of 'the rights of the individual.'"[19]

In 1932, Wright had won a small battle merely by participating in MoMA's International Style show. His presence confirmed him to be not just a past master but a living force, one whose designs would take hold after prosperity returned. He was carrying his arguments to the press and the public. But his major clients were faltering.

Guthrie had big problems. After the *New Yorker* profiled Wright, playing a major role in his rise, it turned to profile Guthrie in January 1931. "Almost everything about Dr. William Norman Guthrie," Geoffrey T. Hellman, the article's author, declared, "is paradoxical." Hellman relished Guthrie's dichotomies: "Although extremely intelligent, he has practically no conception of the limitations of others; although a minister, he has very little interest in humanity; although genuinely concerned with religion, he will stoop to showman's tricks to make it popular; although he has been an insatiable reader and student all his life, he still has an unsophisticated mind." Guthrie was then in the midst of his ongoing battle with the Episcopal system at large, and Hellman, at least, admired him for this. Like Wright's, the rector's idiosyncrasies became endearing. "In spite of his occasional Latin outbursts, and the fact that one of his favorite words is 'jackass,' he is essentially sweet-tempered."[20]

The *New Yorker's* coverage also coincided with problems at St. Mark's Church in-the-Bowery. While Guthrie's radical agenda to Americanize the Episcopal Book of Common Prayer over the past ten years had attracted attendance, an increase in the number of parishioners and income from them lagged. "I trust that Wisconsin is happier than this terribly depressed undertakers' center," he wrote Wright in 1932. "We are wondering whether we shall have enough income to pay taxes, not to feed ourselves. We raised large public funds by a kind of hold-up for the unemployed, and we fire employees right and left, which is extraordinarily inconsistent."[21]

Accusing him of "mismanagement," Guthrie's own vestry board tried to oust him in the same year. He overcame the mutiny, but his ritual services never regained the publicity or attendance of the 1920s, and his days as rector at St. Mark's were numbered.[22]

With the St. Mark's tower and, by now, San Marcos in the Desert doomed, Wright was still strapped for funds. "We are cutting up bedsheets for handkerchiefs," he wrote Darwin Martin, "and have had no new clothes for four years." His only possible source of revenue among the few designs in progress was a house for Nancy and Malcolm E. Willey. Inspired by Wright's *Autobiography,* Nancy asked him if he would design an affordable house in Minneapolis for her and her husband, an administrator at the University of Minnesota. Though the design would go through two phases, it would be an important transition toward what Wright would call the Usonian home.[23]

The year 1932 marked an upward momentum for Wright: his *Autobiography* had appeared, and he published *The Disappearing City,* which allowed him to develop further his anti-urban concept for Broadacre City and his attack on European urbanism. In the book, he articulated the basic principles for Broadacre City, and he added illustrations to further convince the reader that the city as it currently existed was decaying. Seen from the air, the city was disappearing in malevolent clouds, with only the tops of the tyrannical skyscrapers poking through; its citizenry was lost in overbuilding; and the pattern of annexation of rural land to a city with a center appeared "futile" and uncontrolled by any rational process. Broadacre City would allow the reemergence of the citizen and his transformation from citizen to denizen of the landscape. The book was a major step forward in defining Wright's position and concepts.

Also in 1932, Wright and Olgivanna finally launched the Taliesin Fellowship. The first contingent of thirty-two apprentices arrived on October 20, representing a cadre of unquestioning acolytes—a labor force that could till the fields, repair buildings (particularly the Hillside Home School), draft his designs, build models, and eventually supervise construction on site. Unpaid, they were in fact paying for the privilege of apprenticing to the master at an annual tuition of $650.[24]

The applicants came from a wide range of socioeconomic backgrounds, and most shared an adulation for Wright and an interest in an unconventional training in architecture. Unconventional they got. The basic educational philosophy was Deweyesque—learning by doing. But learning would extend beyond work at a drafting board. In a typical day they might draw or work on models, but also till fields, harvest vegetables, cook, and clean. All of this occurred in a setting whose social and spiritual life was increasingly dominated by Olgivanna. She still adhered to Gurdjieffian notions, while Wright mandated the professional formation from philosophy to design method. He gave periodic talks, but daily activities were funneled from Wright to his chief draftsman, who in turn assigned tasks to the apprentices. Though few would acknowledge its reality, the Fellowship soon became a commune that demanded fidelity and strict adherence to the Wrights' demands. Students who felt uneasy or disappointed left usually after a short stint; those who loved the Wrights stayed, many for the rest of their lives. The Fellowship was modeled on the two-tiered medieval guild: the apprentices, just starting their training, and the fellows, who had "graduated" from apprenticeship. As with the guilds of old, only one master dominated the shop.

In that first winter of the Fellowship's founding, Wright set apprentices to cutting wood and starting a long reconstruction of the boarded-up Hillside Home School, located on the other side of Taliesin. Assigning drafting tasks to the new apprentices, he finalized the first version of the Willey house drawings in early 1934. A second version of the design that was built represented the prototype of the Usonian house, containing several of its elements: rot-resistant cypress trim, bricks, and a central "workspace," which replaced the kitchen.[25]

In January, to escape the winter and his recurrent pneumonia, Wright brought his family and apprentices to the desert, where Chandler greeted them at the Hacienda Inn. Wright soon charged the apprentices with building a multisectioned model, measuring almost thirteen square feet, of Broadacre City, the physical representation of Wright's vision for anti-urbanity. Part of the funds for producing the model came from the Pittsburgh department store magnate Edgar Kaufmann, whose son Edgar Jr. was one of Wright's apprentices.[26]

Drawing on the conceptual basis in *The Disappearing City*, developed in his Princeton lectures and other writings, Wright at last gave physical form and definition to Broadacre City in the model. Its essential components included a four-square-mile settlement for 1,400 families, organized by the disposition of its buildings, highways, and parks, and by control of its roads to maximize convenience in work and leisure, intended to provide safety on highways and in industry. The standard elements were farms "correlated" with production and sale; non-polluting factories; decentralized schools; monorails; a controlled traffic system, providing for separation of classes of vehicular traffic; warehouses incorporated into highway structures; and cost-saving houses, described as "generally of prefabricated units," with much glass, "roofless rooms," and rooftop gardens.

The residents of Broadacre City would live in a variety of dwelling types, with each family having its own acre of ground. Wright provided for the individual through smaller factories, farm cooperatives, hotels, a controlled traffic system, automobiles, flying machines (Wright's so-called aerotors), and design centers with communal arrangements for artisans supported by industry and the community. The prevailing ethos was that small is good: "small farms, small factories, small homes for industry, small schools on home grounds, all working in coordination."

Wright set out principles for Broadacre City that were to extend throughout the nation: every man, woman, and child deserved to own an acre of ground as long as they used it or lived on it, and every adult, Wright argued, was entitled to own at least one automobile. According to Wright, the design "presupposes that the city is going to the country" and that the "country" would consist of four sections of land on which "the hills come down to the plains and a river flows down and across the plain." In this he was relying on the traditional systems of American land division—a full section, the township of the public-land survey, subdivided into acre units, with the 640 acres of the section having a density of about 2.2 families per acre—but these systems had rules and principles.[27]

At the outset there was no client for the project except Wright himself and his own personal vision of the democratized American. He conceived of Broadacre City to be a universally adaptable plan or one that did not yet exist, its locations "everywhere" and "nowhere." Wright envisioned a form that could change with different topographies, climates, and social customs.

The physical form of Broadacre City was, however, inseparable from its ideological content. On the one hand, a socioeconomic agenda defined it. On the other hand, reactions to the direct experience of New York City and *urbanisme* drove it forward. The central principles were "general decentralization" and "architectural reintegration of all units into one fabric." These principles were generated by the increase in automobile transportation; by communication via radio, telephone, telegraph, and power transmission; and by standardized machine production. Implicit in this conception was the principle of condensing all jurisdiction of cities and towns into the county as the local governing body. The sizes and seats of existing counties would be retained, but municipal village governments would be abolished. Wright assumed counties had an average size of thirty to fifty square miles.[28]

Ironically, while Broadacre City contained decentralized activities, it hypothesized a centralized government as a means of limiting bureaucracy and linking local and county officials more directly to the federal government. In this system of localized county government, central control would be extreme: land distribution, for example, would be controlled by the agent of the state, the architect, who would be the "arbiter of organic architecture."

The rules that defined Broadacre City were stated as a series of negations, posed as a manifesto on printed posters. Broadacre City was to have:

No private ownership of public needs
No landlord or tenant
No "housing." No subsistence homesteads
No traffic problems. No railroads. No streetcars
No grade crossings
No poles. No wires in site
No headlights. No light fixtures
No glaring cement roads or walks
No tall buildings except in isolated parks
No slum. No Scum.
No public ownership of private needs
No major or minor axis.[29]

Broadacre City played other fundamental roles in Wright's work. It fit into tripartite arrangements of conceptual concentric spheres. At the largest scale was Usonia—the great domain of North America itself, capable of subdivisions spanning the continent. Within it were a multitude of Broadacre Cities, each responding to regional topography and climate and connected with a multimodal transport system. Broadacre City provided a physical and ideal context for Wright's development of building types, particularly the Usonian houses, the core building type of the endeavor, and culmination of his efforts to design economical dwellings. Broadacre City as idea and model also became the repository of the unbuilt projects, the dreams Wright had yet to fulfill, from filling stations to model farms, from sports arenas to museums. The Modern Cathedral and the St. Mark's tower were inserted as miniatures into the model, awaiting their realization at a larger scale. The site model became in Wright's hands a dynamic conceptual tool, altered over time, and he updated his texts accordingly.

Not only did Wright and the apprentices fabricate the buildings for a whole model at a micro scale, but they made models at larger scale of the basic elements: small farms, bridges, and, in particular, the varieties of residences. In the development of these models, the Usonian home went from an ambition to a physical building type with flexibility. It too would be defined by principles and rules: zoned living instead of discrete rooms that distinguished public (living and dining) and private (bedrooms and bathrooms); a concrete floor slab with an integral heating system; replacement of the kitchen with a workspace; furnishings integrated into walls to save space; and a new accommodation for modern transportation: the carport. Generally, the Usonian home would have no basement, a straightforward palette of limited building materials—brick, wood siding (often cypress, for its resistance), patio doors, and clerestories—and one story, often with the ceiling of the living zone pushed up slightly higher than the adjacent spaces. The homes could have a variety of roof types, from flat to pitched to shed (or slanted). With clear and consistent principles, Usonian houses could draw from a variety of simple but effective plan configurations: they could have their constituent elements organized in a straight line, or turned into an L-shape, which could be flipped or rotated depending on the needs of site and climate. While many of the floor plans used a rectilinear grid with squares as units for their organization, they could also work with angular grids, using diamond-shaped or trapezoidal modules. In these nonrectilinear plans, the designs could splay open instead of relying on right angles.

Just as Wright's clear articulation of the principles of the Prairie period house in 1908 had allowed for rich variation—like Bach composing variations with a limited set of notes—his clear articulation of the principles of the Usonian house provided the basis for variations on the theme for the next two decades. Along with the Prairie home, it would become Wright's major contribution to domestic housing, one that would have great impact particularly in the postwar era and become an actor in mid-century modern American design.

In 1935, as a continuation of the challenges he'd presented to New York, Wright brought the Broadacre City model to Gotham, to be displayed at the Industrial Arts Exposition, organized by the National Alliance of Art and Industry. With its density increasing, New York City represented the total opposite image to Wright's spread-out vision of a four-square mile, low-density settlement in the country. Occurring in the midst of the Depression, with building activity at a standstill, Wright's agenda seemed at the time like a fantasy.[30]

A publicity campaign directed by Riis and Bonner, commissioned by the organizers, had produced generally positive, if brief, newspaper coverage. In his *New Yorker* column "The Skyline," Mumford praised Wright's "conception of a whole community" with "both a generous dream and rational plan," but privately he expressed to Wright that he preferred German housing solutions. The comment—a subtle forerunner of a split brewing between the two—troubled Wright.[31]

When pressed, left-leaning critics, like art historian Meyer Schapiro, attacked Broadacre City as naïve. Wright waffled and claimed with ambivalence that it was just a polemical ideal. Polemic or not, Broadacre City became a central focus for the rest of his career. The St. Mark's tower and the Modern Cathedral would also feature in the drawings of the Broadacre City as Wright would develop them over the next twenty years.[32]

Edgar Kaufmann not only helped to bring the Broadacre City model to fruition, but he also became Wright's first major client since Guthrie had commissioned him in the late 1920s. Kaufmann's charge to design a weekend home for himself, his wife Liliane, and son Edgar Jr. on a rustic site in rural Pennsylvania launched the creation of Fallingwater, a major monument of twentieth-century architecture.[33]

Whereas Guthrie had nourished dreamy visions, Kaufmann brought reverie into built reality. Intended as a family weekend home in Mill Run, Pennsylvania, the house had concrete cantilevered slabs protruded from rock over a waterfall, giving the house its name. A wealthy Jewish businessman's reaction to his exclusion from Waspy Pittsburgh society, a testament of vibrant interaction between architect and patron, and a demonstration of Wright's organic motifs expressed in concrete, native stone, and glass, the house became iconic. Within our staging of Wright as the champion of American modernism, Fallingwater represented Wright's ultimate domestic refutation of the International Style. Both Fallingwater and the typical International Style buildings had flat roofs, thin planar projections, cantilevers, glass, and steel—all synonyms for "modern architecture"—but the similarities end there. Fallingwater stands apart because it interacts with its site, protruding laterally from it. Even when an International Style building did engage its location, as did Mies's Tugendhat house in Brno, for example, no Functionalist building created an interface between building and setting with the vibrant color and texture of Fallingwater. And no domestic building of the International Style would equal its renown. Sensing its imminent importance, the Museum of Modern Art rushed to exhibit images of Fallingwater and published a photo study of it.[34]

A year after Wright exhibited Broadacre City in New York, the architect attracted his second major client, Herbert ("Hib") F. Johnson Jr., grandson of the founder of the S. C. Johnson & Son Company. The business had prospered during the Depression by selling Glo-Coat, a self-polishing floor wax, so in 1936, Johnson selected Wright to design his new administration buildings in Racine, Wisconsin.[35] Considered an icon today within the canon of modernism, the building's design straddled the streamlined American *moderne* style, and Wright's organic vernacular, apparent in its lotus-shaped columns and curved corners. The building's open plan was a forerunner of the modern office interior, and the details of Pyrex, brass, brick, and red concrete flooring created a sumptuous palate as grand as that of any traditional corporate headquarters. Wright would later add a research tower with the same curving motifs (though it would not prove successful as a functioning space for research chemists). For Hib Johnson and his wife, Wright also designed "Wingspread," at Wind Point, adjacent to Racine. The vast residence, organized as a pinwheel spinning around a three-story-high multi-hearth octagonal fireplace, was built of pink sandstone, red brick, and cypress. It was the most expensive residence he had yet built, enclosing 14,000 square feet in floor area, a size that dwarfed any scale for familial intimacy.[36]

A third significant client approached Wright in 1936, but from the modest end of the financial spectrum: Herbert Jacobs, a newspaperman in Madison, asked if Wright could design his family's home for $5,000. With the Willey house as his preliminary version, Wright unveiled the Jacobs house as the first pure, built Usonian house, a model of economy adapted for the social changes of the late Depression and informed by sensitive use of evolving technology while still tying the house to its site. It was, in brief, the answer to his quest for *the* standard home for middle-class America.[37]

The revenue from design fees had allowed Wright to return with family and apprentices to the Arizona desert in the winters of 1935 and 1936. The following year, 1937, they camped out as they had at Ocatillo, on Maricopa Mesa, east of Scottsdale, Arizona, and Wright bought a mesa of several hundred acres below McDowell Peak. The planning began for Taliesin West, the Fellowship's winter home. After site preparation, construction of buildings began in 1939. Like all of Wright's homes, it served as a testing ground for design, and in this case one that melded organic architecture and the Fellowship's lifestyle. From then onward, Wright and the Fellowship made the pilgrimage twice yearly between Taliesin in Wisconsin and Taliesin West in Arizona. They spent summer and fall in the former, and winter and spring in the latter.[38]

Wright had gone from pariah to patriarch, appearing as if he were the Establishment itself while simultaneously acting as its gadfly. *Life* magazine published Wright's work and his comments almost annually from 1938 onward. He not only had a following, he had fans. In the early 1940s, Gertrude Kerbis, a student at the University of Wisconsin at Madison, was so inspired by an article about Wright in *Life* that she hitchhiked to Taliesin and sneaked into the building. Enchanted by its rooms, she hid in the house and spent the night undetected. When she awoke, she recalled later, "I had decided I was going to be an architect." Kerbis had a long and successful career.[39]

One shift in this relentless progress toward celebrity status in architecture took place when Wright shifted his allegiance from the *Architectural Record* to the *Architectural Forum,* under the editorship of Howard Myers. Time Inc. took over publishing the *Forum* in 1937, transforming the venerable magazine into a major proponent of modern architecture. It became the next major vehicle for disseminating Wright's work—and for further burnishing his persona. The magazine declared Wright "the year's most inventive architect" and would use his status to promote its thematic agenda for 1938.[40]

In January, the *Forum* published a special edition—handsomely produced and spiral bound—written and designed entirely by Wright. The issue provided a compendium of the architect's building philosophy, and included over twenty new and unpublished works, as well as a bibliography and an anthology of quotations from his favorite writers and inspirations, Thoreau and Whitman. It was as if Wright had in his pocket his own mini-publisher, willing to display and promote his work, as he wanted it, around the country. Wright was now effectively in control of his own myth—as his detractors pointed out. Here was the self he had created.[41]

Immediately after the special issue of the *Forum* appeared, *Time* magazine put Wright on the cover of its January 17, 1938, issue, pronouncing him to be "the greatest architect of the 20th Century." (Almost a year later, *Time* made Adolf Hitler "Man of the Year.") Launched in 1923, *Time* was the first national weekly news magazine, designed to communicate that news by means of individual personality. Framed by the magazine's iconic red border, Wright was the first architect (indeed the first artist) to make the cover. In the color photograph by Valentino Sara, he looks vibrant and youthful, his head turned slightly, his eyes sparkling and playful. Behind him hangs a beautiful colored perspective of Fallingwater, and to his right is a *Pang Tang,* a funerary Chinese sculpture, from his personal collection.[42]

The *Time* article appeared under the heading "Science: Usonian Architect." "Last week the significance to modern architecture of Frank Lloyd Wright's new buildings was recognized in an issue of the *Architectural Forum* which broke all precedents for that magazine," the essay began. Wright was clearly interviewed for the profile piece. His diplomacy and self-curation comes through: "His obvious and arrogant courage," the article stated, "has the abstract indestructability of a triangle." The article proceeded with a general overview, one that Wright had amplified to burnish the glint of success: "In California, Texas, Wisconsin, Minnesota and Pennsylvania superb new buildings have grown from his plans."

Time's positioning of Wright in the public eye was more accurate: "To the U.S. man-in-the-street 15 years ago, the name Frank Lloyd Wright meant, if anything, the builder of a hotel in Tokyo which by some engineering magic withstood the great earthquake of 1923. To the U.S. man-in-the-subway, his name was associated with the scandalous episodes ground from the inhuman interest mill of the tabloid newspapers." But the perception had changed. American architects who took up the International Style had realized what European architects had long understood—that Wright was "a master spirit." The article described his *Autobiography* as combining "magnificent self-revelation with the most stimulating discussion of architecture ever heard in the U.S."

The standard bio followed. It began with the conventional stories of family origins, childhood, and the success of the Prairie period. The article then outlined the downtimes of the 1920s after the Taliesin murders and gave an overview of the problematic 1920s. "Since then, bobbing up for the third time," the article continued, "Frank Lloyd Wright had done perhaps his most amazing work," proceeding to mention the St. Mark's tower and the San Marco resort as "more radical and inventive than any even proposed in functionalist Europe." The projects had never gotten off the ground because of the Depression. Ocatillo, "Wright's desert camp of canvas and boxwood," was described as "one of his most brilliant pieces of geometrical design." (The camp had vanished shortly after construction, but that detail mattered little.) Wright was triumphant, the article continued, with the Johnson Wax Administration Building, which "had been built like an expensive watch" and loaded with astounding technical innovations, from its skinny "dendriform" columns to its horizontal glass tubing and its ventilation, achieved "through two circular ducts or 'nostrils' rising through the building." Although critics might cite the building's cost overruns as a defect, *Time* assured its readers "out of more than 150 clients, only three or four have been seriously dissatisfied over money or anything else." The source of this figure was undocumented.

The coverage concluded with *Time* pointing to the Jacobs house in Madison, Wisconsin, as Exhibit A and Broadacre City as Exhibit B in Wright's new vision for America, Usonia. They appraised the creator of this vision without reservation: "Gracious, mischievous and immaculate at 68, Frank Lloyd Wright has little of the patriarch about him except his fine white hair." Here he was in the "'centre line' of Usonian independence that runs through Thoreau and Whitman."

While *Time* missed the mark slightly—Wright, who still gave out an erroneous birth date, was indeed a patriarch and actually seventy years old—it implied pivotal questions. If Wright aligned himself with nineteenth-century figures Thoreau and Whitman, what relevance did he have to U.S. culture as the world appeared to be coming apart? And, beyond the reputation of the man as a personality, how influential was his work in America and around the globe?

The account in place by the end of the 1930s would remain relatively unchanged for decades. An amalgam of Wright's *Autobiography,* Woollcott's *New Yorker* profile, and *Time's* recognition, it drew on and reiterated his self-created version of his life and career. Wright only needed to embroider the edges. Woollcott's pronouncement of Wright as America's only living genius had been confirmed. In the space of ten years, he had gone from Hollis, Queens, to global celebrity.

A year later, MoMA began planning the first comprehensive exhibition in America to cover Wright's entire career. Billed as "The Show to End All Shows," it was scheduled for the fall of 1940 and conceived—perhaps unsurprisingly at this point—in collaboration with Wright. As the installation approached, the museum announced Wright's arrival in a press release titled "Greatest Living Architect Comes to Museum of Modern Art." He was treated like royalty as he descended upon the institution on November 10, 1940, preceded by two trucks sent from Taliesin filled with eighteen large models. With the models came a crew of his apprentices to help "the Master install the exhibition which will do honor to a great and living prophet in his own time and country." Wright's exhibition, on view from November 13, 1940, to January 5, 1941, was part of a duo of major fall shows on "Great Americans," the other being "D. W. Griffith, American Film Master." The juxtaposition implied that architecture existed on equal footing with film, perhaps the most transformative invention of the twentieth century and certainly the most dominant in the popular imagination. The press release touted Wright's "creative freshness" and "perennial youth."[43]

The combination of fact and fantasy fixed the myth of Frank Lloyd Wright in place, though the catalogue intended for the exhibition lay unpublished. Hitchcock reviewed the exhibition in his most balanced and insightful writing to date. "The size of the present show is worthy of Wright's importance," Hitchcock wrote in the scholarly *Art Bulletin*. "But its intelligibility is inadequate." Why, he asked, was Wright's work, though famous, hard for people to understand? In answering the question, Hitchcock pointed to the differences between the long-established early work in the Prairie style, the "decorative work" of the middle period, the "excessively fantastic" designs of the late 1920s, and the comfortable modernity of his recent projects. This diversity of aesthetics, paired with dispersed locales, made Wright's canon hard to grasp as a whole. "These are all to the eastern critic very far away," Hitchcock noted. He also faulted the exhibition for using original drawings, particularly perspective sketches. His graphic techniques appealed to the connoisseur, but the sketches were unintelligible to the public. Photographs and floor plans, as Hitchcock and Johnson had shown at the International Style show, were the way to illustrate modern architecture.[44]

To Wright, the inadequacies of the exhibition were only annoyances. The exhibition confirmed him as a star whose work would frequently be displayed in New York. From 1932 to 1959, his work was exhibited in seventeen venues across the city. Ten of those took place at MoMA, making him the museum's most exhibited architect.[45]

Wright could continue to rely on Henry-Russell Hitchcock for support. While Philip Johnson found Wright irritating and promoted Mies van der Rohe as the champion of modern architecture, Hitchcock grew from being an initial skeptic of Wright's work to a historian with expertise, culminating in his writing *In the Nature of Materials: The Buildings of Frank Lloyd Wright, 1887–1941*. Working closely with Wright, who supplied both the title and the details, Hitchcock assembled four hundred illustrations and pithy textual analyses loaded with insights. The book became the standard text on the architect for the next forty years; generations of architecture students would learn about Wright from it. However, it had two shortcomings: the black-and-white illustrations failed to convey the integral color palette of Wright's architecture, so its sensuality and connection to nature remained elusive; and because it ended with 1941, the book gave the impression that Wright's career after that was, with the exception of the Guggenheim Museum, of little interest.[46]

Hitchcock also attempted to narrate Wright's influence abroad from 1910 to 1925 in an article in *Parnassus*. "But," he noted, "it is a matter which ought to be pursued further." Though often cited later, the article could not benefit from unraveling Wright's Wasmuth saga, which recasts Wright's influence in Europe and Europe's influence on him.[47]

In 1941, Hitchcock's publisher, Duell, Sloan and Pearce, published the first anthology of Wright's own writings, *Frank Lloyd Wright on Architecture*. Edited by Frederick Gutheim, the book compiled versions of Wright's original manuscripts. Gutheim, who had studied at the Universities of Wisconsin and Chicago, had long admired Wright and would continue to promote his works.[48]

In the early 1940s, nothing appeared to stand in Wright's way—except the war that was already consuming Europe and lurking on the country's horizon. Wright was an isolationist. He had earlier told a London audience not to worry about Hitler. Wright had supported the America First Committee and was enthusiastic about Charles Lindbergh and Henry Ford, who were famously pro-Nazi and anti-Semitic. Wright himself parroted a pathetic anti-Semitism, as seen in tracts he wrote in *Christian Century*. By the time the United States entered the war on December 17, 1940, his apprentices all knew that Wright virulently opposed conscription. "Over his dead body" would they go to war.[49]

Though his political position may have come from personal conviction, other factors were at work. Wright was aware that with war, he would lose clients and new commissions. At the outbreak of the conflict, his architectural commissions had been booming. In the years since the founding of the Fellowship, he had received commissions for seventy-five houses as well as a nonresidential commission. By the end of 1940, Wright had more projects in progress than ever. After Pearl Harbor, however, the war reduced his commissions.[50]

Wright also saw that a draft for the war could deplete him of the workforce on which he had become dependent. He would be shorthanded to implement a new vision he'd been outlandishly proposing, to divide the whole United States into two new states, Usonia and Usonia South, with "pro-war" New York and Washington, D.C., "quarantined into "New England." Furthermore, if America entered the war, it would strip the country of the resources needed to turn the "country into an architect-governed Usonia."[51]

Twenty-five apprentices protested to the local draft board, which turned down all their requests for deferments. Despite claims that Wright was attempting to do war work with proposals for defense housing, that the creation of Broadacre City was in the national interest, or, finally, that his apprentices deserved a farm exemption, the local draft board began calling them up. Nineteen were in uniform by 1942, but others objected. Over the next two years, four objectors were arrested and jailed, including Jack Howe, Wright's chief draftsman, who spent almost three years incarcerated in Minnesota.[52]

The war had other immediate impacts. Gas rationing prevented the annual migration to Arizona, but more serious was the FBI's beginning to investigate the architect's "seditious" activity. Wright's antiwar stance also created a bitter schism with Lewis Mumford, his friend and advocate in New York. "Are you still in the Neville Chamberlain period?" Mumford chided in one letter, referring to the British prime minister following an appeasement strategy in dealing with Hitler. Wright wrote another letter in which he used "gangster" to refer not to Hitler but to those who opposed him. This was too much for Mumford. "Period politics are as bad as period architecture." The friendship shattered. "The Chinese say it well," Wright wrote Mumford. "He who runs out of ideas first strikes the first blow." The bitterness of the rift heightened for Mumford when his son, Geddes, died in combat in Italy in October 1943. Wright and Mumford did not speak to each other for ten years.[53]

Meanwhile, Wright's relationships with his other major New York friends continued but diminished in intensity. As his career and reputation soared, some of his companions faltered. After a long tenure at St. Mark's Church in-the-Bowery and rocky last years, Guthrie retired to his home in Stamford, Connecticut, and began writing his own autobiography. Perpetually verbose, he produced several drafts, but none were published. By the mid-1930s, many had considered him the father of modern sacred dance, and his daughter Phoebe Guthrie toured the St. Mark's dance troupe to perform at Protestant churches and the Chautauqua circuit of adult education gatherings.[54]

Wright and Guthrie remained in touch. "Yours is perpetual spring with daffodillies / Most of the others are just old dull sillies," Guthrie crooned in a poem to "Frank Lloyd Wright, fair Laird of Taliesin," which concluded, "Yours, on my birthday writ / With love and pride, and not a spit of wit." Over the subsequent years, Wright frequently sent Guthrie invitations to visit Taliesin. Their warmth for each other persisted as Guthrie faded into poor health and obscurity. He died on December 9, 1944. At St. Mark's, he had set the tone of the East Village's future as a draw for artists and iconoclasts, and a vital center for the counterculture movement twenty years later.[55]

Not a spit of wit—It's hard to imagine how such an unorthodox and controversial life could be encapsulated. The *New York Times* portrayed this "Crusader for Candor" as a "vibrant speaker, a poet and a writer on many subjects." A champion of the unorthodox, the underdog locked in perpetual tension with his vestry, he represented the "introduction of a black sheep into the churchyard" that "attracted thousands of people in the city and brought many into the church." A black sheep in the big city—a fitting description for both the rector and his architect friend. Wright's iconoclastic status had positive overtones, but the local *Churchman*'s obituary called Guthrie "a disturbing genius" and found him a troubling figure.[56]

Guthrie's role in Wright's personal and professional life slipped into oblivion. He had been a figure whose intimacy with Wright had no equal. From the 1910s onward, he told Wright the brutal truth as he saw it, from the detriments of Wright's adultery to the arrogance of his position as an architect. Fighting his own battles against the Episcopal establishment, Guthrie's life had matched Wright's public drama. He was also the most esoteric of Wright's friends and clients, and his pantheistic views of universal religion paralleled the exoticism of Wright's wife, Olgivanna. In Guthrie, Wright found a kindred spirit—a student of native American ritual, of Eastern mysticism, and of archetypal symbolism—and, unlike most of his clients, a knowledgeable devotee of the global history of architecture. Like Wright, he was intellectually dexterous, writing plays, lectures, treatises, books, and hundreds of sermons. His zeal lead to ridiculousness, noted by his critics. But his vision catapulted Wright at the exact moment he needed it in the 1920s. He believed Wright had a divine gift for creativity and, despite self-defeating tendencies, he did everything he could to enable it. Guthrie, who'd washed up on the shores of Manhattan in the early 1910s, transplanted from the oddities of Scotland, Tennessee, and peripatetic wanderings, played out the whole drama of his career in New York. In that drama, and his relentless quest for success as he saw it, he embodied New York. And in that embodiment, he showed Wright that the city was a place for dreams and ambition, a platform and battleground for artistic vision.

Aleck Woollcott also faded from Wright's life, but with notoriety. He too had been the subject of a *New Yorker* profile. In the spring of 1939, after his column "Shouts and Whispers" had concluded, the magazine published a spread over three weeks about the man. Written by Wolcott Gibbs, the then-current theater critic, its title was "Profile: Big Nemo." The subtitle was Latin for "nobody" and recalled "Little Nemo," the early-century cartoon character who fantasized grand adventures, recounted them, but woke up in bed realizing he'd gone nowhere. Gibbs's portrait was a fusillade against the older critic's narcissism; following Woollcott's biography, the article presented a manipulative man with a grotesque "royal stomach." Woollcott came off as a brilliant yet revolting figure who in the end had nothing of substance to say. Among the milder assessments, Gibbs concluded, "his greatest success will always lie, as it did when he was an actor, in his tireless, eloquent, and extraordinarily diverse performance of the character called, Alexander Woollcott."[57]

Though Woollcott used his soapbox to praise his friends, he often turned his verbal rapier on others, and now his own magazine had done the same to him. Deeply hurt, he wrote his friend and former editor Harold Ross: "To me you are dead. Hoping and believing I soon will be the same." By 1939, when the profile appeared, Woollcott had taken a hiatus from writing and was spending time on an island he had bought as a retreat. Still gluttonous, his health suffered, but he pursued his passions, returning to acting and radio broadcasting. On stage he acted in such unmemorable plays as *Brief Moment* and *Wine of Choices,* though he had the title role in *The Man Who Came to Dinner,* George S. Kaufman and Moss Hart's play in which Woollcott lampooned himself. He died of a heart attack during a radio broadcast on January 23, 1943. Here was a man whose voice became familiar to millions on his *Town Crier* broadcast, whose quick wit peppered the pages of the *Times* and the *World,* a man who earned riches through the zest of his personality alone. The *New Yorker* softened when it published Woollcott's obituary in "Talk of the Town." "His famous ability to coil and strike was part of his infinite charm," it recollected, "and his quarrelsome and unwholesome tongue was a foil to his good deeds, which were many and which he jealously kept secret while painstakingly publicizing his vices. . . . It is a great consolation to us who feel his loss very much, that he died with his boots on."[58] Woollcott had championed Wright at the critical moment in his emergence from the doldrums. He helped put Wright on the map in New York and, via his *New Yorker* profile, across the country. They had become close friends, each regaling in and enjoying the outsized ego of the other, like kindred spirits. So different—the urbane showman and the Midwestern outsider—but bonded in their idiosyncrasies. Without Woollcott, Wright's ascent would have been slower. Their mutual admiration bordered on tenderness.

With the wartime schism with Mumford and the deaths of Guthrie and Woollcott, Wright had lost three figures—all of them New Yorkers—who had played major roles in rescuing him during the doldrums of the late 1920s. But a redemption from so many losses was in progress, a commission for the most important building of his career, and once again New York would be its source.

12

ZENITH

Frank Lloyd Wright received a letter from Hilla Rebay on June 1, 1943, just days before his seventy-sixth birthday. "Could you ever come to New York and discuss with me a building for our collection of non-objective paintings?" "I feel that each of these great masterpieces should be organized into space and only you so it seems to me would test the possibilities to do so." Baroness Hildegard (Hilla) Rebay von Ehrenwiesen, formerly a painter and, as of 1930, curator of the Solomon R. Guggenheim Foundation's collection of nonobjective art, went on to say she had had seen the exhibit Mendelsohn had arranged in Berlin and had met Maginel in Greenwich Village. And she had read Wright's books. All of this gave her the sense that for the project she had in mind, "no one else would do." What she needed was "a fighter, a lover of space, an originator, and a wise man."[1]

How could Wright not have been taken by Rebay's letter? "I appreciate your appreciation," he replied. "I would like to do something such as you suggest for your worthy foundation." Within a month, the contract for the project arrived at Taliesin.[2]

Such was the start of the Guggenheim Museum, the longest project of Wright's career, surpassing the Imperial Hotel with its protracted genesis and challenges. The eighty-two-year-old Solomon Guggenheim, Rebay, and Wright combined forces to produce a landmark of modernist culture. Many would argue that this building fundamentally altered how architects saw themselves and their role. In the fifteen years following the first contact, Wright's career would ascend to pinnacles few artists achieve, particularly in late age. The Wright of the last decades is largely the figure that the public thinks of today: arrogant, brilliant, larger than life, and instantly recognizable, with his long silver hair, sparkling eyes, and impish smile, offering a caustic comment or clever aside, or ode of self-praise. Wright's late period gives us the Wright who appeared on a U.S. postage stamp. Within its frame, the circle of our story moves toward closure.[3]

The new museum needed a program, a budget, and a site. Rebay provided the program: a Museum of Non-Objective Painting for a collection housed in temporary quarters. Solomon R. Guggenheim provided an initial budget of $1 million; it would rise to $3.5 million when finally completed. But no location was specified. One proposed site was between 52nd and 53rd Streets near the new Museum of Modern Art, but competition between Solomon Guggenheim and the Rockefeller family, which was both building Rockefeller Center and supporting MoMA, made that too close for comfort. Rebay, in particular, thought that MoMA, under the directorship of Alfred Barr Jr., was "already dated in so many ways."[4]

The rivalry between Guggenheim and MoMA was adversarial. The institutions were competing for primacy as the purveyors of modern art, with differing agendas and differing collections. Wright also took sides. Despite MoMA's interest in capitalizing on his work through its exhibitions, he saw MoMA as his enemy, particularly as Philip Johnson increasingly controlled its curatorial direction for architecture.

The location of Guggenheim's museum therefore took on singular importance. Wright, who was contractually charged with finding the site, took advantage of the familiarity he'd developed with New York and its environs over the previous decades. For specific advice, he turned to Robert Moses, his distant cousin and the all-powerful head of the parks commission.[5] In July 1943, Wright suggested to Guggenheim, with Moses's encouragement, an eight-acre site in Riverdale in the Bronx. Facing the Hudson River, it would be part of the Henry Hudson Memorial Park. Locating the building in nature, he told Guggenheim, would be "a genuine relief from the cinder heap old New York is bound to become." Wright added that visitors would access the site by "helicopter and motor travel," which would "become quite universal after the war." By proposing this site, Wright showed that his ideal preference was for building a solitary object set in nature. His noting the public's increased mobility reflected the principles he'd developed for Broadacre City and fit with Moses's plans for directing population growth to the area as an aspect of the changing face of the metropolitan region and the increasing density of Manhattan (fig. 53). Other sites recommended by Moses were considered: between Madison Avenue and 36th Street near the Morgan Library, and a lot on Park Avenue between 69th and 70th Streets. But the selection remained up in the air.[6]

Though he had no confirmed site, Wright began searching for the concept and shape of the building. The concept would come early and stick, but development took time. Wright began with a hexagonal floor plan. He then turned to the example he'd previously developed as a primary form sitting in nature: the Automobile Objective for Gordon Strong in the mid-1920s. The project, which Wright had stored in miniature in the Broadacre City model and retained in drawings, became the major source of what would follow. From late 1943 to early 1944, the museum was a spiral in the form of a ziggurat, the very figure that Gordon Strong dismissed as archaic and inorganic.

In an epiphany, Wright turned the ziggurat on its head to produce the defining image. He wrote the word backwards on a drawing—"taruggiz"—a witty way to show that the building itself had been inverted. To Wright, the form's very archaism suggested that it was primal, universal, and timeless, and by inverting the archetypal form, he opened it to new

Fig. 53 Manhattan, August 10, 1945.

meaning. The design would be refined in six versions over the next twelve years, but its basic concept as a spiral remained unchanged to create the upwardly swelling turban of ribbons we know today. Throughout these studies, color played a major role. Wright had his draftsman make perspective studies with the building colored pink, blue, peach, and red—anything but white, the standard non-color of the International Style.[7]

Progress continued while the country was at war. In March 1944 the Guggenheim Foundation purchased a lot on the south corner of Fifth Avenue at 89th Street; it would acquire the rest of the block between 88th and 89th Streets seven years later to provide the present configuration. Wright created an elaborate model that also showed the interior. He presented the Modern Gallery (the museum's working name between 1945 and 1952) to the public at the Plaza Hotel in New York on September 20, 1945 (fig. 54). The building, as modeled, filled the Fifth Avenue site, but the drum was located on the northwest corner of 89th Street and Fifth Avenue. Wright described the building as a spring and declared that after

Fig. 54 Wright, Hilla Rebay, and Solomon Guggenheim with model of the Guggenheim Museum, Plaza Hotel, 1945.

the first atom bomb hit New York, the building would not be destroyed: "It may be blown a few miles up in the air, but when it comes down it will bounce!"[8]

Institutional changes began affecting Wright and the design process. The Guggenheim Foundation bought more art between 1948 and 1949, expanding the collection. Solomon Guggenheim died in 1949. Hilla Rebay resigned under pressure in 1951 as director of the foundation. Over the years her relationship with Wright had become strained, as she often expressed ambivalence and indecision about Wright's design moves. He increasingly felt that her "European" advisers and friends reduced her enthusiasm about him. She persistently pushed the work of the painter Rudolf Bauer and the Bauhaus artist László Moholy-Nagy, whom Wright bitterly disliked. Wright resisted and resented.

Harry Guggenheim, Solomon's nephew, became president of the Guggenheim board and thus the client for the project. James Johnson Sweeney was named director to succeed Rebay in 1952, at which time the museum's name was changed from the Museum of Non-Objective Painting to the Solomon R. Guggenheim Museum, its current name.

Sweeney's appointment was an ominous event for Wright; Sweeney had come from being a curator at MoMA, enemy territory. The *Bauhauslers*—German émigré architects like Walter Gropius and Marcel Breuer, among others, and their promotors at MoMA—were increasingly attacked by Wright, who saw them as opponents of his museum.

And Wright viewed Philip Johnson, who was at best ambivalent about Wright, and Hitchcock, who'd so publicized Wright, as partisans. He caustically wrote Hitchcock that as Gropius "is a scientist, not an architect nor an artist, so you are an historian, not an interpreter nor an artist." They were a dangerous threat to the American agenda: "As Bauhaus propaganda goes (now), the day of the Great Architect in America is over," Wright wrote Hitchcock. "We Americans now by way of Hitchcock and Johnson, sell ourselves to European standardizations and team work of plan factories when the great Architecture of the individual free should be our real concern."[9]

Work on the design development continued in the midst of these changes—and threats. Wright had flipped the drum to its current location at the southwestern corner, nestled off the corner of East 88th Street, where it would be built. He finalized the drawings in 1952, but major challenges lay in the future to get the building constructed.

Returning to stay in New York was a necessity: the Guggenheim project needed his presence. Olgivanna and Wright had been staying at the Plaza Hotel whenever they visited New York for over twenty years. By 1953 the couple were spending so much time there that they began to lease rooms in the Plaza.

In the spring of 1954, Wright and Olgivanna began redesigning their New York home, a double suite in the northeast corner of the Plaza Hotel. Hollywood film producer David O. Selznick and wife had moved out, and the Wrights moved in (fig. 55). They removed the last vestiges of French detailing by Christian Dior and began making their own renovations, which occurred between June and December, in exacting detail. Red velvet curtains fronted the windows. The shades' pull cords were weighted with clear crystal spheres. The curtains framed the circular mirrors that Wright had inserted in the existing window arches and pulled them forward to conceal indirect lighting behind them. Gold Japanese papers set in panels with pale rose borders activated the walls. Furnishings included tables, easels, and chairs lacquered black, with red edges. Their colors complemented the purple upholstery and the table where Wright had placed a Korean dragon jar from his collection. And,

Fig. 55 "Taliesin East," the Wrights' suite at the Plaza Hotel, New York, c. 1954.

of course, into one corner he inserted his beloved baby grand piano. Howard Myers, their friend and editor at *Architectural Forum,* called it "Taliesin the Third"; others aptly called it "Taliesin East."[10]

Wright loved the Plaza's historic interiors and esteemed Henry Hardenbergh, the original architect. "Whenever we were seated for lunch in the Edwardian Room," Olgivanna recalled, "Mr. Wright never failed to point out to me the beauty of the painted ceiling. We occasionally went to the Persian Room which originally was decorated by Joseph Urban, his colleague and friend." Changes to these spaces annoyed Wright. He complained when the hotel removed frescoes from the lobby, closed the glass ceiling of the Palm Court, and covered the Italian marble mosaics with carpets.[11]

In spring of 1954, when Wright arrived for his prolonged stay, McCarthyism was in the air, and the dismissal of three Hunter College professors with communist leanings made the front page of the *New York Times*. The city had emerged from the stall of the mid-1940s and was entering a postwar boom that would change its architecture fundamentally and reveal it as the global capital. Air France advertised nonstop flights between New York and Mexico for $99. Fifth Avenue became home to "airline alley," a series of storefront offices for the booming commercial airline industry; these were often lush retail spaces where one could buy a ticket in style. Gone were any versions of the playful polychromy, textured surfaces, and complex massing of the Art Deco and *moderne* buildings. And ornament? Nonexistent except for a rare exception in the work of Edward Durell Stone. The cost of elaborate detailing became a burden. The Depression and war led architects to lose confidence in their early efforts to define an independent American modern architecture. The shift by practitioners from prewar to postwar—not limited to New York—was often a shocking turnaround. In the late 1950s, E. J. Kahn, who throughout the 1930s built the "wedding cake" structures of midtown Manhattan, would design, with his partner Robert Allan Jacobs, the Frederick Douglass Houses. Spanning four city blocks in the Upper West Side, this low-income rental housing comprised a monolithic series of brick structures, blocky and varying in heights. Similarly, the Alfred E. Smith Houses, designed six years earlier, featured twelve brick buildings, each following the same cruciform plan. Mass housing in Europe provided the precedents.

If any single building complex caught the moment of where modern architecture was heading, it was the United Nations Headquarters. Finished in 1952, it was designed by an international committee with American Wallace K. Harrison as leader. The ensemble of buildings situated a slab-like skyscraper and a squat, concave secretariat building alongside the East River. Wright had no role in designing this symbol of postwar global collaboration. Instead, Le Corbusier's ideas transmitted (and diluted) through followers like the Brazilian architect Oscar Niemeyer had triumphed (fig. 56).[12]

The UN complex revealed the parallel universes of architecture as the 1950s opened: Wright in his organic domain, along with a cluster of young practitioners who were developing a distinctive midcentury version of America modern, and the rest of modern architecture, which embraced the International Style as the new vehicle of corporate identity and the future guide for addressing the "crisis of the city" through urban renewal. With the 1952 completion of Skidmore, Owings & Merrill's Lever House, the "Internationalist" model of the skyscraper was gaining ground (fig. 57). Buildings were boxy. Sleekness and austerity were in.

Wright arrived in New York during this transformation not in secret, as he had on his first visit in 1909, but as America's first celebrity architect. Jane King Hession and Debra Pickrel in their book *The Plaza Years, 1954–1959,* have so effectively documented the period that the details need only be outlined here. Clearly this "Ingenious Giant," as Woollcott named him, was astride the city. From 1954 to 1959, Wright's life at the Plaza Hotel was a whirlwind. It was a time that combined entertaining celebrities, nurturing Wright's public profile, and overseeing not only the Guggenheim, but other projects. From this combination of residence, office, and studio, Wright held court, conducted business, and monitored his projects.[13]

The Wrights entertained celebrities and potential clients, from newlyweds Marilyn Monroe and Arthur Miller to King Faisal II of Iraq. They too were stellar figures with egos writ large. At an architectural luncheon honoring Wright in 1952, Wright declared, "I early decided that an ar-

Fig. 56 United Nations Complex, New York, 1955.

chitect must be either honestly arrogant or hypocritically humble." He had taken this stance early in his career, and if it had not always helped him get clients, it fit perfectly with the persona he projected from New York in the 1950s.[14]

Fig. 57 Lever House, 390 Park Avenue, New York.

Television moguls pounced on the dapper, photogenic, and uninhibited Wright; the octogenarian became the subject of numerous appearances and interviews. This phenomenon introduced him to millions of Americans as a media figure, the only architect whose name the public knew. The roster of Wright's appearances ranged from Hugh Downs's *Conversations with Elder Wise Men* for NBC in May 1953, to Mike Wallace's two-part interview with the ninety-year-old Wright in September 1957. Wright even appeared on *What's My Line,* the television show on which blindfolded celebrities tried to guess the occupation of the mystery guest. These media appearances have allowed succeeding generations to see the man and hear his voice in his advanced years.[15]

Olgivanna described a typical week as "filled with engagements," such as a personalized tour of the *International Festival of Art* at the Seagram Building, dinner with Harry Guggenheim and wife, visits from Carl Sandburg, and various interviews. The city energized the couple. In one NBC broadcast interview, Olgivanna described her husband on camera: "Mr. Wright looked noble and handsome, his talk was like fresh mountain streams."[16]

Olgivanna recalled lovingly the "little things" of their New York life. "I also hear the pigeons outside on the sill of the Plaza windows—forever cooing and fighting each other. I hear Mr. Wright saying, 'Look at that speckled pigeon—he is the boss—the rest are afraid of him.' And we watched him first strut on the thin iron rail, then take off for flight over the traffic signals among the blackened skyscrapers."[17]

Living in New York also allowed Wright to escape the underlying tension that had settled into the Taliesin Fellowship. Now in his late eighties, suffering from cataracts, he relied increasingly on Jack Howe, his chief draftsman, and Curtis Besinger, Howe's assistant, to execute the designs he sketched out. Olgivanna ran the day-to-day operations when they were at the Taliesins with an emphasis on the Fellowship's members participating in the "Work," her Gurdjieffian principles of dance, movement, and spiritual activities. A schism developed between fellows focused on studio production under Wright and those devoted more to Mrs. Wright and her exotic rituals. The cohesion of the early Fellowship dissolved, as did the fluidity of the design process. Because Wright continuously wanted to change his designs even after they were set in final drawings, he disrupted due dates and workflow. To reduce this problem, the fellows began producing multiple sets of drawings, with ones he could alter and others kept as a record of the changes.[18]

Accentuating Wright's presence in New York was the appearance of a major retrospective of his work, *Sixty Years of Living Architecture.* Created

by Wright and executed by his apprentices, the exhibition was intended to be a comprehensive multimedia event that would compensate for
the shortcomings of the MoMA exhibition of 1940. It had previewed in
Philadelphia in January 1951 and then moved to the Palazzo Strozzi in
Florence, where Wright was made an honorary citizen. After it toured
Europe, this extravaganza opened in New York in October 1953 (fig.
58). Wright installed it in two parts, an exhibition pavilion and a full-
scale model Usonian house, both erected on the site of the Guggenheim
Museum before its construction had started (figs. 59, 60). The Usonian
home, the only house Wright built in Manhattan, would be the centerpiece of this and subsequent traveling exhibitions. Transcending models,
drawings, and photographs, the house, which could be disassembled and
shipped, gave the public a chance to experience a Wrightian home.[19]

The show opened to widespread press coverage. Mumford was an obvious reviewer; based in New York, he was at the pinnacle of his career as a
social and cultural critic. Wright had tried to mend their rift several times,
pleading with Mumford to visit him at Taliesin, but Mumford declined.
Mumford still saw him, as he wrote to a friend, as "arrogant, violent, des-
potic," and "high-handed." "I've missed you Lewis," the architect mused.
"Yours *is* an Emersonian mind *but on your own terms.*"[20] Mumford softened

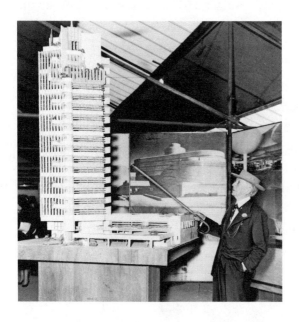

Fig. 58 Exhibition
installation, *Sixty Years of
Living Architecture*, 1953.
Wright is standing with
the Price tower model, the
former tower for St. Mark's
Church in-the-Bowery.

Fig. 59 (opposite, top)
Entrance to *Sixty Years of
Living Architecture* exhibi-
tion, New York, 1953.

Fig. 60 (opposite, bottom)
Usonian model house,
*Sixty Years of Living
Architecture* exhibition,
New York, 1953.

in replying: "The way in which you continue to flourish, like the Biblical bay tree, gives me immense pleasure," he wrote. "Though the honors that are now pouring into your lap are belated they at least give some measure of the mark you left upon all of us."[21]

Their friendship never revived. Wright personally toured Mumford through the *Sixty Years of Living Architecture* exhibition, but a chasm remained. After the visit, Mumford wrote in his memoirs that while he appreciated Wright's work over that of Le Corbusier's, he "realized as never before how the insolence of genius sometimes repelled me." When Mumford reviewed the exhibition in the *New Yorker,* he described the buildings as monuments to Wright's ego, not in the service of others. Wright responded angrily, calling Mumford an "ignoramus."[22]

At the same time, Wright pressed forward with his publishing agenda. By the early 1950s when Ben Raeburn, owner of Horizon Press, became the publisher of his collected writings, Wright found another collaborator who produced his work in impressive formats and with handsome graphics. The Prairie period became cohesive when Grant Carpenter Manson published *Frank Lloyd Wright to 1910: The First Golden Age.* Along with Hitchcock's book, Manson's became a standard reference for decades. Wright now had both word and image under his control, effectively allowing for the historicizing of himself while he was still very much alive. His own books proliferated, but many of his publications repeated or republished earlier material sometimes to the point of boredom or confusing a reader about what was new and what was repetition. Two books, however, provided valuable points of reference at the end of a long career. *A Testament* (1957) was less windy than usual. One part synthesized important recollections as he approached ninety. Included in his reveries was a return to his old love of the primal, his attraction to archetypes as they existed across time in global culture: "I remember how as a boy, primitive American architecture—Toltec, Aztec, Mayan, Inca—stirred my wonder, excited my admiration.... Mighty primitive abstractions of man's nature. . . . Architecture intrinsic to Time, Place and Man." Ever pushing a polemic, the second part presented with a foldout illustration for his vision for a mile-high skyscraper, "The Illinois," intended for Chicago. Facetious but worked out in detail, it included atomic elevators and showed a dramatic evolution in scale and technology from the St. Mark's tower. Thumbing his nose at Chicago architects, he wanted to show the direction architects should be going.[23]

Wright's last book, *The Living City,* published in 1958, focused on Broadacre City. A rewritten version of *The Disappearing City* and *When Democracy Builds,* it featured Broadacre City in its most ideal and idyllic form. In Wright's final vision, he updated the plan and added drawings to show still unbuilt projects and the latest modes of transport, including one-person helicopters. The primal role of the St. Mark's tower for Wright was clear when in the final drawings of Broadacre City for *The Living City,* he restored the building to its original St. Mark's appearance.[24]

Looking at the updating of Broadacre City returns us to consider Wright's sense of urban space and therefore New York. "Every city is after-the-fact an overgrown village. No city is deliberately planned," Wright told his wife. His plan was simply to replace the function of the city with a settlement in a pristine landscape. His urban interventions elsewhere—from Pittsburgh to Madison to Phoenix—took the form of megastructures. He made no plan for New York City. It was beyond redeeming yet still provided the stage set for great ideas and dreams. It was, as William R. Taylor had pointed out, a place where ideas were commerce, and those who generated them with bravado were its stars.[25]

In essence, Wright was an anti-urbanist. Despite later claims, he did not design America's cities. With few exceptions he designed complexes, civic centers, and some large buildings whose scale was urban, but he did not envision and focus on the urban totality as did Le Corbusier. For better or worse, the ideas of Le Corbusier—not Wright—propagated globally as modern icons of "renewal" from the postwar years until deep in the 1960s.[26]

In addition to commenting in interviews or lectures, Wright wrote relentlessly about the city, occasionally from the perspective of Taliesin West, which gave him some distance from his subject. One of his unpublished manuscripts begins, "The great city of New York, capital city of these United States, shows to all the Americas the danger of excess success." "Seen there is the fate of a charming old-time Knickerbocker village driven mad by big business." Noting that an article in *Time* magazine had quoted a successful New York skyscraper-broker as saying "the Slab's the thing," Wright replied, "Well, every graveyard, if it could, would say amen to that."[27]

Such attacks on the city—and there had been many over his long lifetime—served Wright well, as they confirmed his stance as a Romantic Outsider, a status in which he thrived. Approval and rejection worked hand in hand. He needed New York to play out his role as prophet and deliverer of Jeremiads. He understood that its machinery for publicity formed his most important creation: the architect himself as commodity. Wright became the first architect as a brand, leading the way for the star architects who followed in the late twentieth century.

The media—in all its dimensions—offered the avenue for stardom and self-promotion leading to the biggest stage Wright could command, and Gotham was its center. In addition to his own books, Wright turned to "shelter" magazines to disseminate his work. He became the most documented architect in history, with his appearances in mass-market publications dwarfing his frequent appearances in professional magazines. *House Beautiful,* newly energized and directed to homemakers, helped catapult Wright into the public sphere. Ironically, it was owned by the Hearst Corporation, successor to the Hearst newspapers that had vilified Wright in the 1920s. In 1955 *House Beautiful* published a special issue, "The Dramatic Story of Frank Lloyd Wright," featuring articles on his work (fig. 61). Elizabeth Gordon edited the issue and played a pivotal role in presenting the architect to the American middle-class public in the 1950s. She promoted "good design" and "better living" and created a variety of initiatives—from Pace Setter Houses to her Climate Control project—to that end. Wright had sent John deKoven Hill, who'd worked on the *Sixty Years* exhibition and was a favored Fellowship assistant and a skillful interior designer, to assist her at their offices at 572 Madison Avenue. Hill's presence as Wright's in-house advocate guaranteed a perfect product. Gordon saw Wright as the embodiment of American Style and the antidote to the European International Style.[28]

House Beautiful both solidified Wright's ideas and commodified him by promoting licensing partnerships. Riding the postwar economic rebound, "Wright, Inc." hit the market. Publications and partnerships led to visions of domestic interiors. A consumer could buy, for example, the Taliesin Ensemble, a compilation of fabrics, furniture, wall decorations, and other domestic goods. The Heritage-Henredon Company produced

Fig. 61 House Beautiful cover, November 1955.

interior furnishings, such as a square sideboard that was divided into a series of quadrants and framed by a key pattern resonant of Wright's ornament motifs. F. Schumacher & Sons produced a line of decorative fabrics and wallpapers in a spectrum running from "Leaf Green," to "Old Gold," and to "Coral," all advertised alongside the architect's own words. Martin-Senour Paints introduced the "Taliesin Palette" of thirty-six color swatches.[29]

With the availability of mass-produced commodities, Wright's own precepts for an organic architecture tailored to the specifics of client and site were thrown to the wind. He had encouraged this and yet sometimes was appalled by it, too. He was horrified at how Schumacher & Sons presented the "Taliesin Line" at the National Republican Club in New York City, and he lambasted the company's decorator as an "inferior desecrator." Wright's architecture was devolving into separate parts, but in its becoming merchandise, Wright achieved his long-held dream of supplying the design of the American democracy. Architecture *as building* was now substituted with the merchandise to fill and cover it. In so doing, Wright reached a new pinnacle of success even as his name broadened and extended what had taken him there. Just as the public identified Henry Ford with the generic automobile, they associated Wright with the generic American house.[30]

The source of Wright's licensing lay in his original incorporation in the late 1920s, when his friends took ownership of his assets to rescue him from bankruptcy. In 1940, the Frank Lloyd Wright Foundation, which still exists, took hold. In the 1950s, the foundation, with Wright as titular president, entered the world of merchandising in tune with the rise of Madison Avenue advertising and multinational corporations. In all these respects, Wright, though born in the middle of the nineteenth century, was a most modern man. A commercial success and glamorous figure, he was, finally, a true New Yorker. More than an artist or an architect, Wright had become a brand.[31]

Wright's presence in New York led to other commissions. He designed the Hoffman Automobile Showroom at Park Avenue and 56th Street that featured a display of Mercedes-Benz autos on a spiral ramp. He built the "Air House," a two-room inflatable structure for the United States

Rubber Company, as a display piece for the International Home Show at the New York Coliseum at Columbus Circle. For the real estate mogul William Zeckendorf, he designed a motel; it remained unbuilt. On Staten Island, Wright took an existing design and transformed it into the Cass house. Called "The Crimson Beech," it was intended to be a building type for those who wanted a Wright design but couldn't afford to commission the architect. As if the genie had escaped the bottle, a developer's project for a self-contained city of 7,500 on Ellis Island quickly emerged after Wright drew a sketch on a napkin. Other, more realistic commissions popped up in nearby Westchester County, New York, and Stamford, Connecticut.[32]

Harry Guggenheim approached Wright about designing a new type of sports pavilion for Belmont Park, the famous Long Island race track. The project encapsulated Wright's latest aesthetic predilection for gossamer roofs and steel cables in tension to create open, light, and airy structures (fig. 62). The Greater New York Racing Association preferred a traditional approach, however, questioning the project's "unsolved engineering problems." Wright was, per usual, indignant. Thirteen million dollars would provide sixty thousand comfortable seats and boxes, Wright claimed, all rationally arranged. The project would include innovations like heated and cooled floor slabs, a "plastic canopy electrically defrosted," natural ventilation, and ample toilets. His design was still turned down. In a huff, Wright announced, "Australia has taken the sketches home with my consent."[33]

Wright's return to New York—as a celebrity and international figure—facilitated the realization of his two dream projects of the 1920s that emanated from the city. Parked for two decades in the virtual world of Broadacre City, the Modern Cathedral and the tower for St. Mark's Church in-the-Bowery were finally realized as buildings in the 1950s, a testament to his tenacity.

The Modern Cathedral that Wright articulated for Guthrie represented much more than a utopian scheme in the history of architectural fantasies. At the scale Wright imagined—the tallest building in the world and large enough to contain one hundred thousand worshippers—the church would have obliterated blocks of Manhattan, and likewise

Fig. 62 Sports pavilion for Belmont Race Track, perspective view, 1956.

obliterated Wright's ambivalence about the city itself. As he worked out the details of its structure, programmed its functions, and colorized its atmosphere, the project had become a creative catharsis for an architect whose life had been dragged through the trenches for years. Wright reduced the original gargantuan scale of the building for the design of the Beth Sholom Synagogue in Elkins Park, Pennsylvania, in 1954 (fig. 63). As had the Reverend Guthrie, Rabbi Mortimer J. Cohen assumed the role of creative collaborator and client. After Cohen explained the tenets of Judaism, Wright turned its symbols into form: the volume recalled Mount Sinai, and primary geometric shapes, diced and polychromed, became the bimah and Ark of the Covenant. Wright used a massive steel tripod frame to support a double-layered roof of white glass and translucent fiberglass that filtered light to the interior. Some critics have dismissed the interior as kitsch. Maybe it is from a modernist perspective, but the building sits comfortably in its site and functions well for its community, filtering light into worship. It was dedicated in September 1959.[34]

From its inception, Wright had remained fixated on the tower for St. Mark's Church in-the-Bowery. He had fought for its realization even after the stock market crash and the onslaught of the Depression. But it too represented ideas that transcended the object itself and the status of merely an unbuilt project. In addition to its presence in his Broadacre City vision, Wright included its renderings and the building model in all of his

Fig. 63 Beth Sholom Synagogue, Elkins Park, Pennsylvania.

exhibitions. He was convinced that the taproot core with its suspended floors was a true innovation in building technology—all of his skyscraper designs would subsequently feature it. For Wright, the building would have not only prefigured all glass skyscrapers but replaced the International Style mode of building as a box of framed structural steel or grid of concrete columns supporting concrete floors.

In 1952, Wright found the opportunity to produce a version of the St. Mark's tower for the headquarters of the H. C. Price Company, an oil services enterprise in Bartlesville, Oklahoma (fig. 64). Wright mixed the St. Mark's apartments with rentable offices and added a commercial base for the showroom of the Public Service Company of Oklahoma, but he retained the basic strategy of the pinwheel and taproot. Constructed from 1953 to 1956, the Price Tower, as it became known, was the only building to which Wright dedicated a monograph, *The Story of the Tower: The Tree That Escaped the Crowded Forest*. The "crowded forest" was Wright's metaphor for New York and its skyscrapers. He had to move the tower from the city to allow its optimal viewing as a solitary object, making it

Fig. 64 Price Tower, Bartlesville, Oklahoma.

the centerpiece of a small town on the Oklahoma plains. Although in actual construction the taproot did not descend as deep into the earth as Wright imagined it would, the structural concept of a concrete core with cantilevered floors remains a viable construction strategy in the twenty-first century. The lesson that a tall building should "turn" and alter its façades in response to its orientation, light, winds, and climates, however, remains often ignored but still relevant to contemporary practice.[35]

Work on the Guggenheim Museum loomed over all these developments. At the culmination of Wright's career, it encapsulated what he thought of New York and represented his final assault in the battle for the soul of American architecture.

Finally, in March 1956, eighty-nine-year-old Wright received, with the intercession of Robert Moses, a building permit for the Solomon R. Guggenheim Museum. On August 16, ground was broken for construction. Wright would often visit the site as construction proceeded and constant technical changes arose. He also had other challenging issues to deal with in terms of public perception. Shortly after getting the building permit, an open letter from twenty-one artists including Willem de Kooning, Adolph Gottlieb, Franz Kline, and Robert Motherwell appeared in the *New York Times* asking the Guggenheim Foundation to abandon the idea of displaying art under natural light along the inclined walls of the ramp. Though James Johnson Sweeney's name did not appear, the director was suspected of supporting the effort.[36] The objection raised a basic and ongoing issue of what has primacy in an art museum, the art or the architecture. Just a mention of the building raised clashing opinions that Wright had to confront. In his ongoing bitter conflict with Sweeney, their dialogue reached a dead end, as Wright wrote Harry Guggenheim, "With Sweeney as guide there, we are not safe, as in fact he knows less about architecture in general and about our museum building in particular than anyone I have met."[37]

Wright last visited the Plaza Hotel on January 27, 1959. Sensing his time was short and fearing further changes by Sweeney and his supporters, he sent a desperate plea to Harry Guggenheim: "I plead with you now not to fail me in completing the work as it was originally conceived." Wright died in Phoenix, on April 9, two months short of his ninety-second birthday.[38]

The Solomon R. Guggenheim Museum opened on October 21, 1959, six months after Wright's death. Critical response to the building was international in scope, but the reviews of the building coincided with a deluge of obituaries. Domestically, Mumford described the museum as "an over massive pillbox." It expressed an "indescribable individuality" but in his opinion remained "sadly unfavorable." In the *New Yorker,* he elaborated what became a common view: "Architecture is not simply sculpture, and this building was meant also to serve as a museum. In that context it is an audacious failure."[39]

In a harbinger of the congealed view of Wright and his history, the *New York Times* outlined his life and work but claimed the Guggenheim Museum was "his first commission in New York." The key roles of the Modern Cathedral, the St. Mark's tower, and Gotham itself in Wright's career had already disappeared by Wright's demise. We now know of their importance.[40]

The decades following his death saw Wright's reputation and interest in his work dip. Aside from the occasional mention of the big monuments, like Fallingwater and the Johnson Wax building, his work appeared marginal as variations of the International Style moved across the globe. The Larkin Building in Buffalo was torn down. The ultimate disrespect occurred with the razing of the Imperial Hotel in Tokyo in 1968. Olgivanna, who tried unsuccessfully to save the hotel, had succeeded her late husband as head of the Frank Lloyd Wright Foundation. She ran it, the Fellowship, Taliesin Associated Architects (Wright's successor firm), and all aspects of licensing until her death in 1985 at the age of eighty-five. The expenses of supporting her; the Fellowship's members, who were fed (though not salaried); as well as the buildings and grounds at Taliesin and Taliesin West often exceeded income. Licensing Wright's name, in addition to selling off assets from time to time—land at Taliesin West (now filled with suburban tract homes), art works, drawings, and finally Wright's archive itself—became a standard practice and the means by which the Frank Lloyd Wright Foundation still gains most of its revenues. Through licensing, consumers can buy Wrightian designs applied to everything from coffee mugs to key chains, from silk scarves to miniature sculptures. A potential client can even license an unexecuted Wright design for a building—house, high rise, or even civic complex—and have it built.

With the Foundation inheriting Wright's major assets, his children by his first marriage to Catherine had been effectively disinherited from considerable assets; relations between them and Olgivanna ranged from frosty to nonexistent. Lloyd Wright, the eldest son and the most talented of the offspring, produced some impressive work but never emerged from his father's shadow; he died of pneumonia in 1978. Maginel, Wright's unsung younger sister, had died twelve years earlier.[41]

The remaining fellows and apprentices continued ongoing projects, sought new work, and focused their devotion on Olgivanna in their efforts to promote Wright's legacy. The apprenticeship system continued while the last generation of fellows who'd worked under Wright remained alive. Though Wright had vehemently rejected creating an architecture school modeled on academic and professional lines, the Fellowship was turned into a professional degree-granting program in 1987, the antithesis of what Wright had envisioned.

By the time of Wright's death, the struggle he'd waged for the soul of American architecture against the Internationalists had concluded. A look around New York City in 1959 reveals the results. The city Wright encountered in the early 1950s was *the* "headquarter town," as developer William Zeckendorf declared, or as *Business Week* dubbed it, the "executive city, a vision of urbanity realized in buildings." The towers of the United Nations complex, Procter and Gamble's Lever House, and the Seagram Building, designed by Mies van der Rohe and finished by 1958 (see fig. 57), employed similar approaches: massing consisted of a vertical, rectangular box clad in a glass curtain wall. Olgivanna described the Seagram Building as "the symbol of pessimism, a tomb—a monument to the dying city." But these buildings and ones like them became, with the imprimatur of the Museum of Modern Art, the models for civic and corporate America—and for the developing world. Examples in Manhattan proliferated: the Pepsi-Cola Building at 500 Park Avenue, designed by Skidmore, Owings & Merrill, was a glassy, curtain-wall structure of matted metal "piping" set atop a series of columns, or *pilotis* in modernist terminology. The Olivetti Typewriter showroom on Fifth Avenue featured scintillating Venetian glass lights and green marble flooring, the same marble that seemed to grow from the ground, forming into pedestals carrying the newest typewriter makes and models. The Corning Glass building at 717 Fifth, completed in 1959 by Harrison, Abramowitz & Abbe, was also a soaring glass wall, delineated in strong vertical lines with aluminum banding. The same firm designed the Time & Life Building. At forty-eight floors, it employed a series of prominent, exterior columns, cladded in a limestone skin.[42]

The city's metropolitan shape was shifting, too. Instead of abandoning the city for the country, as Wright proposed for Broadacre City, large-scale restructuring—the beginning of urban renewal—was in vogue. While Wright was struggling with building the Guggenheim Museum, Robert Moses had become efficient at tearing open the urban fabric to insert multilane freeways through scores of neighborhoods. He transformed the city, creating not only major transportation infrastructure, but also 658 playgrounds, 416 miles of parkway space, and 13 bridges. Massive public housing complexes rose under his hand and shifted the city's demographic profile. None of these developments showed Wright's influence. Instead, they transmitted, often with misinterpretations, the urban planning ideas that Le Corbusier and his colleagues had been trying to propagate in Europe and beyond.[43]

New York bore witness to the results of a protracted battle: the International Style had triumphed over Wright's organic architecture. His defeat is loaded, like his life, with irony and paradox. New York was dually the anti-city and the rebirth city. Wright embraced the city that both celebrated and rejected him; he loved and thrived in it while relentlessly attacking it. Except for the Guggenheim Museum, Wright left no major building in New York. The skyscraper box that he had railed against become the logo of corporate America, embodied in New York where his taproot version never took. Despite claims otherwise, America's suburbs did not replicate Broadacre City. Though it percolated into the ideas of midcentury modernist architects, his Usonian home did not become the standard model of mass production housing or permeate the country's building stock. A prolific postwar housing industry and small but robust cadre of midcentury practitioners provided its homes, not Taliesin. The world had moved on, but Wright appeared to fight the same battles.[44]

That lone exception, however, was powerful. A building as monumental as the Guggenheim Museum is layered with meaning. For Wright it was a symbol, a refutation, and a confirmation. As a personal symbol, it embodied the city with which he had a complex fifty-year relationship, providing a permanent monumental marker of identity where permanence was not a given. Its abstraction—so fundamental to modernism—and its primal form turned it into a universal and timeless icon.

As a refutation, the museum defied the urban grid and fabric of New York, inserting a freestanding object that both disrupts and rises above its context in a gesture of defiant liberation. Making building as sculpture changed the status of architects, moving them from builders to artists. Simultaneously, the building operates as Wright's final assault on the International Style, and for once triumphs over his opponents with a monument greater than any of their works.

Finally, despite the museum's being seen by its first director and his successors for thirty years as problematic for the display of modern art, the building took on a new role by the late 1980s: the brand of the Guggenheim Museum as a globalizing institution. Suddenly, instead of a millstone, Wright's building itself became an asset, an ultimate confirmation. The change occurred with the rejection of orthodox modernism—a perception of International Style as nonfunctional, vapid, and sterile, as Wright had maintained—and the rise of postmodernism with its yearnings for comfort, tradition, and even ornament. The moment coincided with the reemergence of an interest in Wright that has only increased. Consequently, among architects, his name is the most recognized in the world. Lacking a clear future, America's built environment still needs guidance, and the question remains: Can Wright's organic architecture inspire the future?

The failed blocks of the International Style have been tumbling down. Will the Guggenheim Museum survive after all those modernist boxes fall? It might not bounce like a spring in a nuclear holocaust, as Wright claimed, but its first sixty years reveal it as timeless as any building could be.

EPILOGUE

House Beautiful honored the passing of the architect with another special issue, "Your Heritage from Frank Lloyd Wright." Myriads awaited it eagerly, among them my parents, Eleanor and Frederick Alofsin. The 1959 issue on Wright, so thick and attractive, was something to treasure. My parents pored over the coverage of Wright's architecture—they saved the issues of *House Beautiful*—and drew directly from it and similar publications. They were planning their own dream home on the eastern boundary of Memphis, Tennessee.[1]

As a ten-year-old boy I understood little of these things, but I did gaze at the pages of *House Beautiful,* ignoring the text, and marvel at Wright's living room at Taliesin. Something about it was irresistible—its dynamism, warmth, contrasting wood and stone. Image after image, from whole rooms to detailed corners, entranced me. The views from interior to exterior landscape were unlike anything I had seen. Without realizing its origins, I would spend my teenage years in our new pinwheeling home imbued with a Japanese aesthetic, one in which inside and outside merged. The irony of my growing up in a home inspired by Wright was doubled as we used to drive on country roads through what had been a great plantation, without knowing this had been the land of the Reverend Guthrie's grandmother, Fanny Wright. Intended to be used to train freed slaves, the land was transformed in the late 1920s to become the Shelby County Penal Farm. When I was a kid it was populated, sadly, mostly with incarcerated black men. Now it has reverted to a vast and beautiful nature preserve, Shelby Farms Park, with its own history lost in time.

We loved Wright's architecture without fully comprehending it or grasping its history. Nor did we understand how New York had helped propel it. For us, living at the edge of nature, the big city was an alien world. That's why the Guggenheim Museum seems something of a miracle—organic form taking root in the least organic and most manmade of all locations. Yet for all that New York was so central to Wright, and in the many ways this book has tried to capture and evoke, the paradox was how, beyond the Guggenheim Museum, he left no tangible architectural mark on the city. New York was where he could dream on a different scale—for his designs and for himself. "Work was hard," Frank reflected in the *Autobiography,* "and sometimes interfered with dreaming studies or studious dreams. . . . At other times, the dreams went on undisturbed beneath or above the routine." And as for so many before and since, New York inspired dreaming.[2]

CHRONOLOGY

1867

July 8: (Richland Center, WI) Frank Lincoln Wright born; later changes middle name to Lloyd, connecting him to his maternal Lloyd-Jones lineage.

1909

September 22: (Chicago) Wright departs for New York City, his first documented visit to Gotham. Wright and Mamah Borthwick Cheney meet at the Plaza Hotel in time for the Hudson-Fulton Celebration.

October 5: (New York) Wright and Mamah leave New York to sail to Europe to prepare Wright's Wasmuth publications.

1910

October 6: (New York) Wright returns from Europe, stays in New York for two days, and then returns to Oak Park, Illinois.

November 15: (New York) Wright arrives to oversee project for Universal Portland Cement Company exhibition. He visits his sisters, cousin, and Tiffany's.

December 14–20: (New York) Wright's pavilion for the Universal Portland Cement Company on view at the First Annual New York Cement Show, Madison Square Garden.

1911

January 16: (New York) Wright sails for Liverpool on RMS *Lusitania* en route to second stay in Europe.

March 30: (New York) Wright returns to United States, begins discussion in Spring Green to buy land for Taliesin.

Summer: (Spring Green, WI) Construction begins on Wright's home and studio, Taliesin, located near Spring Green.

October 16: (Taliesin) Wright informed of possible commission for Imperial Hotel, Tokyo.

1913

January 11: (San Francisco) Wright and Mamah Borthwick sail to Japan to pursue commission for Imperial Hotel. Wright has no contract; project delayed by death of Meiji emperor.

Late May: (Taliesin) Wright and Mamah return from Japan; commission in limbo.

1914

August 15: (Taliesin) Tragedy with death of Mamah, her children, and others.

December 12: (Chicago) Miriam Noel contacts Wright. They begin an affair immediately.

1916

December 28: (Vancouver) With contract settled, Wright and Miriam sail to Japan for work on Imperial Hotel, their first of five trips.

1919

October: (New York) During a four-month return from Japan, Wright visits the city to sell Japanese wood-block prints.

1921

Early July: (New York) Wright spends two weeks in the city, again to sell Japanese woodblock prints. Returns to Los Angeles for final inspection of Aline Barnsdall's project on Olive Hill.

July 30: (San Francisco) Wright and Miriam sail back to Japan, stopping in Honolulu.

1922

April 24: (New York) The Reverend William Norman Guthrie asks Bishop William T. Manning for permission to change the order of church service. Outraged, Manning prohibits any teacher or representative of a non-Christian religion to speak or take part in any service at St. Mark's.

August 20: (Taliesin) Wright and Miriam return from Japan, via Seattle; final trip for both.

October 5: (Taliesin) Wright broaches idea with son Lloyd of working together on West Coast; Wright has no work.

October 27: (New York) Wright is en route to the city to see Bosch Reitz at the Metropolitan Museum of Art. Wright intends further sales of Japanese prints to pay expenses at Taliesin. Bosch Reitz informs Wright that prints Wright had sold were retouched.

November 13: Wright finally obtains divorce from wife Catherine.

1923

February: (West Hollywood) Wright living and working in rented house at 1284 Harper Avenue in Sherman; staff consists of himself, his son Lloyd Wright, Kameki Tsuchira, and Rudolf M. Schindler.

February 9: (Oconomowoc, WI) Wright's mother, Anna Lloyd-Wright, dies.

March—July: (West Hollywood) Various projects, mostly speculative: Doheny Ranch project; Commercial Building; Lake Tahoe summer colony.

September 1: (Tokyo) Imperial Hotel opens coincident with Great Kantō earthquake.

September: (Los Angeles) Wright moves office to 1600 Edgemont Street (Residence B, at Barnsdall's Olive Hill complex).

October: (Taliesin) Wright returns to reopen a studio and claims he will soon have other studios in Chicago, Hollywood, and Tokyo.

November 19: (Taliesin) Wright and Miriam Noel marry.

1924

February 2: (Los Angeles) Wright's assistant Rudolf Schindler informs Richard Neutra that Wright is in Los Angeles through the month.

April 14: (Chicago) Louis Sullivan dies; Wright attends the funeral two days later and meets Richard Neutra there.

May: (Taliesin) Miriam Noel leaves Wright.

September 2: (Chicago) Gordon Strong in touch with Wright about designing an "Automobile Objective" on Sugarloaf Mountain, near Washington, D.C.

October: (Taliesin) Richard Neutra arrives at Taliesin; will stay through early February 1925.

November 3–4: (Taliesin) German architect Erich Mendelsohn visits Wright.

November 30: (Chicago) Wright meets Olgivanna Hinzenberg.

December: (New York) Wright makes weeklong trip to city "for business."

1925

January: (Taliesin) Olgivanna moves in and becomes pregnant.

February 17: (New York) Olgivanna introduces Wright to members of her Gurdjieffian circle.

April 12: (New York) Guthrie gives Easter sermon describing "a shrine of worship for all people," the core idea for the Modern Cathedral Wright will design. Wright knows of the project and makes sketches, but the work is limited.

April 19: (Taliesin) Alexander Woollcott visits Wright.

April 20: (Taliesin) Wright's home burns for second time.

July 10: Wright files for divorce from Miriam; protracted skirmishes begin between them.

October 14: (Chicago) Gordon Strong rejects Wright's design for his "Automobile Objective."

December 2: (Chicago) Olgivanna gives birth to Iovanna Lazovich Lloyd Wright and is harassed by Miriam in hospital.

Early December: (Hollis, NY) Wright and family take refuge with Olgivanna's brother Vlado and his wife Sophie.

1926

January: (Puerto Rico) Wright takes Olgivanna to Puerto Rico so she can recover from postpartum depression.

March: (Taliesin) Wright returns from Puerto Rico with his family to his Wisconsin homestead.

June 3: (Taliesin) Miriam storms Taliesin but is blocked at the gate.

April 19–20: (Buffalo and Derby, NY) Wright visits Darwin and Isabelle Martin to see site for their cottage.

August 31: (Chicago/Taliesin) Miriam sues Olgivanna. Wright, Olgivanna, and her two daughters go into hiding in rented bungalow, near Wayzata, MN.

September 6: (Spring Green, WI) Bank of Wisconsin forecloses on Wright's mortgage and takes possession of Taliesin.

October 20: (Lake Minnetonka, MN) Wright arrested and charged with violation of Mann Act.

October 22: (Minneapolis) Wright and Olgivanna released from jail.

November: (Minneapolis) Wright awaits clarification of legal issues.

December: (New York) Wright and his family take refuge with Maginel Wright Barney, the architect's sister, at 41 West 12th Street in Greenwich Village.

1927

January–May: (New York) Wright and Olgivanna rent apartment on East Ninth Street, near the Lafayette Hotel. Guthrie and Wright begin discussing plans to build a tower for St. Mark's Church in-the-Bowery.

January 6–7: (New York) Auction of Wright's Japanese print collection.

January 16: (New York) Alexander Woollcott intercedes for Olgivanna

with Colonel "Wild Bill" Donovan
to resolve her immigration issues.

January: (New York) Wright and Guthrie
resume contact.

February 8: (New York) Elizabeth
Coonley Faulkner invites Wright
and Olgivanna to dinner in
Greenwich Village.

March 3: (New York) Wright, Olgivanna,
and Alfred Orage meet to discuss
Gurdjieff. The writers e. e.
cummings and John Dos Passos
join the meeting.

March 4: (Minneapolis) Wright's charges
of violating Mann Act dropped.

April: (Derby, NY) Wright visits Martins'
site on Lake Erie.

Early May: (New York) Wright departs
the city after his longest stay to date;
returns with Olgivanna to Taliesin.

May 5: (Taliesin) Wright provides Guthrie with initial description of the
tower design for St. Mark's.

August 6: (Madison, WI) Wright, Inc.
registered in Wisconsin.

August 7: (Taliesin) Wright confirms
interest in working with Leerdam
Glasfabriek in Holland.

August 26: Wright and Miriam divorce.

Fall: (Taliesin) Wright working alone
with no draftsmen at Taliesin.
Maintains contact with friends and
colleagues in New York, including
Guthrie, Frankl, and Woollcott.

September 13: (Taliesin) Wright provides
Darwin Martin with encouraging
account of Taliesin life.

October 19: (New York) Guthrie
continues positioning Wright to get
a formal appointment for the St.
Mark's tower commission.

October 26: (New York and Taliesin)
Wright and Guthrie discuss further

the Modern Cathedral project.
Wright's first sketch for it is dated
February 1926.

November 12: (Milwaukee) *Milwaukee
Journal* publishes exposé of Wright's
scandals.

November 25: (Taliesin) Wright wor-
ries the St. Mark's tower project is
doomed.

1928

January 2: (Phoenix) Albert Chase
McArthur hires Wright to consult
on textile-block construction for
Arizona Biltmore Hotel. Discussion
of St. Mark's tower on hold.

January 13: (Spring Green, WI) Bank of
Wisconsin orders Wright to leave
Taliesin and insists he pay all debts
or they will sell.

January–May: (Phoenix, AZ) In first
visit, Wright consults on design of
the Arizona Biltmore Hotel.

April 5: (Phoenix) Wright receives
contract to design San Marcos in
the Desert resort for Alexander
Chandler.

May: (Phoenix) Wright departs, having
defined concept for San Marcos
resort.

May: (Spring Green, WI) Bank of
Wisconsin announces plans to sell
Taliesin at auction. Wright heads to
La Jolla, California, for the summer.

July 30: (Spring Green, WI) Bank of
Wisconsin buys Taliesin at auction
for $25,000 with intention of selling
it to a group of Wright's friends.

August 25: (Rancho Santa Fe, CA)
Wright and Olgivanna marry and
return to Arizona.

September 27: (Phoenix) Wright departs
for Wisconsin.

Early October: (Taliesin) Wright regains access to home, studio, and farm. The stability allows him to relaunch an architectural office.

November 8: (New York and Taliesin) Guthrie and Wright resume discussion of their two projects: the Modern Cathedral project for which Wright begins to produce fantastical drawings based on Guthrie's suggestions, and the tower project for St. Mark's Church in-the-Bowery. The former recedes in importance, while the latter becomes a joint obsession.

December 19: (Taliesin) Wright writes son Lloyd to encourage him and tells of progress in work and life.

December 26: (Taliesin) Wright discovers 1,500 copies of his *Sonderheft* and 100 sets of Wasmuth folios in his basement. He hopes to sell them for a quick profit.

December 31: (New York) Guthrie rhapsodizes on the Modern Cathedral. Wright defines his vision in drawings, three of which are extant.

1929

January 8: (New York) Guthrie informs Wright of positive movement for his commission for the St. Mark's tower; the vestry board wants to see him in person prior to awarding the commission officially.

January 15: (Taliesin) Wright with family and crew leave for Arizona.

End of January: (Chandler, AZ) In his second extended visit to Arizona, Wright and staff begin construction of Ocatillo and work on San Marcos resort.

February 23: (Phoenix) Arizona Biltmore opens; Wright attends event.

March 3: (New York) Contempora Inc. invites Wright to speak at exhibition of work of Erich Mendelsohn.

March 4: (Phoenix) Wright resumes work on St. Mark's tower.

Late March: (Ocatillo) Work complete on the desert camp.

May 24: (Ocatillo) Wright and family leave Arizona by car.

June 18: (New York) Wright arrives in the city to attend Contempora's Exhibition of Art and Industry honoring his friend Erich Mendelsohn.

[c. June 20]: (New York) Wright presents Horace Holley his designs to date for the St. Mark's tower; Guthrie is absent, on vacation.

June 22: (New York) Wright appears with architect and delineator Hugh Ferriss on WOR radio.

June 26: (Taliesin) Wright returns home after extended cross-country trip by car.

July: (Taliesin) Wright continues work on sketches for St. Mark's tower.

September 6: (Taliesin) Wright informs Horace Holley that the St. Mark's design is fully developed. The architect begins recording his impressions of the desert.

September 27: (New York) A. Lawrence Kocher proposes Wright exhibit his work at the Architectural League of New York.

October 11: (New York) Wright speaks at AUDAC lunch.

October 13: (New York) Wright gives Guthrie and members of the St. Mark's vestry board a preview of the tower drawings.

October 16: (Chicago) Wright leaks word of the tower project to newspapers before it is approved, embarrassing Guthrie and Holley. News media spread the story widely. Wright returns to Taliesin for final preparation of Tower drawings.

October 19: (New York) *New York Times* reports on "Odd-Type Buildings" at St. Mark's.

October 29: (New York) "Black Tuesday" as stock market crashes.

November 4: (New York) Wright gives final presentation of tower project for St. Mark's Church in-the-Bowery. Timing and lack of money will doom the venture.

November 6: (Taliesin) Wright returns home and awaits word from St. Mark's vestry board.

December: (New York) Though the plans for the St. Mark's tower are unapproved, the architectural press begins publishing them.

December 26: (New York) Regardless of the flux on the Tower project, Horace Holley is delighted with the layouts for typography that Wright had sent for the inside pages of his magazine, *World Unity*.

1930

January 3: (Minneapolis, MN) Miriam Noel dies.

February 3: (Princeton, NJ) Wright receives invitation for Kahn Lectures at Princeton University; he proposes his forthcoming New York exhibition to accompany the lectures, his first traveling show.

March 21: (New York) Wright attends unspecified meetings.

April 1: (Taliesin) Wright finishes drafts of his Princeton lectures. The architect and staff work on preparing photographs and models, organizing the material for travel.

May 5: (New York) Wright stops in the city en route to Princeton.

May 6–14: (Princeton, NJ) Wright gives his Princeton lectures, published the following year as *Modern Architecture: Being the Kahn Lectures*.

May 12–22: (Princeton, NJ): Wright's exhibition *The Work of Frank Lloyd Wright, 1893–1930* on view at Princeton.

May 15: (New York) Wright debates Ralph Walker, who'd just returned from Germany, on modern architecture at the Architectural League of New York.

May 16: (New York) Wright has lunch with Lewis Mumford, Douglas Haskell, and Joseph Urban.

May 22: (Princeton, NJ) Wright's exhibition closes at the university and is sent to the Architectural League of New York, arriving by May 26.

May 26: (New York) Wright plans to return before his testimonial.

May 28: (New York) The Architectural League of New York sponsors testimonial for Wright. *The Work of Frank Lloyd Wright, 1893–1930* is on view.

May 29–June 12: (New York) Wright's exhibition at Architectural League of New York is open to the public.

June 29: (New York) *New York Times* publishes extensive feature on Wright.

July 1: (Berlin) Heinrich de Fries publishes "Neue Pläne von Frank Lloyd Wright" [New Plans by Frank Lloyd Wright] in *Die Form*, the first appearance of several of Wright's projects; American architectural editors take note.

July 19: (New York) Alexander Woollcott publishes Wright's profile, "The Prodigal Father," in the *New Yorker*. The piece provides a canonical definition of the architect.

October 1–2: (Chicago) Wright gives two public lectures at the Art Institute of Chicago; these will be published July 1931.

1931

February 23: (New York) Launching a series of lectures, Wright speaks at the Twentieth Century Club in Brooklyn, followed by speaking at the Women's University Club in Manhattan; AUDAC, and the School of Social Research.

February 26: (New York) AUDAC organizes a meeting to protest Wright's exclusion from the "Century of Progress"; rancor was the only result.

February 27: (New York) Guthrie declares the tower project could never be built on the St. Mark's site; Wright persists in arguing with him.

March 7: (Eugene, OR) Wright lectures at University of Oregon in conjunction with his traveling exhibition *The Work of Frank Lloyd Wright, 1893–1930*.

March 12: (Seattle, WA) Wright lectures at the University of Washington with his traveling exhibition in place.

May 9–31: (Amsterdam) *The Work of Frank Lloyd Wright, 1893–1930* seen at the Stedelijk Museum.

June 17–July 12: (Berlin) *The Work of*

Frank Lloyd Wright, 1893–1930 seen at the Prussian Academy of Fine Arts.

July 13: (Grand Rapids, MI) Wright lectures at international conference on interior decoration.

September 19: (New York) Wright and Olgivanna sail to Rio de Janeiro, spending three weeks there to judge competition entries for Christopher Columbus Lighthouse.

1932

February 10: (New York) *Modern Architecture*, the International Style exhibition, opens at Museum of Modern Art.

February 14: (Chicago) Wright lectures to overflowing crowd at Chicago City Club.

March 23: (New York) International Style show closes in New York and begins touring the United States.

March 30: (New York) Longmans Green publishes Wright's *Autobiography*; it meets with immediate critical success.

October 20: (Spring Green, WI) Taliesin Fellowship officially opens with arrival of apprentices.

1934

December 18–19: (Pittsburgh/Bear Run, PA) Wright visits site at waterfall over which he will locate Fallingwater; requests a survey of the area, securing commission for the famous house.

1935

January 10: (Taliesin) Wright and Edgar J. Kaufmann confer on the design of Fallingwater.

April 15–May 15: (New York) Broadacre

City model exhibited, Industrial
Arts Exhibition, Rockefeller Center.

December 17 (Buffalo, NY) Darwin
Martin, Wright's friend and patron,
dies.

1936

July 23 (Racine) W. F. Johnson Jr.
requests that Wright proceed with
plans and sketches for a $200,000
office building for S. C. Johnson &
Son, Inc., launching the design for
the Johnson Wax Administration
Building.

1937

(Scottsdale, AZ) Wright obtains land for
construction of Taliesin West, winter
home of Wright, his family, and the
Taliesin Fellowship.

1938

January: (New York) *Architectural
Forum* begins promoting Wright's
work.

January 17: (New York) *Time* magazine
puts Wright on its cover, confirming
the celebratory trajectory his career
will take for the next two decades.

1939

(Maricopa Mesa, AZ) After site work,
construction begins on buildings for
Taliesin West.

1940

November 13: (New York) *Frank Lloyd
Wright: American Architect* exhibition at the Museum of Modern Art;
it runs through January 5, 1941.

November 29: (Taliesin) Wright's assets
reorganized into the Frank Lloyd
Wright Foundation.

1943

June 29: (Taliesin) Wright signs contract
for Guggenheim Museum.

1945

September 20: (New York) Wright
presents model of Guggenheim
Museum at Plaza Hotel.

1952

June 10: (Taliesin) Harold Price Sr. and
building committee visit Wright to
commission office tower for H. C.
Price Company, Bartlesville, OK.
Wright will use his design for the
tower for St. Mark's Church in-the-
Bowery with minor modifications to
create Price Tower.

1953

November 10: (Bartlesville, OK) Construction of Price Tower begins.

October 22: (New York) Traveling exhibition *Sixty Years of Living Architecture: The Work of Frank Lloyd
Wright*, 1071 Fifth Avenue (site of
Guggenheim Museum), opens in
New York after touring; it runs
through December 13.

December 17: (New York) Wright
accepts commission to design the
Beth Sholom Synagogue, Elkins
Park, Pennsylvania. He will transform his Modern Cathedral for
Guthrie, with a reduced scale and
modifications, for the new temple.

1954

June–December: (New York) Wright and
Olgivanna renovate suite in Plaza
Hotel to create Taliesin East.

1955

(New York) *House Beautiful* promotes
    licensee partnerships.

1956

August 16: (New York) Construction
    begins on Guggenheim Museum.

June 3: (New York) Wright appears
    on the NBC television quiz show
    What's My Line?

February 10: (Bartlesville, OK) Price
    Tower dedicated.

1957

May 4–12: (New York) *Showcase for
    Better Living*, International Home
    Building Exposition, Fiberthin
    Air House.

September 1 and 28: (New York) Broad-
    casts of Mike Wallace interviewing
    Wright in two-part series.

1958

May 3: (New York) Plan for Greater
    Baghdad exhibited at Iraqi Consul-
    ate.

October 29: (New York) Wright's work
    included in *International Festival
    of Art* November 23 exhibition at
    Seagram Building.

1959

January 27: (New York) Wright's last visit
    to the Plaza Hotel, his final view of
    Gotham.

April 9: (Phoenix, AZ) Wright dies, two
    months short of his ninety-second
    birthday.

June 9: (New York) Traveling exhibition,
    Form Givers at Mid-Century, at
    Metropolitan Museum of Art,
    through September 6.

September 20: (Elkins Park, PA) Beth
    Sholom Synagogue dedicated.

October 21: (New York) Solomon R.
    Guggenheim Museum opens to
    the public.

ABBREVIATIONS

PEOPLE

AB	Aline Barnsdall
AW	Alexander Woollcott
AJC	Alexander J. Chandler
ALW	Anna Lloyd Wright
DH	Douglass Haskell
DDM	Darwin D. Martin
EL	Emil Lorch
EM	Erich Mendelsohn
FLW	Frank Lloyd Wright
GH	George Howe
GS	Gordon Strong
HH	Horace Holley
HdF	Heinrich de Fries
HRH	Henry-Russell Hitchcock
JLW	John Lloyd Wright
LM	Lewis Mumford
LW	Frank Lloyd Wright Jr.
MN	Miriam Maude Noel
OLW	Olgivanna Lloyd Wright
PLF	Philip La Follette
PTF	Paul T. Frankl
RH	Raymond Hood
WNG	Reverend William Norman Guthrie
WTM	Bishop William T. Manning

PUBLICATIONS

A	Frank Lloyd Wright, *An Autobiography: Frank Lloyd Wright* (New York: Longmans, Green and Co., 1932)
AR	*Architectural Record*
BSS	Joseph M. Siry, *Beth Sholom Synagogue: Frank Lloyd Wright and Modern Religious Architecture* (Chicago: University of Chicago Press, 2011)
C	William Allin Storrer, *Frank Lloyd Wright Companion*, rev. ed. (Chicago: University of Chicago Press, 2006)
CDT	*Chicago Daily Tribune*
CW	*Frank Lloyd Wright Collected Writings,* ed. Bruce Brooks Pfeiffer, 5 vols. (New York: Rizzoli, in association with the Frank Lloyd Wright Foundation, 1992–1995)

DfAL	David G. De Long, ed., *Frank Lloyd Wright: Designs for an American Landscape, 1922–1932* (New York: Harry N. Abrams, 1996)
HY	Bruce Brooks Pfeiffer, *Frank Lloyd Wright: The Heroic Years, 1920–1932* (New York: Rizzoli, 2009)
JSAH	*Journal of the Society of Architectural Historians*
TF	Roger Friedland and Harold Zellmann, *The Fellowship: The Untold Story of Frank Lloyd Wright & The Taliesin Fellowship* (New York: HarperCollins, 2006)
LY	Anthony Alofsin, *Frank Lloyd Wright: The Lost Years, 1910–1922: A Study of Influence* (University of Chicago Press, 1993)
LOLW	*From Crna Cora to Taliesin, Black Mountain to Shining Brow: The Life of Olgivanna Lloyd Wright,* comp. and ed. Maxine Fawcett-Yeske and Bruce Brooks Pfeiffer ([Novato, CA]: Oro Editions, 2017)
M	Herbert Muschamp, *Man About Town: Frank Lloyd Wright in New York City* (Cambridge, MA: MIT Press, 1983)
MM	Brendan Gill, *Many Masks: A Life of Frank Lloyd Wright* (New York: Ballantine Books, 1987)
NYT	*New York Times*
OE	Kathryn Smith, *On Exhibit: Frank Lloyd Wright's Architectural Exhibitions* (Princeton, NJ: Princeton University Press, 2017)

ARCHIVES

Avery	Frank Lloyd Wright Foundation Archives (Museum of Modern Art, New York | Avery Architectural and Fine Arts Library, Columbia University, New York). Additional materials in the Avery Drawings and Archives Collection, Avery Architectural and Fine Arts Library, Columbia University, New York.
FLWF	Frank Lloyd Wright Foundation Archives, Taliesin West, Scottsdale, Arizona.
GA	Guthrie Archive: William Norman Guthrie Papers. Andover-Harvard Theological Library, Harvard Divinity School, Cambridge, Massachusetts.
LC	Prints and Drawings Collection, Library of Congress, Washington, D.C.
SUNYB	Darwin D. Martin Papers, MS 22.86-052, University Archives, State University of New York at Buffalo, Buffalo, New York.

NOTES

Unless indicated otherwise, the letters and documents cited are located in the Frank Lloyd Wright Foundation Archives (The Museum of Modern Art | Avery Architectural & Fine Arts Library, Columbia University, New York).

INTRODUCTION

1. Wright's comments to Lloyd Wright as reported by Merle Armitage in Harvey Einbinder, *An American Genius: Frank Lloyd Wright* (New York: Philosophical Library, 1986), 253. The catalogue of Wright's critique against the city was compiled by Herbert Muschamp in *Man About Town: Frank Lloyd Wright in New York City* (Cambridge, MA: MIT Press, 1983), 15. Muschamp's sources include Frank Lloyd Wright, *The Future of Architecture* (reprint, New York: New American Library, 1970), 181–189, passim; and Wright, *The Living City* (reprint, New York: New American Library, 1970), 59–60, passim. Wright has also been quoted describing New York as "Prison towers and modern posters for soap and whiskey," with the source usually attributed to Wayne Andrews, "Of His Own Choosing," *NYT,* 27 November 1955, 323. The sentiment rings true, but Wright's words don't appear in Andrews's article. For Gotham's origins and definition, see William R. Taylor, *In Pursuit of Gotham: Culture and Commerce in New York* (New York: Oxford University Press, 1992), xvii.

2. Robert A. M. Stern, Gregory Gilmartin, and Thomas Mellins, *New York 1930: Architecture and Urbanism Between the Two World Wars* (New York: Rizzoli, 1987), 29. For a synopsis of Art Deco, see the exhibition catalogue *The Jazz Age: American Style in the 1920s,* ed. Sarah D. Coffin and Stephen Harrison (New Haven: Yale University Press, 2017). A critique of the artifacts, jewelry, and bibelots as objects for an audience that was too high-end and too glamorous appeared: Roberta Smith, "A Show's Secret Star," *NYT,* 7 April 2017, and "Unnamed, Art Deco Steps Out with Plenty of Company in 'The Jazz Age,'" *NYT,* 16 April 2017. In 2018, a major exhibit on Art Deco architecture is planned to open in the Chicago History Museum, "Modern by Design: Streamlining America," with an accompanying catalogue edited by Robert Bruegmann. The multiauthored book generally argues, as I do, that Art Deco, rather than being frivolous, was a major development in the evolution of American modern architecture.

3. Henry-Russell Hitchcock, "Frank Lloyd Wright at the Museum of Modern Art," *Art Bulletin* 23 (1941): 75. Hitchcock refers to his article "Frank Lloyd Wright's Influence Abroad," *Parnassus* 12 (1940): 11–15. For my treatment of Wright's primitivist phase, see *Frank Lloyd Wright: The Lost Years, 1910–1922: A Study of Influence* (Chicago: University of Chicago Press, 1993), 121–122, 153–220. For primitivism's appeal to

modern artists, see Yves le Fur, *Picasso Primitif,* exh. cat. (Paris: Flammarion, 2017).

4. Reyner Banham, "The Wilderness Years of Frank Lloyd Wright," *RIBA Journal,* December 1969, 512, 514.

5. Kenneth Frampton, "Introduction," in *CW,* 2:9.

6. Frank Lloyd Wright, *An Autobiography* (New York: Longmans Green, 1932). Unless indicated otherwise, all citations in Wright's *Autobiography* refer to the 1932 edition. For a history of the *Autobiography,* see *CW,* 2:102–104. A revised and enlarged edition followed in 1943, and a third expanded edition was published in 1977.

7. *A,* 363.

CHAPTER 1. POINTS OF DEPARTURE

1. For Martin and Wright's relationship, see Jack Quinan, *Frank Lloyd Wright's Martin House: Architecture as Portraiture* (New York: Princeton Architectural Press, 2004); *LY,* 28, 66–68, 70–78.

2. Lyndon P. Smith, "The Home of an Artist-Architect: Louis H. Sullivan's Place at Ocean Springs, Miss.," *AR* 17 (1905): 471–490, and "Work of Frank Lloyd Wright, Its Influence," *AR* 18 (1905): 60–65; FLW, "In the Cause of Architecture," *AR* (1908): 155–221.

3. Russell Sturgis, "The Larkin Building in Buffalo," *AR* 23 (1908): 311–321. Wright wrote a reply to rebut Sturgis, but the critic died before he could send it, and Wright kept the reply, unsent, in his files.

4. For the pioneering study of Wright's early career, see Grant Carpenter Manson, *Frank Lloyd Wright to 1910: The First Golden Age,* foreword by Henry-Russell Hitchcock (New York: Reinhold, 1958). For Wright's love affairs treated as a novel, see T. Coraghessan Boyle, *The Women* (New York: Viking, 2009).

5. Wright transferred his practice to Hermann von Holst, an architect he hardly knew but who had an office in Steinway Hall in Chicago, as Wright had for several years (*LY,* 27–28).

6. For a history of the Plaza Hotel, see Curtis Gathje, *At the Plaza: An Illustrated History of the World's Most Famous Hotel* (New York: St. Martin's, 2000); Mike Wallace, *Greater Gotham: A History of New York City from 1898 to 1919* (New York: Oxford University Press, 2017), 298, passim.

7. For Wright's appreciation of the Plaza Hotel, see OLW, *Shining Brow* (New York: Horizon, 1960). Published the year after Wright's death, Olgivanna's book provides, among other recollections, the freshest accounts of their life in New York. The material was updated and expanded in *The Life of Olgivanna Lloyd Wright: From Crna Gora to Taliesin, Black Mountain to Shining Brow,* comp. and ed. Maxine Fawcett-Yeske and Bruce Brooks Pfeiffer ([San Francisco]: Oro, 2017), 85–87, passim.

8. For a comprehensive history of the city in this period, see Wallace, *Greater Gotham; Encyclopedia Britannica,* s.v. "New York."

9. A. C. David, "The New Architecture: The First American Type of Real Value," *AR* 28, no. 6 (1910): 4.

10. For New York as a cultural crucible, see William R. Taylor, *In Pursuit of Gotham: Culture and Commerce in New York* (New York: Oxford University Press, 1992), vvii–xviii.

11. "Europe's Songbirds Flitting to America," *NYT,* 3 October 1909; "Feast of Lights Ends Pageant," *NYT,* 3 October 1909. For illumination and modern architecture, see Dietrich Neumann and Kermit Swiler Champa, *Architecture of the Night: The Illuminated Building* (Munich: Prestel, 2003).

12. Wright claimed on a passport application that he had left the United States on 3 October 1909, but no ocean liners departed from New York on that Sunday. The couple may have left a day earlier on Saturday on the SS *Amerika,* with Hamburg as its port of destination, or more likely on the far more luxurious 706-foot SS *Kaiser Wilhelm,* which departed on October 5 for Bremen. "Shipping News," *NYT,* 2–5 October 1909; dates drawn from Wright's passport application, 15 July 1910, Florence, issued as an "emergency passport" on 20 July 1910. My thanks to Janet Parks of the Avery Library, who drew my attention to the application. For Wright's visit to Germany, see *LY,* 29–62; for Wright's art collection, see Anthony Alofsin, *Frank Lloyd Wright: Art Collector* (Austin: University of Texas Press, 2012).

13. *CDT,* 7 November 1909; for updates to Wright in Italy, see Filippo Fici, "Frank Lloyd Wright in Florence and Fiesole, 1909–1910," *Frank Lloyd Wright Quarterly* 22, no. 4 (2011): 4–17; and Giampaolo Fici and Filippo Fici, *Frank Lloyd Wright: Fiesole 1910* (Fiesole: Minello Sani, 1992).

14. The complete details of Wright's Wasmuth saga appear in Anthony Alofsin, "Frank Lloyd Wright: The Lessons of Europe, 1910–1922," Ph.D. diss., Columbia University, 1987; for brief remarks, see *LY,* 88–92.

15. See Alan Crawford, *C. R. Ashbee: Architect, Designer, and Romantic Socialist* (New Haven: Yale University Press, 1985); FLW to CRA, 31 March 1910, Ashbee Collection, Avery Library; *LY,* 52.

16. WNG to FLW, 1 May 1910, GA.

17. FLW to ALL, 4 July 1910, Frank Lloyd Wright Archive, ms. 1502.281.002, pp. 1–4. My thanks to Ron McCrea for providing a copy of this letter.

18. FLW to ALL, 4 July 1910; for sensational coverage in the press, see *LY,* 30.

19. For Wright's European travels in summer 1910, see *LY,* 29–62.

20. Wright's "emergency passport" application indicated Wright's plan to return to the United States within two months, by 15 September 1910, of his claimed departure on 3 October 1909.

CHAPTER 2. FLEETING GLANCES

1. The SS *Bluecher* set sail from Southampton on 26 September 1910. "Shipping Mails,"

NYT, 6 October 1910; *LY,* 64; Nicole Puglise, "Manhattan Is Apparently Less Dense Today Than It Was in 1910," *New York Observer,* 25 September 2014; Fran Capo and Art Zuckerman, *It Happened in New York City: Remarkable Events That Shaped History* (New York: Morris, 2010), 82, quoting Charles McKim on Pennsylvania Station.

2. *NYT,* 6 October 1910, passim; "Saks and Gimbel's, a Merchandising Legend," *NYT,* 14 November 2015.

3. For Little and Wright's house design for him, see *LY,* 54, 68–70, 72, 78. According to Donald Hoffmann, W. E. Barnard, the contractor, built the Robie house from spring 1909 to spring 1910. Roof work continued into summer 1910. Inside work—trimming, plastering, and millwork—continued through fall 1909 and into winter 1910, and furnishings were added into the fall of 1910 (Donald Hoffman, *Frank Lloyd Wright's Robie House: The Illustrated Story of an Architectural Masterpiece* [New York: Dover, 1984], 27, 31n11, 31n12). Hoffmann asserts that between October 1909 and May 1910 Wright made "at least eight more trips" to the Robie house site, citing the Niedecken-Walbridge Co. ledgers (32–33, 33n13). As Wright left Oak Park on 20 September 1909, and did not return until 8 October 1910, Hoffmann's assertions are in error. George Niedecken may have made these trips, but not Wright. Furthermore, my analysis of the progress photographs taken by Barnard (now in the Special Collections, University of Chicago Library) indicates that only the foundation was in place by the time Wright left. The bulk of construction and final furnishing therefore occurred in Wright's absence under the direction of Hermann von Holst, Niedecken, and Marion Mahony.

4. *LY,* 70–71, 73, 79–81. At the Metropolitan Museum of Art, the Coonley Playhouse triptych window (1912), have accession numbers 67.231.1,2,3; for the playhouse, see *C,* 175; Anthony Alofsin, "The Coonley Playhouse Windows: A Parallel Abstraction" (New York, Sotheby's, 2018) 198–203.

5. *LY,* 67–68, 308.

6. "Shipping and Mails," *NYT,* 16 January 1911. FLW to DDM, 21 January 1911, SUNYB. Internal evidence indicates that Wright misdated the letter "1910." Writing on stationery with the seal of the RMS *Lusitania,* Wright missed sending his letter to Martin from shore because a letter from the "consul" had arrived the morning of 16 January and rushed his departure. For the *Lusitania,* see Eric Larson, *Dead Wake: Last Crossing of the Lusitania* (New York: Crown Publishers, 2015).

7. FLW to DDM, 13 January 1911, SUNYB; *LY,* 73–78. See also DDM to FLW, 18 January 1911, SUNYB.

8. "Memorandum of Agreement Between Frank Lloyd Wright and E. Wasmuth, A. G. 13 February 1911," SUNYB; *LY,* 317–318. Wright had planned to sail on 7 March 1911, but work with the *Wasmuth Verlag* delayed him. Wright's departure and arrival dates are derived from analyzing the "Shipping and Mails," *NYT,* 27 March–1 April 1911, passim; FLW to DDM [telegram], 3 April 1911, SUNYB.

9. See Anthony Alofsin, "Taliesin: To Fashions Worlds in Little," *Wright Studies* 1

(1991): 44–65; "Taliesin I: A Catalogue of Drawings and Photographs," *Wright Studies*, vol. 1. (1991), 98–141; Ron McCrea, *Building Taliesin: Frank Lloyd Wright's Home of Love and Loss* (Madison: Wisconsin Historical Society Press, 2012), 25, 32; and Barbara Miller Lane, "An Introduction to Ellen Key's 'Beauty in the Home,'" in *Modern Swedish Design: Three Founding Texts,* ed. Lucy Creagh, Helena Kåberg, and Barbara Miller Lane (New York: Museum of Modern Art, 2008), 30–31. Miller Lane corrected previously published dates about Mamah's return, including my own. For Key's ideology, see Ellen Key, *The Morality of Woman: And Other Essays* (Chicago: Ralph Fletcher Seymour, 1911), 5 (quote).

10. *LY,* 121–122. For Wright's interest in the spiritual resonance of primary forms, see FLW, *The Japanese Print: An Interpretation* (Chicago: Ralph Fletcher Seymour Company, 1912; reprint, New York: Horizon Press, 1967); and *LY,* 153–220.

11. Primitivism in New York in the 1910s is covered in Ann M. Tartsinis, *An American Style: Global Sources for New York Textile and Fashion Design, 1915–1928* (New Haven: Yale University Press, 2013). Primitivism in the 1910s was more potent than we have assumed. Tartsinis demonstrates that Native American and non-Western sources became a rich trove for a new design aesthetic promoted in New York's museums and through designers who used indigenous art as an antidote to European fashion from 1915 to 1928. The appropriation and emulation of primitivist sources can be seen from today's vantage point of political correctness as colonialist, patronizing, or ethnographically misunderstood. The criticism could apply to Wright's dear friend Guthrie with this interest in non-Western, archaic, and esoteric sources as spiritual inspiration. But such views don't negate historical fact: Wright's motivations were of their time and, if romantic, at least idealistic.

12. For Midway Gardens, see Paul Kruty, *Frank Lloyd Wright and Midway Gardens* (Champaign: University of Illinois Press, 1998); *LY,* 137–140.

13. For the Imperial Hotel, see *LY,* 270–280.

14. Details courtesy of Paul V. Turner, personal communication with the author, 5 November 2013. See also Paul V. Turner, *Frank Lloyd Wright and San Francisco* (New Haven: Yale University Press, 2016), 12–16. For Wright's *San Francisco Call* building project, see Anthony Alofsin, "The Call Building: Frank Lloyd Wright's Skyscraper for San Francisco," in *Das Bauwerk und die Stadt: The Building and the Town, Essays for Eduard F. Sekler* (Vienna: Böhlau, 1994), 17–27; and Alofsin, "The Call Building: Frank Lloyd Wright's First Skyscraper," *Journal of Organic Architecture + Design* 4, no. 1 (2016), a special issue edited by Randolph C. Henning, Eric M. O'Malley, and William B. Scott Jr. The building has often been misidentified as the Press Building due to a note on a drawing written by Henry-Russell Hitchcock; Wright never used the term.

15. In 1932, Sigfried Giedion, the leading polemicist of international Functionalism, observed in *Cahiers d'Art* that European innovations in the early 1900s in reinforced concrete—the modernist material par excellence—had occurred independently of

Wright, "who was only known in Europe ten years later thanks to Berlage" (Sigfried Giedion, "Les Problèmes de l'architecture a l'occasion d'un manifeste de Frank Lloyd Wright aux architectes et critiques d'Europe," *Cahiers d'Art* 7, no. 1–2 [1932]: 72; translation mine).

16. *LY,* 96–100. The sensational nature of the Taliesin fire and murders has generated several topical treatments. See McCrea, *Building Taliesin,* 188–203; Nancy Horan, *Loving Frank* (New York: Random House, 2007); and William Drennan, *Death in a Prairie House: Frank Lloyd Wright and the Taliesin Murders* (Madison: University of Wisconsin Press, 2007).

17. For a review of Horan and Drennan's books, see Anthony Alofsin, "Loving Frank by Nancy Horan; Death in a Prairie House: Frank Lloyd Wright and the Taliesin Murders by William R. Drennan [book reviews]," *JSAH* 69, no. 3 (2010): 450–451.

18. Maginel Wright Barney, *The Valley of the God Almighty Jones* (New York: Appleton-Century, 1965), 146–147.

19. Barney, *Valley,* 147; *A,* 131.

20. *TF,* 39; *A,* 234–238; *A,* 200–204; *MM,* 234–238.

21. *TF,* 39–40.

22. Wright had met Barnsdall in Chicago in 1914, and she bought the Olive Hill site in Los Angeles in 1919; *C,* 210–213. For a monographic study, see Kathryn Smith, *Frank Lloyd Wright: Hollyhock House and Olive Hill: Buildings and Projects for Aline Barnsdall* (Santa Monica, CA: Hennessey & Ingalls, 2006).

23. For the Henry J. Allen house in Wichita, Kansas (1916), see *C,* 208–209. For the American System-Built projects, "American System-Built Houses: Iterations of an Idea," *JOAD* 3, no. 2 (2015), whole issue; Michael Osman, "American System-Built Houses: Authorship and Mass Production," in *Frank Lloyd Wright: Unpacking the Archive,* ed. Barry Bergdoll and Jennifer Gray (New York: Museum of Modern Art, 2017), 148–155.

24. For the chronology of Wright's travels to Japan, see Kathryn Smith, "Frank Lloyd Wright and the Imperial Hotel: A Postscript," *Art Bulletin* 67, no. 2 (1985): 296–310; republished and updated as "Frank Lloyd Wright and the Imperial Hotel: A Chronology," *Save Wright: Wright in Japan,* ed. Edith Payne, 6, no. 1 (2015): 2–7. The issue is subsequently cited as *Wright in Japan.*

25. For discord, see *MM,* 237–264; Wright's "Contract" with Miriam Noel, is dated 1 February 1918, microfiche W007C07, Avery.

26. ALW to MN, 1 July 1918; ALW to MN, 1 August 1918.

27. Julia Meech, *Frank Lloyd Wright and the Art of Japan: The Architect's Other Passion* (New York: Harry N. Abrams, 2001), 131–175.

28. *Antique Colour Prints from the Collection of Frank Lloyd Wright,* The Arts Club of Chicago, Exhibition, Fine Arts Building, 12 November–15 December 1917 (Chicago: The Arts Club of Chicago, 1917); WNG to FLW, 30 November 1917, bMS

680/35, 170. GA.

29. Meech, *Art of Japan,* 133; Julia Meech, "Frank Lloyd Wright and Japanese Prints," in *Frank Lloyd Wright at the Museum of Metropolitan Art* (New York: Metropolitan Museum of Art, 1982), 48–56, 146, reprinted from *Metropolitan Museum of Art Bulletin* 40, no. 2 (1982).

30. For reports on the Imperial Hotel, see Antonin Raymond to FLW, 20 July 1919, and Noémi Raymond to FLW, 17 August 1919. The relationship between Wright and the Raymonds was initially intimate and personal, but it turned sour when Wright fired Raymond in 1921. See *Antonin Raymond: An Autobiography* (Rutland, VT: Charles E. Tuttle, 1973); and Mari Sakamoto Nakahara and Ken Tadashi Oshima, *Crafting a Modern World: The Architecture and Design of Antonin and Noémi Raymond* (New York: Princeton Architectural Press, 2007).

31. Meech, *Art of Japan,* 146–151.

32. "Japanese Fear US," *CDT,* 20 August 1922.

33. FLW to Sigisbert Bosch Reitz, 17 October 1922, and Sigisbert Bosch Reitz to FLW, 26 October 1922, in Meech, *Art of Japan,* 170, 175.

34. Meech, *Art of Japan,* 168.

35. Wright's office in Los Angeles consisted of his son Lloyd Wright; Kameki Tsuchiura, a young Japanese architect who had worked with FLW on the Imperial Hotel and had brought his wife Nobu to assist; and Rudolf M. Schindler, a young Austrian architect who had started working for Wright in 1918. For Wright in Los Angeles, see Robert L. Sweeney, "Frank Lloyd Wright Chronology, 1922–1932," in *DfAL,* 185–192; for Lloyd Wright, see Alan Weintraub, *Lloyd Wright: The Architecture of Frank Lloyd Wright, Jr.* (New York: Harry Abrams, 1998) with essays and text by Thomas S. Hines, Dana Hutt, and Eric Lloyd Wright; for an overview, see Thomas S. Hines, *Architecture of the Sun: Los Angeles Modernism, 1900–1970* (New York: Rizzoli, 2010).

36. For the textile-block houses, see *LY,* 295–298; Robert Sweeney, *Wright in Hollywood: Visions of a New Architecture* (New York: Architectural History Foundation, 1994); Jeffrey M. Chusid, *Saving Wright: The Freeman House and The Preservation of Meaning, Materials, and Modernity* (New York: Norton, 2011).

37. *A,* 222.

38. Jabez K. Stone, "The Monument: The Most Talked About Hotel in the World; Tokyo's Unique Survival of Disaster," *Japan* 13 (1924): 13–17, 37, 40–41, 43, 45; cited in Robert L. Sweeney, *Frank Lloyd Wright: Annotated Bibliography* (Los Angeles: Hennessey & Ingalls, 1978), 30. For early criticism of the Imperial Hotel, see Louis Christian Mullgardt, "A Building That Is Wrong," *Architect and Engineer* 71 (1922): 81–89. For the building's structural system, see Joseph Siry, "Frank Lloyd Wright, Truscon and the Construction of the Imperial Hotel," *Wright in Japan,* 14–17; and "Shindo Akashi's Frank Lloyd Wright in Imperial Hotel: An Excerpt," translated from the Japanese, in *Wright in Japan,* 4–7.

39. *DfAL*, 188; "Wright of 'Love Bungalow' Fame Obtains Divorce," *CDT*, 15 November 1922. For the Doheny Ranch development, see *DfAL*, 16–30; for the Lake Tahoe summer colony, see *DfAL*, 47–56.

40. His first statement in the series was FLW, "In the Cause of Architecture," *AR* 23 (1908): 155–221; FLW, "In the Cause of Architecture, Second Paper," *AR*, 35 (1914): 405–413; FLW, *Experimenting with Human Lives* (Chicago: Ralph Fletcher Seymoure, 1923); FLW, "The New Imperial Hotel, Tokio, Frank Lloyd Wright, Architect," *Western Architect* 32 (1923): 39–46, pls. 1–14; FLW, "In the Wake of the Quake; Concerning the Imperial Hotel, Tokio," *Western Architect* 32 (1923): 129–132.

41. *TF,* 96–99.

42. *A,* 274; *TF,* 42–71; *LOLW,* 14–69.

43. *TF,* 98–99.

44. *TF,* 99–100. The reasons for Wright's short visit are unclear; he could have been tending to print sales or visiting Maginel, whose husband was ill.

45. *TF,* 102; Dione Neutra, *Richard Neutra: Promise and Fulfillment, 1919–1932: Selections from the Letters and Diaries of Richard and Dione Neutra* (Carbondale: Southern Illinois University Press, 1986), 135.

46. *TF,* 77–83; *NYT,* 29 February 1924, 12, 14.

47. *TF,* 85–87 and 617n86; *TF,* 94, 96; *TF,* 90–91.

48. *TF,* 105, 117. Wright had met Toomer in November 1924 when the writer traveled to Chicago to check on Olgivanna's health.

49. *TF,* 105; *A,* 299. The major project that fell through was for the National Life Insurance Company in Chicago; see *DfAL* 68, 70, 83, 100, 116.

CHAPTER 3. NADIR

1. *A,* 271–273.

2. David Lloyd Wright to FLW, 29 April 1925, 272, 274.

3. FLW to Judge Fake, 8 August 1925.

4. "Wrights Withdraw Divorce Suits, but Hint at Another," *Reading Times,* 28 November 1925.

5. *LOLW,* 18.

6. For my description, I rely on Image #716-A, 10-26-28, Jamaica Ave. E between Hollis Ct. Blvd. & 212th Street, from the New York City Municipal Archives, and Kenneth T. Jackson, ed., *The Encyclopedia of New York City* (New Haven: Yale University Press, 1995), 551.

7. *NYT,* 15 December 1925, 2; "Walker Gets Ready for Reorganization; Architects to Aid," *NYT,* 15 December 1925, 1.

8. *A,* 275.

9. FLW, "In Bondage," typescript, with pencil and ink annotations, paginated 327–335, Frank Lloyd Wright Manuscript Collection, Avery Library; identified in the Avery Catalogue as "[An Autobiography, 1932] [fragments]." FLW, "In Bondage," 327 (quote). While Wright had given a lecture in Chicago in 1918 ("Chicago Culture," reprinted in *CW*, 1:154–161) that attacked its culture and nouveau riche, his New York critique was much broader.

10. "In Bondage," 328–329.

11. "In Bondage," 328.

12. "In Bondage," 331, 334.

13. "In Bondage," 335.

14. Wright included "The Usonian City" in *A*, 314–325; *A*, 315 (quote). The term "Usonian" also appeared in an excerpt published in 1940 as "1927: The Pictures We Make"; Wright's text: "'*The American Way.*' Nationality is a craze with us. But why this term 'America' has become representative as the name of these United States at home and abroad is past recall. Samuel Butler fitted us with a good name. He called us Usonians, and our Nation of combined States, Usonia. Why not use the name? It expresses well our character and is a noble word. That I presume is why no one uses it. It is truly significant. Therefore objectionable if not painful." See Frederick Gutheim, ed., *Frank Lloyd Wright on Architecture: Selected Writings, 1894–1940* (New York: Grosset & Dunlap, 1940), 100. Butler did not use the term; James Duff Law coined it in 1903. See James D. Law, *Here and There in Two Hemispheres* (Lancaster, PA: Home Publishing, 1903), 111–112.

15. FLW, "The Usonian City," in *A*, 314–325 (quote on 315).

16. *A*, 321, 323.

17. The essay, published as "The Pictures We Make," is discussed in chapter 4.

18. *TF*, 114; *A*, 275–276; *A*, 290. Wright stated that upon returning from Puerto Rico he and Olgivanna went to Washington to sort out Olgivanna's immigration problems, but he may have antedated the visit by a year. Documentary evidence indicates the couple went to Washington in late winter or spring of 1927. See *HY*, 158, for Olgivanna's description of sights at the U.S. capital.

19. *HY*, 146–148; for an overview of the Skyscraper Regulation project, see Neil Levine, *The Urbanism of Frank Lloyd Wright* (Princeton, NJ: Princeton University Press, 2016), 143–156.

20. For a thorough survey of Wright's architecture in the 1920s, see *DfAL*. First mention of the National Life Insurance Co., Albert M. Johnson Chairman, 2 February 1924; 19 July 1924 contract; final presentation drawings completed 1925 and abandoned by Johnson that year; Wright did receive $20,000 in fees for it. *HY*, 98, 107–108, 123.

21. For Gordon Strong (1869–1954) and his project with FLW, see Mark Reinberger, "The Sugarloaf Mountain Project and Frank Lloyd Wright's Vision of a New World," *JSAH* 43, no. 1 (1984): 38–52.

22. Reinberger, "The Sugarloaf Mountain Project," 39; GS to FLW, 2 September 1924; GS to FLW, 22 September 1924; Strong met Wright through their mutual friend, Alfred MacArthur, who had apparently recommended Wright for the National Life Insurance Company commission.

23. *DfAL*, 80–100; *HY*, 108.

24. GS to FLW, 8 September 1925; FLW to GS, 22 September 1925.

25. GS to FLW, 14 October 1925.

26. GS to FLW, 14 October 1925.

27. FLW to GS, 20 October 1925.

28. Wright visited 19–20 April 1926 to see the location for the country residence notably for Isabelle Martin. The Martins had bought a site in 1926 on edge of Lake Erie in Derby, New York. Wright had made preliminary drawings for the house in May and visited the site in August of that year. He made a second site visit in April 1927 with construction under way during his stay in New York. He would make a third visit from 15–16 June 1927, and a fourth visit on 15 June 1929. For the dates of Wright's visits, see Graycliff estate chronology, http://graycliffestate.org/timeline.cfm. See also Paul Lubienecki, *Frank Lloyd Wright's Graycliff: Architecture as Sacred Space* (Lewiston, NY: Edwin Mellen, 2017), 37, passim. Martin commissioned Wright for a family mausoleum, named Blue Sky, intended for Forest Lawn Cemetery in Buffalo to bring the Martin family together for eternity. Discussion began in 1925 and would continue for three years; it was not built while they were alive but constructed later at the cemetery.

29. "Storms Taliesin in Vain," *NYT*, 4 June 1926; "Issue Warrant for Wright," *NYT*, 5 June 1926; "Mrs. F.L. Wright Sues Dancer," *CDT*, 31 August 1926, 5.

30. *A*, 276.

31. *A*, 277.

32. *LOLW*, 91. A different account claims that Wright, Olgivanna, and the two young daughters set out in his Cadillac in September 1926—driving in style despite his debt; *HY*, 150; *A*, 278. For Little, see *LY*, 54, 72, 78; and Edgar Kaufmann, Jr., "Frank Lloyd Wright's Architecture Exhibited: A Commentary by Edgar Kaufmann, Jr.," *Metropolitan Museum of Art Bulletin* 40, no. 2 (1982): 26–28.

33. "Hinzenberg Seeks Child," *NYT*, 4 September 1926; "Police Search for Wright," *NYT*, 6 September 1926; "Sues Wright for $250,000," *CDT*, 10 October 1926; *A*, 279; *LOLW*, 91–92.

34. *A*, 280.

35. *A*, 279–287.

36. For the *Wisconsin State Journal* front page, 21 October 1926, see *LOLW*, 93.

37. For Nash, see *History of Minneapolis, Gateway to the Northwest: Chicago-Minneapolis,*

vol. 2, ed. Rev. Marion Daniel Shutter, D.D., LL.D. (The S. J. Clarke Publishing Co., 1923), 301–302; and "Murder in Minneapolis," *CDT,* 2 February 1936, 5.

38. *A,* 285.

39. *A,* 286. The Thayers and the Devines visited the jail to see about Olgivanna and to take the children out briefly.

40. *A,* 286.

41. *TF,* 11.

42. R. L. Hopkins [President, Bank of Wisconsin] to FLW, 5 November 1926; *A,* 287.

43. *TF,* 119–120; *HY,* 154; *TF,* 119–120; DDM to FLW, 24 November 1926. For Schevill (1868–1954), see "Guide to Ferdinand Schevill Papers, University of Chicago Library," http://www.lib.uchicago.edu/e/scrc/findingaids/view.php?eadid=ICU .SPCL.SCHEVILL&q=Schevill. His brother-in-law was the sculptor Karl Bitter.

44. No institutional history of the Frank Lloyd Wright Foundation has yet been written. See *TF,* 354.

45. AB to FLW, 20 December 1926; *A,* 279; JLW to FLW, 25 October 1926. William Hanson Jr. to FLW, 28 October 1926, Avery; Ferdinand Schevill to FLW, 19 December 1926. For Wright's son's recollections, see John Lloyd Wright, *My Father, Frank Lloyd Wright* (New York: Dover, 1992).

46. Jane Porter to FLW, [November/December] 1926.

CHAPTER 4. REFUGE

1. Mike Wallace, *Greater Gotham: A History of New York City from 1898 to 1919* (New York: Oxford University Press, 2017), 1048–1052 (quote on 1052).

2. Robert A. M. Stern, Gregory Gilmartin, and Thomas Mellins, *New York 1930: Architecture and Urbanism Between the Two World Wars* (New York: Rizzoli, 1987), 244–258. For the culture of the 1920s as a reverberation of the dramatic changes in New York in the preceding two decades, see Wallace, *Greater Gotham,* 1049–1051.

3. Stern, Gilmartin, and Mellins, *New York 1930,* 359, 692; Jeffery Meikle, *Design in the USA* (Oxford: Oxford University Press, 2005), 102.

4. "Aeolian Hall Opening," *NYT,* 13 October 1912.

5. John Taylor Boyd Jr., "A New Emphasis in Skyscraper Design," *AR,* 52 (1922): 497.

6. For the zoning regulation of 1916, see Levine, *Urbanism,* 135–137.

7. Patricia Morton, "Primitivism," in the *Encyclopedia of Twentieth Century Architecture* (Chicago: Fitzroy Dearborn, 2003), 1061–1062; *Guide to New York City Landmarks,* comp. Andrew S. Dolkart (New York: National Trust for Historic Preservation, 1992). New York Landmarks Preservation Commission entry number 214, 130 West 30th Street, 1927–28. Cass Gilbert's own architectural evolution is telling: by 1928 he fused neo-Gothic details with simplified, geometric masses at the New York

Life Building. Surmounted by a gilded pyramidal "cap," the New York Life Building charts the slow change from revivalist skyscrapers into a more abstracted Art Deco.

8. See Le Corbusier, *Urbanisme* (Paris: Crès & Cie, 1924). For the context of urbanism in France, see Jean Louis Cohen, *France,* trans. Christian Hubert (London: Reaktion, 2015), 45–50, 108–117; for dictionary definitions, see Levine, *Urbanism,* xvi–xvii.

9. Cervin Robinson and Rosemarie Haag Bletter, *Skyscraper Style: Art Deco New York* (Oxford: Oxford University Press, 1976), 92 [Mumford's quote in plate section]; Le Corbusier, *Towards a New Architecture* (New York: Payson & Clark, 1927), translation of 13th French edition of *Vers Une Architecture* (1927) with introduction by Frederick Etchells. Wright's review is discussed in Chapter 10.

10. Stern, Gilmartin, and Mellins, *New York 1930,* 576–577; Christopher Gray, "Streetscapes/The American Radiator Building: A 1924 Precursor of Art Deco," *NYT,* 20 February 1994.

11. For a discussion of the various terms associated with Art Deco and its dating, see Robinson and Bletter, *Skyscraper Style,* 41–45. "Art Deco was not used here extensively until after the impact of the 1925 Paris exposition was felt. To be sure, a few early examples were erected between 1923 and 1927, but the style gained its greatest popularity between 1928–1931" (43).

12. Robinson and Bletter, *Skyscraper Style,* 96 (quote); Jewel Stern and John A. Stuart, *Ely Jacques Kahn, Architect: Beaux-Arts to Modernism in New York* (New York: Norton, 2006); Robinson and Bletter, *Skyscraper Style,* 17.

13. For examples of Maginel's illustration style, see Ella Flagg Young and Walter Taylor Field, *The Young and Field Literary Readers: Book One* (Boston: Ginn, 1916).

14. Mary Jane Hamilton, "Nantucket in the Art of Maginel Wright," *Historic Nantucket* 56, no. 3 (2007); Nantucket Historical Association, http://www.nha.org/history/hn/HN-summer07-wright.html. My thanks to Mary Jane Hamilton for providing details of Maginel's biography.

15. ALW to FLW, 1 August 1920; "Hiram Barney, Jurist and Financier, Dead," *NYT,* 6 July 1925, 11.

16. "Mrs. Maginel Wright Barney, 84, Illustrator and Craftsman, Dies," *NYT,* 19 April 1966, 41.

17. Hamilton, "Nantucket in the Art of Maginel Wright," n.p.

18. I draw my description from the plaques on historic buildings on Maginel's block of West 12th Street. For the cityscape around West 12th Street, see Mimi Sheraton, "West 12th Street, by the Numbers," *NYT,* 20 October 2006 [Arts and Design section]; and *AIA Guide to New York City,* 5th ed., ed. Norval White, Elliot Willensky, and Fran Leadon (Oxford: Oxford University Press, 2010), 148–149.

19. John Loring, *Joseph Urban* (New York: Harry N. Abrams, 2010); Mary Beth Betts, "The American Architecture of Joseph Urban," Ph.D. Dissertation (UMI Dissertation Services [2000] 1999); Randolph Carter, *Joseph Urban: Architecture, Theatre,*

Opera, Film (New York: Abbeville Press, 1992). For Joseph Urban and the fate of the Wiener Werkstätte, see Christian Witt-Döring and Janis Stagg, *Wiener Werkstätte, 1903–1932: The Luxury of Beauty* (Munich: Prestel, 2017).

20. *LOLW,* 94–94.

21. *HY,* 154.

22. *HY,* 154–155; *LOLW,* 85. Lindbergh's ticker-tape parade in Manhattan took place on 13 June 1927.

23. See E. B. White, *Here Is New York* (New York: The Little Book Room, 1949); also originally published in *Holiday* magazine, 1949, reprinted in *Empire City: New York Through the Centuries,* ed. Kenneth T. Jackson and David S. Dunbar (New York: Columbia University Press, 2002). John Sloan's 1927 painting, *The Lafayette,* is in the collection of the Metropolitan Museum of Art (Accession Number: 28.18).

24. *TF,* 119; *HY,* 158. The details of Olgivanna's arrest vary. She stated an immigration officer stopped her at their apartment near the Lafayette Hotel for having an expired visa and that she would be deported. She did not mention being taken into custody, but stated that Wright was furious at her being arrested.

25. AW to Colonel William Joseph Donovan, 16 January 1927; *HY,* 158. Donovan found more important pursuits later as founder of the Office of Strategic Services, the wartime intelligence agency.

26. AW to William Joseph Donovan, 16 January 1927.

27. *HY,* 158. For Olgivanna's account of Donovan and visiting Washington, D.C., see *LOLW,* 87–88.

28. Samuel Hopkins Adams, *A. Woollcott: His Life and His Words* (New York: Reynal & Hitchcock, 1945), 29, 54.

29. Adams, *Woollcott,* 77; Taylor, *Gotham,* 142, 171; Adams, *Woollcott,* 99. Woollcott finished working at the *World* in 1928.

30. Adams, *Woollcott,* 313, 227–234, 150.

31. For the Round Table, see Adams, *Woollcott,* 118–127, 161; Margaret Case Harriman, *The Vicious Circle* (New York: Rinehart & Co., 1951); Donald Leslie Johnson, *The Fountainheads: Wright, Rand, the FBI and Hollywood* (Jefferson, NC: McFarland, 2005), 121–124 (quote on 122); "Woollcott Dies After Heart Attack in Radio Studio During Broadcast," *NYT,* 24 January 1943. Brendan Gill, a *New Yorker* writer of the next generation, sneered that Woollcott "combined a foul mouth with a sentimentality so extreme that he was sometimes referred to even by friends as 'Louisa May Woollcott.'" Brendan Gill, *Here at the New Yorker* (New York: Carroll & Graf, 1987), 202.

32. Charles MacArthur came from Chicago, where he wrote for the *Chicago Tribune* and the *Chicago Daily News.* His brother Alfred was an insurance executive who worked for Albert M. Johnson, Wright's client for the ill-fated National Life Insurance Building project. Charles and Alfred's other brother John D. MacArthur, after

kicking around in various businesses, would become an insurance mogul and ultimately establish the John D. MacArthur Foundation. Wright knew Charles through Alfred and his connection to the National Life Insurance Building project. The Chicago MacArthurs were very much the kind of well-heeled clients Wright needed and to whom he occasionally pitched his projects. As the correspondence shows, Wright and Woollcott enjoyed needling MacArthur, making sarcastic remarks about him like a pair of teenage boys.

33. AW, "Profiles: The Prodigal Father," *New Yorker,* 19 July 1930, 25.

34. *Woollcott,* 298.

35. LM to FLW, 23 August 1926; LM to FLW, 23 August 1926. Mumford's *Wendingen* essay that prompted the initial communication was titled "The Social Back Ground of Frank Lloyd Wright," in *The Life-Work of the American Architect,* ed. H. Th. Wijdeveld (Santpoort, Holland: C. A Mees, 1925). For their complicated and at times tense relationship, see Robert Wojtowicz, "Lewis Mumford, Wright and the Politics of Community," *SaveWright* 7, no. 2 (2016): 10–13; Robert Wojtowicz and Bruce Brooks Pfeiffer, eds., *Frank Lloyd Wright and Lewis Mumford: Thirty Years of Correspondence* (New York: Princeton Architectural Press, 2001); and for a general treatment, see Donald L. Miller, *Lewis Mumford: A Life* (New York: Grove Press, 2002).

36. Paul T. Frankl, *Autobiography* (Los Angeles: Doppel House, 2013); Christopher Long, *Paul T. Frankl and Modern American Design* (New Haven: Yale University Press, 2007), 23, 70, 76 (with quote from Edwin Avery Park, *New Backgrounds for a New Age* [New York: Harcourt, Brace, 1927], 168), 90, 111–113.

37. *TF,* 117, 118, quoting correspondence between OLW and Maude Devine.

38. *TF,* 118, quoting correspondence between OLW and Maude Devine.

39. *TF,* 121–122.

40. *TF,* 118; Elizabeth C. Faulkner to FLW, 8 February 1927.

41. *TF,* 122; AW to FLW, 5 March 1927; *TF,* 122.

42. The rectory's address was 232 East 11th Street (Guthrie owned the townhouse immediately adjacent to it at 230 East 11th Street). The rectory burned in 1979 but was later renovated for occupancy by a cluster of groups involved in historic preservation, including the Greenwich Village Society for Historic Preservation, and an apartment for the St. Mark's rector. ("POSTINGS: Renovating the Rectory of St. Mark's in-the-Bowery; Home for a Rector, and More," *NYT,* 8 March 1998 [Real Estate section]).

43. *CW,* 1:215, 216.

44. *CW,* 1:217, 218. Wright sent a copy of the essay to George Bye, his agent, to see if he could place it with a magazine. The architect also returned to the original title, "Prelude to the City," and considered it for inclusion in the early version of his auto-

biography when it was called *From Generation to Generation.* None of these versions of "In Bondage" were published in his lifetime. The complete essay was published posthumously as "The Pictures We Make" (1927) in *CW,* 1:215–220.

45. "Graycliff Chronology," http://graycliffestate.org/timeline.cfm; *TF,* 122.

46. *TF,* 122; PLF to FLW, 12 June 1927.

47. "Mrs. Wright Releases Architect by Divorce," *NYT,* 27 August 1927, 17. For Wright's divorce, see *HY,* 159; *TF,* 123.

48. "Mrs. Wright Releases Architect by Divorce," *NYT,* 27 August 1927, 17.

49. WNG to FLW, 27 August 1927.

50. P. M. Cochius to FLW, 7 February 1927; FLW to P. M. Cochius, 7 August 1927. (Pfeiffer's date of 7 September 1927 [*HY,* 159] is incorrect.) Cochius, director of Leerdam Glasfabriek, mentioned to Wright that K. P. C. de Bazel, the distinguished architect, interior designer, and Theosophist scholar who had died in 1923, had been Leerdam's previous lead designer.

51. FLW to P. M. Cochius, 11 December 1928. Cochius visited Taliesin in November 1928 (Robert Sweeney, "Chronology," in *DfAL,* 196); Wright later signed a contract with Leerdam and sent it to Cochius, who was visiting New York.

52. FLW to JLW, 26 September 1927; FLW to H. M. Stevenson Company, 30 September 1927. Wright contacted his son John in Michigan City, Indiana, where he had set up a studio.

53. FLW to DDM, 13 September 1927.

54. FLW to Llewellyn Wright, 26 September 1927.

55. FLW to AB, 3 October 1927; AB to FLW, 16 November 1927. In August 1927, Barnsdall had given the Hollyhock House to the California Art Club for fifteen years as its new gallery and headquarters. Six years earlier, in 1921, she had complained that the complex had never satisfied her and that she never felt well in it. In the interim, however, she began to see it as a place of beauty. See *HY,* 159.

56. Wright shared his dilemma with William R. Heath, Martin's friend and a former client in Buffalo for whom Wright designed a house in 1904: "The right thing as you say and I know—for me—is my duty to my child and her mother, is to keep them close—(we have never been separated long since we came together—), and it is before any other obligation whatsoever. EVEN MONEY!!!" (FLW to William R. Health, 20 October 1927, Avery; quoted in *HY,* 158.)

57. "The School the Wright Scandals Wrecked," *Milwaukee Journal,* 12 November 1927, 3.

58. FLW to PTF, 3 October 1927; PTF to FLW, 26 September 1929. The clients, a Mr. Rogers and Mrs. Schwinger, were considering renting a space at 537 Fifth Avenue for a branch of their "California Shop." The rent was too high to proceed.

59. AW to FLW, 3 December 1927.

60. FLW to AW, 7 December 1927.

CHAPTER 5. URBAN VISIONS

1. See [WNG et al.], *St. Mark's-in-the-Bouwerie: A Vital Expression of Present-Day Religion in New York City* [New York: St. Mark's Church, 1929/1930], offprint, 16 pp., original in bMS680/322(3), GA. Intended for fundraising, the document provides a comprehensive overview of the church's history, Guthrie's endeavors, and the vestry board's aspirations. For the church history, see Joseph Siry, *Beth Sholom Synagogue: Frank Lloyd Wright and Modern Religious Architecture* (Chicago: University of Chicago Press, 2012), 65. For the building and its history, see National Register nomination, "St. Mark's Historic District," National Register of Historic Places Inventory/Nomination Form, 14 January 1969, http://www.gvshp.org/_gvshp/resources/doc/SNR_SM.pdf.

2. Tisa J. Wenger, "The Practice of Dance for the Future of Christianity: 'Eurythmic Worship' in New York's Roaring Twenties," in *Practicing Protestants: Histories of Christian Life in America,* ed. Laurie Maffly-Kipp, Leigh Schmidt, and Mark Valeri (Baltimore: Johns Hopkins University Press, 2006), 222–249 (quote on 222–223).

3. *New York World,* 24 March 1924, n.p. Newspaper clipping transcribed and retained by Guthrie, bMS 680/32, GA.

4. Wenger, "Dance," 230, quoting WNG.

5. My account relies on the brilliant and thorough study by Joseph Siry, his chapter "Rev. William Norman Guthrie and Wright's Steel Cathedral" in *BSS,* 63–104. Unless cited otherwise, subsequent quotes are from *BSS.*

6. *M,* 52; *BSS,* 75, quoting WNG.

7. For Guthrie's drawings of his proposed cathedral, see *BSS,* figs. 2.5, 2.6, and 2.7 (pp. 75, 77). The original sketches are in bMS 680, box 28, GA.

8. *BSS,* 58.

9. *BSS,* 80–81.

10. FLW to WNG, 26 October 1927. Wright's first sketch was dated February 1926 without collateral confirmation. See *HY,* 159, 162; *M,* 47.

11. *BSS,* 81, quoting FLW to WNG, 9 November 1928; FLW to WNG, 25 November 1928.

12. *BSS,* 81, quoting WNG to FLW, 31 December 1928.

13. I contest the conventional title for the project. Many writers, including Joseph Siry (*BSS*) and Herbert Muschamp (*Man About Town: Frank Lloyd Wright in New York City* [Cambridge, MA: MIT Press, 1983]), refer to it as the "Steel Cathedral." As early as 1942 Henry-Russell Hitchcock called the project "Steel Cathedral embracing minor cathedrals" (*BSS,* 81) without documentation. But the cathedral was largely

glass with its skin propped up by an internal steel tripod. The descriptions indicate that it was intended to be luminescent, not a demonstration of steel per se. In a letter between Wright and Guthrie from 9 November 1928, the architect refers to the rector's "manuscript describing the Modern Cathedral" (FLW to WNG, 9 November 1928). At other times they call it a Universal Cathedral, but never a Steel Cathedral. Because "Modern Cathedral" was Wright and Guthrie's original designation for the project, it is the title I am using throughout this book.

14. *BSS*, 74.

15. For Wright's concept and symbolism of primary geometry, see FLW, *The Japanese Print* (1912), reprinted in *CW*, 1:117.

16. *M*, 49, 55.

17. Frank Lloyd Wright, *The Future of Architecture* (New York: Horizon, 1953; repr. New York: New American Library, 1970), 204.

CHAPTER 6. DESERT DIALOGUE

1. *MM*, 237.

2. For Wright's projects in Death Valley, see *DfAL*, 66–68, passim; Neil Levine, *The Architecture of Frank Lloyd Wright* (Princeton, NJ: Princeton University Press, 1996), 173–185.

3. *A*, 293; *DfAL*, 100; and Bruce Brooks Pfeiffer, "Frank Lloyd Wright's Encounter with the Desert," *Frank Lloyd Wright Quarterly* 16, no. 1 (January 2005): 6. Albert Chase McArthur (1881–1951) had been in Wright's Oak Park office, 1907–1909. Wright did a bootleg house for his father, Warren McArthur Sr., at 4852 S. Kenwood Avenue (1892). The father also connected Wright to another early client, Edward E. Boynton, for whom the architect designed a house in Rochester, New York, in 1908. Warren Jr., Charles, and Albert McArthur are easily confused with Alfred and Charles MacArthur, Wright's other friends in Chicago, but the families aren't related.

4. WNG to FLW, 20 February 1928, bMS 680/35 (21), GA; WNG to FLW, 27 February 1928, bMS 680/35, GA. For the building history of the Arizona Biltmore Hotel, see *HY*, 142–143, 166, 202; *DfAL*, 100–101, 102, 108; *C*, 226–229.

5. Sweeney, *Hollywood*, 254; *DfAL*, 101, 116, 191–195, 198–200, and passim; Levine, *Architecture*, 107–201, 206–215; *A*, 302. The Canadian-born Alexander Chandler had moved to the Arizona territory in 1887 to practice as a doctor of veterinary surgery, but became impressed with the possibilities of irrigating the Salt River valley. He founded the town of Chandler, located in Maricopa County, in 1911, built the San Marcos Hotel as a winter resort in 1913, and took on development projects in his role as president of several Chandler companies. See *Who's Who in Arizona, 1938*, s.v. "Chandler," 38; Rufus K. Wyllys, *Men and Women of Arizona* (Phoenix: Tucson Pioneer, 1940), 80.

6. FLW to DDM, 6 April 1928; FLW to DDM, 1 June 1928. In the mid-1920s, the

addition of a dedicated railroad stop followed by the opening of an airport put Chandler, Arizona, on the map. Sweeney, *Hollywood,* 142; Levine, *Architecture,* 200, 463.

7. FLW to AJC, 30 April 1928; FLW to DDM, 1 June 1928; Sweeney, *Hollywood,* 144, citing letter from AJC to FLW, 25 September 1928; *MM,* 301.

8. *MM,* 298; *TF,* 133.

9. *MM,* 301.

10. PTF, *New Dimensions: The Decorative Arts Today in Words and Pictures* (New York: Payson and Clark, 1928); Christopher Long, *Paul T. Frankl and Modern American Design* (New Haven: Yale University Press, 2007), 86–89, 113; PTF, *Autobiography* (Los Angeles: Doppel House, 2013), 79–84; PTF to FLW 28 August 1928; Frankl, *Autobiography,* 90–99.

11. PLF to FLW, 3 August 1928; *HY,* 171.

12. FLW to AJC, 18 December 1928; FLW to AJC, 31 December 1928. See also Brian A. Spencer, "Ocotillo," *Journal of the Taliesin Fellows,* no. 34 (2009): 15, 16. According to Spencer, Wright sent letters to Henry Klumb in St. Louis, George Kastner and Cy Jahnke in Milwaukee, Donald Walker and James Yee in Chicago, and Merrill Nusbaum in Cleveland in late October, requesting that they send him drawings to review. By my count, Wright had studios in Oak Park, Taliesin I, the Imperial Hotel, Los Angeles (in multiple locations), and Taliesin II. In addition, he occasionally maintained an office in Chicago.

13. JLW to FLW, 11 December 1928; FLW to FLW Jr., 19 December 1928.

14. PLF to FLW, 26 December 1928; FLW to PLF, 26 December 1928; FLW to Chandler, 31 December 1928.

15. For Wright's misspelling, see Spencer, "Ocotillo," 14, 21n1.

16. See Spencer, "Ocotillo," 16, 18–20. In addition to the six draftsmen, the group included nursemaids Clara Daigle and Emma Louise Taggatz; Will Weston, carpenter and handyman; Weston's wife, Ann, who would serve as cook; his daughter Nettie and son Marcus, who was in the eighth grade and would continue school in Chandler; along with Svetlana. The wife of the neighboring rancher, Mrs. Smoot, drove the children to school.

17. Henry [Heinrich] Klumb, "Wright, the Man," translation of text by Heinrich de Fries, MS 1008.065, Frank Lloyd Wright Manuscript Collection, Avery. See also Edgar Tafel, *Frank Lloyd Wright, Recollections by Those Who Knew Him* (Mineola, NY: Dover, 1993), 96–98; Levine, *Architecture,* 464; Spencer, "Ocotillo," 17, 19.

18. Spencer, "Ocotillo," 17; *DfAL,* 111.

19. "The Arizona Biltmore Hotel, Phoenix, Arizona. Albert McArthur, Architect," *AR* 66 (1929): 19–55.

20. *A,* 302. Wright used alternate spellings, including the phonetic "Sahauro." Our text defaults to "Saguaro."

21. *HY,* 180–181, 80, 112–114; *DfAL,* 137–138.

22. FLW to LM, 12 May 1929; LM to FLW, 12 May 1929.

23. P. Lester Wiener to FLW, 3 March 1929, Avery. "Contempora" listed among its art-ists and founders Bruno Paul, a German progressive architect and designer of interi-ors and furnishings; Lucian Bernhard, a German graphic artist, interior designer, and former professor; and Rockwell Kent, an American painter of landscapes. The mix of Paul, Bernhard, and Kent seems incongruous, but it characterized the heterogeneous condition of modernism in 1929 and represented the modernist vision to connect art and industry with the machine as the symbol of a brave new world. Weiner has received inadequate recognition as a pioneering modernist. He was later the partner of Josep Lluís Sert, and the two figures created master plans for several cities in Co-lombia, including Bogota.

24. Mendelsohn's visit occurred 3–4 November 1924, the month after Richard and Di-one Neutra arrived to stay working at Taliesin; the Neutras departed February 1925 (Sweeney, "Chronology," *DfAL,* 190). For Mendelsohn's previous visit to Wright, see Anthony Alofsin, *Frank Lloyd Wright, Europe and Beyond* (Berkeley: University of California Press, 1999), 8nn11–15, 216–217.

25. OLW quoted in *HY,* 187; *HY,* 191; Sweeney, *Hollywood,* 148, citing the "Architect Leaves Home for Wisconsin," *Chandler Arizonan,* 30 May 1929; *LOLW,* 96–99. By the time Wright had left, he and his crew had erected fourteen or fifteen wood and canvas shelters, but the structures' fate was precarious. On 2 June 1929, a fire, the nemesis of all of Wright's residences, broke out. The caretaker, George Weldon, saved much of the property, but the camp gradually dissolved back into the desert.

26. *A,* 308, 301–312.

27. *A,* 302, 304.

28. *A,* 305, 307, 308.

29. *A,* 303; "In the Cause of Architecture: Arizona," 29 June 1929, Frank Lloyd Wright Manuscript Collection, Ms. 2401.013 A, 9 pp., typescript, Avery; *A,* 394.

30. *A,* 306.

31. *A,* 308, 305, 307–308.

32. *A,* 315, 316, 311.

33. Merle Armitage, the avant-garde book designer and theater impresario in Los Ange-les, recounted that he and Lloyd Wright were present for the dinner in the desert at which Wright made his remarks. See *Texas Quarterly* 5 (1962): 85, cited in Einbinder, *American Genius,* 417; Einbinder, *American Genius,* 251–253; *TF,* 145; and FLW, "Living in the Desert Part Two," Wright Manuscript Collection, Ms. 2401.238 D, 17 pp., typescript with edits, n.d., c. 1940 or later, Avery.

34. Reyner Banham, "The Wilderness Years of Frank Lloyd Wright," *RIBA Journal,* December 1969, 518.

CHAPTER 7. SPINNING TOWER

1. FLW to WNG, 5 May 1927.

2. WNG to FLW, 19 October 1927, bMS 680/35 (19), GA. With respect to keeping Wright's ideas secret lest they be stolen, Guthrie added, "America doesn't believe in original ideas and certainly they need patenting—our ideas they don't want. They prefer ideas that have been tried out, and tried in the community where they can see them in steel and cement. Your ideas are not even on paper."

3. WNG to FLW, 19 October 1927, bMS 680/35 (19), GA.

4. National Spiritual Assembly of the Bahá'ís of the United States and Canada and Universal House of Justice. *The Bahá'í World: A Biennial International Record* (New York: Baha'i Pub. Committee, 1970), 849, 850.

5. WNG to FLW, 19 October 1927, bMS 680/35 (19), GA.

6. WNG to FLW, 19 October 1927, bMS 680/35 (19), GA.

7. FLW to WNG, 26 October 26, 1927.

8. FLW to WNG, 26 October 26, 1927.

9. WNG to FLW, 29 October 1927.

10. HH to FLW, 2 November 1927.

11. FLW to HH, 10 November 1927.

12. FLW to WNG, 25 November 1927.

13. WNG to FLW, 20 February 1928, bMS 680/35 (21), GA.

14. *HY,* 164–173; WNG to WTM, 25 April 1928, bMS 680/34 (71), GA; WNG to FLW, 8 November 1928, bMS 680/35 (22), GA.

15. FLW to WNG, 9 November 1928.

16. For the Baptists' conversion of their building site and air rights to rental spaces, see *BSS,* 74.

17. WNG to FLW, 12 November 1928, bMS 680/35 (23), GA.

18. WNG to FLW, 12 November 1928, bMS 680/35 (23), GA.

19. FLW to WNG, 20 November 1928, bMS 680/35 (24), GA.

20. Though there is no indication that Wright or Otto Kahn knew each other personally, Otto Kahn would fund the series of Princeton lectures in which Wright participated. See Neil Levine, "Introduction," *Modern Architecture: Being the Kahn Lectures for 1930* (repr. Princeton, NJ: Princeton University Press, 2008), xi–xvi; for Corbett, see Paul D. Stoller, "The Architecture of Harvey Wiley Corbett," master's thesis, University of Wisconsin–Madison, 1995; Levine, *Urbanism,* 136, 402n57.

21. FLW to HH, 2 January 1929; WNG to FLW, 31 December 1928; WNG to FLW, 8 January 1929. Holley kept pressure on the vestry board to appoint Wright to the commission: HH to FLW, 4 January 1929, and HH to FLW, 23 January 1929.

22. FLW to WNG, 4 March 1929.

23. Levine, *Architecture,* 464.

24. FLW to WNG, 4 March 1929; WNG to FLW, 11 March 1929, bMS 680/35 (25), GA; FLW to Donald Walker [telegram], 18 June 1929; *HY,* 191; and for Wright's visit to the Martin site on 15 June 1929, see the Graycliff chronology at http://graycliffestate .org/timeline.cfm.

25. *A,* 311, 314.

26. *NYT,* 18 June 1929, 1, 12, passim.

27. PTF to FLW [telegram], 17 June 1929; P. Lester Wiener to FLW, 28 June 1929. See "Contempora Exhibition of Art and Industry," 18 June 1929, Avery. While the exhibition featured Erich Mendelsohn, it also included the French fashion designer Paul Poiret; Vally Wieselthier, a Viennese ceramicist sculptor; and Julius Klinger, an Austrian painter and graphic artist. The group also included the currently unidentified Joseph Singel.

28. "Discussion of Modern Architecture by Frank Lloyd Wright and Hugh Ferrisss," 22 June 1929, Box 505, Item 2401.062 D, 8 pp., Avery. Ferriss was the recent author of *The Metropolis of Tomorrow* (New York: Ives Washburn, 1929). For more on Ferriss, see Carol Willis, "Drawing Towards Tomorrow," in the reprint edition (Princeton, NJ: Princeton Architectural Press, 1986). All quotations are from "Discussion of Modern Architecture."

29. HH to FLW, 6 September 1929.

30. FLW to AJC, 9 July 1929, quoted in *HY,* 191; FLW to Donald Walker [telegram], 25 June 1929.

31. WNG to FLW, 4 July 1929, bMS 680/35 (26), GA; WNG to FLW, 14 July 1929, bMS 680/35 (27), GA.

32. FLW to WNG, 6 July 1929.

33. FLW to Brooks Brothers, 5 August 1929.

34. HH to FLW, 6 September 1929; FLW to HH, 7 September 1929.

35. FLW to WNG, 5 October 1929.

36. PTF to FLW, 26 September 1929. A luncheon was originally proposed, but Wright's event would become a gala dinner. Wright suggested having a symposium—led by the architect himself (FLW to PTF, 30 September 1929). C. Adolph Glassgold [AU-DAC secretary] to FLW [telegram], 4 October 1929. Wright informed Paul T. Frankl that he will come to New York on 15 October 1929 (FLW to PTF, 3 October 1929); FLW to Maginel Wright Barney, 5 October 1929; FLW to HH, 5 October 1929; "City Brevities," *NYT,* 12 October 1929, 26.

37. *NYT,* 11 October 1929, passim.

38. FLW to LLW, 29 October 1929.

39. WNG to FLW, October 1929 (Undated and missing page 1).

40. WNG to FLW, October 1929 (Undated and missing page 1).

41. For a typical Associated Press report, see "Plan Inverted Pyramid Flats," *Ogden Standard-Examiner* (Ogden, Utah), 18 October 1929, 5; *Time* 14 (28 October 1929): 62.

42. George C. Gallati, "Frank Lloyd Wright's Friends Offer Aid for Work," *Daily News* (Canonsburg, PA), 18 October 1929, 16; *Outlook and Independent,* 30 October 1929, 36; "Wright's Pyramids," *Time* 14, no. 18 (28 October 1929): 68; "What Architects Are Talking About," *American Architect* 136 (1929): 53–4.

43. Warren Shepard Matthews to FLW, 17 October 1929.

44. "Odd-Type Buildings to Overlook Church," *NYT,* 19 October 1929.

45. The situation was already confusing, as this would be the second corporation claiming to take control of Wright's assets and save him from financial woe: "Eccentric Architect Incorporates Himself," *Ames Daily Tribune* (Ames, Iowa), 21 September 1929, 3; Donald Hoffmann, *Frank Lloyd Wright, Louis Sullivan, and the Skyscraper* (Mineola, NY: Dover, 1998), 90n10; WNG to FLW, 16 October 1929, bMS 680/32 (15), GA. The vestry committee outlined an endowment of $1 million to "effect a property development" and to carry on the church's religious activities. The amount was later reduced to $500,000 but never raised.

46. FLW to WNG, 21 October 1929.

47. WNG to FLW, 23 October 1929, bMS 680/35 (28), GA.

48. FLW to WNG, 28 October 1929. Wright elaborated: "As a victim and beneficiary of much so-called publicity,—take it from me—that publicity is always premature or belated. I have never known of any that was opportune."

49. Bruce Bliven to FLW, 24 October 1929; Bruce Bliven [*New Republic*] to FLW, 24 October 1929. Bliven started work at the *New Republic* in 1923 and was editor in chief from 1930 to 1953. He was also the father of Bruce Bliven, a longtime staff writer for the *New Yorker*. See "The Papers of Bruce Bliven," University of Iowa Libraries, Iowa City, Iowa, available at https://www.lib.uiowa.edu/scua/msc/tomsc600/msc566/iaauth_bliven.html.

50. FLW to Bruce Bliven, 29 October 1929.

51. FLW to LLW, 29 October 1929.

52. For confirmation of the date of the vestry board meeting, Monday evening, 4 November 1929, see HH to FLW, 28 October 1929. Wright claimed he was preparing a set of ozalid prints, rendered in color, that he hoped to send to New York before the meeting. FLW to WSM, 28 October 1929; FLW to Warren Matthews, 30 October 1929, bMS 680/35 (29), GA (quote). Wright also confirmed with Guthrie that he was indeed coming to New York and would arrive for the vestry meeting with "two completed sets of studies and all the information you could require, hoping to satisfy everybody concerned, particularly you." FLW to WNG, 31 October 1929, bMS 680/35 (30), GA.

53. Guthrie had set 1 December 1929, as the target date for public symposium. His friend Edward L. Tilton, architect of the U.S. Immigration Station on Ellis Island, had suggested inviting William A. Boring, his former partner who was director of Columbia University's School of Architecture; Harvey Wiley Corbett, the Art Deco master; Cass Gilbert, architect of the Woolworth Building; and Whitney Warren, the wizard behind the design of Grand Central Terminal. Guthrie saw this event as a kind of "popular propaganda." Furthermore, the august company would raise Wright's status beyond a mere outsider and position him as if he were a player on the New York scene. Except for Wright, none of the invited architects were told they were setting the stage for St. Mark's official public announcement of the project planned a week later on 8 December. Guthrie, of course, wanted Wright's approval of the idea, but that did not keep him from pressing Wright on pragmatics. "The question is," he asked, "whether your plan can be put through our building department and whether it can be financed, and I am quite sure that the beauty will go a long way toward overcoming the evil effects of conventional criticism." WNG to FLW, 23 October 1929, MS 680/35 (28), GA; FLW to WNG, 28 October 1929. Wright was receptive to Guthrie's idea: FLW to HH, 28 October 1929.

CHAPTER 8. COMMAND PERFORMANCE

1. "Financial Markets," *NYT,* 4 November 1929, 18, 36.

2. "Elevated Train Stops for a Dog," *NYT,* 4 November 1929, 1

3. "Open New Galleries for Sculpture Show," *NYT,* 4 November 1929, 52.

4. FLW to Arthur J. Hopper, 28 September 1929, Avery. Wright intended for the glass skin to expand and contract with heat and cold.

5. In an earlier version of the scheme, Wright had placed the spacious bedroom on one side of the floor and a "Boudoir" on the other, transforming the New York practice then in use of providing a "dressing" for a one-bedroom apartment. The space had included a day bed, dressing table, chest of drawers, and hassock. After taking into account the realistic needs of potential renters, however, the architect later swapped out the luxurious dressing area for a second bedroom, a far more practical response to the church's need to make these units a paying operation.

6. WNG to FLW, 6 November 1929, bMS 680/35 (31), GA. Guthrie followed up on the discussion about the impact of the project on nearby houses. The arguments with Matthews were tedious and protracted. See FLW to WSM, 30 October 1929; WSM to FLW [telegram], 8 November 1929; FLW to WSM, 9 November 1929, bMS 680/35 (29), GA. Wright still had to play ball with Matthews, though he couldn't resist a few jabs:

"I notice your official title seems to be Warren Shepherd [*sic*] Matthews. I have always envied the two-name architects and [should] be Lloyd Wright. Had I known as much thirty years ago as I do now I should have been. Warren Matthews is an appealing name to me, like Raymond Hood, Cass Gilbert, Norman Shaw. History holds no instances of a three-name architect having survived as such. Instinctively I put War-ren Matthews on the plans as indicated of personality and achievement entitling the owner of the name to distinction and merit. . . . If you want this changed to Warren Shepherd Matthews kindly let me know. In intending to do you honor I may have been guilty of a faux pas." (FLW to WSM, 3 December 1929)

7. FLW to HH, 14 December 1929. The church had prepared a thorough report that looked at the status of its existing properties, acquisition costs for new properties, expenses, and potential financial returns—the kind of due diligence required to make the development happen. See "Report of the Properties Committee. St. Marks in the Bouwerie, New York City, Referring to Plot Plan of Our Block, December 11, 1929," 7 pp., typescript, St. Marks in the Bouwerie Collection, document folder, Avery. Wright repeated to Guthrie what he told Holley about Chicago's interest in the towers, adding that he assumed the New York City building department was satisfied and that, though their buildings had to drop back to twelve stories, they would still be very beautiful (FLW to WNG, 14 December 1929).

8. "What Architects Are Talking About," *American Architect* 136 (1929): 53–54.

9. "What Architects Are Talking About," *American Architect* 136 (1929): 53–54.

10. "Saint Mark's Towers, the Glass House for America," *AR* 67 (1930): 1–4.

11. The "offenders" who had published the St. Mark's project included, among others, World-wide Photos, the Associated Press, the United Press, and "C.C.C."; John Ford to FLW, 24 January 1930; clipping, "Architect Plans Glass House in Manhattan," 21 January [1930], p. 2 of unidentified newspaper; both documents in Better Homes in America Records, Box 11, folder 5, Hoover Institution Archives, Stanford University; FLW to DH, 5 February 1930. My thanks to Jennifer Tait for providing the references to Ford and Better Homes in America. Ford and his wife, Katherine Morrow Ford, later wrote *Modern House in America* (New York: Architectural Book Publishing, 1940), a pioneering survey of a broad range of modern residences in the United States.

12. DH to FLW [telegram], 15 January 1930; FLW to HH, 25 January 1930. FLW to HH, 17 February 1930; FLW to WNG, 25 February 1930; also in Brooks Bruce Pfeiffer, ed., *Letters to Clients* (Fresno: Press at California State University, 1986), 287.

13. FLW to WNG, 26 February 1930; also cited in Pfeiffer, *Letters to Clients,* 289.

14. WNG to FLW, 5 March 1930; FLW to WNG, 7 March 1930. Wright asked for input from a New York architect in whom Justin Miner, a key figure in financial matters, and the vestry would have confidence, but Miner had been ill for three and half months and had not replied, a further impediment to action (FLW to Justin Miner [telegram], 31 March 1930; HH to FLW 18 April 1930). For how Wright may never have been paid, see *HY,* 212.

15. WNG to FLW, 20 May 1930, and WNG to FLW, 9 June 1930, both quoted in Donald Hoffmann, *Frank Lloyd Wright, Louis Sullivan, and the Skyscraper* (Mineola, NY: Dover, 1998), 71.

16. FLW to WNG, 9 February 1931; also cited in Pfeiffer, *Letters to Clients,* 289, 290; WNG to FLW, 27 February 1931.

17. FLW to WNG, 28 March 1931. Communication between Wright and Guthrie continued throughout the spring and summer of 1931 even while Guthrie vacationed on the SS *Republic.*

CHAPTER 9. PIVOT POINT

1. *A,* 295; *HY,* 204; *TF,* 147.

2. Ellen Moody, "Conserving and Exhibiting the New York Models," in *Frank Lloyd Wright: Unpacking the Archive,* ed. Barry Bergdoll and Jennifer Gray (New York: Museum of Modern Art, 2017), 226–232.

3. For Wright's mention of the Princeton lectures, see FLW to WNG, 1 May 1930; WNG to FLW, 10 May 1930.

4. LM to FLW, 11 March 1930. Wright added, "We need a human antidote to the inspired madness of Buckminster Fuller; + even Hitchcock may let his eyes convert him to what his intelligence objects!"

5. Karl Jensen [Wright's secretary] to Richard Lloyd Jones, 21 March 1930, notes that Wright is returning at the end of the week. The details of Wright's agenda are unconfirmed: they could have included a lecture at a women's club, a push for his book project at the *Architectural Record,* a futile effort for St. Mark's, or a visit to Woodstock, New York, in conjunction with a commission for a new theater; FLW to E. Baldwin Smith, 1 April 1930.

6. FLW to E. Baldwin Smith, 1 April 1930.

7. FLW to LM, 14 April 1930; LM to FLW, 19 April 1930.

8. Drawing on the extensive research of Robert Judson Clark, Neil Levine wrote a new introduction to FLW, *Modern Architecture: Being the Kahn Lectures for 1930* (reprint, Princeton, NJ: Princeton University Press, 2008), ix–lxxi (quote on xx).

9. FLW, *Kahn Lectures,* 103, 109.

10. Levine, "Introduction," in FLW, *Kahn Lectures,* xx–xxi; [Sherley W. Morgan] to FLW, 3 June 1930.

11. For Guthrie on the lectures, see WNG to FLW, 20 May 1930. See also Kathryn Smith, *On Exhibit: Frank Lloyd Wright's Architectural Exhibition* (Princeton, NJ: Princeton University Press, 2017), 46–47, 233.

12. PTF to FLW, 13 January 1930; FLW to PTF, 25 January 1930. Frankl also planned a visit to Taliesin; William Lescaze to FLW, 10 April 1930. For Howe, see Robert A. M. Stern, *George Howe: Toward a Modern American Architecture* (New Haven: Yale University Press, 1975); for Lescaze, see Arthur J. Pulos, *William Lescaze: The Rise of Modern Design in America* (Syracuse, NY: Syracuse University Library Associates, 1984); Lorraine W. Lanmon, *William Lescaze, Architect* (Philadelphia: Art Alliance Press; London: Associated University Presses, 1987); Caroline R. Zaleski, *Long Island*

Modernism, 1930–1980 (New York: Norton, 2012).

13. Parker Hooper [*Architectural Forum*] to FLW, 25 March 1930; FLW to Parker Hooper, 1 April 1930. The article appeared as FLW, "The Logic of Contemporary Architecture as an Expression of this Age," *Architectural Forum* 52 (1930): 637–638.

14. In haste, Wright had left New York for Taliesin, carelessly missing a dinner date he had with Norman Bel Geddes. Geddes wrote the architect on 5 December 1929: "Also, whatever happened to our dinner engagement? I expected you to dinner the Monday following our talk" (Norman Gel Geddes to FLW, 5 December 1929). Wright issued a cursory apology: "We left too soon to come back to you on Monday but I should have dropped you a note telling you this long before" (FLW to Norman Bel Geddes, 14 December 1929; [Roger William] Riis to FLW, 12 March 1930, Avery). The firm was the publicist for the company and had received Geddes's approval for contacting Wright. See Roger William Riis and Charles W. Bonner Jr., *Publicity: A Study of the Development of Industrial News* (New York: J. H. Sears & Co., 1926). For the agency, see Scott M. Cutlip, *The Unseen Power: Public Relations: A History* (New York: Routledge, 1994). FLW to [Roger William] Riis [Riis and Bonner], 1 April 1930. For the Fair, see Adnan Morshed, "The Aesthetics of Ascension in Norman Bel Geddes's Futurama," *JSAH* 63, no. 1 (2004): 74–79; Barbara Szerlip, *The Man Who Designed the Future: Norman Belle Geddes and the Invention of Twentieth-Century America* (Brooklyn, NY: Melville House, 2017).

15. For Kathryn Smith's treatment of the Architectural League events, see *OE*, 44–48. She comes to same conclusion I draw: "The exhibition and attendant events at Princeton University and the Architectural League, especially the latter, had the intended effect: a rehabilitation of Wright's public image" (*OE*, 48). She speculates, however, that Joseph Urban was the "key figure" behind the league's action and exaggerates his role in the events. The origin of the invitation from the "Little Napoleons" and the correspondence between Ray Hood, among others, and Wright shows that an awareness of Wright's presence was much more extensive among practitioners in New York.

16. *OE*, 44–45; "1927: League Moves into New Quarters," Architectural League of New York, http://archleague.org/2010.

17. RH to FLW, 16 May 1930. For Hood, see Walter H. Kilham, *Raymond Hood, Architect: Form Through Function in the American Skyscraper* (New York: Architectural Book Publishing Co., 1973). The League's invitation is reproduced in *OE*, 47 (fig. 2.7):

THE ARCHITECTURAL LEAGUE

OF NEW YORK

announces an exhibition

of renderings, drawings, and types of ornament by

Frank Lloyd Wright

MAY 20 to JUNE 12, 1930

Approach and setting by

JOSEPH URBAN

18. FLW to Donald Walker [telegram], 22 May 1930. Wright had previously sent Walker from Taliesin to Princeton to install the exhibition. See Architectural League of New York to FLW, 16 April 1930; FLW to HH, 22 April 1930; *OE*, 44–48.

19. *NYT*, 28 May 1930, 13, with advertisement for the building on p. 45. The opening occurred on 27 May.

20. "Frank L. Wright Honored Here," *NYT*, 29 May 1930, 28.

21. Henry Saylor "Editor's Diary, Wednesday, May 28," *Architecture* 62 (1930): 105, quoted in *OE*, 47, 251n35. Smith speculates (*OE*, 47) that the event was "incongruous" and merely the effort of Joseph Urban to help his friend Wright. The correspondence surrounding the testimonial does not point singly to him as the source. Though Urban and Wright were friends, Urban later reneged on providing funds for the Taliesin Fellowship.

22. FLW to OLW [telegram], 30 May 1930.

23. FLW to LW, n.d., cited as ca. 3 June 1930 in *OE*, 51n37.

24. FLW to RH, 2 June 1930; RH to FLW, 26 June 1930; RH to FLW, 7 July 1930.

25. William Lescaze to FLW, 20 June 1930; Ely Jacques Kahn to FLW, 20 August 1930; Ralph Walker to FLW, 21 November 1930; Ralph Walker to FLW, 16 December 1930.

26. EL to FLW, 12 June 1930. Emil Lorch was an active figure in the Midwest for creating a progressive outpost at Michigan. He maintained contact with a variety of European modernists and was sympathetic to Wright's work and his ideology. For their ongoing dialogue, see EL to FLW, 9 July 1930; EL to FLW, 14 July 1930.

27. FLW to LM, [June] 1930, Avery (misdated in index to correspondence as 3-1-30). More than that, he claimed that there was "a genuine desire" to involve him in some way with the Chicago fair: "What that way is I don't know yet. Corbett, Walker, Hood, and Kahn give me this much advance notice."

28. LM to FLW, 1 July 1930.

29. Everett V. Meeks to FLW, 30 July 1930; Katherine Atwater to FLW, 23 September 1930; Katherine Atwater to FLW, [late September 1930]; Katherine Atwater to FLW, 2 October 1930; *HY*, 208. Smith covers the exhibition's domestic and international tours in detail in *OE*, 48–66, 233.

30. FLW to WNG, 28 March 1931.

31. *HY*, 208; *OE*, 233; Louise Mendelsohn to FLW, 22 January 1931.

32. *CDT*, 8 September 1929, p. B2. The newspaper announced Wright and Barry Byrne would talk on 10 September at the Architects Club of Chicago, organized by the Chicago Chapter the American Institute of Architects.

33. R. Plimpton to FLW, 13 February 1931 (quote); Harold Stark to FLW, 24 January 1931; (invitation from) Harold Stark to FLW, 11 August 1930. For Wright's lectures, see Levine, "Introduction," in FLW, *Kahn Lectures*, xxi.

34. H. I. Brock, "A Pioneer in Architecture That Is Called Modern; Frank Lloyd Wright, Who Proposes a Glass Tower for New York, Has Adapted His Art to the Machine Age," *NYT,* 29 June 1930, 11, 19.

35. HH to FLW, 3 July 1930.

36. AJC to FLW, 21 July 1930.

37. Adams, *Woollcott,* 309; "Woollcott Dies After Heart Attack in Radio Studio During Broadcast," *NYT,* 24 January 1943, 1, 43; Adams, *Woollcott,* 161.

38. AW, "Profiles: The Prodigal Father," *New Yorker,* 19 July 1930, 22–25.

39. AW, "Prodigal Father," 23.

40. AW, "Prodigal Father," 24–25.

41. AW, "Prodigal Father," 25.

42. FS to FLW, 28 July 1930; WNG to FLW, 29 July 1930; LM to FLW, 24 August 1930; Don Anderson to FLW, 31 July 1930.

43. FLW to AW, 31 July 1930.

44. FLW to Kihachiro Okura, 29 July 1930. Wright sent similar sentiments to his former chief assistant at the Imperial Hotel: "But America is awakening to the importance of what I have done and is likely to keep me busy" (FLW to Arata Endo, 29 July 1930). For Einstein, see FLW to EM [telegram], 13 February 1931; *HY,* 213; Milton Cameron, "Albert Einstein, Frank Lloyd Wright, Le Corbusier, and the Future of the American City," Institute for Advanced Studies, "Institute Letter," Spring 2014, https://www.ias.edu/articles/spring14 and https://www.ias.edu/ideas/2014/cameron-einstein. For Ford, see WNG to FLW, 6 November 1929.

45. *HY,* 219–220. On the sail to Brazil, the Wrights enjoyed the shipboard company of Eliel Saarinen, the Finnish architect who represented Europe in the judging; Olgivanna states they stayed six weeks in Brazil (*LOLW,* 114–117). For details, see Adriana Irigoyen, "Frank Lloyd Wright in Brazil," *Journal of Architecture* 5, no. 2 (2000): 137–157.

CHAPTER 10. WRIGHT AS WRITER

1. Kenneth Frampton, "Introduction," *CW,* 2:9.

2. My inventory of the FLW Manuscript Collection, Avery, indicates that between 1918 and 1927, Wright produced only four manuscripts. The total between 1927 and 1932 excludes his writings for "In the Cause of Architecture" and his *Autobiography.*

3. For Wright's role in the debates about modern architecture in the mid-1920s in Europe and the publications about him, see Anthony Alofsin, "Frank Lloyd Wright and Modernism," in *Frank Lloyd Wright, Architect,* ed. Terence Riley with Peter Reed (New York: Museum of Modern Art, 1994), 39–47.

4. The Wasmuth Verlag, Wright's publisher in Berlin in the early 1910s, remained on

the sidelines in later years. It issued a reduced facsimile of the Wasmuth folios around 1924–1925. Poor in quality, limited in numbers, it was printed without Wright's permission.

5. For De Fries (1887–1938), see Roland Jaeger, *Heinrich de Fries und sein Beitrag zur Architekturpublizistik der zwanziger Jahre* (Berlin: Gebrüder Mann, 2001).

6. HdF to FLW, 10 October 1925: De Fries sent color plates to Wright of his book, *Aus dem Lebenswerk,* noted difficulties in printing the reproductions, and said the drawings were damaged in transit. For the review of De Fries's book by Greta Dexel, 12 December 1926, see Alofsin, "Frank Lloyd Wright and Modernism," 41, 56n45.

7. FLW to H. Th. Wijdeveld, 30 October 1925, confirming receipt of the copy of *Wendingen* in Bruce Brooks Pfeiffer, ed., *Frank Lloyd Wright: Letters to Architects* (Fresno: Press at California State University, 1984), 57; Donald Longmead and Donald Leslie Johnson, *Architectural Excursions: Frank Lloyd Wright, Holland and Europe* (Westport, CT: Greenwood, 2000), 97; H. Th. Wijdeveld to FLW, 25 April 1926.

8. Jean Badovici, "Entretiens sur l'architecture vivante: l'art de Frank Lloyd Wright," *L'Architecture Vivante* 2 (1924): 26–27, pls. 34–35. An illustration of the Millard House, "La Miniatura," appeared in *L'Architecture Vivante* (1927), pl. 31; Jean Badovici, "Frank Lloyd Wright," *L'Architecture Vivante* (1930): 49–76, pls. 26–50 (included in Badovici, ed., *Frank Lloyd Wright: Architecte américain* [Paris]: Albert Morancé, 1932).

9. Jean Badovici, "Frank Lloyd Wright," *Cahiers d'Art* 1, no. 2 (1926): 30–33.

10. André Lurçat to FLW, [late September] 1927; FLW to DDM, 13 September 1927; FLW to PTF, 1 October 1927; FLW to PTF, 3 October 1927. In the small world of transatlantic interplay, Jean Lurçat, André's brother, was a guest of honor at AUDAC in New York, Wright's umbrella organization for modern design (DH to Members of AUDAC, 29 November 1930). Douglas Haskell was secretary of AUDAC at this time.

11. André Lurçat to FLW, 29 October 1927; Christian Zervos to FLW, 9 November 1927.

12. Christian Zervos to FLW, 9 November 1927. For Le Corbusier's entry, see *Kenneth Frampton's Modern Architecture: A Critical History* (Singapore: Thames & Hudson, 1992), 159–160.

13. Christian Zervos to FLW, 9 November 1927.

14. "Frank Lloyd Wright," *Cahiers d'Art* 2, no. 9 (1927): 322–328; "Etats-Unis," *Cahiers d'Art* 2, no. 10 (1927): xiii; HRH, "Introduction," in *Frank Lloyd Wright* (Collection "Les Maitres de l'architecture contemporaine," no. 1) (Paris: Cahiers d'Art, 1928), 1–6. The monograph included illustrations of Wright's work completed between 1902 and 1923. Quotes and references to Hitchcock's introduction come from my translation. For Wright's comment about Harvard graduates, see Edgar Tafel, ed., *Frank Lloyd Wright: Recollections by Those Who Knew Him* (Mineola, NY: Dover, 1993), 256. For

an expanded biography of Henry-Russell Hitchcock, see Helen Searing, ed., *In Search of Modern Architecture: A Tribute to Henry-Russell Hitchcock* (New York: Architectural History Foundation; Cambridge, MA: MIT Press, 1982).

15. HRH, "Introduction."

16. HRH, "Introduction."

17. FLW to HRH, [November 1928], dated inaccurately as "1/1/1926" in Avery.

18. Robert Benson, "Douglas Haskell and the Modern Movement in American Architecture," *Journal of Architectural Education* 36, no. 4 (1983): 2–9; DH to FLW, 11 August 1928. DH, "Organic Architecture: Frank Lloyd Wright," *Creative Arts* 3 (1928): li–vii.

19. DH, "Building or Sculpture? The Architecture of 'Mass,'" *AR* 67 (1930): 366–368; FLW to DH, 21 April 1930; DH to FLW [telegram], 24 April 1930, Avery; FLW to M. A. Mikkelsen [telegram], 21 April 1930.

20. George T. Bye to FLW, 8 March 1927.

21. FLW, "Why the Japanese Earthquake Did Not Destroy the Hotel Imperial," *Liberty* 4 (1927): 61–66; for an example of positive response, see Cleaver Thayer to FLW, 27 November 1927; FLW, "Taliesin: The Chronicle of a House with a Heart," *Liberty* 6 (1929): 21–22, 24, 26–29.

22. For commission of the essays, see M. A. Mikkelsen to H. H. Saylor [editor of *Architecture*], 7 July 1930.

23. *HY*, 15; FLW, "In the Cause of Architecture I: The Logic of the Plan," quoted in *CW* 1:249.

24. FLW to M. A. Mikkelsen, 30 September 1927. Wright paid for the subscriptions of Lucien Hanks, Llewellyn Wright, H. Th. Wijdeveld, Erich Mendelsohn, and H. P. Berlage. He instructed Mikkelsen, however, to bill Norman Guthrie, Andrew T. Porter, Darwin D. Martin, William R. Heath, Franz Aust, Kameki Tsuchiura, Werner Moser, and Rudolph Schindler for their own subscriptions.

25. The correspondence about Wright's trying to get the *Architectural Record* to publish his essays as a book is extensive. See, for example, FLW to M. A. Mikkelsen, 17 February 1930; FLW to DH, 17 February 1930; DH to FLW, 10 April 1930; FLW to A. Lawrence Kocher [*Architectural Record*], 10 March 1930.

26. A. Lawrence Kocher to FLW, 28 March 1930. Wright's agreement with the *Record,* dated 4 May 1927, stipulated that all articles be submitted by 1 October 1928; DH to FLW, 25 August 1930. Kocher was editor at *Architectural Record* through 1938 and led in moving its coverage exclusively to building techniques, particularly prefabrication. See Anna Goodman, "Making Prefabrication American: The Work of A. Lawrence Kocher," *Journal of Architectural Education* 71, no. 1 (2017): 22–33.

27. M. A. Mikkelsen to H. H. Saylor, 7 July 1930, Avery. Scribner's published the journal *Architecture* from 1917 to 1936. After considering publishing Wright's material as *Creative Matter in the Nature of Materials,* it was decided in 1931 that in the economic

recession, his design made the book too expensive for architects and students to purchase (*HY,* 218–219). The *Architectural Record* eventually reprinted the articles, including articles from a symposium on Wright: *In the Cause of Architecture,* ed. Frederick Gutheim (New York: Architectural Record Book, [1975]).

28. HH to FLW, 21 September 1927.

29. FLW, "Towards a New Architecture," *World Unity* 2 (1928): 393–395, quoted from *CW,* 1:317. Le Corbusier later described the George Washington Bridge as "the only seat of grace in the disordered city" (Le Corbusier, *When the Cathedrals Were White* [New York: Reynal & Hitchcock, 1947], 75.)

30. Robert Morss Lovett to FLW, 28 September 1927.

31. Bruce Bliven to FLW, 8 November 1929.

32. Jean Badovici, ed., *Frank Lloyd Wright: Architecte américain* (Paris: Albert Morancé, 1932), a review of material previously published in *L'Architecture Vivant.* The copies arrived at Taliesin in January 1931. See also Heinrich De Fries, "Neue Plane von Frank Lloyd Wright," *Die Form: Zeischrift für Gestaltende Arbeit* 5, no. 13 (1930): 342–349.

33. Robert L. Leonard and C. Adolph Glassgold [AUDAC] to FLW, 16 July 1930. The committee also thought Wright's concepts were similar to the new "laws" of those that Raymond Hood had sent them. Wright's involvement was first mentioned in Robert L. Leonard to PTF, 12 June 1930; PTF to FLW, 17 June 1930; FLW to C. Adolph Glassgold [telegram], 24 July 1930; FLW to C. Adolph Glassgold [telegram], 28 July 1930. The *Annual* did publish Wright's essay "Principles of Design" (1931), 101–104. After Wright's article appeared in the *Annual,* Douglas Haskell, who was serving as secretary of AUDAC, asked Wright for a set of the illustrated drawings; the *Studio* in London might be able to publish them, and "they circulate all over Europe" (DH to FLW, 10 December 1930).

34. FLW to Harry M. Beardsley [*Chicago Daily News*], 28 October 1929.

35. Sheldon Cheney to FLW, 30 January 1930; Maude T. Cheney to FLW and OLW, 8 February 1930. The Cheneys published *Art and the Machine* in 1936, in which they saw a "spreading machine age consciousness" in the visual arts in paintings like Charles Demuth's *My Egypt,* with its two massive grain elevators, and Charles Sheeler's photographs of the Rouge River plant of Ford Motor Company (Stern, Gilmartin, and Mellins, *New York 1930,* 290).

36. Mary Fanton Roberts [*Arts and Decoration*] to FLW, 3 January 1930; FLW to Mary Fanton Roberts, 7 January 1930; John Taylor Boyd Jr., "A Prophet of the New Architecture," *Arts and Decoration* 33 (1930): 56–59, 100, 102, 116.

37. Julius Hoffmann to FLW, 2 March 1930. Hoffmann sent the request to Wright at an out-of-date office address in "Chicago"—but Wright still managed to receive his correspondence. The book was titled *The New Interior in Europe and America.* On Margold, see Renate Ulmer, *Emanuel Josef Margold: Wiener Moderne, Künstlerkolonie Darmstadt, Corporate Design für Bahlsen, neues Bauen in Berlin* (Stuttgart: Arnoldsche,

2003); "Emanuel Josef Margold" in *Stadtlexikon Darmstadt* (Stuttgart, 2006), 601. He had been a student of Josef Hoffmann, the Secessionist designer in Vienna and co-founder of the Wiener Werkstätte.

38. FLW, *Modern Architecture: Being the Kahn Lectures for 1930* (Princeton, NJ: Princeton Architectural Press, 1931); FLW, *Two Lectures on Architecture* (Chicago: Art Institute of Chicago, 1931).

39. FLW, "One Day in New York," FLLW MS, 2401.076, 12 pp., typescript, Avery.

40. FLW, "One Day in New York," 1, 2, 5, 11.

41. *HY*, 226; FLW, *The Disappearing City* (New York: William Farquhar Payson, 1932); rewritten and included in *When Democracy Builds* (Chicago: University of Chicago Press, 1945) and in *The Living City* (New York: Horizon Press, 1958) as well as a posthumous edition titled *The Industrial Revolution Runs Away* (New York: Horizon Press, 1969).

42. *HY*, 214; Jane Porter to FLW [December 1926/January 1927].

43. Asa Briggs, *A History of Longmans and Their Books, 1724–1990* (London: British Library and Oak Knoll Press, 2008), 416–417, 547, 556. Briggs noted that Longmans, Green did not aggressively pursue American opportunities. Curiously, Wright's name does not appear in Briggs's appendix of their authors.

44. The correspondence on negotiating a contract between Wright and his publisher is extensive. See, for example, A. L. McCarthy to FLW, 27 August 1930; Frank E. Hill to George T. Bye, 25 November 1930.

45. *HY*, 220.

46. Carolyn A. Barros, "Figura, Persona, Dynamis: Autobiography and Change," *Biography* 15, no. 1 (1992): 1–28. My thanks to Willa Granger for pointing to this source.

47. *MM*, 323–324. Gill mixed admiration with ribald skewering of the architect: Wright was "incorrigible in his failure to perform the feat of thinking hard—of driving his mind past the cozy lowlands of A, B, and C into the comparatively distant and chilly heights of D, E, and F" (*MM*, 325).

48. *San Francisco Chronicle*, 10 April 1932, quoted in *CW*, 2:13. For additional reviews, see *HY*, 226; *New York Times Book Review*, 3 April 1932, quoted in *CW*, 2:13–14; *Saturday Review of Literature*, 23 April 1932, quoted in *CW*, 2:13–14.

49. Transcript, "The Mike Wallace Interview," 1 September 1957 and 28 September 1957. Harry Ransom Center, University of Texas at Austin, available at http://www.hrc.utexas.edu/multimedia/video/2008/wallace/wright_frank_lloyd_t.html.

50. Frampton, "Introduction," *CW*, 2:7.

CHAPTER 11. PHOENIX RISING

1. FLW to WNG, 9 February 1931, photocopy, bMS 680/35 (32), GA. Wright informed Guthrie he was coming to New York starting 23 February for talks at the 20th

Century Club, Brooklyn, Tuesday; Women's University Club, Wednesday; meeting of AUDAC Thursday, and lecture at Art Center, Friday, "School of Social Research [New School of Research]"; *A,* 335–344.

2. *A,* 336. Levine, *Urbanism,* 405n18, speculates that Wright "more than likely" knew of Fuller's 1928 design for a high rise and Raymond Hood's high-rise design on a pedestal. No documentation supports the speculation. The relationship between Wright and Fuller remains, however, a subject worth further research. For Fuller, Hugh Ferriss, and Norman Bel Geddes, see Adnan Morshed, *Impossible Heights: Skyscrapers, Flight, and the Master Builder* (Minneapolis: University of Minnesota Press, 2015).

3. The back story is more complex than Wright allowed in his *Autobiography.* He had offered Raymond Hood his assistance as a consultant to push for the modern architecture "that ought to be ours and is" in the World's Fair in Chicago. Having been excluded from actually participating, Wright still wanted to have a say in what was displayed and saw Hood, who was on the commission for the Fair, as a vehicle to that end (FLW to RH, 2 June 1930). He claimed to Mumford that there was "a genuine desire" to involve him in some way with the Chicago Fair: "What that way is I don't know yet. Corbett, Walker, Hood, and Kahn give me this much advance notice" (FLW to LM, [June] 1930). Hood had tried to involve Wright, but others on the committee, particularly Harvey Wiley Corbett, opposed him, and Hood had to inform Wright he was too much of an individualist to participate (RH to FLW, 10 June 1930; RH to FLW, 26 June 1930). For the Fair, see Lisa Schrenk, *Building a Century of Progress: The Architecture of Chicago's 1933–34 World's Fair* (Minneapolis: University of Minnesota Press, 2007), and Cheryl Ganz, *The 1933 Chicago World's Fair: Century of Progress* (Urbana: University of Illinois Press, 2008).

4. Invitation to members of AUDAC, 26 February 1930; "Wrightites v. Chicago," *Time* 17 (1931): 63–64.

5. *A,* 338.

6. *A,* 339–344.

7. *HY,* 218.

8. See Jason Farago, "Men of MoMA Who Furnished Your Modernist Home," *NYT,* 8 September 2017, C16, exhibition review of *Partners in Design: Alfred H. Barr, Jr. and Philip Johnson,* Grey Art Gallery, New York University, 8 September–9 December 2017.

9. David Hanks, ed., *Partners in Design: Alfred H. Barr, Jr. and Philip Johnson,* exh. cat. (New York: Monacelli Press, 2015), 138. Hitchcock began as more literary and published than Johnson, but not all critics approved of him. According to Wright, the Princeton crowd thought little of "cocksure Hitchcock" (FLW to LM, [June] 1930, Avery [misdated index to correspondence as 3-1-30]). When the art historian, Princeton graduate, and Princeton instructor Donald Drew Egbert reviewed Hitchcock's *Modern Architecture: Romanticism and Reintegration* (1929), he eviscerated it for narrowly defining modernists as only those who use reinforced concrete as a building

material. Challenging this reductive view, Egbert pointed out a range of "ultra-modernists" Hitchcock had excluded, including Frank Lloyd Wright. See Donald Drew Egbert, [Review of *Modern Architecture*, 1929], *Art Bulletin*, 12, no. 1 (1930): 98–99. Egbert attended Wright's Princeton lectures.

10. Hanks, *Partners in Design*, 7, 138; for the Barr and Johnson apartments, 66–109; quotes from exhibition wall panels. After Southgate, Johnson had two other residences in the neighborhood, which included Beekman Place and Turtle Bay. Later, around 1950, he would design a guest house for the Rockefellers at 242 East 52nd Street; he later lived there from 1971 to 1979. Lescaze's residence followed the aesthetics of Le Corbusier but kept the pre-existing internal floor arrangements.

11. The role of *Modern Architecture: International Exhibition,* which popularized the "International Style" moniker, has been thoroughly explored, including Wright's role in it. The primary references include the exhibition catalogue by Alfred H. Barr Jr., Henry-Russell Hitchcock Jr., Philip Johnson, and Lewis Mumford, *Modern Architects* (New York: Museum of Modern Art and Norton, 1932), and the accompanying book by Henry-Russell Hitchcock and Philip Johnson, *The International Style: Architecture Since 1922* (New York: Norton, 1932). For a reconstruction of the exhibition, see Terrence Riley, *The International Style: Exhibition 15 and the Museum of Modern Art* (New York: Rizzoli and Columbia Books on Architecture, 1992). See also Hugh Howard, *Architecture's Odd Couple: Frank Lloyd Wright and Philip Johnson* (London: Bloomsbury, 2016), and *OE,* 66–85.

12. FLW to LM, 19 January 1932, quoted in *HY,* 224. After leaving Wright's employ, Neutra had found success in southern California designing in a Functionalist mode that was inflected with a Wrightian sensitivity to site. For Neutra, see Barbara Lamprecht, *Richard Neutra: The Complete Works* (New York: Taschen, 2000), and Thomas S. Hines, *Richard Neutra and the Search for Modern Architecture,* 4th ed. (New York: Rizzoli, 2006).

13. FLW to Philip Johnson, 19 January 1932, quoted in *HY,* 224.

14. LM to FLW, 21 January 1932, quoted in *HY,* 224.

15. LM to FLW, 21 January 1932, quoted in *HY,* 224. In his foreword to the 1966 edition of *The International Style,* Hitchcock benefited from hindsight: "Thus by the mid-thirties the Style was effectively rivaled—or rejected—both by older and by younger architects during just those years when it was spreading most widely through the western world." He added that he and Johnson had been "moving away" from the notion in different ways and that he had come to "the conclusion that International Style is over." Henry-Russell Hitchcock and Philip Johnson, *The International Style* (reprint, New York: Norton, 1966), ix.

16. FLW to George Cranmer, 20 February 1932, quoted in *HY,* 225–226.

17. FLW, "The House on the Mesa," MS 2401.120, 2 pp., handwritten by FLW with his edits, n.d. Wright worked on the text in two additional variants: MS 2401.120

B, "The House on the Mesa," 9 pp., typescript version of A, marked "superseded"; and MS 2401.120 C, "The House on the Mesa," 6 pp., "final" version of typescript, carbon copy.

18. Le Corbusier, "A Noted Architect Dissects Our Cities," *New York Times Magazine,* 3 January 1932, 10–11, 19; FLW, "Broadacre City: An Architect's Vision," *New York Times Magazine,* 20 March 1932, 8–9. I explored the subject extensively in "Broadacre City: The Reception of a Modernist Vision, 1932–1988," in *Center: Modernist Visions and the Contemporary American City* 5 (New York: Rizzoli, 1989), 8–43. I pointed out the dialogue between Wright and Le Corbusier as it appeared in dueling articles in the *New York Times Magazine* in 1932. I also emphasized the critical reactions to Broadacre City and Wright's inability to defend it from Marxist critiques. In reviewing the standard literature on Broadacre City, Levine (*Urbanism,* 406n34) misrepresented my position as focusing exclusively on the stock market crash as the motivation for Broadacre City. As shown throughout this book and the *Center* essay, a multitude of factors contributed to Wright's concepts. His reaction to Le Corbusier was one of them, but not the sole focus, as claimed by Levine.

19. "Frank Lloyd Wright Tells of the Broadacre City," *City Club of Chicago Bulletin* 25 (1932): 27, 29.

20. Geoffrey T. Hellman, "Profiles: Lights, Please!," *New Yorker,* 31 January 1931, 22, 25.

21. WNG to FLW, 24 February 1932.

22. Wenger, "Dance," 246–249.

23. *HY,* 227; see Jane King Hession and Tim Quigley, *John H. Howe: From Taliesin Apprentice to Master of Organic Design* (Minneapolis: University of Minnesota Press, 2015), 24.

24. Stern, *Howe,* ix; *HY,* 221, 230–235; *TF,* 177–238.

25. Stern, *Howe,* 18. Klumb turned the Willey drawings over to Howe as one of his last duties before leaving; the built version was completed in 1933; *C,* 236.

26. Stern, *Howe,* 25–26. For a clarification of the details for making the Broadacre City model, which was funded in December 1934, see *OE,* 90–91.

27. John Sergeant, *Frank Lloyd Wright's Usonian Houses: The Case for Organic Architecture* (New York: Whitney Library of Design, 1976), 123n11.

28. FLW, "The New Frontier: Broadacre City," *Taliesin* 1:1 [*sic*], October 1940; *Democrat Tribune Press* (Mineral Point, WI), 11.

29. Wright's slogans were prominent in the posters for the 1935 exhibition; see "Broadacre City, Frank Lloyd Wright, Architect," *American Architect* 146 (1935): 55.

30. For a thorough discussion of the Broadacre City model at Rockefeller Center, see *OE,* 87–101.

31. Quotes by Mumford and Wright from *OE,* 100.

32. "Models New Type of City for Self-Contained Group," *NYT,* 27 March 1935; for critical reactions, see Alofsin, "Modernist Visions," 24–28.

33. See Franklin Toker, *Fallingwater Rising: Frank Lloyd Wright, E. J. Kaufmann, and America's Most Extraordinary House* (New York: Knopf, 2003); Richard Cleary, *Merchant Prince and Master Builder: Edgar J. Kaufmann and Frank Lloyd Wright* (Pittsburgh: Heinz Architectural Center, Carnegie Museum of Art, 1999); *C,* 236–239; Banham, "Wilderness Years," 518.

34. *A New House by Frank Lloyd Wright on Bear Run, Pennsylvania* (New York: Museum of Modern Art, 1938); *OE,* 112–121.

35. See Jonathan Lipman, *Frank Lloyd Wright and the Johnson Wax Buildings* (New York: Rizzoli, 1986).

36. *C,* 250–251; *MM,* 373–376.

37. For the Jacobs house, see *C,* 241–242; for the Willey house, see *C,* 236.

38. Meryle Secrest, *Frank Lloyd Wright: A Biography* (New York: Knopf, 1992), 451; Stern, *Howe,* 35–40; *TF,* 335–337, 340–341; *C,* 253–255.

39. Wright's work or comments in *Life* appeared in 1938, 1939, 1942, 1945, 1946, 1950–1953, 1955–1957, and 1959. For Kerbis, see Blair Kamin, "Gertrude Kerbis, Groundbreaking Architect, Dies at 89," *Chicago Tribune,* 16 June 2016.

40. Howard Myers, editor of the *Architectural Forum,* became the publisher of much of Wright's work, supplanting the dominance of the *Architectural Record.* Douglas Haskell succeeded Myers at *Forum* in 1953; see Stern, *Howe,* 35. The *Architectural Forum* folded in 1974. See Witold Rybczynski, "The Glossies: The Decline of Architectural Magazines," *Slate,* 15 November 2006, http://www.slate.com/articles/arts/architecture/2006/11/the_glossies.html

41. "Frank Lloyd Wright," *Architectural Forum* 68 (1938): 1–102; 88 (1948): 65–156, editor's note, 54; "A Four-Color Portfolio of the Recent Work of the Dean of Contemporary Architects, with His Own Commentary on Each Building," *Architectural Forum* 94 (1951): 704–108, also issued as an offprint.

42. *Time* 31, no. 3 (17 January 1938): cover, 29–32. *Pang Tang* means "fat Tang lady." The figure is a funerary *mingei,* and for the Chinese was a fashionable upper-class status symbol. The Frank Lloyd Wright Foundation sold it (with Olgivanna's approval) in 1967 at Parke-Bernet Galleries, New York, for $425. My thanks to Margo Stipe and Julia Meech for identifying the sculpture (Margo Stipe to author, personal communication, 2 June 2016). The drawing in the background was one of several copies showing this dramatic rendering of Fallingwater.

43. Press Release no. 401108-67, Museum of Modern Art, 4 pp., typescript, Museum of Modern Art Exhibition Archives, available at MoMA website.

44. HRH, "Frank Lloyd Wright at the Museum of Modern Art," *Art Bulletin* 23 (1941): 73–76. Hitchcock's review contained the most perceptive analysis on Wright that had appeared to date. For a less critical review, see Frederick A. Gutheim, "First Reckon

with His Future: Frank Lloyd Wright's Exhibit at the Modern Museum," *Magazine of Art* 34 (1941): 32–33. Gutheim was preparing at that time the first edition of Wright's collected writings. For a history of the exhibition, see *The Show to End All Shows: Frank Lloyd Wright at the Museum of Modern Art,* 1940 Studies in Modern Art 8, ed. Peter Reed and William Kaizen, essay by Kathryn Smith (New York: Museum of Modern Art, 2004), 129–147.

45. Stern, *Howe,* 125; Arthur Drexler to author, personal communication, 10 April 1980. For the complete list of Wright's MoMA exhibitions during his lifetime, see *OE,* 233–239. MoMA mounted a major retrospective on Wright titled *Frank Lloyd Wright: Architect,* 16 February–10 May 1994. The museum put on a subsequent exhibition intended to celebrate its acquisition in 2012 of the Wright archive in partnership with Columbia University: *Frank Lloyd Wright and the City: Density vs. Dispersal,* 1 February–1 June 2014, and a second celebratory exhibition, *Frank Lloyd Wright at 150: Unpacking the Archive,* took place 12 June–1 October 2017.

46. Hitchcock did write "The Later Work of Frank Lloyd Wright, 1942–1959," a superficial commentary on his designs after 1942. It was published in *Architecture: Nineteenth and Twentieth Centuries* (London: Penguin, 1958) and reprinted, unillustrated, in Hitchcock, *In the Nature of Materials: The Buildings of Frank Lloyd Wright, 1887–1941* (Cambridge, MA: Da Capo, 1975). Wright's late work and many unexecuted projects began being published only in the mid-1980s. See, for instance, Bruce Brooks Pfeiffer, *Treasures of Taliesin: Seventy-Seven Unbuilt Designs* (San Francisco: Pomegranate, 1985), and the monumental series by Bruce Brooks Pfeiffer and Yukio Futagawa, *Frank Lloyd Wright: The Complete Works,* 12 vols. (Tokyo: ADA Edita/Global Architecture, 1984–88).

47. HRH, "Frank Lloyd Wright at the Museum of Modern Art," *Art Bulletin* 23 (1941): 75. Hitchcock refers to his own "Frank Lloyd Wright's Influence Abroad," *Parnassus* 12 (1940): 11–15.

48. *Frank Lloyd Wright on Architecture: Selected Writings, 1894–1940,* ed. Frederick Gutheim (New York: Duell, Sloan and Pearce, 1941). Eric Pace, "Frederick Gutheim Is Dead at 85: Expert on Planning and a Writer," *NYT,* 4 October 1993.

49. For Wright's isolationism, see *TF,* 348–373; *TF,* 357 (quote).

50. Stern, *Howe,* 39.

51. *TF,* 364, 254.

52. Stern, *Howe,* 43–45.

53. Stern, *Howe,* 43, 45–46; Miller, *Mumford,* 248. See also Donald Leslie Johnson, *The Fountainheads: Wright, Rand, the FBI and Hollywood* (Jefferson, NC: McFarland, 2005).

54. Wenger, "Dance," 246–249.

55. WNG to FLW, 7 March 1932. See Ada Calhoun, *St. Marks Is Dead: The Many Lives of America's Hippest Street* (New York: Norton, 2015).

56. "Dr. Guthrie Dead; Retired Rector, 76," *NYT,* 10 December 1944, 53; Guy Emery Shipler, "Guthrie of St. Mark's: Highlights in the Career of a Disturbing Genius," *Churchman* 159, no. 1 (1945), whole issue. Shipler was editor of *The Churchman,* published in New York, bMS 680/32 (66), GA.

57. Wolcott Gibbs, "Profiles: Big Nemo—I," *New Yorker,* 18 March 1939, 24–29; Gibbs, "Big Nemo—II," *New Yorker,* 25 March 1939, 22–27; Gibbs, "Big Nemo—III," *New Yorker,* 1 April 1939, 22–27. As Woollcott's biographer put it, the profile had emphasized "his more grotesque and displeasing qualities with too little recognition of his underlying character" (Adams, *Woollcott,* 221–222). Gibbs, then theater critic at the *New Yorker,* had personal bias. On numerous occasions, in print and in person, Gibbs expressed an intense dislike for Woollcott as both an author and as a person. In a letter to James Thurber, Gibbs wrote that he thought Woollcott was "one of the most dreadful writers who ever existed." See Thomas Kunkel, *Genius in Disguise: Harold Ross of the New Yorker* (New York: Random House, 1995); Gibbs, "Profiles: Big Nemo—III," 27.

58. Adams, *Woollcott,* 222. Woollcott took up radio broadcasting in 1929 while he was working as a staff writer at the *New Yorker.* See "Woollcott Dies After Heart Attack in Radio Studio During Broadcast," *NYT,* 24 January 1943; "The Talk of the Town," *New Yorker,* 30 January 1943, 8.

CHAPTER 12. ZENITH

1. Hilla Rebay to FLW, 1 June 1943, as quoted in Bruce Brooks Pfeiffer, ed., *Frank Lloyd Wright: The Guggenheim Correspondence* (Fresno: Press at California State University, 1986), 4. Hilla and Maginel had met at the Belcourt, a Parisian bistro (later known as Frutti di Mare), located at 67 Second Avenue and East Fourth Street in the Village. For more on Rebay, see Joan M. Lukach, *Hilla Rebay: In Search of the Spirit in Art* (New York: George Braziller, 1984); and Pfeiffer, *Guggenheim Correspondence,* 7–11. The literature on New York's Guggenheim Museum is extensive. For an insightful synopsis, see Francesco Dal Co, *The Guggenheim: Frank Lloyd Wright's Iconoclastic Masterpiece* (New Haven: Yale University Press, 2017).

2. FLW to Hilla Rebay, 10 June 1943, in Pfeiffer, *Guggenheim Correspondence,* 4–5. The contract was dated 29 June 1943 (Pfeiffer, *Guggenheim Correspondence,* 8–9).

3. The number of scholarly studies, picture books, and journalistic accounts relating to Wright in the postwar years is expanding. In addition to works cited elsewhere in the notes, a sampler includes Donald Leslie Johnson, *Frank Lloyd Wright Versus America: The 1930s* (Cambridge, MA: MIT Press, 1990); and *Frank Lloyd Wright: The Crowning Decade, 1949–1958,* ed. Bruce Brooks Pfeiffer (Fresno: Press at California State University, 1989).

4. Dal Co, *Guggenheim,* 34–36.

5. The definitive treatment: Robert A. Caro, *The Power Broker: Robert Moses and the Fall of New York* (New York: Vintage Books, 1975); a counter view: Hilary Ballon and

Kenneth T. Jackson, eds., *Robert Moses and the Modern City: The Transformation of New York* (New York: Norton, 2007).

6. Dal Co, *Guggenheim,* 23, 26.

7. Dal Co, *Guggenheim,* 48–49; Christopher Grey, "The Building Wore Red," *NYT,* 24 June 2009.

8. Dal Co, *Guggenheim,* 22, 52, and 71, quoting *Architectural Forum,* January 1946.

9. Dal Co, *Guggenheim,* 36–37.

10. Jane King Hession and Debra Pickrel, *Frank Lloyd Wright in New York: The Plaza Years, 1954–1959* (Salt Lake City: Gibbs Smith, 2007), 16–27, 129n32; *M,* 98–100; OLW, *Shining Brow,* 173; *M,* 99, quoting OLW; Hession and Pickrel, *Plaza Years,* 16. See also "The Plaza Hotel: History," http://www.theplaza.com/history.

11. OLW, *Shining Brow,* 173, 172; *LOLW,* 174–176.

12. See Victoria Newhouse, *Wallace K. Harrison: Architect* (New York: Rizzoli, 1989).

13. Pickrel and Hession updated their monograph with a series of blogs in 2017, available at http://www.metropolismag.com. Debra Pickrel, "When Frank Lloyd Wright Lived at the Plaza Hotel," *Metropolis,* 17 July 2017 (with unpublished interviews); Pickrel, "How Frank Lloyd Wright Would Have Transformed Ellis Island," *Metropolis,* 11 July 2017; Pickrel, "Mike Wallace on His 'Heart-Starting' 1957 Interview with Frank Lloyd Wright," *Metropolis,* 15 June 2017; Jane King Hession and Debra Pickrel, "Wright in New York: Looking Back on Frank Lloyd Wright's Final Years," *Metropolis,* 8 June 2017; Pickrel, "Remembering Frank Lloyd Wright's Demolished Car Showroom," *Metropolis,* 9 May 2013.

14. "'Honestly Arrogant' F. LL. W. Restates Lifelong Creed," *AR* 111 (1952): 14.

15. Stern, *Howe,* 45. For Wright's appearance on *What's My Line,* the CBS game show, on 3 June 1956, see https://www.youtube.com/watch?v=cMXK_KtUVm4. For the Mike Wallace interview, see "Transcript, The Mike Wallace Interview," 1 September 1957 and 28 September 1957, Harry Ransom Center, University of Texas at Austin, http://www.hrc.utexas.edu/multimedia/video/2008/wallace/wright_frank_lloyd_t.html.

16. OLW, *Shining Brow,* 22–35. Wright's week concluded with a quick trip to Philadelphia to visit Beth Sholom Synagogue. See also *LOLW,* 176–178.

17. OLW, *Shining Brow,* 171.

18. Stern, *Howe,* 78, 92. Wright suffered a stroke in 1958 (Robert McCarter, *Frank Lloyd Wright* [London: Reaktion, 2006], 198).

19. The exhibition *Sixty Years of Living Architecture* was on view from 22 October to 13 December 1953. For a synopsis of the genesis of the show and its tours, see *OE,* 169–209.

20. FLW to LM, 10 July 1951, quoted in Robert Wojtowicz and Bruce Brooks Pfeiffer, eds., *Frank Lloyd Wright and Lewis Mumford: Thirty Years of Correspondence* (New York: Princeton Architectural Press, 2001), 196.

21. *MM*, 415; LM to John Gould Fletcher, 10 April 1946, 188–189; LM to FLW, 28 June 1951, both letters quoted in Wojtowicz and Pfeiffer, *Thirty Years of Correspondence*, 195.

22. Miller, *Mumford*, 188; *TF*, 488.

23. In the late 1930s and early 1940s, Manson was turning his Harvard doctoral dissertation—the first on Wright—into the first American monograph on the architect's early work. He generously gave much of his material to Hitchcock, who used it in his book *In the Nature of Materials*. Manson's pioneering study appeared later as *Frank Lloyd Wright to 1910: The First Golden Age* (New York: Wiley, 1958); it became the standard introduction to Wright's "Prairie period." Horizon Press's first book with Wright was *The Future of Architecture* (1953); Horizon also published his last book while alive, *A Testament* (1957). For Wright's quote on primitivism, see *A Testament*, reprinted in *CW*, 5:155. Wright saw Taliesin West as archetypal. To a neighbor who'd written that "the satisfying primitive forms [of] Taliesin" had given him much, Wright replied: "You are perfectly right in feeling the primitive in Taliesin West. . . . [It] is as original as the Maya but far beyond it" (FLW to Fowler McCormick, n.d. [1950s], quoted in *OLLW*, 129). Horizon Press continued publishing Wright's work after his death, including another edition of his *Autobiography* (1977). For more on Raeburn, see David Cay Johnson, "Ben Raeburn, 86, Publisher of the Known and Aspiring," *NYT*, 23 April 1997.

24. FLW, *The Living City* (New York: Horizon Press, 1958). See Anthony Alofsin, "Broadacre City: Ideal and Nemesis," *American Art* 25, no. 2 (2011): 21–25. Some of Wright's other projects conceived in the early 1930s were built later, including the theater he originally designed for Woodstock, New York, that was eventually built in Dallas, Texas. See Ann Abernathy, "Of Time and the Theater," *Frank Lloyd Wright Quarterly* 27, no. 2 (2016): 4–11.

25. OLW, *Shining Brow*, 41.

26. Wright's complex of Baghdad was an exception, a fantasy from tabula rasa, as was his early project for Bitterroot Valley, Montana. The premise of Neil Levine, *The Urbanism of Frank Lloyd Wright* (Princeton, NJ: Princeton University Press, 2016), is that Wright was an urbanist. For the limitations of Levine's claims, see Robert McCarter, "The Urbanism of Frank Lloyd Wright [by] Neil Levine [book review]," *JSAH* 75, no. 4 (2016): 506–507; and Paul Goldberger, "Not an Urbanist, Only a Genius," *New York Times Magazine*, 13 February 1994, 48–49.

27. The manuscript exists in multiple drafts and revisions, and is designated simply as "[New York]." I quote from MS 2401.423 F, marked final and signed by Wright, Taliesin West, Phoenix, 1 December 1952, Frank Lloyd Wright Manuscript Collection, Avery.

28. Monica Penick, *Tastemaker: Elizabeth Gordon, House Beautiful, and the Postwar American House* (New Haven: Yale University Press, 2017), 131–140. Hill had joined the Fellowship in 1938 as its youngest member and, with Wright's encouragement,

focused on interior design. He worked on sixty-nine projects and approximately twenty interiors with Wright (ibid., 131–132).

29. Hession and Pickrel, *Plaza Years,* 57–59.

30. Hession and Pickrel, *Plaza Years,* 61.

31. *M,* 88–89. On 29 November 1940, the Frank Lloyd Wright Foundation was founded with Wright as the corporation president and Olgivanna as vice president (*TF,* 354). In 1952 the foundation lost its assumed nonprofit tax status. The State of Wisconsin demanded back payments, and the IRS sued Wright for $20 million in unpaid taxes (*TF,* 501–503).

32. For Wright's Ellis Island project, see Greg Goldin and Sam Lubell, *Never Built New York* (New York: Metropolis, 2016), 114–117. For Wright's other projects in the region, see John L. Rayward residence (1955), New Canaan, Connecticut, *C,* 410–411; Maximilian Hoffman residence (1955), Rye, New York, *C,* 418–419; William and Catherine Cass house (Erdman Prefab #) (1959), Richmond (Staten Island), *C,* 440–441; Hession and Pickrel, *Plaza Years,* 124, passim.

33. Hession and Pickrel, *Plaza Years,* 103. The architect wrote about the racetrack project at length in an unpublished manuscript dated June 1956. "About a year ago," Wright began, "Harry *Guggenheim,* racing a special interest—convinced that the public is not getting the breaks it deserves at the races, said 'do something about this.' I started with this idea of steel in tension—a light canopy suspended from bastions and piers—but, other urgencies crowded it out" ("The New Sports Pavilion," carbon, 6 pp., typescript, dated "Taliesin, June 30th, 1956," MS 2401.362, Avery). Wright also retained in his files a clipping that was relevant to the project, Audax Miner, "The Race Track: Country House," *New Yorker,* [1941?] (MS 2401.255 B, Avery).

34. For the definitive comprehensive study of Beth Sholom, see *BSS,* 309–556; for date of contract, 17 December 1953, see *BSS,* 384; for dedication in September 1959, *BSS,* 489.

35. See Anthony Alofsin, *Prairie Skyscraper: Frank Lloyd Wright's Price Tower* (New York: Rizzoli, 2005), exh. cat. for *Prairie Skyscraper: Frank Lloyd Wright's Price Tower,* 14 October 2005–15 January 2006, Bartlesville, Oklahoma. The exhibition traveled to Yale University, the National Building Museum, Washington, D.C., and the Chicago Architecture Foundation. See also FLW, *The Story of the Tower: The Tree That Escaped the Crowded Forest* (New York: Horizon Press, 1956).

36. FDC, *Guggenheim,* 1–2.

37. FDC, *Guggenheim,* 1, 101.

38. *M,* 99; FDC, *Guggenheim,* 104; For Wright's death, see Stern, *Howe,* 99, 101; *MM,* 499.

39. FDC, *Guggenheim,* 1; *TF,* 489; FDC, *Guggenheim,* 3, 6.

40. "Frank Lloyd Wright Dies: Famed Architect Was 89," *NYT,* 10 April 1959.

41. Maginel died in 1966 at the age of eighty-five, Robert Llewellyn died in 1986 at the age of ninety-two, and David Samuel Wright died in 1997 at the age of 102.

42. Robert A. M. Stern, Thomas Mellins, and David Fishman, *New York 1960* (New York: Monacelli, 1995), 10; for social and architectural context, see pp. 61, 337–338, 374–376, 380, and 398. For Olgivanna's impressions, see OLW, *Shining Brow,* 22.

43. Paul Goldberger, "Robert Moses, Master Builder, Is Dead at 92," *NYT,* 30 July 1981, A1.

44. For Wright's attitudes toward New York in the 1950s, see Robert Twombly, *Frank Lloyd Wright: His Life and Architecture* (New York: Wiley, 1979), 386–388.

EPILOGUE

1. "Your Heritage from Frank Lloyd Wright," *House Beautiful* 101 (1959).

2. *A,* 25.

SOURCES

The origins of this book go back to my doctoral dissertation, "Frank Lloyd Wright, The Lessons of Europe" (1987). As the late Vincent Scully said about his own dissertation, "At that time, no one liked 19th Century architecture." The same could have been said about scholarly interest in Wright in the mid-1980s. "My aim was to rehabilitate it," Scully explained. "That's what dissertations should do: bring back great areas of human experience that have been jettisoned." Inspired by Scully, I set out to find what had been jettisoned in Wright's "human experience." Fortunately, the Frank Lloyd Wright Archives at Taliesin West, near Scottsdale, Arizona, had opened to provide scholarly access to its holdings, and I was able to conduct research and live among the Taliesin Fellows for extended periods of time.

The dissertation became the basis of *Frank Lloyd Wright: The Lost Years* (1993). That work picked up where Grant Manson left off when he defined the Prairie period in his classic *Frank Lloyd Wright to 1910: The First Golden Age* (1958). In rediscovering what had been "lost" to history, I identified the next dozen years as Wright's primitivist phase. Wright's interest in primitivism paralleled that of other European artists, from Gauguin to Picasso, who pursued universal values assumed to exist in the purified forms of ancient and non-Western cultures. Like other primitivists, Wright relied on an idealized vision of an age of innocence, and his convictions propelled exotic projects like Midway Gardens in Chicago and the Imperial Hotel in Tokyo in the 1910s. But Wright was unique among American architects in this inclination.

When Wright returned to America from Japan in 1922, his primitivist phase had peaked and began to recede gradually. The architect had to reconstruct his personal and artistic lives as he was newly influenced by the terrains of California and the high deserts of the Southwest. In the mid-1920s, when New York took its firm grip on him, he had to somehow legitimize himself when esoteric ideas would only detract from the efforts. However, he never abandoned his belief in the "spell power" of archetypal forms—it only moved beneath the surface, behind what Brendan Gill called one of Wright's masks.

To pursue those subjects thirty years ago, I needed to study his drawings and his letters. Through the generosity of the late Bruce Brooks Pfeiffer, founder of the Frank Lloyd Wright Archives, I gained the first unfettered access to the whole archive at Taliesin West. While living among the members of the Fellowship, I pored over the original drawings with Bruce, adding for the first time unique accession numbers to each sheet. To me, the drawings, most of which were unpublished, were an endless revelation. But letters were another matter. Wright carefully saved copies of his letters and those he received, as well as drafts of his manuscripts, throughout his career. But the correspondence was unorganized when I encountered it in 1984. To make the letters usable for researchers, I created—with the support of the Getty Center for the History of Art and the Humanities—the digital index to over one hundred thousand documents. A print version was derived from it and published in five volumes as *Frank Lloyd Wright: An Index to the Taliesin Correspondence* (1988). Its appearance has allowed subsequent generations of scholars and others to conduct scientific research on Wright using his vast correspondence.

When I began pursuing Wright into the 1920s, the correspondence provided a vital source—indeed the core of the work that followed. Over the decades I read the letters to and from Wright, and to make sense of their complexity, I created a detailed chronology that tied together correspondence, related documents, and even notes and dates on Wright's drawings; I have included here a very abbreviated version. This short list benefited from the careful work of scholars Kathryn Smith, Robert L. Sweeney, Jane King Hession, and Debra Pickrel; their publications are cited in the notes. Simultaneously, I looked at and documented all the projects and designs Wright produced from 1922 to 1932. They attested to Wright's continual creative reinvention despite personal trauma. The artistic evolution of his architecture hovered as an inchoate project in itself, while the story that kept moving forward was more biographical than a monograph on buildings and projects. The detailed study of all the buildings and projects was put aside to give primacy to Wright and New York, an account that was previously unknown.

In 2012, research that began at the Frank Lloyd Wright Archive at Taliesin West moved to Columbia University when the Frank Lloyd Wright Foundation sold the physical archive (though retaining intellectual rights) to the Museum of Modern Art and Columbia University in New York. Wright's models went to MoMA, and everything else to the Avery Architectural and Fine Arts Library. A major trove of my research material came from the William Norman Guthrie Archive at the Andover-Harvard Theological Library in Cambridge, Massachusetts. I also benefited from studying drawings and photographs in the Prints and Photographs Division of the Library of Congress. Period newspapers, magazines, and journals provided not only valuable accounts of Wright's activities but also ambience and context.

Though based largely on archival and primary sources, this book benefited from the work of historians and critics who have marveled at and diced the life and work of Frank Lloyd Wright. Before becoming the controversial architectural critic for the *New York Times,* Herbert Muschamp had the prescience to realize a story existed between Wright and the city. His *Man About Town: Frank Lloyd Wright in New York City* (1983) introduced the subject. Operating with intuition and insight and using secondary sources to extemporize, he hit all the right notes. His viewpoint was that of a critic; mine is more that of a historian. Muschamp did not benefit, however, from the documentary materials—letters, drawings, and manuscripts—that definitively shape the image of Wright as flaneur in New York. For his vitality, exuberance, and imaginative insights, I owe Muschamp a laurel of thanks. My book differs from his pioneering effort by uncovering a more complex story and by weaving together Wright's life and work in documentary detail. Aware that the definitive study of Wright's life has yet to be written,

I often turned to the extant biographies, particularly Brendan Gill's *Many Masks: A Life of Frank Lloyd* (1987).

Several more focused studies provided definition and insight. Joseph Siry's *Beth Sholom Synagogue: Frank Lloyd Wright and Modern Religious Architecture* (2012) contains the first detailed exploration of Wright, Guthrie, and their joint projects. Siry's consummate work supported the structure—and often details—for my discussions of the architect and his extraordinary client. I benefited particularly from Siry's analyses of the Modern Cathedral and the tower for St. Mark's Church in-the-Bowery. Roger Friedland and Harold Zellman's *The Fellowship: The Untold Story of Frank Lloyd Wright & the Taliesin Fellowship* (2006) marshalled details and fact that had not appeared elsewhere and was a useful source. Bruce Brooks Pfeiffer's *Frank Lloyd Wright: The Heroic Years, 1920–1932* (2009) looked at the period chronologically. His account of the period as "heroic" helped to guide my treatment. *Frank Lloyd Wright: Designs for an American Landscape, 1922–1932* (1996), edited by David DeLong, was indispensable for references to Wright's work in the 1920s, as it explores the marvels of Wright's creative efforts at the time. In *Frank Lloyd Wright in New York: The Plaza Years, 1954–1959* (2007), Jane King Hession and Debra Pickrell brought to light Wright's special affection for the Plaza Hotel. Robert A. M. Stern, Gregory Gilmartin, and Thomas Mellins, *New York 1930: Architecture and Urbanism Between the Two World Wars* (1987), remains a monumental overview and basic architectural reference; it assisted me in creating the context for Wright's adventures in the city. Though including a vast range of building types, it properly highlights the role of the skyscraper as well as urbanistic visions of the future. Its copious illustrations give the visual context to envision Wright in New York.

The richness of cultural histories about New York is splendid and expanding. The New York that Wright confronted resembled the Gotham defined so cogently by cultural historian William R. Taylor in his book *In Pursuit of Gotham: Culture and Commerce in New York* (1992). For the city's early history, I also turned to Edwin G. Burrows and Mike Wallace's *Gotham: A History of New York City to 1898* (1998). Wallace's sequel, *Greater Gotham: A History of New York City from 1898 to 1919* (2017), provides voluminous documentation of the consolidation of the city and set the stage for the 1920s. Donald L. Miller's *Supreme City: How Jazz Age Manhattan Gave Birth to Modern America* (2014) features a cast of characters, both celebrities and buildings. Jules Stewart's *Gotham Rising: New York in the 1930s* (2016) complements this survey. David Reid's *The Brazen Age: New York City and the American Empire: Politics, Art, and Bohemia* (2016) looks at the turbulent yet culturally rich years 1945–1950 but also casts back to the previous decades. Two classic studies remain valuable: Ann Douglas's *Terrible Honesty: Mongrel Manhattan in the 1920s* (1995) and E. B. White's *Here Is New York* (1949). My standard reference was *The Encyclopedia of New York City*, 2nd. ed., edited by Kenneth T. Jackson (2010).

At times I reviewed broad surveys and histories of modern architecture to remind me of the contexts in which Wright's career evolved. Among them were Martin Filler's *Makers of Modern Architecture: From Frank Lloyd Wright to Frank Gehry*, vols. 1 and

2 (2007, 2013); Kenneth Frampton, *Modern Architecture: A Critical History,* 4th ed. (2007); and William J. R. Curtis, *Modern Architecture Since 1900,* 3rd ed. (1996).

In 2017, around Wright's sesquicentennial birthday, new publications reinforced the themes of this book and added new layers of detail. Francesco Dal Co's *The Guggenheim: Frank Lloyd Wright's Iconoclastic Masterpiece* (2017) is a masterful synopsis of the museum's history and a sophisticated analysis of its construction and meaning. Because it is so synthetic and insightful, I relied on it in discussing Wright and the history of the Guggenheim Museum. Kathryn Smith's *Wright on Exhibit: Frank Lloyd Wright's Architectural Exhibitions* grounded the long history of Wright's exhibitions with elaborate detail. She corroborates the important role the Museum of Modern Art and, by extension, New York itself played in resurrecting Wright's career. Monica Penick's *Tastemaker: Elizabeth Gordon, House Beautiful, and the Postwar American Home* deepens our understanding of Wright's work in the context of the 1950s by exploring the role Gordon played in promoting him. Bruce Pfeiffer's final book was a devoted tribute and documentation: *From Crna Cora to Taliesin, Black Mountain to Shining Brow: The Life of Olgivanna Lloyd Wright.* It adds unpublished material about the couple and at times brings New York into sharp focus with detailed and glowing accounts of the city.

The vast literature on Wright ranges from coffee table extravaganzas to detailed academic tomes. I have focused in this book on monographs and articles that support our theme. I regret not including references to a number of fine scholarly studies and contextual works. I owe these authors a debt of thanks, as their works have also influenced my studies on Wright. In addition to the sources mentioned above, general readers will discover a helpful survey in Robert McCarter's *Frank Lloyd Wright* (2006). For the panorama of Wright's built work, consider William Allin Storrer's *Frank Lloyd Wright Companion,* rev. ed. (2006) and his *Architecture of Frank Lloyd Wright: A Complete Catalogue,* 4th ed. (2017).

ACKNOWLEDGMENTS

This book benefited from the kindness of friends. Michael V. Carlisle, my literary agent at InkWell Management, believed in the project from the outset. The MacDowell Colony offered refuge and support when I worked on the prospectus and initial chapters of this book. Pat Cloherty supplied her guest cottage in Garrison, New York, when I began writing its final chapters. Katherine Boller, my editor at Yale University Press, saw the book's potential and encouraged its publication.

I owe a debt to the University of Texas at Austin for its ongoing support of this book and my work in general. The endowment of the Roland Gommel Roessner Professorship of Architecture in the School of Architecture helped fund research, writing, and obtaining illustrations. I was fortunate to have a series of brilliant research assistants at different stages of the project: Katherine Nye, Willa Granger, and Hannah Simonson. I learned much from each of them.

The staff at several archives provided access and permissions to use their materials. My foremost thanks go to Margo Stipe, Director and Curator of Collections, Frank Lloyd Wright Foundation. Bruce Brooks Pfeiffer, Oskar Munoz, and Indira Berndtson offered generous assistance over the years. The archivists of the Avery Fine Art and Architecture Library, Columbia University, facilitated my many visits to their collections. Without the assistance of Shelley Hayreh, Nicole L. Richard, Margaret Smithglass, and Janet Parks, this book would not have achieved its final form. Jessica Suarez, Curator of Manuscripts and Archives, and Frances O'Donnell, former curator, opened the William Norman Guthrie papers at the Andover-Harvard Theological Library, Harvard University. Lauren Robinson helped in tapping the rich photographic collections at the Museum of the City of New York. Mari Nakahara, Barbara Natanson, and their staff colleagues of the Prints and Photographs Division of the Library of Congress facilitated research. Generous archivists answered queries and their institutions provided illustrations: *House Beautiful* and the Hearst Corporation, Milwaukee Public Library, Monmouth University, National Bahá'í Archives, New-York Historical Society, New York Public Library, and New York City Municipal Archives.

The thorough observations of two insightful anonymous readers assisted in clarifying the text. Thomas Mellens shared his insights after reading the final draft as part of our ongoing dialogue about the varieties of modern architecture in New York City. Heidi Downey, Sarah Henry, and Raychel Rapazza at Yale University Press moved the project from a manuscript to a book.

Several colleagues and scholars helped answer my questions and shared their insights and their own research. I owe special thanks to Joseph Siry, the pioneering and generous scholar whose research on Wright and Guthrie underpinned my own work. Steven Mansbach has always enthusiastically encouraged my scholarship. Others helped in diverse ways: Donald Albrecht, Gideon Bosker, David De Long, Kelly Dyson, R. Scott Gill, Dixie Guerrero, Mary Jane Hamilton, Guy Haskell, Jack Holzheuter, Wendy S. Israel, Christopher Long, Ron McCrae, Eric O'Malley, Francesco Passanti, Debra Pickrel, Monica Penick, Cathryn Jakobson Ramin, Witold Rybczynski, Robbi Siegel, Patti Smith, William Allin Storrer, and Paul V. Turner.

Lastly, I thank my wife, Patricia, for her love and support.

ILLUSTRATION CREDITS

The photographers and the sources of visual material other than the owners indicated in the captions are as follows. Every effort has been made to supply complete and correct credits; if there are errors or omissions, please contact Yale University Press so that corrections can be made in any subsequent edition.

Fig. 1: Wisconsin Historical Society, WHi-3970.

Fig. 2: Detroit Publishing Company Photograph Collection, Prints & Photographs Division, Library of Congress, LC-DIG-det-4a23880.

Fig. 3: Queensboro Bridge, Bridges/ Plant & Structures Collection, bps_iv_0969. Courtesy NYC Municipal Archives.

Fig. 4: Photographer unknown. Museum of the City of New York. X2010.11.10769.

Fig. 5: William Norman Guthrie papers, bMS 680/1, Andover-Harvard Theological Library, Harvard Divinity School, Cambridge, Massachusetts.

Figs. 6, 10, 17, 29, 44, 51, 61: The Frank Lloyd Wright Foundation Archives (The Museum of Modern Art | Avery Architectural & Fine Arts Library, Columbia University, New York).

Fig. 7: *Chicago Daily Tribune*.

Fig. 8: Wisconsin Historical Society, WHi-3971.

Figs. 9, 18: Collection of the New-York Historical Society.

Fig. 11: Jamaica Avenue, Borough President Queens Collection, bpq_0716-a. Courtesy NYC Municipal Archives.

Figs. 12, 24–26, 32–36: The drawings of Frank Lloyd Wright are Copyright © 2017 Frank Lloyd Wright Foun-

dation, Scottsdale, AZ. All rights reserved. The Frank Lloyd Wright Foundation Archives (The Museum of Modern Art | Avery Architectural & Fine Arts Library, Columbia University, New York).

Fig. 13: *Helena Daily Independent*. Courtesy of Newspapers.com.

Fig. 14: Minneapolis Newspaper Photographs Collection, Hennepin County Library.

Fig. 15: Photography Collection, Miriam and Ira D. Wallach Division of Art, Prints and Photographs, The New York Public Library, Astor, Lenox and Tilden Foundations.

Fig. 16: Beecher Ogden, Museum of the City of New York. X2010.11.3537.

Fig. 19: Carl Van Vechten Collection, Prints & Photographs Division, Library of Congress, LC-USZ62–121914.

Fig. 20: Lewis Mumford Collection, Monmouth University.

Fig. 21: Samuel H. (Samuel Herman) Gottscho (1875–1971)/Museum of the City of New York. 88.1.1.551.

Fig. 22: Courtesy of Milwaukee Public Library.

Fig. 23: Historic American Buildings Survey, Prints & Photographs Division, Library of Congress, HABS NY,31-NEYO,3–1.

Fig. 27: Brian Spencer Collection. The

Frank Lloyd Wright Foundation Archives (The Museum of Modern Art | Avery Architectural & Fine Arts Library, Columbia University, New York).

Fig. 28: Prints & Photographs Division, Library of Congress, LC-USZC4–2201.

Fig. 30: Photographer unknown. Photograph courtesy of National Bahá'í Archives, United States.

Fig. 31: Photographer unknown, Public domain. MNY219544. Museum of the City of New York X2010.11.5273.

Figs. 37, 38: *Architectural Record,* with permission from the Frank Lloyd Wright Foundation, Scottsdale Arizona.

Fig. 39: No copyright holder identified. Originally published by Wide World Photos, Inc./Museum of the City of New York. X2010.11.5273.

Figs. 40, 41: The Frank Lloyd Wright Foundation Archives (The Museum of Modern Art | Avery Architectural & Fine Arts Library, Columbia University, New York). Photograph by Gilman Lane.

Fig. 42: The Frank Lloyd Wright Foundation Archives (The Museum of Modern Art | Avery Architectural & Fine Arts Library, Columbia University, New York). (FLWFA 3100.0015)

Fig. 43: Permission granted by the Frank Lloyd Wright Foundation, Scottsdale Arizona. (FLWFA 3100.0032)

Fig. 45: Henry-Russell Hitchcock, 193?/unidentified photographer. Henry-Russell Hitchcock papers, 1919–87. Archives of American Art, Smithsonian Institution.

Fig. 46: Courtesy of Camp Treetops.

Fig. 47: Copyright Irving Underhill. Courtesy of Prints & Photographs Division, Library of Congress, LC-USZ62–123573.

Fig. 48: *Architectural Record.*

Figs. 49, 50: Courtesy of Universitätsbibliothek Heidelberg.

Fig. 52: Digital Image © The Museum of Modern Art/Licensed by SCALA/Art Resource, NY.

Fig. 53: Wurts Bros. (New York, N.Y.). Museum of the City of New York. X2010.7.1.8860.

Fig. 54: New York World-Telegram & Sun Newspaper Photograph Collection, Prints & Photographs Division, Library of Congress.

Fig. 55: Copyright © 2017 Pedro E. Guerrero Archives.

Fig. 56: Photography: Port Authority of New York Archives CP-13370; collection, Museum of the City of New York.

Fig. 57: Wurts Bros. (New York, N.Y.). Museum of the City of New York. X2010.7.1.13482.

fig. 58: *New York World-Telegram & Sun* Newspaper Photograph Collection, Prints & Photographs Division, Library of Congress, LC-USZ62-116654.

Figs. 59, 60: Copyright © 2017 Pedro E. Guerrero Archives.

Fig. 62: Photographs in the Carol M. Highsmith Archive, Prints & Photographs Division, Library of Congress, LC-HS18089.

Fig. 63: Photographs in the Carol M. Highsmith Archive, Prints & Photographs Division, Library of Congress, LC-HS503-1735.

Fig. 64: With permission, *House Beautiful* magazine. Image courtesy of Monica Penick.

INDEX

Page numbers in *italic* type indicate illustrations. Buildings and projects by Wright are indexed as main entries by name.

cantilevered construction, 57, 58, 125, 141, 146, 150, 226, 261
Capitol Theater, New York, 69, *70*
Carlton, Julian, 35
Carnegie Music Hall, New York, 18
Carrère & Hastings, 69
Cass house (Wright), 257
Cathedral of St. John the Divine, New York, 101
Cellini, Benvenuto, 209
Century Theatre (formerly New Theatre), New York, 18
Chamberlain, Neville, 234
Chandler, Alexander J., 112–13, 115, 117, 131, 138, 176–77, 222, 228, 295n5
Charles Scribner & Sons, 170, 309n27
Cheney, Eduard, 11
Cheney, Mamah Borthwick. *See* Borthwick, Mamah
Cheney, Maude, 203; *Art and the Machine,* 309n35
Cheney, Sheldon, 142, 203, 206; *Art and the Machine,* 309n35; *The New World Architecture,* 203
Chicago City Club, 219
Chicago Daily Tribune (newspaper), *36,* 42, 61
Chicago Sunday Tribune (newspaper), 35
Chicago Tribune (newspaper), 21, 146
Chicago Tribune Tower, 73
Christian Century (magazine), 233
Christian Science, 10
Chrysler, Walter P., 149, 169
Chrysler Building, New York, 75, 106, 156, 169
Churchill, Henry, 172
Churchman (magazine), 235
cities: desert in contrast to, 111, 123; European *urbanisme* and, 55, 72, 147, 219, 221, 223; Le Corbusier and, 72, 148; machine metaphor applied to, 53–55, 166; rural areas

vs., 80, 166; Wright's comments on, 54–55, 123, 148, 166, 204–5, 219, 220–24, 253. *See also* Broadacre City (Wright)
civic architecture, 16–17, 20, 253, 318n26
Cochius, Petrus Marinus, 92–93
Cohen, Mortimer J., 258
color, 9, 10, 227, 232, 241, 256
Commercial National Bank and Trust Company, 149
Contempora, 119–20, 297n23
Contempora Exhibition of Art and Industry (1929), 137, 299n27
Conversations with Elder Wise Men (television show), 248
Coonley, Queene and Avery, 30, 89
Cooper, James Fenimore, 18
Corbett, Harvey Wiley, 120, 134, 161, 170, 301n53, 311n3
cornices, 199
Corning Glass building, New York, 264
Cortissoz, Royal, 167
Coward, Noel, 178
Coward-McCann, 206
Cranmer, George, 216
Creative Arts (magazine), 193
Christopher Columbus Lighthouse competition, 182, 274
cummings, e. e., 88
Cunard line, 14, 31
Curie, Marie, 80
curtain-wall construction, 156, 263

Daigle, Clara, 296n16
Daily Princetonian (newspaper), 166
dance, Guthrie's presentation of, 99–101, 102, 234
Darmstadt Artists' Colony, 203
Darwin D. and Isabelle Martin house (Wright), 9
decentralization, 55, 205, 223
De Fries, Heinrich, 186–87, 200; *Frank Lloyd Wright: Aus dem Lebenswerke*